FOUNDATION FOR ENDANGERED LANGUAGES

in association with

Ryukyuan Heritage Language Society
琉球継承言語会

FEL XVIII Okinawa

Indigenous Languages: their Value to the Community

弥勒世果報創いるしまくとぅば

豊かな社会のための言語

Proceedings of the 18th FEL Conference

Okinawa International University
Ginowan City
Okinawa, Japan

17 – 20 September 2013

Editors:
Patrick Heinrich and Nicholas Ostler

Published by

Foundation for Endangered Languages
Batheaston Villa
172 Bailbrook Lane
Bath BA1 7AA
England

ISBN 978-0-9560210-6-9

Cover design: Daiju Kojima
Cover photo: Karen Walzer

Table of contents

Index of Authors

Index of Languages (Worldwide)

All languages, and some groups, mentioned in papers are indexed. Reference is to the first page.

Index of Languages and Dialects (in Ryukyu Islands)

All dialects, languages, and some groups, mentioned are indexed. Reference is to the first page.

Language Endangerment in the Contemporary World: Globalisation, Technology and New Media

Patrick Heinrich

Ca' Foscari University
Palazzo Vendramin, Dorsoduro 3462 Venice 30123 Italy
[patrick.heinrich@unive.it]

Nicholas Ostler

Foundation for Endangered Languages
172 Bailbrook Lane, Bath BA1 7AA England
[nicholas@ostler.net]

Introduction

The 2014 FEL Conference is held in Okinawa, the main island of the Ryukyu Islands in the extreme southwest of the Japanese Archipelago. Six mutually unintelligible Ryukyuan languages are spoken there.

The Ryukyuan languages are part of the Japonic language family, which also includes Japanese and the Hachijo language. The Ryukyuan languages separated from Japanese sometime before the 7th century and preserve several phonological distinctions already lost in Old Japanese. It is a probable inference that settlers from some part of Kyushu moved into the Ryukyu Islands from the 8th century on, and that the Ryukyuan languages developed on the basis of Kyushu Japonic and Hachijo on the basis of Eastern Japonic.

This makes these languages not daughter languages of Japanese but sister languages. What languages were spoken before in the Ryukyus and how they influenced the formation of the Ryukyuan languages remains as yet unknown.

It was only after the Meiji Restoration in 1868 and the establishment of a modern nation state that Japanese were spread in these islands. Japanese was however spread with such fervor that all Ryukyuan languages are set to become extinct by 2050 if no counter-action is taken. In fact, all Ryukyuan languages are either definitely or severely endangered today.

It is only recently that attempts have been made to slow or reverse the shift against the Ryukyuan languages, and language revitalization efforts are still at a nascent stage. Given this situation in the Ryukyus, FEL XVIII seeks to discuss the societal benefit of maintaining indigenous languages in order to outline and clarify the benefits indigenous languages offer the communities speaking them. There is nothing to be gained from language loss for communities speaking an endangered language. Quite the contrary: maintenance of indigenous languages, if it can be achieved, would offer many advantages.

There are many ways in which indigenous languages profit their speakers. They fall into four larger categories:

1. Indigenous languages can be employed for **cultural effects** such as song, poetry, speech events, ceremonies or festivals. As a matter of fact, performing arts, Ryukyuan *shimauta* folk songs and *kumiwudui* opera, is one of two domains remaining intact for the Ryukyuan languages today (the other is indigenous religion).

2. Indigenous languages may also enhance **economic progress**. In recent years, Ryukyuan languages can increasingly be often found on local food products, on restaurant menus and in the linguistic landscape. The rationale behind this phenomenon is economic. Local products and services employing local languages promise better revenues.

3. Indigenous languages offer a **wealth of knowledge** to their speakers. Since these languages have been formed in a particular geographic and cultural environment, these languages are carriers of the local knowledge of this specific language ecology. Such knowledge pertains to climate, customs, beliefs, vegetation and so on. Needless to say, indigenous languages also inform linguists about issues such their origin, development and contact, ensuring a more comprehensive understanding of language in general.

4. Indigenous languages also serve as a powerful tool for **indigenous empowerment**. All endangered languages are spoken by communities dominated in one way or another by a more powerful community. It is the language of this powerful community which is replacing the indigenous language. Maintaining endangered languages goes hand in hand with establishing a new, more balanced relationship between shifting and dominating communities. In the Ryukyu Islands, domination comes from 'mainland' (*hondo*) Japan. Besides language endangerment this domination also manifests in problems relating to the school curricula and textbooks, but most prominently in the long-standing 'military base-problems' (*kichi mondai*) of Okinawa.

This range of topics is unified by the feature that these various issues all point to ways in which indigenous languages best profit the community.

The resulting conference – unlike FEL conferences in previous years – has two streams.

One is focused specifically on the Ryukyuan languages. This begins with the Keynote session and the Special session, and finishes in the three sessions with Japanese numbering, イ *i,* ロ *ro* and ハ *ha.* (Except for the Keynote papers, items in this stream are only reproduced in English as abstracts. Many of these presentations were given in Japanese.)

The other stream treats endangered languages worldwide, and is numbered in ordinary western (so-called "arabic") numerals from 1 to 8.

Okinawan

Keynote Session

Three Japanese linguists review the position of the Ryukyuan languages. Ishihara looks at measures of the endangerment of the languages considered as a homogeneous group, while Maeda tells the story of Amami, one of the northern group. Miyara reviews the historical devekopment of the languages as far as is known, and also gives a linguistic analysis, at various levels, of what makes the Ryukyuan languages different from Japanese, as well as from each other.

Special Session: Okinawan in Hawai'i

This session is devoted to the use of Okinawan language in the Pacific islands of Hawai'i. Hijirida starts from the Okinawan language class at the HUOA Hawai'i Okinawa Cultural Center, and attempts to use this as an illustration of Okinawan language revitalization efforts, cultural events and community activities in Hawai'i more generally. Iwasaki gives his impressions derived from teaching a course largely to Japanese-fluent students without Okinawan heritage. Kindred reviews the state of teaching Okinawan throughout Hawaii by focusing on three specific situations.

Okinawan Sessions: イ *i,* ロ *ro ,* ハ *ha*

The first session broaches three very distinct topics, united by the thought that these theoretical studies can be applied to give a clearer image of Ryukyuan languages as a target for learning. Miyahira presents evidence for an Okinawan idiom which is used to build *rapport* in conversational situations. Nishioka considers the diversity of possibilities to represent the Ryukyuans in writing, derived from Chinese, Japanese and western, and makes a practical proposal. Van der Lubbe shows how higher-level features can be used to characterize the distinctive properties if a Ryukyuan dialect.

The second session is also varied in content, but this time the focus is on innovation in theoretical approach, rather than applicability. Jarosz considers how a study of high-level conceptual entities – proverbs and metaphors – shows up the value of the dialect Miyakoan. Higa considers how the situation of Okinawans displaced in Hawai'i ("diasporans") may be favourable to survival of the language, both because there is no pressure to integrate with Japanese, and because of the example of revitalization activities for Hawai'ian itself. Ando shows how Okinawan suffixes preserve cognitive distinctions that have been merged in the Japanese case particle *ni,* and muses on the relative importance of space versus animacy in determining the semantics of these relators.

The third session focuses on literary aspects of Okinawan. Yonaha considers the various reasons for which "surtitles" (glosses projected at the side of the stage, as in traditional Chinese opera) can be of value to theatre performances, to clarify the original language for some, as well as to translate it for others. And Keoni Ikeda ponders on how to get the phatic distinction between speaking in Okinawan and speaking in Japanese across in (predominantly English) translations.

Worldwide

Session 1: Knowledge carriers

Ding shows how Prinmi, a language of SW China without a written tradition, preserves knowledge of stars and the local flora and fauna, which were also prominent in the speakers' ancestral religion. By contrast, the languages' carrier role may be trumped by present attitudes. Hudson and Henderson talk of how contemporary beliefs about who is historically significant have affected the survival chances of four languages of Honduras, almost independently of the actual past experienced by their communities. Nash focuses on another interaction of remembered past with a future under construction by looking at the wider effects when Aboriginal Australian words are chosen to provide scientific terms for newly discovered species.

Session 2: The extra effort

Keegan and Mato reviews the conscious difficulty of using technology in Māori rather than English, and how it can be overborne by a deliberate pride in using the ancestral language. Nakagawa investigates the Okinawan language Tokunoshima, and finds that preservation of cultural heritage may be stronger than actual success in maintaining the language.

Session 3: Revitalization planning

Simpson describes new initiatives in Australia to give learners access to indigenous languages, distinguishing and comparing the approaches to languages still vital and to those mainly valued for their roles as emblems. She also identifies challenges they share as language programmes, and some potential solutions. Franchetto, Nonato and Souza share ideas gained from a recent collaboration between Australia and Brazil, with flexible models of interaction among government, civil society and language communities, illustrated by plans for three Brazilian languages.

Session 4: Losses and gains

Gruzdeva and Länsisalmi use the similarities and differences between the largely extinct neighbouring languages of Nivkh in Sahalin and Ainu in Hokkaido to discuss concepts of *super-diversity* and *[quotes] "mother-tongues"*, building a new philosophical view of endangerment and revitalization. Jamshedov considers the ambiguous status of Shughnani among the languages of the Pamirs, a local lingua franca and yet still only precariously represented in education.

Session 5: Knowledge advantages

Ngara describes how knowledge in the Maa language may act as a buttress to the Masaai people and their cullture, under threat from modern developments in Kenya. Reid, Nunn and Sharpe recount how Aboriginal legends provide evidence about changes in sea-level and coast-line of over ten thousand years ago. Lusekelo tells of the hazard to the knowledge implicit in the Hadzabe personal naming system as they increasingly accept joke names from Swahili or Judaeo-Christian names since their Christian conversion. Make Jobo considers a study of proverbs in the Wolaita language of Ethiopia, concluding that they have a valuable role to play in formal education.

Session 6: In school: "could do better"

Fujita-Round comments on the weak showing of local ethnography and language in the schools of Miyako, a Ryukyuan island. Wilson notes a missed opportunity: the scarcity of instruction in indigenous culture in large urban schools in Canada.

Session 7: Societal well-being

Walsh, Marmion and Troy gather and present evidence of the economic, educational, health and social benefits to the community of the revilalization of Australian aborisinal languages. Zuckermann and Walsh postulate language as core to a people's well-being, and hypothesize that language reclamation often results in mental health empowerment, as evidenced in a current reclamation project with the Barngarla people of the Eyre Peninsula, S. Australia. Pinharanda-Nunes and Lee are concerned for the creole language Papiah Kristang, interested in a dubious relation between the promotion of Kristang (e.g. for tourism) and genuine cultural activities developed in the Malacca Portuguese community. Sugita offers theoretical analysis of the crucial role of language in the sedimentation of knowledge within a community, and hence the community's general development, taking her evidence from Okinawa and Amami in the Ryukyus.

Session 8: Social and cultural settings

Anderson and Uribe-Jongbloed note how the improvement that has recently come about in Colombia's official policies of respect for indigenous communities have so far not been reflected in popular attitudes and action; they propose beneficial changes, aimed at spreading responsibility more widely. Kamasungua cites the Yui language and community of Papua New Guinea as a clear case where the language supports community traditions and hence community-consciousness. Funegra relates the story of the Quechua-language magazine *Noqanchis* in Cuzco, Peru, its effect on the perceived "cool" of Quechua, and hence its positive effect on the use, and general prominence, of the language. Finally, Ngara and Oguda set the relation of language and cultural support within a long history: they note the relative eclipse of Ngasa in Tanzania by its neighbouring languages, and make a cultural case for its promotion.

Final Thanks and Acknowledgements

In organizing FEL XVIII, we received much support which we gratefully acknowledge. Peter Simpson organized the sessions at Okinawa International University and hosted us there, while Masahide Ishihara from the University of the Ryukyus organized the first day at the Convention Center and the excursion to Kudakajima. Okinawa International University and the University of the Ryukyus supported the symposium with international symposium grants. Kiyoshi Hara from Joshibi University of Arts supported the symposium with funds which are part of his Japanese Society for the Promotion of Science project on written and spoken communication in Asia. Byron Fija from Okinawa Christian University organized the music program on the first day and provided from the Japanese map printed on the back of the proceedings. Tatsuro Maeda, Yuko Sugita and Shino Miyara also helped at various stages in the preparation of the symposium. We are also grateful to the following colleagues for chairing the sessions of the symposium: Chris Davis, Shinako Oyakawa, Fija Byron, Jack Wendel, Michinori Shimoji, Biba Sethna, Kate O'Callaghan, Kensuke Okamura, Tjeerd de Graaf, Michael Bradley, Kiyoshi Hara, Chris Moseley and Yuto Niinaga. A hearty thanks also to the students of Okinawa International University and the University of the Ryukyus for their help in holding the symposium, and to Mamoru Akamine from the University of the Ryukyus for sharing his knowledge on the history and the religion of the Ryukyus with us during the excursion to Kudakajima. The local newspaper Ryukyu Shinpo and Okinawa Times offered us space for a column on language endangerment, and so did Japan Times. Thanks indeed for all this support – *Ippee nifee deebiru!*

Endangerment of the Indigenous Languages in Okinawa Prefecture, Japan

Masahide Ishihara
University of the Ryukyus
Nishihara, Okinawa
[ishihara@ll.u-ryukyu.ac.jp]

Introduction

The purpose of this presentation is twofold. One is to talk about linguistic diversity in the Okinawa Prefecture, and the other is to talk about the fact that this diversity is endangered. There are five "indigenous" languages spoken in the prefecture: Kunigami, Okinawa, Miyako, Yaeyama, and Yonaguni. Each of these languages has varieties or dialects, which deepens diversity further. In addition, a lot of people speak so-called Japanese "neo-dialects", such as *Uchinaa-Yamatuguchi* ('Okinawan-Japanese'), which has intensified linguistic diversity in the prefecture even further. Some Okinawan people may speak Okinawan, *Uchinaa-Yamatuguchi* and Standard Japanese. In recent years, however, linguistic diversity has decreased owing to the fact that ever fewer people speak their "indigenous" languages.

In this presentation, I will first briefly talk about linguistic diversity in Okinawa Prefecture, then I will discuss how endangered the indigenous languages are. In conclusion, I shall address a particular issue that the people of Okinawa have to decide.

Linguistic Diversity

Okinawa Prefecture consists of three archipelagos: Okinawa, Miyako and Yaeyama. In addition to Japanese known as *kokugo* 'national language', *hyōjungo* 'standard language' or *kyōtsūgo* 'also standard language', different indigenous languages are spoken in these chains. Furthermore, Yaeyama Archipelago includes the Island of Yonaguni, which has its own language. Karimata (2014) says that communication is impossible between natives of Yonaguni and Ishigaki, an island in Yaeyama, if they speak in their respective *shimakutuba* ('community languages'); the same between those of Miyako and Okinawa. In addition, it is said that communication is impossible between natives of Miyako and Yaeyama. The fact that a person from an island cannot talk in his/her own community language to a person from another island demonstrates that Okinawa Prefecture with its many islands has significant language diversity.

There are two languages spoken in Okinawa Island, which has the greatest area in the prefecture. They are Kunigami and Okinawa. Karimata (2014) says that a person from Naha, located in the south, may not be able to talk with a person from Nakijin, located in the north, when they speak in their own community languages.

Due to dialectal differences, difficulty in communication may occur even between speakers of Okinawan, which has the largest number of speakers and is considered to be the major language of the prefecture by a lot of people. For example, *aii, aijaa, aiyoo, aihyaa, appii, afii, ahii, apii, yakaa, yakumii,* and *yacchii* all mean 'older brother' in dialects of Okinawa spoken in the central and southern parts of the Okinawa Island (Karimata, 2014: 266-267). In addition, Kunigami has its own diversity as presented in Nago-shi (2006). There are two types of adjectives: one has *-san* form, while the other has *-han* form. For example, there two adjective forms for 'big': *magi-san* and *magi-han.*

There is another factor that has promoted linguistic diversity in the prefecture. Okinawa was annexed by Japan in 1879, and since Japanese-language education started in the following year, Okinawan people have created a new kind of Japanese dialect known as Uchinaa-Yamatuguchi, or 'Okinawan Japanese'. It may sound like Japanese, but there are slight differences in grammar or lexicon, or in both. For example, an Okinawan may say *neenee-ga keeki tabeyotta*, '(I saw) my elder sister ate a cake'. *Neenee* is an Okinawan-Japanese term for Standard Japanese *ane* 'older sister'. The *V-yotta* form is used only when the speaker witnessed the event; in other words, it is an evidentiality expression. Standard Japanese does not have this kind of expression. Most Okinawans speak daily in this new dialect, and some even confuse this variety with Standard Japanese.

As briefly described above, Okinawa Prefecture has an intricate linguistic diversity, where Japanese, indigenous community languages, and Uchinaa-Yamatuguchi are spoken. However, this diversity is now being lost. The major cause is the decline in the number of community language speakers. In the following section, I talk about the endangerment of indigenous languages of the prefecture.

Assessing the extent of Ryukyuan language endangerment[1]

This section presents an assessment of Ryukyuan language endangerment in Okinawa Prefecture, employing the nine factors proposed by UNESCO Ad

---

[1] This section is a shortened version of Ishihara (2014).

Hoc Expert Group on Endangered Languages in a methodological document entitled "Language Vitality and Endangerment" (UNESCO 2003), hereafter referred to as LVE. LVE identifies nine factors to be used in assessing language endangerment encompassing three major areas: language vitality, language attitudes, and urgency for documentation. These nine factors have to be taken together to evaluate a language's overall situation.

Of the nine factors, six are involved in the evaluation of language vitality. These are intergenerational language transmission (Factor 1), absolute number of speakers (Factor 2), proportion of speakers within the total population (Factor 3), shifts in domains of language use (Factor 4), response to new domains and media (Factor 5), and availability of materials for language education and literacy (Factor 6).

Factor 1: Intergenerational language transmission

Factor 1 simply refers to the fact any language will become endangered and eventually become extinct if it is not transmitted from one generation to the next, i.e. from parent to child at home. Recent surveys such as Ishihara (2014), Okinawa Prefecture (2013) and Ryūkyū Shinpō (2012) report that the number of speakers in younger generations is rapidly decreasing. In fact, there is a general consensus among the people that the community languages are spoken by grandparents and older generations, and that the parent generation may still understand the language, but they hardly speak it at any occasion to their children or among themselves. This is the situation that is assessed at grade 2, which equates to being "severely endangered", in LVE.

Factors 2 and 3: Absolute number and proportion of speakers within the total population

In its LVE framework, UNESCO (2003) emphasizes the importance of absolute number of speakers of the language in question (Factor 2) and the proportion of the total population who have spoken competence (Factor 3). Needless to say perhaps, it is rather difficult to give a precise count of how many people speak a given language, and hence also to calculate the proportion of speakers. However, a fairly accurate estimate can be obtained by using census data in combination with the information in the literature about speaker proficiency, taking "speakers" to mean productive bilinguals, whom we know to be aged 60 or above at the time of writing (see Anderson, to appear), the total number of speakers of community languages can be estimated to stand at 353,651 for five Ryukyuan languages combined spoken in Okinawa Prefecture, i.e. around 350,000 (Okinawa Prefecture 2013b). Using this method of calculation, the number of speakers represents a small proportion at around a quarter of the

total population of Okinawa Prefecture, which again corresponds to grade 2 ("severely endangered").

Factor 4: Shift in domains of language use

Factor 4 assesses language vitality and endangerment in terms of shift in domains of language use. UNESCO (2003: 9) states, "where, with whom, and the range of topics for which a language is used directly affects whether or not it will be transmitted to the next generation." In other words, language maintenance is about maintaining contexts where the language may be used. The survey conducted by the present author (Ishihara, 2014) shows that the community language is mostly spoken in private domains, that is, among family members, relatives, and friends. Furthermore, it is rarely used as a medium of communication in workplaces or neighborhoods. As we have already seen above, the language is seldom used by the parental generation towards children [2]. Therefore, the degree of endangerment for Factor 4 corresponds to "limited or formal domains" (grade 2). It should be noted here that language endangerment is not static but a process and that in this case, too, further decline must be predicted at this stage. That is, when the elderly people who speak the community languages in private domains such as the home and community pass away, these domains will be completely taken over by Japanese.

Factor 5: Response to new domains and media

Factor 5 assesses language vitality with respect to response to new domains and media. UNESCO (2003: 11) defines six degrees of endangerment for this factor. In Okinawa, school education, printed publication and mass media can be considered as new domains for the Ryukyuan languages. Recently, there are some schools where children can study the languages to some extent. Furthermore, newspapers, magazines, books and other printed materials have also been exclusively printed in Japanese until recently. In the past two decades, some books have been published in the community language only, or as bilingual works employing both the community language and Japanese. In addition to local radio or TV programs broadcast in the community language like *Minyō de chuu wuganabira* "Good Afternoon with Folksongs" which has been broadcast for more than thirty years now, there is now a program in Okinawan called *Uchinaa de asobō* "Let's play with Okinawa", on NHK Educational TV. It is a five-minute program in which school-age children can learn the Okinawan language. The Internet hosts several important new domains of language use. For example, Kiyoshi Higa teaches the Okinawan language on the Internet using his blog (Higa, 2012), where he gives

---

[2] A survey conducted by Okinawa Prefecture (2013a) shows similar results: Children do not have opportunities to hear the languages of their communities.

explanations of grammar and lists of vocabulary. This blog is bilingual, written in Okinawan and Japanese.

As presented in this subsection, the languages of the Ryukyus have regained some lost domains, entered domains they have never been used in, and spread in new internet-based domains. However, neither the number of domains nor the amount of language use in each domain is large at present. Therefore, the assessment for Factor 5 is grade 2 ("coping").

Factor 6: Materials for language education and literacy

For this factor, UNESCO's (2003: 12) LVE does not posit any explicitly named degrees of endangerment but merely allots grades from 5 to 0. Education is crucial for the revitalization of the languages of the Ryukyus. Adults and children who want to learn how to use the languages may be taught at school or learn by themselves. As long as they learn how to speak by repeating what their teachers say at school, they may not need written materials[3]. However, let us note here that if one wants to learn to speak a language, recorded expressions or video clips uploaded on the Internet are of crucial help. They may also reinforce what one learns from a teacher without using printed materials.

For the people of Okinawa Prefecture who want to learn how to read and write their community languages, some kind of written materials with which they can study are definitely needed. Several written materials have been published in the past two decades, some of which are accompanied by a CD. However, almost all the materials published so far have instructions written in Japanese, while examples are written in the Ryukyuan language using orthographies based on the Japanese

At present, Okinawan children do not read materials written in Ryukyuan languages at school. Children are not given literacy education in the community languages as a part of the school curriculum. Literacy education in the Ryukyus is conducted in Japanese, and it is aimed at developing and improving skills in reading and writing Japanese only. In the rare cases in which some kind of Ryukyuan language proficiency is being developed, it takes place at home or in extracurricular classes. In 2013, there was a new initiative by the Naha City Board of Education which published a guidebook entitled *Chikati ashiba na shimakutuba* ('Let's Enjoy Using Community Language'). Students at all the elementary and junior high schools in Naha City were

given this guidebook and encouraged to have conversations with their parents and/or grandparents in *shimakutuba*.

On the basis of what has been discussed in this subsection, Factor 6 is assessed at grade 2. There exist materials written in Ryukyuan languages, but the number of printed materials is very small and most of them are intended to be read by adults, not by children, partly owing to the fact that literacy education in the languages is not included in the school curriculum.

Factor 7: Governmental and institutional attitudes and policies

The second category of factors in LVE is language attitudes. This is important for assessing the degree of endangerment or vitality of an endangered language because language choices are governed by attitudes. UNESCO (2003) proposes two factors relating to language attitudes, differentiating between attitudes of the government, and attitudes of the people.

Factor 7 assesses the vitality of an endangered language with respect to governmental support for revitalization. In the Ryukyuan case, Okinawa Prefecture did not support existing revitalization efforts and demands of revitalization movements until a few years ago; however, Okinawa Prefectural Museum and Art Museum has constantly organized events related to revitalization of the indigenous languages of the prefecture. Moreover, financial backing of such efforts is particularly weak. The Ryukyuan languages are not official languages of Okinawa Prefecture, nor are they taught at schools as part of the official curriculum. Furthermore, the prefectural or municipal governments do not provide assistance in teacher training at present. However, there exists some governmental support, at least on a symbolic level. For example, the Okinawan prefectural government has confirmed that the languages of the Ryukyus constitute the core of Ryukyuan culture (Okinawa Prefecture, 2005, 2012). Furthermore, in 2006 the prefectural assembly of Okinawa established an ordinance known as *Shimakutuba no hi ni kansuru jōrei* ('Ordinance to Celebrate the Community Language Day'). This can be seen as evidence that the prefectural government of Okinawa is not indifferent to the endangerment of the Ryukyuan languages (Ishihara, 2010b). However, neither the prefectural government nor the assembly seems to have any roadmap, policy or the necessary know-how for the revitalization of the Ryukyuan languages at the present. While both claim to support the idea of revitalization, these good intentions have yet to manifest in concrete policies and actions. There was a small step forward in 2013, however. Okinawa Prefecture conducted a prefecture-wide survey on language use and language attitudes for the first time in Okinawan history (Okinawa Prefecture, 2013a). It seems that the prefectural government is now more

---

[3] Currently, most of the teachers of the Ryukyuan languages are in their seventies or above and most of them have not studied applied linguistics or language teaching at higher education institutions. They belong to NPOs or other kind of organizations. Before they start teaching, they get together to learn teaching methods and compile teaching materials. This situation is problematic because their teaching methods and materials may not be based on tried and tested applied linguistic theories.

willing to take action to promote revitalization of the community languages.

According to UNESCO's (2003: 13-14) LVE framework, Okinawa is assessed as "passive assimilation" (grade 3) in terms of this factor. UNESCO's description of this degree of support reflects the current situation in the Ryukyus: "No explicit policy exists for minority languages; the dominant language prevails in the public domain."

Factor 8: Community members' attitudes towards their own language

For Factor 8, UNESCO (2003: 14-15) does not posit specific forms of support, but allocates grades ranging from 5 to 0. Community members' attitudes towards their own language may be the most crucial in determining the chances of maintenance or revitalization of the language. Ishihara (2014) and Okinawa Prefecture (2013) show that the majority of the respondents want to speak their community language in the future may reveal a generally positive societal attitude towards the maintenance of heritage languages. These survey also demonstrate that majority of the respondents want their children and/or grandchildren to be able to speak the community language. Obviously, in order to have children and grandchildren speak the community language, language transmission would need to be restored in the home. It is therefore assumed that a positive response to this question may reflect a generally positive attitude towards future grassroots revitalization efforts.

From what are presented in Ishihara (2014) and Okinawa Prefecture (2013), it is clear that the majority of the respondents have positive attitudes towards the community languages and want them to be maintained. Most of the people surveyed expressed the wish to speak the languages, and also hope for their children and/or grandchildren to inherit them. However, when asked about the likelihood of community language maintenance, almost half of the respondents were skeptical. In view of this, Factor 8 may be most appropriately be assessed at grade 3.5, that is, somewhere between grade 4 ("[m]ost members support language maintenance") and grade 3 ("[m]any members support language maintenance; many others are indifferent or may even support language shift").

Documentation urgency assessment

The third and final category for assessing language endangerment is concerned with the amount and quality of language documentation. Documentation is important for language maintenance and revitalization because it lays an important basis for the development of teaching materials such as grammar books, textbooks, recordings and videos. Dictionaries are also the outcome of documentation. Even if a language is set to become extinct in the near future, documenting the language has its merits. According to UNESCO:

> Documentation of such a language is important for several reasons: 1) it enriches the intellectual capital; 2) it presents a cultural perspective that may be new to our current knowledge; and 3) the process of documentation often helps the language resource person to reactivate the linguistic and cultural knowledge. (UNESCO, 2003: 7)

UNESCO (2003: 16) defines six levels of documentation for Factor 9. In the case of the Ryukyuan languages, a lot of printed materials have been published. There are grammar books such as Miyara (2000), Shimoji (2009) and Yoshiya (1999), and dictionaries such as Handa (1999), Kokuritsu Kokugo Kenkyūjo (1963), and Nakasone (1983). Textbooks such as Nishioka *et al.* (2000) have accompanying CDs, in which examples are pronounced by native speakers. However, there is very little audiovisual recording of natural speech that is easy to access. Therefore, the assessment of the nature of documentation is "fair" and the grade is 3. UNESCO (2003: 16) describes this level as follows "There may be an adequate grammar, some dictionaries, and texts, but no everyday media; audio and video recordings may exist in varying quality of or degree of annotation."

Conclusion

As described in the preceding sections, Okinawa's linguistic diversity is being lost, and the indigenous languages will certainly vanish unless some measures are taken to reverse the language shift. One possible first step may be efforts to strengthen existing domains of use, thereby creating opportunities for people to use the community language. These domains include the home, school, neighborhood and social gatherings such as festivals. Furthermore, the Ryukyuan languages will co-exist with Japanese. The solution for revitalization against a backdrop of such co-existence is the development of complementary functions between Ryukyuan and Japanese, which should result in societal bilingualism. In this ideal situation, all speakers would be bilingual and none of the languages involved would be considered inferior and therefore unnecessary. This development of distinct functions for Japanese and Ryukyuan languages, then, is the ultimate goal towards which any measures of Ryukyuan language revitalization must aim. The longer such a development is delayed, the more difficult it will become to maintain and revitalize the Ryukyuan languages. This paper reveals the urgency with which the task of reversing language shift must be undertaken, but it also gives hope that language revitalization is possible if positive language attitudes are promoted through concrete support for using and transmitting the Ryukyuan languages.

References

Anderson, M. (2014). Language shift and language loss. In M. Anderson & P. Heinrich (Eds.), *Language Crisis in the Ryukyus*. Newcastle upon Tyne: Cambridge Scholars Publishing.

Handa, I. (1999). *Ryūkyūgo jiten* [Dictionary of the Ryukyuan Language]. Tōkyō: Daigaku Shorin.

Higa, K. (2012). *Higa Kiyoshi no Uchinaaguchi kōza – bun de oboeru Uchinaaguchi* [Kiyoshi Higa's Course on Okinawan. Memorizing Okinawan in Sentences]. Online available at: http://blogs.yahoo.co.jp/bunshou_uchinaaguchi (accessed on 3 May 2014).

Ishihara, M. (2010a). Ryūkyū shogo o meguru gengo seisaku [Language Policies on the Languages of the Ryukyus]. In M. Ishihara, I. Kina & S. Yamashiro (Eds.), *Okinawa, Hawai. Kontakuto zōn toshite no tōsho* [Okinawa and Hawai'i. Islands as Contact Zones] (pp. 71-90). Tōkyō: Sairyūsha.

Ishihara, M. (2014). Language vitality and endangerment in the Ryukyus. In M. Anderson & P. Heinrich. *Language Crisis in the Ryukyus*. Newcastle upon Tyne: Cambridge Scholars Publishing.

Karimata, S. (2014). Shometsu kiki gengo no kyōiku kanōsei o kangaeru [One thought on possibility of education of endangered languages] In Y. Fujita, K. Toguchi & S. Karimata (Eds.) *Tōsho chi'iki no arata na tenbō* [New Perspectives of Islands] (pp.263-279). Fukuoka: Kyūshū University Press.

Kokuritsu Kokugo Kenkyūjo (1966). *Okinawago jiten* [Dictionary of the Okinawan Language]. Tōkyō: Ōkurashō Insatsukyoku.

Miyara, S. (2000). *Uchinaaguchi Kōza. Shurikotoba no shikumi* [Lecture on Okinawan Language. The Structure of the Shuri Dialect]. Naha: Okinawa Times.

Moseley, C. (Ed.) (2009) *Atlas of the World's Languages in Danger* (3rd edition). Paris: UNESCO. Online available at: http://www.unesco.org/culture/en/endangeredlanguages/atlas (accessed 3 June 2014).

Naha City (2013). *Chikati ashibana shimakutuba* [Let's Enjoy Shimakutuba]. Naha: Okinawa Jiji Shuppan.

Nakasone, S. (1983). *Okinawa Nakijin hōgen jiten* [Dictionary of Nakijin Dialect of Okinawa] Tōkyō: Kadokawa Shoten.

Nishioka, S., Nakahara, J.,Ikari, F. & Nakajima, Y. (2006). *Okinawago no nyūmon. Tanoshii Uchinaaguchi* [Introduction to the Okinawan Language. Diverting Okinawan Language]. Tōkyō: Hakusuisha

Ogawa, S. (2014). Orthography development. In P. Heinrich, S. Miyara and M. Shimoji (Eds.), *Handbook of the Ryukyuan Languages* (pp. 575–590). Boston: Mouton de Gruyter.

Okinawa-ken (2005). *Okinawa bunka shinkō shishin* [A Guide to Promotion of Okinawan Culture]. Naha: Okinawa-ken.

Okinawa-ken (2011). *Jūmin kihon daichō nenreibetsu jinkō* [Basic Resident Register Population by Age Group]. Available online at: http://www.pref.okinawa.lg.jp/site/kikaku/shichoson/2422.html (accessed on 3 May 2014).

Okinawa-ken (2012). *Okinawa 21 seiki vishon – akihon keikaku* [Okinawa 21st Century Vision. A Basic Plan]. Naha: Okinawa-ken.

Okinawa-ken (2013a). *Shimakutuba kenmin undō suishin jigyō – kenmin ishiki chōsa* [Prefectural Campaign for Promotion of Shimakutuba. A Prefecture-wide Survey on Language Attitude]. Naha: Okinawa-ken.

Okinawa-ken (2013b). *Jūmin kihon daichō nenrei-betsu jinkō* [Basic Resident Register Population by Age Group]. Available online at: http://www.pref.okinawa.lg.jp/site/kikaku/shichoson/2422.html (accessed on 3 May 2014).

Ryūkyū Shinpō (2012). *2011 Okinawa kenmin ishiki chōsa* [2011 Survey of People's Attitudes in Okinawa Prefecture]. Naha: Ryūkyū Shinpō.

Shimabukuro, R. (2008). Ryūkyūgo ni kansuru ishiki chōsa to Ryūkyūgo fukkō no kanōsei [Survey of Awareness about Ryukyuan Languages Possibility of their Restoration]. M.A. Thesis, Graduate School in Humanities and Social Sciences, University of the Ryukyus.

Shimoji, M. (2009). A Grammar of Irabu, a Southern Ryukyuan Language. Ph. D. Dissertation, Department of Linguistics, Australian National University.

UNESCO Ad Hoc Expert Group on Endangered Languages (2003). *Language Vitality and Endangerment*. Online available at: http://www.unesco.org/culture/ich/doc/src/00120-EN.pdf (accessed on 3 May 2014).Chercheur, J.L. (1994).

Language Endangerment in the Amami Islands

Tatsuro Maeda
Tokyo University of Foreign Studies
[airoption@gmailcom]

(Translated by Kensuke Okamura, Dokkyo University)

Introduction

UNESCO added the Amami language to its list of endangered languages in 2009. That caused a great surprise and puzzlement among the residents on the Amami Islands. Before then, there had been no specific names for the indigenous language there. The language was called *shimaguchi* ('community language'), which is similar to the name *shimakutuba* for the indigenous languages in Okinawa, but it has been just a few decades since it began to be widely used (Maeda, 2006: 5-6). Until then, and even now, the most popular name which the residents use to mention the language is *hōgen* ('dialect'). Local people still have little or no language awareness that the Amami language is a language in its own rights. Negative evaluation of the language as being "useless" or "insignificant" remain like a stain in their mind.

Furthermore, the Amami Islands administratively belong to the Kagoshima Prefecture, although the Amami language is one of the Ryukyu languages. This fact greatly affects the historical background of the Amami language and also the present efforts of language revitalization. The political and psychological distance from Okinawa, where other Ryukyuan languages are spoken in close geographic proximity, and the control by Kagoshima from the 17th century are crucial factors in the endangerment of the Amami language.

The purpose of this paper is clarify the "endangerment" of the Amami language. There is no doubt that the degree of language endangerment in Amami is of such extent that the future existence of the language is in peril. However, it has rarely been discussed what this endangerment entails for whom. In other words, our discussions on language endangerment have very often been simply based on the assumption that "the residents in an area hope that their language will continue to exist or will be revitalized." On the basis of the Amami language, I would like to discuss this point.

Historical and social background of the Amami Islands and the Amami language

Even since the Ryukyu Kingdom was formed in the 15th century, Shuri (today a part of Naha City), the political capital of the kingdom, had ruled the Amami Islands. Because of the geographical closeness, there must have been exchanges between the inhabitants of these islands, but few written records testifying this are left. The period before the control of the Ryukyu Kingdom is regarded as a mythological age called *Amaminyu* (literally 'the world of Amami'). The period of the control of the Ryukyu Kingdom, on the other hand, is called *Nahanyu* ('the world of Naha'). The two periods are clearly distinguished in this way (Maeda, 2006: 11-12). The military invasion by Satsuma (Kagoshima) in 1609 had a massive historical impact on the present situation of the Amami Islands. Satsuma colonized the Amami Islands, forcing the residents to a single crop agriculture (sugar cane) in order to produce value-added brown sugar. Farmers suffered under the exaggerated production targets and as a consequence food production for the residents was restricted. The result was a situation where people often died of hunger, and this in turn created a class of slaves. Satsuma could also buy arms by selling the brown sugar from Amami. In the event, it dominated the Amami Islands until it became Kagoshima Prefecture after the Meiji Restoration (Sakida, 2012).

Although the Amami Islands became a part of Japan after the Meiji Restoration, in practice they remained a colony of Kagoshima. They both depended economically on Kagoshima and they also continued to be economically exploited. In 1940 the same system of tax, administration, school etc. as the Japanese 'mainland' (*hondo*) was introduced in the Amami Islands and they were also integrated into the Japanese army draft system. These hard circumstances brought about a surplus workforce, and as a result the islands experienced massive labor emigration to the mainland in the 1920s, especially to Osaka and Kobe, then the biggest industrial areas in Japan. An inflow of labor from the Korean peninsula and Okinawa also happened at the same time. The migrant workers communities still exist in these cities today. The economy of the Amami Islands depended on these migrant workers and the money they sent home, and this has also not changed.

As a result of this, the Amami people were placed at the bottom of the society in the mainland and experienced much discrimination. The Amami language was considered as one of the reasons for discriminating against them.

In school, "dialect-correction" was promoted in the Amami Islands before and during World War II. The Japanese government tried to spread the view that the 'national language' (*kokugo*) was Standard Japanese and that it was important for every Japanese citizen to speak it in order to become a modern state. In most cases, this view led directly to an oppression of the dialects of the Amami language. Okinawa and the Amami Islands, where language different from Japanese are spoken, share this experience. However, the difference between them is that the educational administration of the Amami islands has been under the control of Kagoshima Prefecture. Especially in 1941, in the period of the Pacific War, the Standard Japanese language education entailed also elements of militaristic education. The textbooks used then in Amami were written for the pupils in Kagoshima and therefore unfamiliar to pupils on the Amami Islands. Teachers who themselves were born there and spoke the Amami language had to forbid the pupils to use this language. Teachers also kept watch on one another, and the influence extended over the entire community in the end. Thus, the intensity and the severity of education in the period of the Pacific War was much more severe in the Amami Islands than in Kagoshima.

The often violent ways in education were in a way "rationalized" by the negative attitudes that Amami emigrants were experiencing on the mainland, and which they then "brought back" to the Amami Islands. Because of the linguistic and cultural differences, the Amami people were often considered "non-Japanese" in the mainland. Hence, they devoted themselves to practice of militaristic education and activities even more than people on the mainland, in order to prove that they, too, were "real Japanese".

Both in their own community and in the places where they had emigrated, the Amami language was looked down upon, and this trend continued after the end of World War II. Until the 1980s, albeit in a less severe manner, children ware told not to use the language in school (Maeda, 2013: 38-39).

School education is not the only reason why the Amami language has been driven to its present stage of endangerment. There is no doubt that it has played a key-role in shaping attitudes towards the local language in the village community. Attitudes which were often more militaristic and conservative than on the mainland had the result that it was considered a "taboo" to doubt one's "Japaneseness". Moreover, the Emperor system continued to have strong support also after the War. The occupation and control of the Amami Islands by U.S. armed forces from 1945 to 1953 further strengthened this strong sense of Japanese nationalism.

Given this historical and social background, it still remains difficult for the people in Amami to build a positive attitude towards their own language. Above all,

for Amami to be accepted as Japanese, the Amami language needed to be seen as a dialect of Japanese.

Relation to Okinawa

After the end of Okinawan political control over Amami in the 17th century, exchange of residents between the Amami Islands and Okinawa still continued. However, an "orientation toward the mainland" has taken root since the Meiji period and this has supported the view that the Amami people are Japanese. In so doing, the view emerged that "We are different from Okinawan people. We are Japanese." Consider a concrete example. It is said that in 1945, when Japan acknowledged defeat, the Amami Islands refused to sigh the capitulation which the U.S. had prepared because it mentioned them as Northern Ryukyu. This means that there was awareness among the Amami people that they "did not belong to Ryukyu, or Okinawa". The thought of the U.S. that Ryukyu was a united community and ruled by Japan compulsorily was obviously "wrong" (Eldridge, 2003). Under the control of the U.S. armed forces, the movement for the return to Japanese control began both in Okinawa and on the Amami Islands. Until 1953, when the Amami Islands returned to Japanese control, there existed limitations for travel and sojourn on the mainland, as an effect of which many residents lost their jobs and went to (U.S.-occupied) Okinawa to work instead. Okinawa remained occupied by the U.S. until 1972. Men were mainly engaged in physical labor at American military bases, and women were engaged in service industries or in prostitution. In Okinawa, too, the Amami people were in a minority and discriminated against.

To this day, the central figures in the Amami return movement are praised and regarded as heroes. Children sing a "song for the return to Japanese control" at school, and the reversion day (on Christmas) is celebrated every year. Amami's "Japanese ideology" that exaggerated the difference between Amami and Okinawa is similar to that once used by Okinawans vis-à-vis Taiwan. Taiwan was a Japanese colony from 1895 to 1945. Also owing to the fact Okinawa was under control of the U.S.A. until 1972, the attitudes of Okinawa and the Amami Islands toward "Japan" vary considerably.

During the control of the U.S. the number of repatriates from the mainland or overseas increased extremely, causing a food crisis in the Amami Islands. The residents thought that a return to Japan would improve this critical situation, and this in turn led to an atmosphere where one could not criticize the return movement or question one's "Japaneseness".

The difference from the present situation of Okinawa

The historical and social background of Amami makes it more difficult to organize a language revitalization movement in Amami than in Okinawa. Thus, the Amami language situation is grave. In this section, it is discussed what is lacking for the Amami language revitalization in comparison to Okinawa. The future of the Amami language depends on how the following problems will be solved.

(1) No original local mass media: Although there are some small FM broadcasters with limited range, Kagoshima controls most available radio or television broadcasts. On the two Amami Islands closest to Okinawa, Yoronjima and Okinoerabujima, Okinawan radio or TV programs can be received. As for newspapers, there is one daily newspaper on Amami Ōshima and one on Tokunoshima. These are differences from Okinawa, which possesses its own broadcasting station in Naha and which produces original programs.

(2) No university: On the Amami Islands, there are no universities except for some very small institutions for agricultural and marine products, medicine as well as incidental facilities such as a satellite campus of Kagoshima University. There exists no scholarly or scientific hub on the Amami Islands. Researchers of the Amami language and culture inevitably come from the outside of the islands and therefore it is hard to return their research results to the community. The other is that there are neither universities nor colleges for high school graduates to enter. If they want to go to university or college, they have without exception to leave the islands.

(3) No specific industries: The Amami Islands and Okinawa are similar in climate, but tourism in the Amami Islands is not as prosperous as that in Okinawa. Commerce and industry are also on a smaller scale in the Amami Islands. With subsidy from the Japanese government, public works are carried out. Many of the working-age population have been leaving the Amami Islands the Meiji period. This has led to a drastic population decline and to social aging of the community.

(4) No autonomy: As mentioned above, the Amami islands are under control of Kagoshima. Discrimination of Kagoshima against the Amami people is not completely eliminated yet. Particularly, Kagoshima's control over education leads to the loss of school as a domains to pass on the Amami language to the next generation. Police officers, bureaucrats and executive teachers etc. are also dispatched from Kagoshima to the Amami Islands.

In fact, Okinawa consists of a number of islands, and therefore, the situations on the Okinawa Island and the others are probably different in significant ways. For example, the situations of the Miyako and Yaeyama islands may be similar to that of the Amami Islands. When we think about "the Ryukyu language" we should never ignore the Amami islands. However, they have been largely forgotten even by Okinawa so far.

Conclusions

The Amami people are conscious of the endangerment of the Amami language. Nevertheless, compared to Okinawa, there are very few people who consider the possibility of language revitalization. To many people in the Amami Islands, reversion to the Amami tradition means a separation from Japan. The sense of security that can be gained by staying one of the Japanese districts is still necessary for the Amami people.

In that situation, however, activities to pass on the Amami culture to the next generation still continue. Just very few young people are willing to study traditional performing arts and music. Nonetheless, the impoverishment of the community is doing severe damage to the languages and cultures. The number of people from which it could be inherited is also in decline. Many people are convinced that the Amami language is a "Japanese dialect" and they do not accept the opinion that it is a language in its own right. Although "being Japanese" was the only way for them to survive, the Amami people were suspected by mainlanders to not "be really Japanese". These memories are hard to get rid of people's minds. The younger generations have a less negative attitude towards Okinawa than the other older generations. For those who take part in the revitalization of the Amami language, Okinawa is the closest role model. If Okinawa reaches out with a helping hand to the Amami islands, regardless of the differences and the past feuds, the revitalization of the Amami language will possibly make faster progress.

Compared to Miyako and Yaeyama islands, which are regarded as a part of Okinawa, the Amami language is linguistically closer to the Kunigami or Okinawan languages. It may be possible to bring about a positive interaction between Okinawa on one hand and the Amami Islands on the other hand.

References

Eldridge, R.D. (2003). *Amami henkan to nichibei kankei – sengo Amerika no Amami/Okinawa senryō to ajia senryaku* [Amami Reversion and US-Japanese Relations. American Occupation of Amami and Okinawa and Asian Strategy]. Kagoshima: Nanpō Shinsha.

Maeda, T. (2006). Amami-Ōshima Setouchi-chō ni okeru "shimaguchi" denshō katsudō [Efforts of language transmission in Setoichi Town in Amami Ōshima]. In Tagengo shakai kenkyūkai (Ed.) *Tagengo shakai kenkyūkai nenpō* Annula [Proceedings of the Study Circle on Multilingual Societies 6].

Maeda, T. (2013). Kagoshima-ken no kokugo kyōiku ni okeru hyōjungo/hōgen ideorogī [Standard language/dialect ideology in national language education in Kagoshima]. In Tōkyō Gaikokugo

Daigaku (ed.): *Nihongo/nihongaku kenkyū* [Study of Japanese and Japanology] 3.

Sakida, M. (2013). *Amami shotō no satō seisaku to tōbaku shikin* [Sugar Policy in the Amami Islands and Funds for Overthrowing the Shogunate. Nanpō Shinsha: Kagoshima.

History and Structure of the Ryukyuan Languages

Shinsho Miyara

901-0213 Okinawa, 592 Zukeran
Kitanakagusuku, Japan
[s7miyara@gmail.com]

Abstract

Ryukyuan languages shared a number of basic vocabulary items of the same origin with Japanese, but they are not dialects of Japanese. A common Ryukyuan-Japanese ancestral language can be traced back beyond the Nara period (AD 710-784) when Japanese started being written. The Ryukyuan languages have been handed down from generation to generation in the Ryukyu Islands for more than a thousand years. In 1879, the Ryukyuan Kingdom was replaced by Okinawa Prefecture against much local resistance, and simultaneously Ryukyuans were claimed to be mere dialects of Japanese. This perspective has crucially contributed to the endangerment of the Ryukyuan languages. To show the differences with Japanese, the typological features of the Ryukyuan language are presented. This is followed by a brief discussion of the morphological and the syntactic properties of Okinawan, the largest Ryukyuan language.

Ryukyuan languages as sister languages to Japanese

Until the appearance of the UNESCO *Atlas of the World's Languages in Danger* (2009), Ryukyuan languages spoken in Okinawa Prefecture had been considered to be dialects of Japanese for many years by Japanese dialectologists, Campbell (1991), Shibatani (2009), and others. The UNESCO view brought a drastic change in the view of indigenous languages spoken in Japan. Six Ryukyuan languages (henceforth "the Ryukyuans") and the Hachijō language are recognized as indigenous languages of Japan now, in addition to the Japanese and the Ainu languages. There is no doubt that the Ryukyuan group is genetically related to Japanese and that these make up two branches of the *Japonic* language family (Serafim, 2003). On the other hand, most of the dialectological studies in Japan have been directed toward the genetic relatedness (i.e., differences and similarities) between Japanese and Ryukyuans under the assumption that they are merely different dialects of one and the same language. However, all Ryukyuan languages are mutually unintelligible with Japanese, and it will be argued below that it is necessary to study them as individual languages with their own linguistic systems. The study of the Ryukyuans should be no more a part of Japanese linguistics, and should take place in an independent field of study, Ryukyuan linguistics.

Starting with a glottochronological study by Hattori (1959), there exist today a series of studies about genetic relationship between Japanese and the Ryukyuans (Nakama, 1992; Yasumoto, 1994; Bentley, 2008, etc.). They largely agree that around 1,500–1,700 years ago Proto-Ryukyuan-Japanese split into the Japanese and the Ryukyuan branches. Their finding conforms to history and linguistic facts. Old Japanese first appeared in such documents of the eighth century as the *Manyōshū* ('Collection of Ten Thousand Leaves'), an anthology of about 4,500 *waka* poems, for 400 years up to 759 CE) and the *Kojiki* ('Records of Ancient Matters', a collection of myths and pseudo-history, 712 CE) in the Nara period (710-784 CE). Insofar as their finding is well-sustained, it is no wonder that there are a great many basic vocabulary items of *Manyō* origin in present-day Ryukyuan languages. In the *Kojiki,* there was not a single instance of *Nippon* or *Nihon* ('Japan'); instead, *Yamato* was the national name of Japan at that time. In the Okinawan language, such words as *Yamatu, Yamatuu, Yamatunchu,* and *Yamatuguchi* are still used to refer to 'mainland Japan', 'mainland Japanese people or products', 'the mainland Japanese people', and 'the Japanese language', respectively. Likewise, *tō-nu kuni* is the Okinawan word for 'China', whose national name was then *tō* (imitating Chinese Tang, AD 618-907)

There is another piece of evidence that splitting into Japanese and the Ryukyuans must have taken place in or before the Nara period, but not in the Heian period (AD 784-1191). It was in the Heian period that narrative prose fiction and essays were written in *hiragana*. There is an Okinawan analogue to the *Manyōshū,* called the *Omoro sōshi* ('Compilation of Thoughts', an anthology of about 1,554 songs and ballads, 22 volumes, 1532, 1613, 1623, 1654 CE), which is written mostly in *hiragana* and rarely in Chinese characters. Because of insufficient understanding of the phonetic quality of *hiragana* reflecting Heian pronunciation, there are many basic inconsistencies in the *hiragana* transcription of the *Omoro sōshi*, though it is an anthology compiled by the Ryukyuan Kingdom. For example, the focus particle *du* is written in such *hiragana* as to (と), do (ど), ru (る), and ro (ろ) (Mamiya, 2005: 9). Such inconsistences make it difficult to understand the songs and ballads compiled in the anthology. If splitting into Japanese and Ryukyuans had taken place at the Heian period, *hiragana* would have been being used among the intellectuals in the Ryukyu Islands.

Any Japanese dialect directly traces back to either the *Kamigata* speech variety or the *Edo* variety which separated in the Edo period (AD 1603-1867); for example, the copula *ʤa*, the negative *nu*, and the past negative *nanda* in the Kamigata speech variety began to be changed into *da*, *nai*, and *nakatta* respectively around the Edo region (Higuchi, 1994). However, this is not the case for Ryukyuan languages; the copula *jan*, the negative *ran*, and the past negative *ran-ta-n* have been used in Okinawan from far back in the past. Basically there are no influences of cultures from the Heian to the Edo period in Ryukyuan languages. It is secure to say that Ryukyuan languages have been transmitted from generation to generation for more than a thousand years in the Ryukyu Islands.

The Ryukyus once formed their own kingdom. However, the Meiji government replaced the Ryukyuan Kingdom with Okinawa Prefecture by sheer force and against much local resistance in 1879, and simultaneously declared the Ryukyuan languages to be dialects of Japanese. Having treated the Ryukyuans as dialects of Japanese for 135 years has endangered these languages. Like English and German as descendants of Proto-Germanic, the Ryukyuans and Japanese have a number of basic vocabulary items of the same origin so that they shared a common ancestor we may call Proto-Japonic at an early period in history.

Typology of the Ryukyuan languages

In order to show the differences between Japanese and the Ryukyuan languages, some phonetic features and phonological characteristics of the Ryukyuans are presented in this section. Most of the contents of the present section are based on Miyara (2014b).

Glottal Stop [ʔ]

The glottal stop [ʔ] is widely distributed among the Ryukyuan languages. It is distinctive in word-initial position as in (1) when immediately followed by semivowels and nasal consonants, but predictable as in (2) when followed by vowels.

(1)   *ʔja:* '2PSG'   vs.   *ja:* 'house'
      ʔwa: 'pig'   vs.   *wa:* '1PSG'
      ʔnni 'rice'   vs.   *nni* 'breast'

(2)   *ʔama* 'there'
      ʔiri 'west'
      ʔuʃume: 'grandfather'

Since any vowel involves the occurrence of [ʔ] in word-initial position, there are no content-words beginning with vowels. That is, any content-word begins with a consonant in the Ryukyuans.

Diachronic change of *p>Φ>h*

Japanese has undergone a historical change of *p>Φ>h* (Ueda 1898). As illustrated in (3), the diachronic change of *p* has not taken place in the Southern Ryukyuans spoken in Miyako, Yaeyama, and Yonaguni, as well as in Okinawan spoken in the northern part of Okinawa main-island, which is called the Kunigami language in the UNESCO (2009) *Atlas of the World's Languages in Danger*.

(3) Shika Yaeyaman
pasɨ 'chopsticks'   *piʃi* 'woman'
pɨni 'a mustache'   *pe:* 'tiptoe'
pusu 'stars'   *po:gɨ* 'broom'

On the other hand, as shown in (4), Shuri Okinawan hold the intermediate stage *Φ* while some others have reached the final stage *h*. As a result, Ryukyuans hold ancient aspects of *p* in the Japonic family.

(4) Shuri Okinawan
Φa: 'leaf'   *Φi:* 'fire'
Φu: 'fortune'   *Φe:* 'manure'
(*Φo*)

Consonant clusters

Ryukyuan languages allow a variety of consonant clusters in word-initial position. For example, in Okinawan, consonant clusters, such as *kkʷ, tʃ, ntʃ, mp, nnd, nndʒ, ŋk, ŋgʷ, nn, mm, ʔmb, ʔndʒ, ʔnn, ʔmm, ʔw,* and *ʔj*, appear mostly in word-initial position, as in (5) and (1).

5)   *kkʷa* 'child'   *tʃu* 'human being'
     Na:Φantʃu 'people from Naha'
     nndaN 'not see'   *nndʒuN* 'see'
     wikigaŋgʷa 'boy'   *ndʒi* 'thorn'
     mpa:mpa: 'being unwilling to do'
     ʔmba 'dried layer of the skin of soybean milk' *ʔmbusaN* 'be heavy'
     ʔmma 'horse'   *ʔndʒasuN* 'let out'

Itō and Mester (1995) discuss three constraints on consonant clusters in Japanese. Ryukyuan phonology does not share a constraint ruling out nasal/voiceless obstruent clusters (**nt, *mp, *ŋk*) and one against single /p/ (only *pp* and *mp* are permitted), but it does have one ruling out voiced obstruent geminates (**bb, *dd, *gg, *zz*).

No mono-moraic content words

When the Yonaguni language is excluded, there are no mono-moraic content words in the Ryukyuan languages. Japanese mono-moraic words in (6) correspond to either bi-moraic ones with long vowels in (6a) or bi-moraic ones with voiceless obstruent geminates in (6b). Note that in (5) there is such an example as *tʃu* 'human being' that corresponds to *hito* in Japanese.

(6) a. (Jps. *ki*) *ʧii* (←/kii/) 'spirit'
      (Jps. *ke*) *kii* (←/kɨɨ/) 'hair'
      (Jps. *ʧi*) *ʧii* (←/tii/) 'blood'
      (Jps. *te*) *tii* (←/tɨɨ/) 'a hand'
      (Jps. *na*) *naa* (←/naa/) 'a name'

   b. (Jps. *ko*) *kkʷa*   'child'

Without the existence of / ɨ / the generality of palatalization cannot be maintained, because the applicability of this rule in (6a) depends entirely on the presence of /i/ versus / ɨ / when preceded by /t d/ or /k g/ (Miyara, 1995).

High Central Vowel Phoneme / ɨ /

Out of five Ryukyuan languages, the Okinawan and the Yonaguni language have no high central vowel [ɨ] though many local varieties of Amami, Miyako, and Yaeyaman languages have one. Very interestingly, it is arguable that these two languages have the high central phoneme / ɨ / as well. The arguments for the existence of / ɨ / in Okinawan are based on a series of studies such as Miyara (1996, 1997, 2000, 2009, 2011), Miyara & Arakawa (1994), and Ōmori (2005). In Miyara (2014b), there appears a possibility of the argument for the existence of / ɨ / in the Yonaguni language. Although a detailed discussion of it will not be repeated here, the postulation of / ɨ / greatly contributes to the generality of palatalization, vowel coalescence, and some other general rules, to the distinction of the underlying representations for many pairs of homophonous words, and to the typological characterization of Ryukyuans. It then becomes possible to say that typologically the Ryukyuan languages have a phonological system with the high central / ɨ / (Miyara, 2011); Northern and Southern Ryukyuan languages have six vowel phonemes /i e ɨ u o a/ and the Yonaguni language has four vowel phonemes /i ɨ u a/.

Northern Ryukyuans, Southern Ryukyuans, the Yonaguni language

Nakasone (1961), Kokuritsu Kokugo Kenkyūjo (1963), Miyara (2011: 28), and others all agreed that there are three larger language groups in the Ryukyuan languages. Northern Ryukyuans include languages spoken in the Amami Islands and Okinawa main island, Southern Ryukyuans include ones spoken in the Miyako and the Yaeyama islands, and the third group is the Yonaguni language. The grouping is based on the fact that [w] in the Northern Ryukyuans corresponds to [b] in the other two groups and that [d] in the Yonaguni language corresponds to [j] in the other two.

Without the postulation of / ɨ / in Okinawan, however, the Amami and the Okinawan languages are different in their vowel phonemes and do not form the same language group contrary to many other similarities between these two languages. Only when Okinawan has the vowel phoneme / ɨ / does it turn out to be the case that Japanese /i/ and /e/ regularly correspond to /i/ and / ɨ / in Northern Ryukyuans, and to / ɨ / and /i/ in Southern Ryukyuans respectively.

The Yonaguni language shows the same vowel correspondences as Northern Ryukyuans in that / ɨ / corresponds to Japanese /e/, and /i/ to Japanese /i/. The distinction of /i/ and / ɨ / in the Yonaguni language is based on the analysis of such examples (Ikema, 1998) as [ʧimu] 'heart' (←/kimu/), [ʧi:] 'milk' (←/tii/), [tiN] 'heaven' (←/tin/), and [diN] 'money' (←/din/), the last two underlying forms of which block the application of palatalization.

Morphology of Okinawan

As a representative morphological case of Ryukyuans, word formations of person types in Okinawan are introduced. Most of the contents of the present section are based on Miyara (2014c).

Vowel lengthening

Lengthening the final vowel of non-verb lexical items turn out to be nouns of person types. Word-final vowels of nouns are lengthened in (7), and stem-final vowels of adjectives in (8). In (8), Okinawan adjective stems end with /s/, but drop this final vowel before being undergoing lengthening of the stem vowel.

(7) *juntaku* 'chattering' → *juntakuu* 'a talkative person'
    ʃima 'a local area' → *ʃimaa* 'a local person / product'
    jamatu 'mainland Japan' → *jamatuu* 'a mainland Japanese, a mainland Japanese product'

(8) /nagas/ 'long' : *Φisa naga-a* 'a long-legged person'
    /magis/ 'big' : *ʧiburu magi-i* 'a big-headed person/thing'

Suffixation

Like the English suffix -*er*, /-jaa/ is added to verb stems to form agentive nominals, as in (9). The agentive suffixation is very productive.

(9) /-jaa/ : *Ɂiju tu-jaa* 'a fish getter, fisherman'
    kusa ka-jaa 'a grass cutting person or machine'
    /umi akk-jaa/ → *Ɂumi Ɂatʃ-aa* 'a sea worker, fisherman'

Suffixation of -*aa* to nouns in (10) and a subsequent deletion of stem-final vowels derive persons with the properties denoted by the nouns though they usually have an unfavorable connotation.

(10) /-aa/: /jukusi-aa/ → *jukus_-aa* 'a liar'
     /tanki-aa/ → *tanʧi-aa* → *tanʧ_-aa* 'a short-tempered person'
     /juntaku-aa/ → *juntak_-aa* 'a chatterbox'

The noun *juntaku* 'chattering' derives two different nominals, *juntakaa* in (10) and *juntakuu* in (7), depending on whether it undergoes the application of suffixation of -aa or that of vowel lengthening.

Suffixation of -nʧu to toponyms in (11) derives a person who takes root in the place.

(11) -nʧu: ʔumi-nʧu 'a fisherman'
              ʔagi-nʧu 'a landlubber'
              ʃima-nʧu 'local people, islanders'

A diminutive suffix -g^{w}aa is always accompanied with tender loving connotation, and suffixed to both animate and inanimate nouns.

(12) -g^{w}aa: ʧiruu-g^{w}aa 'dear Chiruu'
                saki-g^{w}aa 'a small amount of sake, my favorite sake'
                majaa-g^{w}aa 'a cute kitten'

It is different from the prefix guma- 'small' in guma-miʧi 'a lane, a path', which is equivalent to ko-miʧi in Japanese.

Prefixation

In Okinawan, almost all Okinawan adjective stems can be altered into prefixes. For example, a prefix guma- 'small' is derived from the adjective gumas-a-n 'is small'. Okinawan derived nouns, such as guma-ʔiju 'a small fish', guma-g^{w}ii 'a low voice', and guma-bu-i 'light rain-falling', and guma-bu-i 'drizzle', are the counterparts of ko-zakana, and ko-goe, ko-bur-i, and ko-same in Japanese. The Japanese prefix ko- has nothing to do with any adjective stem. Japanese has no such productive word formation process of deriving suffixes from adjective stems.

In (13a), guma-a 'a small thing' is derived through vowel lengthening in (8) from the adjective stem /gumas/, and then the suffix -g^{w}aa in (12) is added to derive guma-a-g^{w}aa. In (13b), the verb stem /Φu/ 'to rain' is first nominalized by a suffix -i to form a derived noun Φu-i 'raining'. The derived prefix guma- is then added to the nominalized form Φ u-i, and by rendaku-voicing guma-bu-i is derived. Finally, suffixation of -g^{w}aa is applied to have a noun with tender loving connotation.

(13)   a. guma-a-g^{w}aa 'a cute little one'
        b. guma-bu-i-g^{w}aa 'drizzle'

Syntax of Okinawan

As a representative syntactic case of the Ryukyuans, focusing in Okinawan is introduced. Most of the contents of the present section is based on Miyara (2014a).

In Okinawan, any finite verb ends with a mood morpheme. There are five different mood forms, which

are related to the speaker's attitude toward an event, such as -N 'indicative (IND)', -ru 'declarative with focus (DFC)', /-mɨ/ (mi~i) 'yes-no question (YNQ)', -ga 'wh-question (WH)', and -ra 'question with focus (QFC)'. When as in (14) the nominative phrase waa=ga is focused by particle du in the declarative sentence, it is generally accompanied by mood element -ru. When as in (15) wh-phrase taa=ga is focused by particle ga, it must be accompanied by mood element -ra.

(14) [$_{CP}$ [$_{TP}$ waa=ga=du   wass-a-ta]-ru]
         1SG=NOM=FOC   wrong-be-PST-DFC
         'It is I who was wrong.'

(15) [$_{CP}$ [$_{TP}$ taa=ga=ga   ʔiʧ-u]-ra]
         who=NOM=FOC   go-PRS-QFC
         'Who in the world will go?'

The scope of negation in (16) is marked by adding a particle /ja/ to the nominative phrase Taruu=ga. This particle varies its form (ja~(a-)a~(e-)e~(o-)o), depending on the morpheme-final short vowel (a, i, u) or consonant n preceded. In (16), ʔure=e and Taruu=ga=a are derived by the application of j-deletion and vowel coalescence from /uri=ja/ and /Taruu=ga=ja/ respectively.

(16) [$_{CP}$ ʔure=e [$_{NEGP}$ Taruu=ga=a ____ na-ran]
         this=TOP Taruu=NOM=/ja/ can.do-NEG-ta-N]
         -PST-IND
         'As for this, it is not the case that Taruu was able to do.'

Three typical cases of phrasal focusing in (14)-(16) are shown as the relationships between focus particles and mood elements or the negative ran. [4]

On the other hand, clausal focusing needs either the main verb /a/ 'be', which as the only argument takes a CP-constituent in (17), or the main verb /s/ 'do', which takes a TP (or vP) in (18).

The two types of verb, /a/ and /s/, are mainly designed to focus or negate these different clausal types by particles du and /ja/, which are usually adjoined to the clause periphery.

(17) ʔure=e [$_{NEGP}$ [$_{CP}$ waa=ga ____ ʔi-ʧa-no]=o
         it=TOP   1SG=NOM   say-PST-IND=/ja/
         ʔa-ran]-i.
         be-NEG-YNQ
         'Isn't it the case that I said so?'

----

[4] Technical note: TP – tensed phrase e.g. Engl. "I go", "I went"; vP – verb phrase e.g. "go", "do it"; CP – complementizer phrase e.g. "that I go", "(for) me to go".

(18) ʔure=e [NEGP [TP waa=ga ____
     it=TOP   ISG=NOM
     ʔi-ʧa]-je=e   s-an]-i.
     say-PST-NMLZ=/ja/ do-NEG-YNQ
     'Isn't it the case that I said so?'

There is a fundamental difference in the adjunction of particles to TP and CP; TP-constituents must be nominalized by -i before the particle /ja/ in (18) is adjoined, but there is no such nominalization process necessary for the adjunction to CP in (17). A past event represented by TP is construed as being focused in (18). What is focused in (17) is a past event that the speaker conceives as a fact.

In (19a), within the embedded clause of vP, there is no mood element -ra to license the clause-internal focused wh-phrase taa=ga=ga 'who=NOM=FOC'. However, it is necessary that the focus particle ga will agree with an interrogative mood element -ra within the bounds of the same clause.

(19) a. *[vP taa=ga=ga   ʔiʧ]-i s-u-ra.
         who=NOM=FOC go-NMLZ do-PRS-QFC

     b. [vP taa=ga=tᵢ   ʔiʧ]-i=gaᵢ s-u-ra.
         who=NOM=   go-NMLZ=FOC
         do-PRS-QFC
         'Who in the world will go?'

Accordingly, as in (19b), the focus particle ga would be raised to the vP-periphery, leaving a trace t with no phonetic reflex in the original position in order to become a clause-mate with the main verb s 'do' having the mood element -ra. This is the case in which as in (15) focused wh-phrases are licensed.

Although the obligatory raising of the focus particle ga to the periphery of vP in (19b) is designed to license the focused wh-phrase, it results in creating such a type of clausal focus constructions as (18). In this case, the main verb s 'do' takes as its complement a vP (or TP) with the focus particle ga. However, what is focused is not the entire embedded clause of vP, but the wh-phrase taa=ga.

Summary

Based on the discussion stated above, Ryukyuan languages are different from Japanese in many ways (with respect to glottal stop [ʔ], consonant clusters, phoneme /ɨ/, word formations of person types, mood elements, focusing, and so forth) while they are closer to Old Japanese than present-day Japanese in many basic vocabulary items. It also has been shown that Okinawan, with the largest speaking population among them, is a language with a developed system of mood and focus.

References

Bentley, J. R. (2008). *A Linguistic History of the Forgotten Islands: A Reconstruction of the Proto-Language of the Southern Ryukyus.* Folkstone: Global Oriental.

Campbell, G. L. (1991). *Compendium of the World's Languages.* New York: Routledge.

Hattori, S. (1954). Gengo nendaigaku, sunawachi goi tōkeigaku ni tsuite [On glottochronology or lexical statistics]. *Gengo kenkyū* [Journal of the Linguistic Society of Japan], 26/27, 29-77.

Higuchi, T. (1994). Gengo no tayōsei [The Diversity of Languages]. In: H. Tanaka, *et al.*, *Nyūmon kotoba no kagaku* [Introduction to the Science of Language] (pp. 111-129). Tokyo: Taishukan Shoten.

Ikema, N. (1998). *Yonaguni kotoba jiten* [Dictionary of the Yonaguni Language]. Yonaguni: Private Publication.

Itō, J. & A. R. Mester (1995). Japanese phonology. In J. Goldsmith (Ed.), *The Handbook of Phonological Theory* (pp. 817-838). Cambridge: Blackwell.

Kokuritsu Kokugo Kenkyūjo (1963). *Okinawago jiten* [Dictionary of the Okinawan Language]. Tokyo: Ōkurashō Insatsukyoku.

Mamiya, A. (2005). *Ōmoro sōshi no gengo* [Language in the Ōmoro Sōshi] Tokyo: Kasama Shoin.

Miyara, S. (1995). Okinawa hontō Shuri hōgen ni okeru kōgaika ni tsuite [Palatalization in the Shuri dialect of Okinawa]. *Human Science* (=The Bulletin of the College of Law and Letters, University of the Ryukyus), 1, 1-34.

Miyara, S. (1996). Chūzetsu kōboin onso /ɨ/-ni taisuru hihan-ni kotaeru [Reply to the critique of the central high vowel phoneme /ɨ/]. *Ryūkyū no hōgen* [Ryukyuan Dialects], 20, 68-85.

Miyara, S. (1997). Chūzetsu kōboin onso /ɨ/-o megutte [Concerning the central high vowel phoneme /ɨ/]. *Gengo kenkyū* [Journal of the Linguistic Society of Japan], 111, 107-129.

Miyara, S. (2000). *Uchinaaguchi kōza – Shurikotoba no shikumi* [Lectures on Okinawan: A grammar of the Shuri dialect]. Naha: Okinawa Times.

Miyara, S. (2009). Two types of nasal in Okinawan. *Gengo kenkyū* [Journal of the Linguistic Society of Japan], 136, 177-199.

Miyara, S. (2011). Japonikku gozoku no naka no Ryūkyū goha – keitō, taikei, oyobi genkyō [Ryukyuan languages in the Japonic language family. Genealogy, system, and the present situation] In P. Heinrich & M. Shimoji (Eds.), *Ryūkyū shogo kiroku hozon no kiso* [Essentials in Ryukyuan Language Documentation] (pp. 12-41). Tokyo: Research

Institute for Languages and Cultures of Asia and Africa.

Miyara, S. (2014a). A generative approach to focusing in Okinawan. In P. Heinrich, S. Miyara, & M. Shimoji (Eds.), *Handbook of the Ryukyuan Languages* (pp. 141-156). Boston: de Gruyter.

Miyara, S. (2014b). Phonological aspects of Ryukyuan languages. In P. Heinrich, S. Miyara, & M. Shimoji (Eds.), *Handbook of the Ryukyuan Languages* (pp. 175-198). Boston: de Gruyter.

Miyara, S. (2014c). Shuri Okinawan grammar. In P. Heinrich, S. Miyara, & M. Shimoji (eds), *Handbook of the Ryukyuan Languages* (pp. 279-404). Boston: de Gruyter.

Miyara, S. & T. Arakawa (1994). Okinawa hontō Yonabaru hōgen ni okeru chūzetsu kōboin onso /ɨ/ ni tsuite [On the central high vowel phoneme /ɨ/ of the Yonabaru dialect of Okinawa]. *Gengo kenkyū* [Journal of the Linguistic Society of Japan], 104, 1-31.

Miyara, T. (1931). Hōgen kenkyū-kara mita Yaeyamago [Yaeyaman from the standpoint of dialectology]. *Kokugo kyōiku* [National Language Education], 16(9). Also in *Miyara Tōsō zenshū* [The Complete Works of Tōsō Miyara] vol. 17 (pp. 292-302). Tokyo: Dai'ichi Shobō, 1982.

Nakahara, Z. and M. Hokama (1965). *Kōhon Ōmoro sōshi* [A Compilation of the Omoro Sōshi]. Tokyo: Kadokawa Shoten.

Nakama, M. (1992). *Ryūkyū hōgen no kosō* [The Old Stratum of Ryukyuan Dialects]. Tokyo: Dai'ichi Shobō.

Nakasone, S. (1961). Ryūkyū hōgen gaisetu [Introduction to the Ryukyuan dialects]. In Y. Endō (Ed.), *Hōgengaku kōza* [Course on Dialectology] vol. 4 (pp. 6-25). Tokyo: Meiji Shoin.

Ōmori, I. (2005). Ōgimi-son Tsuha hōgen no on'in no kenkyū [A Phonological Study of the Ogimi-Tsuha Dialect]. M.A. Thesis, University of the Ryukyus.

Serafim, L. A. (2003). When and from where did the Japonic language enter the Ryukyus? A critical comparison of language, archaeology, and history. In A. Vovin and T. Nagata (Eds.), *Perspectives on the Origins of the Japanese Language* (pp. 463-476). Kyoto: International Research Center for Japanese Culture.

Shibatani, M. (2009). Japanese. B. Comrie (Ed.), *The World's Major Languages* (pp. 741-763). New York: Routledge.

Ueda, K. (1898). Gogaku sōken dai-yon – *p*-onkō) [Linguistic Notes 4. On the *p* sound]. *Teikoku bungaku* [Imperial Literature], 4(1), 41-46.

Yasumoto, Y. (1994). Nihongo no kigen [The origin of Japanese]. *Nihongo-ron* [Theory of Japanese], 2(11), 12-35.

Okinawan Language Transmission in in Okinawan Community in Hawai'i

Kyoko Hijirida

1105 Palekaiko Street
Pearl City, Hawai'i, USA
[hijirida@hawaii.edu]

This presentation is focused on the Okinawan language class at the HUOA Hawai'i Okinawa Cultural Center located in Waipahu, Hawai'i.

It provides an overview of Okinawan language revitalization efforts, cultural events and community activities in Hawai'i. It points out future concerns and issues regarding the Okinawa language revitalization, activities, and new developments.

HUOA Okinawa Language Class

In 1990, The Hawai'i United Okinawa Association (HUOA) established the Hawai'i-Okinawa Cultural Center, and three years later the Cultural Center offered its first Okinawan language class to revitalize, promote, and benefit the local Okinawan communities.

However, active interest in this Okinawan language class has been progressing slowly and limited to those who are already engaged in learning Okinawan arts, dances, and cultural activities such as *Sanshin* (a three-stringed banjo-like instrument), Okinawan music, traditional dances, food, cooking, etc. Ordinary people and contemporary Okinawan descendents do not show much concern or keen awareness about the possibility of losing the Okinawan native language.

The Fall and Rise of Okinawan Language in Hawai'i

Because Okinawan immigrants to Hawai'i arrived much later than Japanese immigrants from the Mainland of Japan, the "late-comers" faced many disadvantages. The Okinawan immigrants had to overcome obstacles, prejudices, use Japanese language, and assimilate the new foreign cultures in Hawai'i. The *issei* – the first generation of Okinawan immigrants – encouraged their offspring to learn Japanese language, customs, and tradition, while adapting to the new economic, social, and cultural environments in Hawai'i.

Immigrants from Okinawa celebrated their 100th anniversary in 2000. The Japanese language radio station, KZOO, now features news, music, and entertainment programs from Okinawa. This new wave of Okinawan cultural influence also helped the University of Hawaii to establish and offer Okinawa Language & Culture courses in 2004 as part of the university language curriculum. It also helped establish the Center for Okinawan Studies in 2008 at the University of Hawai'i at Manoa.

Future Concerns and Issues

The successful revitalization of the Okinawan language is important for the future of Hawai'i. The heritage, tradition, and culture of Okinawa are vitally important for the economic benefits for Okinawan people in Hawai'i, in view of their continuing prosperity, economic developments, and cultural values.

Through interactions with the faculty of University of Hawai'i language program and Okinawan traditional arts teachers, the language instructors in the local community may be further enhanced and explored with new strategies and actions. It should seek further support and encouragement from the Okinawa Prefecture in order to increase additional people exchanges, language teacher trainings, cultural promotions, joint seminars and symposia.

References

Hijirida, K. (2006). Okinawan language and culture course: Its contents and curriculum implementation at the University of Hawaii. *Immigration Studies* 2. Immigaration Research Center, Okinawa.

Ishihara, M. (2007). Linguistic cultural identity of Okinawans in the U.S. In Joyce Chinen (Ed.) *Uchinaanchu Diaspora Memories, Continuities, and Construction Social Process in Hawaii* 42, 231

Okinawan Classes at University of Hawai'i, Manoa

Shoichi Iwasaki

Department of East Asian Languages and Literatures
University of Hawai'i, Manoa
[iwasaki9@hawaii.edu]

Teaching the language and culture of Okinawa in Hawai'i provides a unique opportunity to examine how educational efforts outside of the homeland community affects both Okinawa and Hawai'i, 5,000 miles apart from each other, through affirmation of the value of the indigenous language and culture. I will discuss how the efforts made at the University of Hawai'i are bringing "value to the original community" from outside, and at the same time bringing "value to the diasporic community" away from the homeland. We will explore how we can take advantage of our unique circumstances to encourage effective language revitalization.

With endorsements from the State Legislature and the UH Board of Regents, the Center for Okinawan Studies (COS) was established at the University of Hawai'i, Manoa, in 2008. The Center sponsors various activities on campus, including lectures, films, dance and music performances, and other cultural and intellectual activities. The UH Manoa library houses the Sakamaki/ Hawley collection which consists of over 4,000 rare Okinawa and Ryukyu related texts, and new volumes are being constantly added to the collection. At the same time, the UH offers several courses that cover Okinawan related topics such as Okinawan dance, Sanshin, Asian American studies, history, and the general language and culture of Okinawa. The Center for Japanese Studies, in response to the community's effort to maintain the Okinawan tradition, has been a strong supporter of the COS.

"Okinawan Language and Culture," a two-semester sequence of courses was first offered in 2004 after careful planning by Professor Serafim, a well-known Ryukyuan linguist, and Professor Hijirida, a native speaker of Uchinaaguchi (Okinawan) and a language education specialist. In addition to the two founding teachers, Dr. Curry, an editor of the Okinawan-English Word Book based on the late Mitsugu Sakihara, has also been teaching these courses. Different teachers bring their own expert knowledge to the class, though the language and the culture components are always the core of the course. I began teaching the course in Spring of 2014. Below is a description of the courses that I currently teach.

For the language component, I use two textbooks. For the first semester of the course, I use an unpublished textbook, *Rikka! Uchinaa-nkai* by Masaaki Sakihara, Shigehisa Karimata, Moriyo Shimabukuro and Lucila Gibo. This is intended for students who have little knowledge of Japanese. Since the requirement for taking the course at UH is at least three years of Japanese language study, basic concepts such as verbal

morphological structure, constituent order, the use of case particles and pragmatic particles are concepts familiar to all students. I bring in typological comparisons between Okinawan and Japanese to enhance their understanding of the language. This also prompts discussion of genetic relations between Okinawan and Japanese. For the second semester, I use *Okinawago no nyūmon* ('An Introduction to Okinawan') by Satoshi Nishioka and Jo Nakahara (Hakusui-sha). This is one of the rare published Okinawan language textbooks written mainly for native speakers of Japanese. Texts, vocabulary lists, grammar explanations are all written in Japanese. To assist the students I provide English translations.

Since it is essential for the students to understand that Okinawan, though endangered, is a living language, I provide ample sound input. Masashi Sakihara, the main author of *Rikka*, has graciously provided me with recordings made by native speakers of the conversations in the textbook. Students memorize all the dialogues guided by these recordings. *Okinawago no nyūmon* comes with professional recordings of all the dialogues as well.

Both of the textbooks are also good resources for introducing Okinawan culture. In addition, since Okinawan culture is alive and well in Hawai'i in the forms of festivals, cultural performances, food, and so forth, we take advantage of real cultural experiences. Students are encouraged to participate in them, and report their experiences in class and in writing.

Since I have been involved in the study of endangered languages using Ikema, a dialect of Miyako Ryukyuan, I include substantial discussion of endangered languages in my classes. This aspect is something new I added to the courses. Although slightly outdated, Crystal's *Language Death* provides an easy entry point for the study. Thereafter, I use various websites such as UNESCO'S page on endangered languages and recent articles specifically written about Okinawan situations (R. Shinzato 2003; Fija *et al.*, 2006; Iwasaki & Ono, 2011 etc.). This aspect of the course is especially relevant for many students in Hawaii, who have been witnessing a revitalization effort of the Hawaiian language in their own community. They are encouraged to compare the linguistic situations in Hawaii and Okinawa.

Since my experience with students taking the courses is still very limited, I cannot report students' reactions in detail, but there are a few interesting observations I can provide at this time.

Last year, I had a very small class of nine students. None of them were so-called Okinawan heritage students, though most were Japanese heritage students. As of this writing, I have not met the thirty or so students who are enrolled in the course for the next semester. Although I understand the risk of "guessing" heritage by last name, it's the best measure before the class begins. I counted only 5 students with Okinawan heritage names. I must mention, however, that the nine students from last year were genuinely interested in Okinawa as they all had Okinawan-heritage friends and acquaintances and interact with them often in their daily lives. I find this situation to result in a very positive attitude towards different languages and cultures. One student told me that he enjoyed learning about the diversity in Japan, one aspect often neglected in Japan related courses.

I should point out, however, that the success of the courses is also due to the university's affirmation of minority languages and cultures. Since the courses satisfy students "diversification" requirement for graduation, many Japanese majors and minors feel encouraged to take these courses.

The Okinawan language courses at UH which introduce Okinawan language and culture to young students thus complement the community based language instruction which is mostly geared toward the older heritage population. It is hoped that the effort at the university and in the community can provide incentive to people in Okinawa to maintain their language, and at the same time these efforts will bring awareness to the situation of language endangerment that is happening in Okinawa among people who live elsewhere.

The community-based teaching of Okinawan is also being done in Los Angeles and probably in South America with Okinawan immigrant history. It is hoped that the teaching of Okinawan will also be encouraged at the level of higher education in these areas.

A Preliminary Needs Analysis of the Teaching and Learning of Okinawan in Hawai'i

Shaun Kindred

Department of Linguistics
University of Hawai'i at Manoa
[skindred@hawaii.edu]

Okinawan Language and Culture in Hawai'i

In general, it can be said that all the languages of the Ryukyu Archipelago stopped being transmitted to younger generations in the 1950s (Heinrich, 2005) and most seem doomed to extinction by 2050, when the last remaining native speakers pass away. However, Ryukyuans, particularly those Okinawans from mainland Okinawa, are unique among indigenous communities. There are hundreds of thousands of Okinawans currently living outside Japan and around 50,000 ethnic Okinawans living in Hawai'i (Nakasone, 2002). Although faced with different educational and social environments from post-war Japan and far removed geographically and culturally from Okinawa, *Uchinaaguchi* (the Okinawan language) has managed to survive in this diaspora.

The development of Okinawan language and culture classes has been slow, perhaps due to a relatively late assertion of a distinct Okinawan identity in Hawai'i. However, Hawai'i provides a strong community, funds, and multiple resources that make it an ideal place to study Okinawan language and culture. The University of Hawai'i, particularly, has one of the most complete collections of resources on Ryukyuan studies outside of Japan. Hawai'i is home to one of the largest branches of the Worldwide Uchinanchu Business Association, supports a Center for Okinawan studies, a two-day cultural festival, and multiple ethnic, religious, cultural, and community organizations.

Language Courses

It has been over five years since an overview of the state of Okinawan language in Hawaii has been presented (Curry, Hijirida & Serafim, 2009), and yet, the educational landscape has considerably changed since that time. In addition, as has been the case in many other endangered language communities and classrooms, there is a worrisome lack of classroom and community evaluations. There are few endangered language classrooms in the world where we have data on the effectiveness of the curriculum and whether or not it is meeting the needs of the students or greater community. None of the Okinawan language programs have been created or reevaluated based on an assessment of the needs of the students and the community.

It is my intention in this paper to give a comprehensive overview of the state of Okinawan language teaching throughout Hawaii by primarily focusing on the evaluation of three current language programs in Hawai'i:

> 1. A biweekly community course at the Hawaii United Okinawa Association's Community Center.

> 2. A biweekly community course taught a Buddhist temple that has had long ties to the Okinawan community.

> 3. The university course series JPN471-472 taught at the University of Hawaii at Manoa.

Needs of the Community

These classrooms and the context in which they are taught are reviewed by way of a needs analysis (NA). A needs analysis (or assessment) is a systematic process for describing the current status of a program, the expected results or the "wants" of a program, and the gaps between the two. It is these gaps that are called the *needs* of a program. Once the needs are found, one can begin to look for solutions to filling the gap by determining the objectives and contents of a course as well as producing, testing, and developing new materials to suit the course.

While NA is commonly used to within fields such as social work, medicine, and management, it also has a long history of positive use within second language program development (West, 1994) and has been used for the University of Hawai'i's own Japanese language program (Iwai *et al.*, 1999). However, while one may say that needs analyses are as necessary to language programs as a doctor's diagnosis is to prescribing the right medicine to a patient, they have not yet been applied to any endangered language programs.

NA is used in this case to not only evaluate the needs of one language course in Hawai'i but to discover what the status of Okinawan language teaching is in Hawai'i, the desires of the community, and the gap between them. There are a variety of models, theories, and methods associated with needs analysis that may be used, but a *triangulation* of sources and methods promoted by Long (2001) is used to improve the reliability and validity of the analysis.

Triangulation of Sources and Methods

Triangulation is a procedure often used by researchers, such as ethnographers, to increase the credibility of their qualitative and naturalistic data. It requires utilizing different sources of data and methods of collecting that data and comparing the results with one another so as to reflect and address the discrepancies and agreements between them. This

Through a triangulation of multiple sources: teaching materials, teachers, students, community members; and multiple methods: oral interviews, participant observations, and questionnaires, I will describe the challenges faced by these groups, their successes, and the unfilled gaps between the desires of the students, the desires of the community, and the realities of the classroom.

Finally, I will briefly touch upon the recent developments in the online education of Uchinaaguchi as well as other promising changes to the state of Okinawan language teaching in Hawaiʻi.

I hope to show that only by properly assessing the needs and values of a language community – how and why the language is important to them and what they desire – can you begin to improve existing programs and formulate ones that accurately address the needs of that community.

Acknowledgements

I would like to acknowledge help of Dr. Stewart Curry, Dr. Kyoko Hijirida, Dr. Shoichi Iwasaki, Norman Kaneshiro, and Eric Wada, without whose assistance this research would not have been possible.

References

Curry, S., Hijirida, K. & Serafim, L. (2009). Documenting, teaching, and revitalizing Uchinaa-guchi: the future of the Okinawan language. In *1st International Conference on Language Documentation and Conservation (ICLDC)* (pp. 1–10). Honolulu. Retrieved from http://hdl.handle.net/10125/5073

Heinrich, P. (2005). Language Loss and Revitalization in the Ryukyu Islands. *JapanFocus*. Retrieved from http://www.japanfocus.org/-Patrick-Heinrich/1596

Iwai, T., Kondo, K., Lim, D. S. J., Ray, G. E., Shimizu, H. & Brown, J. D. (1999). *Japanese Language Needs Analysis 1998-1999. NFLRC* (Vol. 13, pp. 1–87). Honolulu. Retrieved from http://scholarspace.manoa.hawaii.edu/handle/10125/8950

Long, M. H. (2001). Methodological issues in learner needs analysis. In M. H. Long (Ed.), *Second Language Needs Analysis* (pp. 19–76). Cambridge University Press.

Nakasone, R. Y. (2002). *Okinawan Diaspora*. Honolulu: University of Hawaiʻi Press.

West, R. (1994). Needs analysis in language teaching. *Language Teaching*, *27*(01), 1–19.

Value of Prinmi: Knowledge of Traditional Culture in a Threatened Language

Picus Sizhi Ding

Dept. of Linguistics, Humanities
University of Hong Kong
Pokfulam, Hong Kong
[picus@hku.hk]

Abstract

Under the pressure of assimilation from Chinese, traditional knowledge embedded in Prinmi is in the process of gradual loss. Certain types of vocabulary open a window into traditional Prinmi culture. These include a separate set of animal names used for a duodecimal cycle based on the Chinese zodiac, a nine-unit system for counting days and years, a five-way grouping of wild animals, detail-oriented practice in naming species, and elaborated sibling terminology based on gender, age difference, as well as gender difference/identicality between the ego and the referent. A number of features involved are similar to what has been observed in some unrelated indigenous languages. Together they offer peculiar perspectives to human's perception of the world dissimilar to mainstream cultures. However, a recent study of simple Prinmi words from thirteen children shows clear signs of language attrition, e.g. widening the meaning of *sheep* for goats and a tendency to use Mandarin for numerals larger than five, basic color terms, and words such as *star, moon, sun, flower, grass, finger* and *milk*, etc. This is caused by the effect of modern schooling in Chinese. The Prinmi case reveals that loss of traditional knowledge is well underway before a language becomes critically endangered.

Introduction

Prinmi is a Tibeto-Burman language of the Qiangic branch spoken in southwest China across northwest Yunnan province and southwest Sichuan province. In this vast area a great number of Prinmi varieties exist with some difficulty in mutual intelligibility among one another. Ding (2014a) groups them into Western Prinmi (spoken in Lánpíng, close to Yunnan's western border with Myanmar/Burma), Northern Prinmi (spoken primarily in Mùlǐ, Sichuan) and Central Prinmi (spoken roughly in the region between the former two groups). The three groups constitute a continuum of language and dialect comparable to that embracing Italian, Spanish and Portuguese, alongside their many 'dialects'. The variety of Prinmi presented in this paper belongs to Central Prinmi, which has the smallest number of speakers among the three major dialect groups.

With regard to official minority nationalities, Prinmi speakers in Yunnan identify themselves as *Pǔmǐ* (普米), while those in Sichuan have been known as *Zàng* (藏), or Tibetans, since their initial ethnic classification in the 1950s (see Harrell, 2001: 193-215).

Situated close to the bottom of ethnic minorities in China in terms of population and power (Ding, 2014b), in recent decades Prinmi has been under threat of loss of traditional knowledge accumulated in a centuries-long history. This paper first looks at endangerment of Central Prinmi. Then vocabulary regarding astrology, time ordinals, fauna and flora, as well as sibling terms will be studied. Finally, language attrition in Prinmi found in children and its relationship to loss of traditional knowledge are discussed.

Central Prinmi as an endangered language

The latest nationwide census of 2010 gives a total population of 42,861 for the *Pǔmǐ* nationality and 42,572 for the *Zàng* nationality in Mùlǐ, Sichuan.[5] The number of native speakers of Prinmi is substantially fewer than the population figures, as considerable language shift has taken place in Yunnan on the one hand, and a portion of the *Zàng* nationality in Mùlǐ on the other, speaks a variety of Khams Tibetan or one of three other (putative) Qiangic languages[6].

An educated estimate for speakers of Central Prinmi is under 5,000, who are widely scattered in villages in Lìjiāng City such as Xīnyíngpán, Jīnmián and Xīchuān (all in southwestern Nínglàng County), Sōngpíng (Yǒngshèng County), as well as Rénhé and other villages further west in Yùlóng County. Natives of these villages are not in frequent contact, even within the same county, due to great distances obstructed by mountains and rivers. Xīnyíngpán is the largest community for Central Prinmi, where the author has conducted fieldwork on and off for the past two decades.

The following criteria are often used to measure language endangerment: number of speakers, age of speakers, transmission of the language to children, and functions of the language in the community/society (Tsunoda, 2005: 9). The number of speakers is considered a crucial factor in language endangerment,

---

[5] All figures for population are cited from official sources for the 2010 Population Census of China; see References.

[6] See Chirkova (2012) for general sociolinguistic settings and debatable issues about Qiangic languages in Mùlǐ.

just as the surviving number of an animal is cited as the indicator of its degree of endangerment. Despite significant similarity in biolinguistic diversity and endangerment, it is a simplistic calculation to gauge language threat based on the absolute number of speakers without making explicit reference to the total population of the region where the language is found.

A language will not be under threat simply because its number of speakers is small. Sumbuk (2006) provides a list of more than 20 languages of Papua New Guinea, each with less than 100 speakers, but these languages are not endangered and their number of speakers has been stable for centuries. Language endangerment is essentially a negative consequence for a smaller language which can no longer keep a balance with other languages in competing for speakers and functions (cf. Nettle & Romaine, 2000: 30). Therefore, it is necessary to contextualize a minority language in order to genuinely evaluate its endangered status.

One feasible solution is to calculate the Indicative Language Size (ILS) of a language, taking into account impact of extensive language contact, if applicable, in society where the dominant and the minority languages compete with each other. The formula goes as follows:

$$\text{ILS} = \frac{Number\ of\ speakers\ of\ a\ language}{Total\ population\ of\ society} \times 100\%$$

In a monolingual society or a language community with little contact with speakers of other languages, the ILS would be 100%. Approximately half of Central Prinmi speakers (i.e. 2,500) reside in Nínglàng County (where the population as of 2010 was 258,869), so the ILS of Central Prinmi in Nínglàng will be 0.966%. The ILS of Prinmi in Yunnan is about 0.07%, based on the conservative estimate that fewer than 75% of *Pǔmǐ* speak the language (42,861 x 0.75 ÷ 45,966,000).

In addition to the small value in ILS, an on-going language shift and apparent language attrition in Prinmi children (see below) all indicate that Central Prinmi is unmistakably in a state of endangerment. A similar trend is also found for Prinmi as a whole in Yunnan.

Traditional knowledge embedded in Prinmi

Ancestors of the *Pǔmǐ* were nomadic people. They gradually adopted a sedentary lifestyle after they had settled in Yunnan. This section looks at some aspects of Prinmi vocabulary as a window into the knowledge of their traditional culture.

Astrological terminology

Having traveled extensively in Nínglàng, my main consultant *Lujinv* is extremely knowledgeable in Prinmi culture. During one of the fieldwork sessions in 1995, he commented that an elderly man in *Cuufxxii* village knew names of many stars in Prinmi, but he had passed away. Nowadays it is unclear whether someone in a remote village might remember a few names for stars in

Prinmi or such naming and related astrological knowledge had been lost forever.

A set of duodecimal animals is still in use in Xīnyíngpán to designate a cycle of twelve years. For elderly people, this system can also be employed to speak of a cycle of days. This chronological system has its origin in the Chinese zodiac, but it was borrowed into Prinmi through Tibetan. The indirect route of borrowing is transparent when the names of animals in the calendar are compared with those used in everyday life in Prinmi and their correspondent words in written Tibetan, as shown in Table 1. For instance, the expression for Year of the Horse is tɕɑ^H wu^H;[7] the second word literally means 'harvest'.

A consonant cluster consisting of a stop and a glide/rhotic in written Tibetan is pronounced as an affricate in modern Tibetan. Given this regular sound change, it is easy to see the connection between the animal terms used in the calendar and those in written Tibetan, except for the case of 'Hare'. Although the ordinary word for 'dog' in Prinmi is almost identical to that found in 'Dog' in the duodecimal set, this is due to the fact that palatalization has also occurred in this cognate word in Prinmi (cf. the archaic kʰɨ^R 'dog', which is found as a frozen form in a few compounds).

Meaning	Ordinary term	In Prinmi Calendar	Calendar term in written Tibetan[8]	
Rat	ɣo^F	tʃʰɨ^{L}be^H	ཅི	*byi* ('rodent')
Ox	kwɜ^H	lõ^H	གླང	*g-lang*
Tiger	ɣo^R	to^H	སྟག	*s-tag*
Hare	ʎju^{L}tsɨ^R	zɨ^{L}bˈi^H	ཡོས	*yos*
Dragon	bˈə^F	bˈə^{L}taj^H	འབྲུག	*'-brug*
Snake	bɑ^{L}lɜj^H	bˈə^{L}dɑ^H	སྦྲུལ	*s-brul*
Horse	gɥɛ̃^{R}	tɕɑ^H	རྟ	*r-ta*
Sheep	zõ^H	zɨ^R	ལུག	*lug*
Monkey	tsɜ^{H}ʑi^L	pˈi^H	སྤྲེལ	*s-prel*
Bird	gɥɛ^{L}tsi^R	dʒɥɛ̃^{R}	བྱ	*bya*
Dog	tʃʰɨ^R	tʃʰi^H	ཁྱི	*khyi*
Pig	tʃʰɥɑ^R	pʰɜ^H	ཕག	*phag*

Table 1: Comparison of the names of duodecimal animals in Prinmi and written Tibetan

Prinmi has a rather simple syllable structure, permitting only open syllables without any consonant cluster. All prefixed letters at the beginning of a syllable in written

---

[7] Prinmi examples are rendered in IPA with tones marked as H(igh), L(ow), R(ising) or F(all) at the end of a syllable.

[8] The Tibetan script is Romanized with the apostrophe representing a glottal stop and the digraphs *kh* and *ph* aspirated stops.

Tibetan is omitted in Prinmi (true also in most modern Tibetan languages). As a result, the morphemes for 'Dragon' and 'Snake' become homophones in Prinmi and a second syllable is added to distinguish them. The emergence of the other two disyllabic terms for 'Rat' and 'Hare' in the Prinmi calendar is unclear.

The use of a separate set of animals for the duodecimal zodiac is extraordinary. Such borrowing from Tibetan has not been observed in other languages in Nínglàng.

A nine-unit system for counting time

As in many indigenous languages (Harrison, 2007: 88-89), the concept of week does not exist in Prinmi. However, there is a set of time ordinals for counting forward and backward from today for as many as four days (cf. Bradley, 2013). None of these words make use of Prinmi numerals.

-4	ɹə^{H}la^{L}ɲi^L	'four days ago'
-3	ɹə^{L}gi^{H}ɲi^H	'three days ago'
-2	ɹə^{H}ni^L	'two days ago'
-1	ʒja^{H}ni^L	'yesterday'
0	pi^{H}ni^L	'today'
+1	sjɛ̃^{L}(ɲi^H)	'tomorrow'
+2	kʰu^{L}sjɛ̃^{R}	'two days hence'
+3	kʰu^{L}di^H	'three days hence'
	kʰu^H«l85»	
+4	«s71»^{L}	'four days hence'

There is a similar set for counting a nine-year span, centered around this year:

-4	ɹə^{H}la^{L}pɨ^L	'four years ago'
-3	ɹə^{L}gi^{H}pɨ^H	'three years ago'
-2	ɹə^{H}pɨ^L	'two years ago'
-1	ʒjɑ^{H}pɨ^L	'last year'
0	pi^{H}pɨ^L	'this year'
+1	ʒjɑ^{L}kʰɑw^H	'next year'
+2	sjɛ̃^{H}kʰɑw^L	'two years hence'
+3	kʰu^{L}sjɛ̃^{L}kʰɑw^H	'three years hence'
+4	kʰu^{L}di^{H}kʰɑw^H	'four years hence'

Morphemes used in counting days and years are alike in Prinmi: their order and meaning are consistent in backward counting in both cases, but not in forward counting. In year-counting a new term is inserted for 'next year', and this causes a shift in the subsequent ordinal meaning of the morphemes in forward counting of years. The discrepancy observed with the year counting reveals that these ordinal morphemes express a relative position in the nine-unit system rather than an absolute ordinal meaning in Prinmi. Moreover, the morpheme ʒja, appearing in both 'last year' and 'next year', is probably a relic of an ancient conceptualization of time which only separates 'present' from 'non-present' (cf. Harrison, 2007: 89 for counting of

days in Sie). Later the two words were set apart through tones and addition of different morphemes for 'year'.

These ordinal-like Prinmi morphemes as well as the analyzable head for 'year' are all bound, occurring exclusively in the time-counting systems.

Grouping of wild animals

In Prinmi culture animals not locally domesticated are regarded as wild animals. According to the main consultant, wild animals can be classified into one of the following five groups:

(I) pɑ^{L}tʃjɛ̃^{H} (the pawed group, mammals with soft feet) such as ʎju^{L}tsi^R 'hare', gɥɛ^F 'fox', po^H 'dhole', sɥi^F 'leopard' and kʰɜ^{L}tõ^H 'lynx';

(II) kʰʉ^{H}tʃjɛ̃^{H} (the horned group, mammals with a pair of horns or antlers, especially for the male) such as pjɛ̃^{L}kwɜ^H 'feral cattle', tsɜ^H 'red deer' and tjɜ^F 'blue sheep';

(III) gwɜj^{L}tʃjɛ̃^{H} (the tusked group, mammals with elongated front teeth, especially for the male) such as lõ^{H}bu^{L}tʃʰi^L 'elephant', tʃʰɥɑ^{L}ne^H 'wild boar' and lʉ^F 'musk deer';

(IV) dõ^{L}tʃjɛ̃^{H} (the winged group, animals with a pair of wings) such as kʰɯ̯ɑ^{L}lɥɛ^R 'turtle dove', kʰjõ^R 'owl' and nɥɛ̃^{R} 'Temminck's tragopan'; and

(V) kwɑ^{L}tʃjɛ̃^{H} (the hoofed group, mammals with hard feet) such as dzi^F 'camel', bᴶõ^R 'rhinoceros' and bᴶe^{L}da^{H}gɥɛ̃^{H} 'zebra'.

This scheme of classification is based on physical attributes of wild animals. Although some group terms are readily translatable into English, e.g. avian for Group (IV) and ungulate for Group (V). The classification as a whole is probably unique to Prinmi. A peculiarity of the Prinmi grouping is the different categorization based on presence/absence of horns or antlers for male ungulates. This horn-based criterion is prioritized over the hoof-based one. Therefore a deer is regarded to belong to kʰʉ^{H}tʃjɛ̃^{H} (the horned group) even though it shares the characteristic of kwɑ^{L}tʃjɛ̃^{H} (the hoofed group).

This grouping scheme is applicable to novel mammals such as zebras and walruses, which can only be seen on television. Admittedly this kind of folk taxonomy and classification is unmatchable to modern scientific models. Many animals such as snakes, frogs, and fishes do not fit in the Prinmi grouping, for example. Nonetheless, such folk classification and grouping of wild animals provide different perspectives on human's understanding of animals in the wild.

Naming of plants

The forest represents an important resource to Prinmi. Many plants are known in traditional Prinmi culture by specific names; this facilitates passing knowledge about

tʃʰjɛ̃ᴴbõᴸ
Yunnan pine
(Pinus yunnanensis)
云南松/
Yúnnán sōng

kʲiᴸɹiᴿ
Chinese white pine
(Pinus armandii)
□山松/
Huáshān sōng

pine (Pinus) 松□/*sōngshù*

Figure 1: Different naming of pine trees in Prinmi and other languages

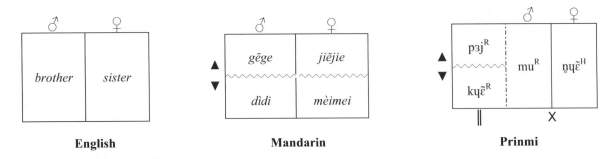

English   **Mandarin**   **Prinmi**

Figure 2: Comparison of sibling terms in English, Mandarin and Prinmi

a particular plant along with its name to young people. For instance, the Yunnan pine (Pinus yunnanensis) is termed tʃʰjɛ̃ᴴbõᴸ in Prinmi and the Chinese white pine (Pinus armandii) kʲiᴸɹiᴿ. They are kept distinct by Prinmi speakers, whereas an average Chinese or English would simply refer to them as 松□/*sōngshù* and pine trees respectively. Since the Yunnan pine is found pervasively in the region, tʃʰjɛ̃ᴴbõᴸ is often used for translating the word *pine* expediently, but this Prinmi word definitely does not bear the general meaning for denoting the genus of pine trees.

Without a general Prinmi term for *pine* and knowledge about the Chinese name for kʲiᴸɹiᴿ, the consultant was unable to tell me what kind of tree it was. To enlighten this ignorant, but curious, linguistics student, one day he showed me a small broken branch of the tree. Upon seeing needles on the twig, I puzzledly asked whether kʲiᴸɹiᴿ was a kind of pine tree like tʃʰjɛ̃ᴴbõᴸ. The following explanation was given. Seeds of kʲiᴸɹiᴿ, but not tʃʰjɛ̃ᴴbõᴸ, can be harvested and sold as pine nuts. Furthermore, kʲiᴸɹiᴿ (five needles) has more needles in a fascicle than tʃʰjɛ̃ᴴbõᴸ (three needles). Such knowledge seems to have been stored in the lexicon together with the distinct names given to these two species of pine trees. The way Prinmi speakers lexicalize these trees stands in stark contrast to that by English (or Chinese) speakers. As illustrated in Figure 1, in Prinmi culture heed is paid to details of individual species, while such details are largely overlooked in cultures, such as English and Chinese, that name the trees at a higher level and elaborated expressions are called for only when it is necessary to distinguish the two by specialists.

To date, there are still many plant names in Prinmi that have remained mysterious to me, as no sample of them is available. These include «l85»«s71»ᴸs«s83»ᴴ (a kind of tree found at both high and low altitudes), t«s51»ᴴs«s04»ᴸ (a kind of plant with white flowers and edible fruit), biᴴsʉᴴ (a kind of plant with edible fruit) and so forth.

Sibling terms

While English has only two words for sibling, Japanese and Chinese languages (Mandarin, Cantonese, or Taiwanese, etc.) have as many as four. The doubling of number is due to the semantic consideration of age difference in addition to gender of the referent. On top of these semantic factors, Prinmi also includes in sibling terms the feature of gender identicality/difference between the ego and the referent. That is, a Prinmi sibling term contains three pieces of crucial information: (i) whether the referent is male or female, (ii) whether the referent is elder or younger than the ego, and (iii) whether genders of the referent and the ego are different or identical. These features are symbolized in Figure 2 in a box notation adopted from

Nerlove & Romney (1967) as follows: (i) ♂ = male, ♀ = female, divided by a solid line inside the box; (ii) ▲ = elder, ▼ = younger, divided by a zigzag line; and (iii) ‖ = same gender, ✕ = different gender, divided by a pecked line.

Because the third semantic factor is context-dependent, Prinmi sibling terms cannot be freely translated into languages such as English and Chinese. The compound $pɜj^{L}kɯ̧ɛ̃^{H}$, for example, may mean either brothers or sisters (i.e. siblings of the same sex) depending on whether the ego is male or female. Conversely, accurate translation of sibling terms into Prinmi requires the gender of the ego to be accessible to the translator. This seemingly complicated system of sibling terminology is not unique to Prinmi; a set of equivalents is found in some Polynesian languages, e.g. Maori and Hawaiian (see Epling *et al.*, 1973). While the semantic feature on gender identicality/difference is observed in many Tibeto-Burman languages (cf. Turin, 2004), the number of sibling term and interface of these three semantic features vary significantly (Ding, 2008).

The Prinmi sibling terminology opens the door to a three dimensional system for kinship terms, where a great diversity of patterning is possible (cf. Nerlove & Romney, 1967).

Language attrition in Prinmi

Yùlóng County has seen many speakers of Central Prinmi shifting their native tongue to Naxi and Yunnan Mandarin. Similar language shift in Nínglàng County is also observed, but on a smaller scale. Young children still acquire Prinmi as their first language in Xīnyíngpán village, for example. However, fresh child data collected from the village in early 2014 show conspicuous language attrition in the vocabulary and phonology of Prinmi.

Thirteen children of Xīnyíngpán, eight boys and five girls, of the age of six, eight (2 children), nine (4), ten (2), twelve (2) and fourteen (2), were invited to partake in elicitation of simple Prinmi words. Pictures were shown on a computer as prompts for 97 words, including numerals, body-part terms, animals (primarily domestic ones), verbs, adjectives, household nouns and nature terms.

None of these young speakers were able to produce all the words in Prinmi. Numerals larger than five were substituted with Mandarin by most of them, with occasional confusion between two Prinmi numerals. Many children did not know how to say *finger* in Prinmi; a few confused *mouth* with *beak*. Color terms such as *red, yellow* and *green* posed a problem for most of them. The Mandarin word for *milk* was typically given to a picture showing a box of milk, as the Prinmi word had slipped their mind. *Flower, grass, star, moon* and *sun* were only known by their Mandarin terms in the speech of most children.

In addition to wholesale replacement of a Prinmi word, interference from Mandarin is discernible from the child data. Some children were able to supply the word $bɨ^{H}tʃjɛ̃^{H}$ 'sunray' after their confident response *tàiyáng* 'sun' was pointed out to be Mandarin. A few, after some hesitation, uttered the compound for *sunray*, rendering the target Prinmi word disyllabic (as in Mandarin), with only an approximate meaning. Nettle & Romaine (2000: 54) note that *sun* is one of the words most resistant to replacement by English among younger speakers of Dyirbal, but this is not the case with Prinmi children.

Another seemingly semantic confusion occurred between the words *goat* and *sheep*. These two animals were presented in this order in the elicitation, as goats were more commonly found than sheep in Xīnyíngpán. Surprisingly, a few children applied the same word $zõ^{H}$ 'sheep' for these two domestic animals. There are two probable reasons. They have forgotten the Prinmi word $tsʰɨ^{F}$ 'goat' and only remember $zõ^{H}$ 'sheep'. As a result, they simply extend the meaning of $zõ^{H}$ 'sheep' to cover also goats, i.e. an instance of over-generalization. Another probability is that these children have regarded $zõ^{H}$ 'sheep' as equivalent to the general term *yáng* in Mandarin, which is taught in school. Therefore, they naturally refer to either of these two animals with the same word. This is analogous to using *pine* to refer to two species of pine trees in Chinese, as shown in Figure 1 above.

The schooling effect can also account for the loss of larger numerals, as children are taught how to count in Mandarin in kindergarten and primary school. Likewise, celestial bodies, flowers and grasses are all among simple items illustrated in picture books used in classroom. Prinmi children will spend hours for learning how to write them in Chinese characters. On the other hand, children's exposure to these terms in Prinmi is relatively limited in everyday life. Monolingual education in Chinese, coupled by exclusive use of Mandarin in broadcast media, is undoubtedly responsible for the language attrition experienced by these young speakers of Prinmi.

Knowledge draining and language attrition

Back in 1997 on my second field trip to Xīnyíngpán, my main consultant remarked once regrettingly that the younger generation spoke an attrited form of Prinmi. Two decades has almost passed when I recently have got a chance to look at some child data of Prinmi. The data confirm that language attrition is well underway in Xīnyíngpán, despite the fact that Prinmi is still transmitted to young children at home.

When a speaker has shifted his native tongue to another language, he cannot be expected to preserve knowledge associated with the bygone language in his mind, cf. Nettle & Romaine's (2000: 54-55) discussion of simplified vocabulary used by younger speakers of Dyirbal. A person who has become a passive or semi-speaker of Prinmi is unlikely to pay attention to subtle difference which distinguishes the Chinese white pine from the Yunnan pine, as he lacks the specific words and relevant knowledge about their difference. Likewise, this now fluent speaker of Mandarin will simply refer to sheep and goats as *yáng*, unless he is asked to name them with specific terms. What is happening to Prinmi is that knowledge embedded in the language about traditional culture has been in the process of gradual draining even before the language becomes moribund or critically endangered.

Like many minority languages of the world, Prinmi has no history of writing. The spoken language represents the sole medium for storing knowledge of traditional Prinmi culture and their perception of the environment around them. As such, when language attrition happens, it affects not only linguistic forms and constructions, but also meaning and knowledge embedded in the language. In preservation of natural languages, it is too late to document a dying language which has lost much of its traditional knowledge. Loss of human knowledge completes with the death of (unwritten) languages, but it commences with language attrition.

Acknowledgements

Numerous Prinmi speakers of all three major dialect groups have helped me to understand their languages over the past two decades. I am grateful to all of them and, in particular, *Bonfbon Lujinv*, who is recognized as one of the best speakers of Prinmi in Niuwozi in virtue of his great knowledge of the Prinmi language and culture. Children from Xīnyíngpán who have helped me recording simple words also deserve special thanks here.

References

Bradley, D. (2013). Time ordinals in Tibeto-Burman. Presented at the 23rd Annual Meeting of Southeast Asian Linguistics Society. Chulalongkorn University, Bangkok.

Chirkova, K. (2012). The Qiangic subgroup from an areal perspective: a case study of languages of Muli. *Language and Linguistics*, 13(1), 133-170.

Ding, P.S. (2014a). *A Grammar of Prinmi: Based on the Central dialect of northwest Yunnan, China*. Leiden: Brill.

Ding, P.S. (2014b). Power and other issues in minority language education in China: the case of Bai in northwestern Yunnan. In F.E. Anderson & C. Volker (Eds.), *Education in Languages of Lesser Power: Asia-Pacific Perspectives* (pp. 47-62). Amsterdam: John Benjamins.

Ding, P.S. (2008). Sibling terminology in Prinmi. Presented at the 41st International Conference on Sino-Tibetan Languages and Linguistics. SOAS, London, UK.

Epling, P.J., Kirk, J. & Boyd, J.P. (1973). Genetic relations of Polynesian sibling terminologies. *American Anthropology*, 75, 1596-1625.

Harrell, S. (2001). *Ways of Being Ethnic in Southwest China*. Seattle: University of Washington Press.

Harrison, K.D. (2007). *When Languages Die: the extinction of the world's languages and the erosion of human knowledge*. Oxford: Oxford University Press.

Nerlove, S. & Romney, A. K. (1967). Sibling Terminology and Cross-Sex Behavior. *American Anthropologist*, 69, 179-187.

Nettle, D. & Romaine, S. (2000). *Vanishing Voices : the extinction of the world's languages*. Oxford: Oxford University Press.

Office for the Population Census of Sichuan Province, Sichuan Provincial Bureau of Statistics. (2012). *Tabulation on the 2010 Population Census of Sichuan Province*. Beijing: China Statistics Press.

Office for the Population Census of Yunnan Province, Yunnan Provincial Bureau of Statistics. (2012). *Tabulation on the 2010 Population Census of Yunnan Province*. Beijing: China Statistics Press.

Sumbuk, K. (2006). Papua New Guinea's languages: will they survive? In D. Cunningham, D.E. Ingram & K. Sumbuk (Eds.), *Language Diversity in the Pacific: Endangerment and Survival* (pp. 85-96). Clevedon: Multilingual Matters.

Tsunoda, T. (2005). *Language Endangerment and Language Revitalization*. Berlin: Mouton de Gruyter.

Turin, M. (2004). Thangmi kinship terminology in comparative perspective. In A. Saxena (Ed.), *Himalayan Languages: Past and Present* (pp. 101-140). Berlin: Mouton de Gruyter.

Talking To The Past: Endangerment, History, and the Economics of Language in Northwest Honduras

Kathryn Marie Hudson

University at Buffalo
Departments of Anthropology and Linguistics
380 MFAC-Ellicott Complex
Buffalo, New York 14261-0026
khudson@buffalo.edu

John S. Henderson

Cornell University
Department of Anthropology
261 McGraw Hall
Ithaca, New York 14853
jsh6@cornell.edu

Abstract

Indigenous languages are closely connected to conceptualizations of identity which, in turn, are commonly based on historically-rooted ideologies. The association between language and history is particularly salient in Mesoamerica due to the sustained academic and public interests in epigraphy and archaeology, though the potential advantages of this connection are not always realized by speakers. Taking the indigenous languages of northern and western Honduras as its case study, this paper explores the complex relationships that exist among language, endangerment, archaeology, history, and the accrual of social and economic capital. This group – which includes Lenca, Ch'orti', Pech, and Garifuna – incorporates both endangered and stable languages; it is our contention that language stability in the region is based, at least in part, on perceived differences in the relationships of these languages to history as constructed by contemporary Hondurans. More specifically, association with a favored past can provide speakers with social capital that can be mobilized economically and can contribute to language survival.

A connection with the Maya past – particularly as it is realized through archaeological research – has afforded Ch'orti' a central place in Honduran history that supports its perpetuation and provides speakers with social capital that can be converted into economic benefit. The non-Mayan Lenca language was never afforded such a status despite its connection to an equally vibrant and archaeologically significant cultural sphere; this historical marginalization of Lenca speakers in constructions of the Honduran past contributed to endangerment by consciously refocusing intellectual, political, and social attentions to bolster the official historical account. Similarly, Garifuna is closely associated with Honduran ethnohistorical politics in a way that encourages language maintenance. Pech, on the other hand, has not been connected to precolumbian history, at least in the public mind, and its speakers are thoroughly marginal to national historical discourses and have little capital of any kind. These case studies will be reviewed to illustrate how the association of language and history relates to endangerment by contributing to or preventing the development of economic and social capital.

Guatemala and far western Honduras, is a member of the Cholan group of Mayan languages. It is a developing language that is used in all domains and taught in primary schools; it is also the focus of ongoing scholarly interest. Pech, also referred to by some as Paya, is spoken in north central and northeastern Honduras. It is a Chibchan language that is now moribund despite some local interest in preservation. Those that continue to use the language are primarily older adults; most individuals are transitioning to Spanish (Lewis, Simmons & Fennig, 2014). Garifuna is a Maipurean language spoken by the so-called Black Caribs, descendants of a mixed population of Carib, Arawak, and African people now living along the Caribbean coast of Honduras, Guatemala, and Belize. It is a developing language used in all domains, though some communities are shifting to Spanish (Lewis, Simmons & Fennig, 2014).

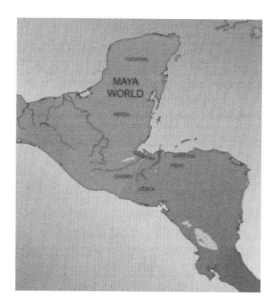

Figure 1:   A map of eastern Mesoamerica

The Indigenous Past in the Imagination of Honduran History and the Construction of a National Identity

The development of new conceptions of Honduran history and of a Honduran national identity began in the nineteenth century and gave rise to a state-sanctioned and -supported historical vision that has had far-reaching consequences for the cultural and linguistic survival of indigenous peoples.   In the aftermath of the dissolution of the ill-fated República Federal de Centroamérica, Honduran intellectual life revolved around the construction of a suitable history and national identity for the new state (Euraque, 2004: 9-36).

From the beginning, this creation of a national identity was founded on a perspective shared by politicians and intellectuals that did not recognize the continuance of significant ethnic and linguistic diversity beyond the Colonial period. In effect, variability among indigenous peoples was erased in the interest of creating an imagined homogeneous indigenous ethnicity that combined with an equally undiversified Spanish culture to create a Honduran mestizo identity. This historical construction was part of a discourse of *mestizaje* that was widely influential in Latin America, particularly in Mexico (Gamio, 2010); by the end of the century the basic notion of Honduras as a mestizo society – along with corollary myths of racial harmony and the absence of racial discrimination – had become hegemonic in Honduran intellectual circles (Euraque, 2004: 33-34). The logic of these constructs dictated that the process of *mestizaje* had been so successful that distinct indigenous ethnic groups had become vanishingly small, and census records reflect the new orthodoxy as people who would once have been categorized as indigenous were progressively tabulated as mestizos (Euraque, 2004: 17-36).

During the twentieth century, even as living indigenous people became increasingly invisible, two new historical constructs harnessed the indigenous past in the service of a new national identity: Lempira, a legendary Lenca leader was elevated to the status of a national hero and archaeology was appropriated to create a national Maya history.

The process through which Lempira, a Lenca cacique who died defending his territory in western Honduras against the Spanish invasion, became a national symbol (Euraque, 2004: 71-87) began in the nineteenth century within the context of the emergence of the Honduran state. Although such a figure is mentioned in at least one document in the Archivo General de Indias in Seville (Joya, 1992: 143), the invention of Lempira as he is conceptualized today was essentially a romantic elaboration of folklore. The motivations that drove this process were likely tied to the need for an identity related to the newly formed state. This state, by virtue of encompassing multiple ethnic and linguistic groups,

required an associated identity that could be shared by all of its citizens if it was to survive the nationalistic tendencies that dominated the 19th and early 20th century and counter the inevitable internal rebellions. Lempira, by virtue of his position as an indigenous individual who fought against a recognized foe, provided an ideal and unifying focus.

In 1915, the new Honduran national anthem solidified Lempira's status as a national hero. A decade later, the decision to name the new national currency after Lempira (Figure 2) reflected the enshrinement of the fully elaborated Lempira, who had been cast as a national hero and now, specifically, as a defender of national territory. It is not a coincidence that the political debates resulting in the naming of the new currency closely followed a foreign intervention in Honduras in the course of which American marines occupied the city of Tegucigalpa (Euraque, 2004: 82). The debates also took place at a time of intense anti-African sentiment in Honduran political circles, especially among pro-labor factions, which were deeply hostile to the immigration of people of African descent in general and the United Fruit Company's increasing reliance on black laborers in particular (Euraque, 2004: 84-86). The state's selection of an indigenous national hero reflected this bias and sent a subtle message of exclusion directed toward the country's African-based populations. It also represented a modified historical narrative in which political agendas and social biases combined to privilege the elite and the indigenous at the expense of a marginalized African-derived group. This narrative pushed the Garifuna and other African groups to the historical margins and instead fostered a historical perspective in which their contributions and accomplishments were generally overlooked.

Figure 2: Lempira note with portrait of the national hero commissioned by the state

Figure 3: Lempira note, reverse with image of ballcourt and stela at Copán

Throughout the same period, conceptions of precolumbian Honduran history focused narrowly on the role of the ancient Maya to the exclusion of other cultural groups. In particular, attention was focused on the spectacular material remains of the city of Copán, which flourished in far western Honduras during the fifth through ninth centuries and represented the southeastern edge of the Maya cultural sphere. Intellectual and popular interest in Copán and the Maya was politically sanctioned by the Honduran government, and the reverse of the one Lempira note (Figure 3) bears an image of the main ball court at Copán and a stela memorializing one of the city's its great kings.

The emphasis on Copán as a reflection of a grand Maya past was by no means representative of the actual archaeological record of Honduras, since the city is located in the far western part of the country, only a few kilometers on the Honduran side of the frontier with Guatemala, and precolumbian material remains in the great majority of national territory were of a very different character. This construct did, however, match the interests and narrow focus of the mostly foreign archaeologists who were working in Honduras on the spectacular remains of Copán, which was the first Maya city to be extensively investigated. It allowed for the appropriation of the academic vision of a homogeneous ancient Maya civilization – reflected in the spectacular architecture, public art, and hieroglyphic texts of Maya cities, mostly located in neighboring countries – into the new Honduran history. Perhaps more importantly, it allowed the state of Honduras to make itself part of an emerging historical narrative that was receiving international attention and acclaim. This afforded the state and its government a kind of status that, in turn, brought financial gain in the form of increased tourism and academic investment.

The fact that academia was, in effect, creating the subject of its study through its processes of analyses was irrelevant. The problematic nature of such a homogenizing category was similarly overlooked, particularly since it fit nicely with the Honduran governmental tradition that encouraged Central American social and political accord. Although the country's efforts to create a politically unified region were unsuccessful, the emerging emphasis on the ancient Maya created a singular historical and cultural identity for the region that connected Honduras with its neighbors and the glories of their pasts. It also aligned with the emerging emphasis on indigenous achievement as a unifying source of state attention, which was first manifest in the selection of Lempira as a national hero. A focus on the Maya allowed Hondurans – and arguably other Central Americans – to create a national identity through an emphasis on their heritage and the accomplishments of their ancestors. That this identity was recognized internationally and deemed worthy of study and support was a reinforcing bonus, though the consequences – including the contemporary appropriation of the cultural homogenization being applied to the past – were overlooked. Even Lempira, who began as a Lenca hero elevated to a national status for his efforts against the Spanish, became more generically indigenous.

Language was a key element in the academic creation of the Maya. Originally used to describe the language of Mayapan, the dominant political center in northern Yucatan in the fifteenth century, the term "Maya" was appropriated as a label for a broadly distributed set of languages when linguists and ethnographers recognized their genetic relationships in the nineteenth century. Archaeologists developed an intuitive sense that language is central to identity into an implicit expectation that language families should correspond to broad cultural groupings, thereby specifically reifying an assumed cultural commonality among Mayan speakers into an imagined enduring and essentialist Maya identity. Even today, definitions of "Maya" as an archaeological category are almost always implicit, beginning with a territory defined by the distribution of Mayan languages: "There are few parts of the world where there is such a good 'fit' between language and culture: a line drawn around the Mayan-speaking peoples would contain all those remains, and hieroglyphic texts, assigned to the ancient Maya civilization" (Coe, 2011: 11). They typically proceed to describe and characterize archaeological sites within these bounds, focusing on a particular complex of architecture, sculpture, and texts that was in fact the apparatus of royal legitimation in Classic period lowland city-states (e.g., Coe, 2011; Hammond, 1982; Sharer, 1994). It thus reflected shared system of political legitimization rather than cultural commonality.

Federico Lunardi, papal nuncio in Honduras in the 1940s, provided the state with an explicit archaeological foundation for its national Maya vision. Lunardi (1948) asserted that all Honduran indigenous peoples were Maya descendants. He even invited a biological anthropologist to measure Lenca people in the hope of finding anthropometric proof of their "Maya-ness" (Euraque, 2004: 63). Building on the prestige attached to Copán in the public mind, he represented all of the nation's archaeological remains as having been produced by the Maya. North American archaeologists working in Honduras in the mid 20th century held and promoted the contrasting orthodox view that the Maya world extended only barely east of Copán. Lunardi was thus marginalized academically, but public intellectuals and government officials in Honduras embraced his ideas enthusiastically. Interestingly, despite the status accorded Sylvanus Morley, Doris Stone, and other North American archaeologists in the country, the official discourse remained the inverse of their academic perspectives. Even Stone, who did extensive field investigations in regions occupied by Lenca speakers (Stone, 1941, 1957) and wrote about the ethnohistory of the ancestors of the Lenca people with whom she worked (Stone, 1948), did not dare to directly challenge Lunardi's interpretations. For Hondurans, Honduran archaeology became Maya. Honduran *indigenismo* ignored most non-Maya people and, consequently, cultural diversity was effectively erased in the present and the past.

Such erasure, though not openly sanctioned by academia, was nonetheless encouraged by the perpetuation of core-periphery interpretive models. The particularities of this process have been discussed elsewhere (see Henderson & Hudson, 2011; Hudson, 2011, 2013; Hudson & Henderson, 2014), but it is worth reiterating that the intellectual marginality implicit within this framework – and the accompanying idea that all achievement flowed from a culturally advanced Maya core into a far less advanced periphery inhabited by non-Maya ethnic groups – reinforced the Honduran belief that their past was rooted in the accomplishments of Copán Maya. These Maya were, in turn, cast as the local representatives of a regional culture; the end result of this process minimized the ancient diversity that existed within Honduran territory and assigned the Maya to an exalted position within the national psyche.

Neo-Maya public architecture in the capital provides a striking material reflection of the official Mayanization project. El Picacho (Figure 4), also known as Parque Naciones Unidas el Picacho, was built on an imposing hilltop overlooking Tegucigalpa. The park was designed around buildings combining elements inspired by the architecture of Copán, Chichén Itzá, Palenque, and other Maya sites. It was inaugurated in 1946 on the occasion of the convening of the Primera Conferencia Internacional de Arqueólogos del Caribe with great intellectual and political fanfare. It was intended to demonstrate Honduras' commitment to public archaeology and is often associated with the country's attempts to be part of the global heritage movement, but its emphasis on the Maya and focus on a replica Maya temple instead made manifest a national commitment to a customized and distinctly Mayan past.

Figure 4: El Picacho, Tegucigalpa

Parque Concordia, near the city center below, features a series of even more bizarre pastiches of precolumbian Maya and other elements (Figure 5). It was originally built in 1883 but subsequently remodeled during the 1930s to reflect a Maya heritage. The buildings focus on structures that combine elements inspired by the architecture of well-known Maya sites such as Chichen Itza and Copan; the end result is an emphasis on a Maya achievement and a commitment to the existence of a singular Maya world.

Figure 5:   Parque Concordia, Tegucigalpa

The Impact Of Imagined Honduran History On Indigenous Peoples And Their Languages

The Mayanization of Honduran history connected the Ch'orti' to the officially favored (i.e. Maya) past made impressively manifest in the monuments of Copán. It has given them a central place in Honduran history and provided them with considerable social capital that can be converted into economic benefit. This capital is seen most clearly in the favored position they occupy within the northwestern part of the country. Although this privileged status is not officially sanctioned, it is implicitly encouraged through the association of Ch'orti' communities with the favored Maya past and the corresponding national and international interest in Ch'orti' culture and language. One needs only to visit the site of Copán and the eponymous nearby town for a brief time to discover that Ch'orti' culture can command considerable attention and thus – by extension – a considerable amount of economic gain. Ch'orti' handicrafts are sold in stores an on street corners, often under the label 'Maya.' Generic Maya-like products of various kinds are also produced to tap into the desire of visitors to take a part of the glorious Maya past home with them.

The economic capital generated by the social capital afforded Honduran Ch'orti' communities has allowed for the reiteration of the national historical narrative and its implicit cultural hierarchy. Ch'orti' villages are relatively more prosperous, and consequently their inhabitants are elevated in the eyes of both their countrymen and the foreign visitors who travel to see them. This reinforces their position as an idealized indigenous identity worthy of its association with an idealized Maya past, and the resulting feedback loop and supports their position as the politically sanctioned face of Honduras. Ongoing academic interest in the Maya, both ethnographic and linguistic, also contributes to this process. Researchers bring attention to the villages they study and create interest in their inhabitants, which in turn creates more social capital and opportunities for economic gain.

This social and economic capital is also occasionally put to political use. Ch'orti' factions have occupied the Copán archaeological park on two occasions, first in 1998 and again in 2000 (Metz, 2010: 299). These actions were partly about a descendant group having a voice in the management of the material remains that reflect the achievements of their ancestors and of the revenues they generate; they also involved an array of issues concerning land and investigation of the assassinations of activists. The archaeological site was the symbolic and practical focus of their efforts, and their association with such a monument to the national past was surely viewed as a means of strengthening the indigenous position on these issues and attracting attention to their cause. It is unlikely that any indigenous group would have dared to make such a visible and vocal statement without the knowledge that they were somehow intimately associated with a place – in this case, Copán – that was crucial to the national sense of self.

The Honduran historical narrative has also created a kind of safety net around the Ch'orti' language through an emphasis of its importance. Although it is impossible to say for certain that any language will be forever free from the threat of extinction, the views of history dominant in Honduras and elsewhere in Central America indicate that Maya languages are often more secure than their non-Maya counterparts. The centrality of Mayan language in academic and Honduran constructions of ancient Maya civilization, in tandem with the recognition that the hieroglyphic texts of Copán were written in an ancestral version of Ch'orti', has contributed to the ability of Ch'orti' speakers to maintain their language. Such ongoing local interest in language use and preservation can be seen, at least in part, as a product of the Honduran historical narrative. By virtue of their association with the favored Maya past, Ch'orti' speakers are able to view themselves, their culture, and their language as valuable and worthy of perpetuation. This kind of pride is crucial to the continuation of a language; the official reinforcement of this provides additional motivation. Furthermore, many scholars influenced by the view that the Maya represent(ed) a kind of cultural core have reinforced this perspective through their selection of research foci. In the case of Ch'orti', as in the cases of many other Maya languages, a variety of lexical, grammatical, and educational resources have been produced (see e.g. Cowie & Martínez S., 1994; Lubeck & Lubeck, 1984a, 1984b, 1989; McNichols, 1977; Oakley, 1966). These works, and the academic interest and prestige associated with their creation, reinforce local perceptions of value and create an intellectual reservoir that aids in the preservation and perpetuation of Ch'orti' and other Maya tongues.

The condition of the region's non-Maya languages and their speakers is considerably bleaker. Although their ancestors can be connected to the Ulúa sphere (Hudson & Henderson, 2014), a cultural tradition that was as vibrant and archaeologically significant as Copán, the Lenca and their language do not enjoy a privileged place in official Honduran history. The elevation of Lempira to the status of national hero makes the marginalization of Lenca speakers even more thoroughly ironic, though part of the reason for this disconnect may be that the decision to name the currency after Lempira was more a racist rejection of African heritage than an embracing of a Lenca legacy. The official Lempira was constructed as a representative of a fictive homogenous indigenous ethnicity -- a single element in the *mestizaje* process. Language, which is one of the most obvious dimensions of cultural identity, is by necessity erased by *mestizaje*. Indeed, *ladino* – a term that is now frequently used in Central America to designate those with a strongly Hispanicized rather than mixed *mestizo* culture – was originally a linguistic label for those who lacked "pure" Spanish cultural heritage but nonetheless adopted Spanish or Vulgar Latin (Piedra, 1987: 313).

The social capital of the Lenca is limited despite their association with a well-documented and elaborate archaeological culture. The Ulúa sphere has never received the scholarly or tourist interest afforded the Maya and, as a result, their descendent populations have been unable to achieve the levels of social and economic security seem among groups such as the Ch'orti'. Although the network of towns known as the Ruta Lenca has become an attraction for those wishing to experience the natural beauty of the western highlands of Honduras and brought some attention to contemporary Lenca populations, it remains a relatively uncommon destination that is overshadowed by Copán and the lure of the Caribbean coast. Additionally, many Lenca live outside of the settlements along this route. Those that do encounter tourists reap few social or economic rewards from these encounters despite the existence of handicrafts – such as the black and white pottery that typifies modern Lenca ceramic production – for sale and the proliferation of guides willing to impart tidbits of ancient Lenca wisdom. This reality reflects the perceptions of interest and importance on the part of tourists and those who cater to their arrangements. The relative lack of social capital prevents the Lenca from attracting the kind of attention necessary to generate economic resources; the resulting lack of economic capital, in turn, precludes the developments of the kind of infrastructure necessary to raise their social and cultural profile.

It seems certain that the Lenca are aware of their position and the lack of value assigned to their cultural identity. Lenca living along the Ruta Lenca often emphasize an imagined Maya identity in an attempt to attract interest and resources, and a loose association of Lenca and geographically or culturally related communities has publically dubbed itself the Maya-Lenca Nation. Individuals claiming to represent Lenca interests often emphasize a Maya connection, and Maya cultural traditions are sometimes appropriated in situations where non-local individuals or tourists are present. The unintended result of these efforts is the reinforcement of the official historical and cultural narrative. By recognizing – and perhaps believing – that their culture is and was somehow inferior to a dominant Maya identity, contemporary Lenca populations are contributing the erosion of their own identity. While cultures invariably change through time and the assumption of an invariable cultural identity is ethnographically unsupported, the need for cultural replacement in an attempt to gain social capital and fend off cultural irrelevance appears to represent a situation in which cultural marginality is imposed.

Ancient Lenca is not part of the myth of precolumbian Honduras, so Lenca speech – with no insulation from the effects of the Mayanization of the past and the *mestizaje* discourse – has been one of the major casualties of the re-invention of Honduran history. The linguistic decline that began with centuries of conflict and resistance was greatly exacerbated by massacres in the early twentieth century that targeted Lenca speakers. In the ensuing decades, the historical narratives that devalue the Lenca vis-à-vis national processes of identity formation and minimize the accomplishments of their ancestors created an environment in which knowledge of Lenca was, at best, a neutral skill and, at worst, a social and economic hindrance. The coalescence of these factors, in combination with the lack of social status given to Lenca individuals and the poverty caused by the resulting dearth of economic resources, created a situation hostile to language survival. The death of Lenca is made more tragic and complete due to the lack of resources created while speakers of the language were still alive. This is due, in large part, to a lack of social and intellectual interest in the language and its speakers that is directly attributable to the biases inherent in the narratives perpetuated by political and academic interests.

The Garifuna were never part of the creation of a new Honduran history. The ancestral Garifuna originated on St. Vincent as a blend of Arawaks, Caribs, and escaped African slaves. At the end of the eighteenth century, the British removed them and deposited them in the Bay Islands off the Caribbean coast of Honduras and, shortly

thereafter, on the northeast mainland (González, 1988). An African heritage is apparent in their phenotypes and in many of their cultural practices but not, surprisingly, in their language; Arawak and Carib vocabulary dominate the lexical repertoire, though European languages have also had been influential. This conflation of historical factors has created a distinct Garifuna identity, though this distinctiveness has not been easily translated into social or economic capital. Honduran intellectuals and politicians had no room in the new national identity for people of African descent. So intense was the perception of African culture as polluting, that one official Honduran geography alleged that Africans were not only a deleterious affect on morals, but had even corrupted the Maya language (Euraque, 2004: 51).

However, Garifuna does not appear to be endangered despite these prejudices. Part of the reason may be that, until very recently, the restriction of Garifuna communities to the coast and their Caribbean orientation afforded their language some insulation from the effects of Mayanization and *mestizaje* by placing them into a conceptually distinct category. The coastal Caribbean identity is viewed by many as largely distinct from the cultural spheres found in the interior, and this view – which is supported by both academic and popular perspectives – has created a kind of buffer zone that facilitated language survival. By affiliating with Caribbean identities, Garifuna communities in Honduras are separated from many of the cultural traditions found in the interior. Furthermore, their affiliation with related communities in Belize reinforces their place in a kind of international cultural consortium that provides additional protection. Although the Ch'orti' are associated with Maya communities outside of Honduras – including Ch'orti' speakers in Guatemala – the benefits of this association are less significant due to the dominance of Maya identities in the national narrative. For the Garifuna, however, the advantages of their international associations are significant. Unlike the Lenca and Pech, who are more geographically constrained and lack perceptible ties to communities beyond their territories, the Garifuna have a cultural range that is perceived to be both more independent and more substantial. Additionally, their connection to Belizean and Caribbean populations creates an enhanced level of international awareness concerning their condition and a subtle pressure to preserve the identity responsible for these ties. The fact that many Garifuna men have found employment on ships, in combination with significant levels of emigration to the United States and elsewhere, has further contributed to this phenomenon. The resulting social capital and position within the Afro-Caribbean sphere generates local interest in language maintenance; it also creates an elevated level of international awareness that reinforces local and governmental perceptions of value.

Issues of race and racial equality, in combination with their cultural ties to other African Diaspora populations, afford the language an additional measure of protection. There is a longstanding and considerable scholarly interest in the various instantiations of the African experience, and the relatively high profile of Garifuna communities in the minds of scholars interested in a range of Diaspora-related topics reinforce the view that the various components of Garifuna identity – including language – are interesting and relevant to understandings of the human experience. A variety of linguistic (e.g. Breton, 1877; Fleming, 1956, 1962; Howland, 1969a, 1969b; Munro, 1998; Suazo, 1994) and ethnolinguistic (e.g. Howland, 1988; Shaw, 1972) have been produced; ethnographic works such as Anderson (2007, 2009), Flores (2001), Franzone (1995), Gonzalez (1988), and Taylor (2012) are also prolific. Such scholarly attention generated a kind of social capital rooted in professional assessments of value – in short, by choosing to study Garifuna language and culture and publically present the results of these studies and worthy of attention, scholars are creating social capital capable of countering the dominant and Maya-centric narratives. Ongoing interest by tourists – some seeking a connection to their African past and others who simply want the thrill of visiting an exotic community representative of an aspect of history familiar to them – generates additional social capital that, in turn, produces economic resources.

Anderson (2007, 2009) points out that the Garifuna view themselves as having a kind of "black indigeneity" in which their African heritage, experiences as Africans in Honduras, and solidarity with the Diaspora coexist in equal measure with their perceptions of association with indigenous Central American identities and experiences. Although this perspective attempts to position Garifuna communities in both the indigenous and African spheres, the Garifuna "are traditionally interpellated as Black, [and] have had to confront a series of negative associations … that resonate far beyond Honduras" (Anderson, 2009: 16). These associations reflect and reinforce traditional racist policies in the country, and perceptions of Blackness – no matter how disparate from the identities perceived by the Garifuna themselves – represent a "form of otherness associated with distinct racial-cultural groups" that is separate from the blanco-mestizo-indio continuum dominant in the discourse surrounding the Honduran national identity (Anderson, 2009: 61). This otherness, though rooted in attempts to reduce the capital available to Garifuna populations, have surprisingly had the opposite effect. England (2010: 297-298) notes that the Garifuna have "the ability to join other members of the African diaspora in anti-racist struggles in one moment, and claim rights to land, bilingual education, and so forth as an autochthonous peoples in another," thus transforming their marginalization into a social and political capital capable of protecting their cultural and linguistic

interests. This appropriation also serves as a counter to the national definition of the Garifuna as a folkloric attraction and allows for local access to some of the revenue generated by this position.

The Pech have been similarly disconnected from precolumbian history, at least in the public mind, and are now thoroughly marginal to national historical discourses. Although they controlled a substantial coastal chiefdom at the time of the Spanish invasion and were able to successfully repel attempts at conquest during the sixteenth century, they were forced into the mountains of northern Honduras following the emergence of the Miskito and the proliferation of Miskito raids on Pech settlements. This migration arguably created a kind of cultural void in which the Pech – now separated from their traditional coastal sphere – were similarly disconnected from their new neighbors. This lack of a cultural anchor put the Pech at a disadvantage and created a substantial obstacle to social or economic betterment; it also created a situation in which the Pech have little perceptible capital of any kind. This dearth can be seen in the ongoing clashes between Pech farmers and ladino campesinos in Capiro-Calentura National Park by creating a situation in which Pech success requires alliances with other, more powerful ethnic groups (for a discussion of these conflicts, see Mollett, 2007). This dependence creates a situation in which the Pech are reliant upon a broader indigenous personality that overshadows their particular identity. This reliance, in turn, absorbs the Pech into the blanco-mestizo-indio continuum described by Anderson (2009) and views their position within the constructed indigenous narrative as superior to their own distinctive identity, thus devaluing Pech culture and language and contributing to their decline.

Academic discourse has largely supported this homogenizing perspective. Many contemporary accounts describe the indigenous individuals who accompanied the canoe captured by Christopher Columbus as Maya even though historical accounts tell us that they came from a region known to have been inhabited by Pech-speaking chiefdoms. Although many researchers have focused broadly on issues of indigenous identity in Honduras and elsewhere in Central America, comparatively little ethnographic or historical attention has been given to the specific study of the Pech and their cultural traditions. Notable exceptions include Conzemius (1928), Davidson (1991), Flores-Mejía (1989a), Flores-Mejía and Griffen (1991), Lanza (1986), and Lunardi (1943); the relatively low profile of these works, however, and their overall scarcity have done little to generate the kind of interest in Pech affairs that can be translated into social or economic capital.

As in the case of the Lenca, the coalescence of these factors, in combination with the general lack of social status afforded Pech individuals and the poverty caused by the resulting dearth of economic resources, has created a situation hostile to language survival. The moribund status of Pech is made more tragic by the relative lack of resources pertaining to the language itself despite some local interest in preservation. Of those resources that do exist, many use the language to explore broader typological or theoretical issues than on the study of the language for its own sake (see e.g. Constenla Umaña, 1991; Flores Mejía, 1989b; Humnick, 1991; Holt, 1986; and Holt & Bright, 1976). Pech-specific works more useful to local communities – including Flores Mejía (1998), Holt (1999), and Lardé y Larín (1941) – are valuable sources of information but have been unsuccessful in fending off the processes of language death. This is due, in part, to the fact that they do little to address local attitudes towards the language. The overall lack of social and intellectual interest in the language and its speakers is directly attributable to the biases inherent in the narratives perpetuated by political and academic interests, and the critically endangered status of the language can thus be attributed to the lack of social and economic capital caused by the perpetuation of a skewed system of historically-rooted judgments of cultural value.

Concluding Remarks

The experience of indigenous communities in Honduras in the nineteenth and twentieth centuries demonstrates that language stability in the region is based in large part on differences in the relationships of these languages to history and national identity as constructed by Hondurans. Most obviously, association with an officially favored past can provide speakers with social capital that can be mobilized economically and that can contribute to language survival. The construction of the precolumbian past of Honduras as Maya has afforded Ch'orti' speakers a focal place in Honduran history that supports the perpetuation of their language and culture; this success is, therefore, a consequence of the capital afforded the Ch'orti' and other Maya groups within the parameters of the Honduran historical narrative.

By contrast, speakers of non-Maya languages have found it harder to negotiate the official historico-cultural landscape. The Garifuna are marginalized by the Mayanization of Honduran history and, by virtue of the African component of their heritage, they have been accorded no role in the national identity. However, their coastal location, Caribbean orientation, and ties to the African Diaspora create some insulation from the effects of Mayanization and *mestizaje* by placing them into a conceptually distinct category. These factors also place them in an international cultural consortium that generates cultural and linguistic interest and protection. The speakers of Lenca and Pech have not been so lucky. The Lenca language had no insulation against the power of the discourse of *mestizaje* which envisions an inevitable process in which distinctive features of indigenous peoples – above all their languages – are erased as they blend with European features. The self-conscious focusing of intellectual, political, and social attentions to bolster the official historical account of a Maya past, and the concomitant marginalization of Lenca speakers in constructions of the Honduran past created a situation hostile to language survival. The Lenca, cognizant of the ethno-politics surrounding the Honduran national identity, have in some cases adopted the term 'Maya' as part of a tradition of cultural replacement of supplementation geared towards the acquisition of social and economic capital. The Pech occupy a geographic area distinct from their traditional homeland and thus experience a kind of cultural disconnect from other groups in region. This created a situation in which the Pech are reliant upon a broader indigenous personality that overshadows their own identity and views their position within the constructed indigenous narrative as superior to their own distinctive identity. In all of these cases, it is the coalescence of history, identity, and social and economic capitals that facilitate or repel processes of language endangerment. A contextualized approach can thus provide a more comprehensive perspective that, in turn, has the potential to preserve and protect the languages threated by the narratives of the modern world.

References

Anderson, M. (2007). When Afro Becomes (like) Indigenous: Garifuna and Afro-Indigenous Politics in Honduras. *Journal of Latin American and Caribbean Anthropology* 12.2, 384-413.

Anderson, M. (2009). *Black and Indigenous: Garifuna Activism and Consumer Culture in Honduras*. Minneapolis, MN: University of Minnesota Press.

Breton, R. (1877[1635]). *Grammaire caraibe, composée par le p. Raymond Breton, suivie du Catéchisme caraibe*. Bibliothèque linguistique américaine, no. 3 (1635 original MS. republication ed.). Paris: Maisonneuve.

Campbell, L.R. (1997). *American Indian Languages: The Historical Linguistics of Native America*. New York, NY: Oxford University Press.

Coe, M.D. (2011). *The Maya*. 8th ed. New York: Thames and Hudson.

Constenla Umaña, A. (1991). *Las lenguas del area intermedia: introducción a su studio areal*. Universidad de Costa Rica.

Conzemius, E. (1928). *Los Indios Paya de Honduras. Estudio geográfico, histórico, etnográfico, y lingüístico*. Paris, France: Paul Geuthner.

Cowie, D., and Martínez, S. (1994). *Precartilla para escolares chortí-hablantes*. SIL International: Instituto Lingüístico de Verano.

Cuddy, T.W. (2007). *Political Identity and Archaeology in Northeast Honduras*. Boulder, CO: University of Colorado Press.

Davidson, W. (1991). Geographical perspectives on Spanish-Pech (Paya) Indian relationships in sixteenth century Northeast Nicaragua. In D. Thomas (Ed.), *The Spanish borderlands in Pan-American perspective, vol. 3, Columbian Consequences* (pp. 227-244). Washington, D.C.: Smithsonian Institution Press.

England, S. (2010) Black and Indigenous: Garifuna Activism and Consumer Culture in Honduras (review). *The Americas* 67(2), 297-298.

Euraque, D.A. (2004). *Conversaciones históricas con el mestiaje y su identidad nacional en Honduras*. San Pedro Sula, Honduras: Centro Editorial.

Fleming, I. (1956). *Garífuna líburu 1*. SIL International: Instituto Lingüístico de Verano

Fleming, I. (1962). *Alfabeto caribe*. Dirección General de Cartografía.

Flores, B.A.T. (2001). Religious education and theological praxis in a context of colonization: Garifuna spirituality as a means of resistance. Doctoral Dissertation, Garrett/Northwestern University, Evanston, Illinois.

Flores Mejía, L. (1989a). *Mitos, leyendas y ritos de los pech*. Tegucigalpa, Honduras: Cooperación Española-PROAVEH.

Flores Mejía, L. (1989b). On Paya causatives. *Estudios de Lingüística Chibcha* 8, 7-15.

Flores Mejía, L. (1998). Aspectos fonológicos y morfológicos del pech importantes en el desarrollo de una ortografía práctica. In A. Herranz *et al.* (Eds.), *Educación bilingüe e intercultural en Centroamérica y México* (pp. 229-241). Tegucigalpa, Honduras: Guaymuras.

Flores Mejía, L. & Griffin, W. (1991). *Dioses, héroes y hombres en el universo mítico de los pech*. San Salvador, El Salvador: UCA Editores.

Franzone, D. (1995). A Critical and Cultural Analysis of an African People in the Americas: Africanisms in the Garifuna Culture of Belize. Doctoral Dissertation, Temple University. UMI Dissertation Services.

Gamio, M. (2010[1916]). *Forjando Patria: Pro-nacionalismo (Forging a Nation)*. Boulder, CO: University Press of Colorado.

González, N.L. (1988). *Sojourners of the Caribbean: Ethnogenesis and Ethnohistory of the Garifuna*. Urbana, IL: University of Illinois Press.

Hammond, N. (1982). *Ancient Maya Civilization*. New Brunswick, NJ: Rutgers University Press.

Henderson, J.S. & Hudson, K. (2011). The Southeastern Frontier. In D. Nichols & C. Pool (Eds.), *Oxford Handbook of Mesoamerican Archaeology*, ed. D. Nichols and C. Pool (pp. 482-494). New York, NY: Oxford University Press.

Holt, D.G. (1986). The development of the Paya sound system. University of Californi, Los Angeles. Doctoral Dissertation, University of California Los Angeles.

Holt, D.G. (1999). *Pech (Paya)*. Languages of the World/Materials, 366. München, Germany: Lincom.

Holt, D.G. & Bright, W. (1976). La lengua Paya y las fronteras lingüísticas de Mesoamérica. In *Fronteras de Mesoamérica, 1. XIX Mesa Redonda de la Sociedad Mexicana de Antropología* (pp. 149-156). México, D.F.

Howland, L.G. (1969a). *Uraga garífunoúti*. SIL International: Instituto Lingüístico de Verano.

Howland, L.G. (1969b). *Uboú jama planéta*. Unión Panamericana.

Howland, L.G. (1988). *Comunicación con los espíritus 'dügü garifuna (Caribe)*. SIL International: Instituto Lingüístico de Verano, Serie grammatical.

Hudson, K.M. (2011). Colonizing the Past: George Byron Gordon and the birth of a Colonialist Archaeology on the Southeastern Mesoamerican Frontier. *Histories of Anthropology Annual* 7, 246-264.

Hudson, K.M. (2013). The Ties that Bind: Archaeology, Politics, and Revolutions of Identity in Mesoamerica's Southeast. *Anthropology: Bachelors to Doctorates* 2(1).

Hudson, K.M. & Henderson, J.S. (2014). Life on the edge – identity and Interaction in the Land of Ulúa and the Maya World. In J. Ikäheimo, A.K. Salmi & T. Äikäs (Eds.), *Sounds Like Theory* (pp. 151-171). Monographs of the Archaeological Society of Finland 2, Helsinki.

Humnick, L.A. (1991). The phonology-morphology interface in Paya: a lexical phonology approach. Masters Thesis, The University of Texas at Arlington.

Joya, O. (1992). Crónica de las crónicas: la conquista de la Provincia de Honduras (S XVI). P*araninfo: Revista del Instituto de Ciencias del Hombre 'Rafael Heliodoro Valle'* 1(2):109-144.

Lanza, R. (1986). *Los pech. Una cultura olvidada*. Tegucigalpa, Honduras: Talleres Guaymuras.

Lardé y Larín, J. (1941). La numeración paya. *Revista del Archivo y Biblioteca Nacionales* 19, 557-560.

Lewis, M. P., G. F. Simons, & C. D. Fennig. (2014). *Ethnologue: Languages of the World, Seventeenth edition*. Dallas, Texas: SIL International. Online version: http://www.ethnologue. com.

Lubeck, D., & J. Lubeck. (1984a). *Cacanic e castilla: chorti - castellano.* SIL International: Instituto Lingüístico de Verano.

Lubeck, D., & J. Lubeck. (1984b). *E libro era jax tua' cacano cache leer tama e lenguaje.* SIL International: Instituto Lingüístico de Verano.

Lubeck, D., & J. Lubeck. (1989). *Método moderno para aprender el idioma chortí: Una gramática pedagógica.* SIL International: Instituto Lingüístico de Verano.

Lunardi, F. (1943). *Los payas, documentos curiosos y viajes: esbozo de un capítulo de la historia de Honduras.* Tegucigalpa, Honduras: Tipografía Nacional.

Lunardi, F. (1948). *Honduras maya: etnología y arqueologĕa de Honduras.* Tegucigalpa, Honduras: Imprenta Calderón.

Metz, B. (2010). Questions of indigeneity and the (re)-emergent Ch'orti' Maya of Honduras. *Journal of Latin American and Caribbean Anthropology* 15(2), 289-316.

McNichols, J. L. (1977). *Alfabeto chortí.* Guatemala: Instituto Indigenista Nacional

Mollett, S. (2007). Entanglements: *campesino* and indigenous tenure insecurities on the Honduran north coast. In P. Vandergeest, P. Idahosa, and P. S. Bose (Eds), *Development's displacements: economies, ecologies and cultures at risk.* Vancouver, Canada: University of British Columbia Press.

Munro, P. (1998). The Garifuna gender system. In Hill, Mistry, & Campbell (Eds), *The Life of Language: papers in linguistics in honor of William Bright.* New York, NY: Mouton de Gruyter.

Oakley, H. (1966). *Chorti.* Janua Linguarum, series practica.

Piedra, J. (1987). Literary whiteness and the Afro-Hispanic difference. *New Literary History* 18(2), 303-332.

Restall, M. (2001). The Janus face of Maya identity in Post-Conquest Yucatan. In U. Hostettler & M. Restall (Eds.), *Maya Survivalism* (pp. 15-23). Markt Schwaben, Germany: Anton Saurwein.

Sharer, R. J. (1994). *The Ancient Maya.* 5th ed. Stanford, CA: Stanford University Press.

Shaw, M. (1972). *Según nuestros antepasados: Textos folklóricos de Guatemala y Honduras.* SIL International: Instituto Lingüístico de Verano.

Stone, D.Z. (1941). *Archaeology of the North Coast of Honduras.* Peabody Museum of Archaeology and Ethnology, Memoirs 9(1). Cambridge, MA: Harvard University.

Stone, D.Z. (1948). The northern highland tribes: the Lenca. In J.H. Steward (Ed.), *Handbook of South American Indians, Vol. 4: The Circum-Caribbean Tribes* (pp. 205-217). Smithsonian Institution, Bureau of American Ethnology, Bulletin 143. Washington.

Stone, D.Z. (1957). *The Archaeology of Central and Southern Honduras.* Peabody Museum of Archaeology and Ethnology, Papers 49(3). Cambridge, MA: Harvard University.

Suazo, S. (1994). *Conversemos en garífuna* (2nd ed.). Tegucigalpa, Honduras: Editorial Guaymuras.

Taylor, C. (2012). *The Black Carib Wars: Freedom, Survival, and the Making of the Garifuna.* Jackson, MS: University Press of Mississippi.

The Value of Scientific Names from (Australian) Indigenous Languages

David Nash

School of Literature, Languages and Linguistics
The Australian National University
Canberra ACT 0200, Australia
[david.nash@anu.edu.au]
Australian Institute of Aboriginal and Torres Strait Islander Studies (AIATSIS)

Abstract

The adoption of endangered words into scientific nomenclature in a small way assists the survival of words that otherwise would be lost. Linnæan biological names are guaranteed as much longevity as science can offer. Biological species are being identified at an increasing rate and there is a corresponding demand for unique names appropriate for these species and other taxa (including of fossils). This need has in Australia increasingly been met by words selected from Australian indigenous languages. Names in general can assist language revitalization by reminding the wider community that the language exists, and by providing a positive way for the community to interact with the speakers or holders of a heritage language. For biological names in particular, indigenous languages are clearly an excellent source, because a relevant word is likely to be available and is likely to be previously unused (meeting the uniqueness requirement). A local word can manifest 'the seamless fit between an indigenous language and its language ecology', and may even, for instance, be phonosemantically appropriate. Each local word so used is a potential link between local language maintenance, traditional ecological knowledge, and science and the wider world. Not only does the adoption of a word into scientific nomenclature assist its survival, but the arrangements around bestowal of these names also provide an opportunity for positive engagement between the speakers or holders of heritage languages, and biologists and naturalists. The limits of this approach are also noticeable in how the existing Australian scientific names have been assigned.

Introduction

Linnæan biological names have accumulated since the mid 18th century. Names have long been drawn from Latin and Greek roots, but these have long been augmented by placenames, commemorative personal names, and descriptive words taken from other languages. The topic of this paper is the adoption in Linnæan names of words from endangered languages, specifically the languages of Australia: nowadays less than a tenth of Australian languages can be classed as 'safe' with respect to intergenerational language transmission (Moseley, 2010).

Biological taxonomy practice is that even when a name is superseded it is not entirely discarded as it is retained in the permanent taxonomic history. Thus a word from an endangered language gets a new and indefinitely long lease of life when it is applied in a Linnæan name. I consider here how successful this avenue has been, and could be, for the benefit of the relevant communities.

Taxonomic background

More than 150 Linnæan names already incorporate a word from an Australian language (Nash, 2014b). An early and fairly well-known example is the word *wombat*, once uniquely attested from an inland language near Sydney, which survives not only in English (and other world languages), but also since 1803 in zoological names *Vombatus* genus, Vombatidæ family (Wilson & Reeder, 2005). The last few decades has seen a proliferation of Linnæan names incorporating a word from an Australian language (and indeed a proliferation of Linnæan names generally). The most recent adoption is the tree genus *Karrabina* (Fortune-Hopkins *et al.*, 2013) from *karabin(y)*, the name in the Yugambeh language of northeast NSW.

From the point of view of the taxonomist, there are a couple of factors assisting the adoption into scientific (Linnæan) nomenclature of words beyond their traditional pool of Latinate adjectives and so on. The first is the requirement for a unique name. Within a genus, a species name obviously needs to be unique. Further, the name of each genus (and higher taxon) is required to be unique within its Kingdom.

The second factor is the immense increase in the number of identified biological species. The increase is predicted to continue for centuries, as most species are yet to be identified:

Assessment of this pattern for all kingdoms of life on Earth predicts ~8.7 million (±1.3 million SE) species globally, of which ~2.2 million (±0.18 million SE) are marine. Our results suggest that some 86% of the species on Earth, and 91% in the ocean, still await description (Mora *et al.*, 2011)

Another estimate, possibly on the high side, is 'a total of 8.7 to 10.6 million species (without including protists and prokaryotes)' (Mora *et al.*, 2013). Alongside this, '~8000 valid species were described annually from 1990 to 2000' (Mora *et al.*, 2013). Drawing on local languages meets the need for a much larger pool of available descriptive terms which might fit the organism being named.

Word ecology

A local word can, in the words of the conference call, manifest 'the seamless fit between an indigenous language and its language ecology'.

If any language is to have a longstanding word denoting a particular organism, surely it will be an indigenous language of the organism's range. Such a local name has agood claim to be appropriate, a good fit with its sense, perhaps because a relevant semantic distinction is made, or perhaps because the word has evident parts. There could also be an informal appreciation of the appropriateness of the name through sound symbolism. That is, the word may be phonosemantically appropriate: when the sound of a word somehow fits its sense. This possibility encompasses onomatopœia, but is considerably wider. This 'pervasive synesthetic sound symbolism' has been studied particularly for fauna terms (Berlin, 2006). Note that fauna and flora terms are common among the words borrowed from local languages into colonising or global languages. An example from outside Australia is English *gecko* (and New Latin *gekko)* " < Malay *gēkoq* (the q is faint) an imitation of the animal's cry." [OED]. The word was assured longevity when Linnæus incorporated it in the zoological name for the Tokay gecko (*Gekko gecko* L), and also the family Gekkonidæ.

A classic example of how a word can survive is the small reptile *skink* /skɪŋk/ *Scincus scincus* Linnaeus 1758 (family Scincidæ) '< classical Latin *scincus* (Pliny) < Hellenistic Greek σκίγκος /skíŋkos/ probably a loanword' [OED]. In other words, the word *skink* originated in an unrecorded ancient language and its survival became ensured when it was borrowed into Ancient Greek, and then into the Linnæan system. There may have been a phonosemantic factor in its longevity.

An early Australian example is *boobook:* 'Bōkbōk, an owl' in the Sydney Language, recorded by William Dawes (Dawes & Anonymous, 2009: B3) by 1793 and soon taken up in the zoological name (and common name) for the Southern Boobook owl, *Ninox boobook* (Latham, 1801: 64); the owl's call sounds like the word.

Authenticity

The link between the Australian word and the Linnæan name is the strongest when the chain of connection is the shortest. In some cases the first scientific record of the organism and of the word are bound up together. In this situation, the scientist is in the locality where the language is spoken and collaborating in some way with speakers. Such were the circumstances of the first vocabulary recorded of Australian language, by Cook and Banks at Endeavour River in 1770. Their journals noted the local word for a 'polecat', respectively *Quoll* and *Je-Quoll,* sc. Guugu Yimidhirr *dhigul* 'native cat', (Haviland, 1974: 220,225).[19] The word was published in *Mustela quoll* by the zoologist Zimmermann in 1777

9

Cook's journal entry http://nla.gov.au/nla. cs-ss-jrnl-hv23-626 and Banks' http://nla.gov. au/nla.cs-ss-jrnl-banks_remarks-268; now understood to denote *Dasyurus hallucatus* Gould 1842, Northern Quoll (Abbott, 2013).

and 1783 (Allen, 1902: 16). Unfortunately (for the word) Zimmermann's names were ruled invalid in 1954, and though there was agitation for its restoration (Mahoney & Ride, 1984), it remains suppressed, though its time as a Linnæan name has supported its currency as the English common name for the marsupial. Aside from *quoll,* the oldest names which have stuck were also obtained by the authors directly from speakers of the relevant language: two mammal species names applied by (Meyer *et al.,* 1793: 28, 33), *Phascogale tapoatafa* and *Canis dingo,* used the two appropriate words supplied by Governor Arthur Phillip from the Sydney Language. These two words have had completely different fortunes. *Tapoatafa* can be recognised as containing *dabuwa* 'white', and does not otherwise survive. On the other hand the word *dingo* /'diŋu/ originally unique to the Sydney Language (no word cognate with *dingo* has been encountered in any other Australian language), was borrowed into English as /"dɪŋgəʊ/, and thence into languages around the world.

In recent years too a Linnæan name has arisen through direct collaboration between speakers of an Australian language and a scientist. The *Karrabina* genus, mentioned above, is apparently one such, assigned only last year. Here are a couple of other examples from recent decades.

• The Alyawarr language word *yakerr* denoting 'desert Flinders' grass, *Yakirra australiensis'* spread to the genus *Yakirra* (distinguished from *Panicum*) by virtue of a botanist's longterm collaboration with Alyawarr people; 'The name *Yakirra* is an aboriginal term for some of the species of the genus (P.K. Latz, personal communication).' (Lazarides & Webster, 1984: 293).

• The fossil mollusc †*Karathele kurtuju* (Kruse, 1998: 37) took its species name from Warlmanpa *kurtuju* 'shield'. The palæontologist was guided by Warlmanpa people during his fieldwork, and when he encountered the previously undescribed fossil species he asked for a descriptive word from their language to use in the name. This example shows clearly that even when an appropriate word is chosen collaboratively from a local language, the word need not have denoted the organism.

At the less authentic end of the spectrum of localisation, since about 1970 there have been a number of instances where a taxonomist has reached for a popular book with an Aboriginal theme and selected a word to use as a name, on the basis of the perceived relevance of the gloss. This has been done without any communication with the relevant language holders and without regard to geography. Here are some examples.

• Around fifty four species of *Onthophagus* dung beetles were named in two publications. 'New species are given Australian aboriginal names with few exceptions. In each case, an effort was made to give the species an appropriate name in a language spoken more or less in the same area as that where the species occurs, or to use the name of the tribe occurring in that area. Words were selected from (Reed, 1965) . . . Names of tribes and the location of their territories were obtained from [(Berndt & Berndt, 1988)]' (Matthews, 1971), also (Storey & Weir, 1990: 783).

- A genus of small dasyurid marsupial new to science was found in arid WA from 1957. The taxonomist named it *Ningaui* because of attributes shared with the 'tiny mythological beings that are hairy, have short feet, and only come out at night to hunt for food all of which is eaten raw' (Archer, 1975: 243). The taxonomist found the word in a section about an island 'off the northern coast' in a popular book (Roberts & Mountford, 1969: 54), and abstracted it from the quite different location and the mythological status. The word is recognisable as *nyingawi* 'short ghosts' (plural of *nyingani*) in the Tiwi language, spoken on wet tropical islands on the north of Australia. The languages where the Ningaui is found would have a term applicable to small rodents or dasyurids (Burbidge *et al.*, 1988), but this was not readily available to the taxonomist. Nevertheless, the zoological *Ningaui* do contribute in a slight way to the survival of the Tiwi word, and there is arguably more community value in *Ningaui* than to be gained from, say, a Græco-Latin coinage.

- *Pedinura mokari,* a marine crustacean was named using *mokari* 'an Aboriginal word meaning new' (Bruce, 2003: 365). The word is actually from Ngarrindjeri, on the coast of SA adjacent to part of the crustacean's range, but the relevance of the meaning 'new' is only that it was new to science, and did not reflect any attribute of the creature.

- Homogenised popular lists of 'euphonious Aboriginal words' have been popular during the 20th century in Australia (Furphy, 2002). These booklets have been a handy source for some taxonomists, but because the source language or region is usually not stated, there is no regard for locality, let alone a chance for engagement between the taxonomist and the speakers of the endangered language. An extreme example is the name of *Murrindisyllis kooromundroola,* a marine bristle worm found off the coast south of Sydney (NSW). The taxonomists (San Martín *et al.,* 2007) coined both the genus and the species names from three separate unsourced words they found in a popular booklet 'of 3,000 pleasant-sounding words from which to choose an appropriate Australian name' (Endacott, 1973), in turn from three disparate Australian languages: *murrindi* 'five' fingers' (Endacott, 1973: 40) from a language yet to be identified (combined with the established genus name *Syllis*), *kooro* 'eyes' from the Mulyara (Muliarra) language of WA, and *mandrulha* 'only two' (literally *mandru* 'two', *-lha* 'only') from the Dieri (Diyari) language of northern SA. All that

remains of the particularities of origin is the taxonomists' justification of the combination as 'referring to the unique pair of eyes' (Nash, 2014a). Admittedly, the tiny organism was retrieved from under the sea out from land in 1990, and is unlikely to have had a particular name in any indigenous language. Nevertheless, the speakers of a source language may have preferred to have been involved in this appropriation of a word of their language.

As an aside, we need to acknowledge instances where a proper name from an Australian language has been used in a Linnæan name. There are instances where this has happened to a personal name and, more commonly, to placenames. An example of the former is the freshwater fish *Hypseleotris barrawayi,* Barraway's gudgeon (Larson, 2007: 116) 'named for the late Sandy Barraway, traditional owner of the Sleisbeck country, who had great knowledge of the fauna and stories associated with that country', and who had collaborated with scientists. An example of the latter is *Guyu wujalwujalensis,* a temperate perch (Pusey & Kennard, 2001) named for Wujal Wujal township near where it was found (and the genus is also local, *guyu* 'freshwater fish (generic)' in Kuku-Yalanji).

These examples illustrate that a good fraction of the Linnæan names adopt a word whose sense encompasses the organism under study, and many do not. Some words have been chosen which indicate a property of the organism (such as colour or shape), and quite a few simply commemorate the indigenous name of the type locality or of a local language.

Some similiarities with placenaming

For the Linnæan names considered here, there are similarities and contrasts with how Indigenous placenames have been adopted by the now-dominant incomers. For one, an original word has generally suffered less mangling in scientific names than in placenames, where *ad hoc* spellings and pronunciation distortions (beyond loan phonology) are rife. Of course this is partly because most scientific names are pronounced only by specialists, and in the context of scientific Latin thereby promoting 'Italian' rather than English vowel qualities. Second, a lot of Australian words adopted into Linnæan biological names have been selected from a dictionary, or other written source comprising a fair sample of the donor language in some kind of consistent orthography, whereas a placename was typically first written down in isolation with a stretch of the haphazard English orthography.

The considerations of authenticity are somewhat parallel to the situation with placenames (Nash, 2003). As with placenames, we can distinguish varying degrees of dislocation between the original word and its adoption into nomenclature. At one extreme, a name is applied to an entity known to the speakers of the language and in a way they would understand. At another extreme, the name is applied to some entity in another region, and with a connection that would be opaque to the language's speakers even were they to learn of the new name. Typically, once the source historical word list was compiled, there were no speakers of the language involved in the subsequent dealings by the wider society in the recorded word. Then an author, landholder, or public employee, in need of a new name (whether for a place, street, company, product, boat, racehorse, etc) has chosen a word from some kind of popular source to apply as a name, and in most cases it is unlikely there was any communication about the name with the language's speakers or their descendants.

Engagement with language holders

The wide variation in the degree of engagement with language holders has been illustrated above. At the weakest extreme, in the latter part of the 20th century, taxonomists have often plucked a general word from some popular compilation of 'Aboriginal words', with or without some regard for locality, and usually with no contact with the donor language community.

The situation can improve. Life scientists could find benefit in adopting some of the participatory research methods from cognate disciplines. Some biologists have continued the practice of earlier times and made direct contact with language communities around their field sites, and indeed these connections have in recent decades been affected by the rise of regional land councils and language centres, and the recognition of traditional ecological knowledge. And there are now Aboriginal organisations which can broker the selection of appropriate nomenclature. For instance, a language revival organisation *Kaurna Warra Pintyandi* (KWP) has been providing a naming service in its region for over a decade, http://www.adelaide.edu.au/kwp/requests/ The forerunner of KWP provided the name Yitpi (a Kaurna word meaning 'seed') for a spring wheat cultivar registered in 2000 (SARDI South Australian Field Crop Evaluation Program, 1999).

Of course it should not be assumed that a language community will want to provide a name for wider use. Sometimes the inquirer could be oblivious to the reasons why some types of word are not suitable. As far as I am aware, in Australia generally an indigenous language community is pleased to be able to steer an inquirer towards a term with wide acceptability.

Even where a name has been assigned in the absence of local engagement, nevertheless we can look to educational value being retrospectively made of the name's local origin. This could happen for instance in the course of school education, in public signage, and visitor information. Admittedly Linnæan names are not a prominent feature in the linguistic landscape, but it can be a matter of local pride when a local word is seen to have some value to others beyond the community of the donor language, even more so when the language

community is aware there was a personal chain of connection with the taxonomist.

Conclusion

Thus there is a continuing demand for unique names appropriate for newly described biological species. Endangered languages are an excellent source for these names, and the adoption of endangered words into scientific nomenclature is one small contribution to the promotion of maintenance and revitalization of endangered languages, and has greater potential when the language community is involved and engaged at the stage of name selection.

Acknowledgements

I am grateful to Jane Simpson for discussion of the topic, and to various linguist colleagues, biologists and palæontologists for alerting me to examples and answering my particular queries. I have used online databases including Mammal Species of the World http://www. bucknell.edu/msw3/, the Paleobiology Database http://fossilworks.org, Wikispecies http://species.wikimedia.org, and the Catalogue of Life http://www.catalogueoflife.org.

Abbreviation

OED = Oxford English Dictionary Second edition, 1989; online version September 2011).

References

Abbott, I. (2013). Extending the application of Aboriginal names to Australian biota: 'Dasyurus' (Marsupialia: Dasyuridae) species. *The Victorian Naturalist,* 130(3), 109–126. http://search.informit.com.au/documentSummary;dn=425523720638389; res=IELHSS.

Allen, J. A. (1902). Zimmermann's 'Zoologiæ Geographicæ' and 'Geographische Geschichte' considered in their relation to mammalian nomenclature. *Bulletin of the AMNH,* 16(2), 13–22. http://hdl.handle.net/ 2246/502.

Archer, M. (1975). *Ningaui,* a new genus of tiny dasyurids (Marsupialia) and two new species, *N. timealeyi* and *N. ridei,* from arid Western Australia. *Memoirs of the Queensland Museum,* 17(2), 237–249.

Berlin, B. (2006). Evidence for pervasive synesthetic sound symbolism in ethnozoological nomenclature. In L. Hinton, J. Nichols, & J. J. Ohala (Eds.), *Sound symbolism* (pp. 76–93). Cambridge, UK: Cambridge University Press. http://books.google.com.au/books?id=Uov84NavOR8C.

Berndt, R. M. & Berndt, C. H. (1988). *The world of the first Australians: Aboriginal traditional life: Past and present*. Aboriginal Studies Press. http://books. google.com.au/books?id=KjYvRxUzzgMC.

Bruce, N. L. (2003). New genera and species of sphaeromatid isopod crustaceans from Australian marine coastal waters. *Memoirs of Museum Victoria,* 60(2), 309–369. http://museumvictoria.com. au/pages/4001/60_2_bruce.pdf.

Burbidge, A. A., Johnson, K., Fuller, P., & Southgate, R. (1988). Aboriginal knowledge of the mammals of the central deserts of Australia. *Australian Wildlife Research,* 15(1), 9–39.

Dawes, W. & Anonymous (2009). The notebooks of William Dawes on the Aboriginal languages of Sydney. http://www.williamdawes.org.

Endacott, S. J. (1973). *Australian Aboriginal words and place names and their meanings.* Melbourne: Acacia Press, 10th edition.

Fortune-Hopkins, H., Rozefelds, A., & Pillon, Y. (2013). *Karrabina* gen. nov. (Cunoniaceae), for the Australian species previously placed in *Geissois,* and a synopsis of genera in the tribe Geissoieae. *Australian Systematic Botany,* 26(3), 167–185. http://www.publish. csiro.au/?paper=SB12037.

Furphy, S. (2002). Aboriginal house names and settler Australian identity. *Journal of Australian Studies,* 26(72), 59–68. http://www.api-network. com/main/pdf/scholars/jas72_furphy. pdf.

Haviland, J. B. (1974). A last look at Cook's Guugu Yimidhirr word list. *Oceania,* 44(3), 216–232.

Kruse, P. D. (1998). *Cambrian palaeontology of the eastern Wiso and western Georgina basins.* Number 9 in NTGS Report. Darwin: Northern Territory Geological Survey. http://www.nt.gov.au/d/ Minerals_Energy/Geoscience/Content/ File/Pubs/Report/NTGSRep9.pdf.

Larson, H. K. (2007). A new species of carp gudgeon, *Hypseleotris* (Pisces: Gobioidei: Eleotridae), from the Katherine River system, Northern Territory. *The Beagle: Records of the Museums and Art Galleries of the Northern Territory,* 23, 111. http://search. informit.com.au/documentSummary;dn= 097570479712945;res=IELHSS.

Latham, J. (1801). *Supplement II to the General synopsis of birds.* York Street, Covent Garden, London: Leigh, Sotheby, & Son. http://www. biodiversitylibrary.org/item/103837, http://www.biodiversitylibrary.org/bibliography/4900 8.

Lazarides, M. & Webster, R. (1984). *Yakirra* (Paniceae, Poaceae), a new genus for Australia. *Brunonia : Australian Systematic Botany,* 7(2), 289–296. http://www.publish.csiro.au.virtual.anu.edu.au/?paper =BRU9840289.

Mahoney, J. A. & Ride, W. D. L. (1984). The identity of Captain Cook's quoll *Mustela quoll* Zimmermann, 1783 (Marsupialia: Dasyuridae). *Journal of the Australian Mammal Society,* 7(2), 57—62. http://books.google.com.au/books?id= 7hCPg7WCir0C&lpg=PA59&ots=5UYA_PvcZv.

Matthews, E. G. (1971). A revision of the Scarabaeine dung beetles of Australia. I. Tribe Onthophagini. *Australian Journal of Zoology Supplementary Series,* 19(9), 3–330. http://www.publish.csiro.au/nid/ 91/issue/3832.htm.

Meyer, F. A. A., Phillip, A., & Bruce, J. (1793). *Systematisch-summarische Übersicht der neuesten zoologischen Entdeckungen in Neuholland und Afrika: Nebst zwey andern zoologischen Abhandlungen.* Leipzig: Dykische Buchhandlung. http: //openlibrary.org/books/OL24130913M.

Mora, C., Rollo, A., & Tittensor, D. P. (2013). Comment on "Can we name Earth's species before they go extinct?". *Science,* 341(6143), 237. http://www.sciencemag.org/content/341/6143/237.3. abstract.

Mora, C., Tittensor, D. P., Adl, S., Simpson, A. G. B., & Worm, B. (2011). How many species are there on Earth and in the ocean? *PLoS Biol,* 9(8), e1001127. http://dx.doi.org/10.1371/ journal.pbio.1001127.

Moseley, C., Ed. (2010). *Atlas of the World's Languages in Danger.* Memory of Peoples. Paris: UNESCO Publishing, 3rd edition. http://www.unesco.org/new/en/ culture/themes/endangered-languages/ atlas-of-languages-in-danger/.

Nash, D. (2003). Authenticity in toponymy. In J. Blythe & R. McKenna Brown (Eds.), *Maintaining the links.*

Language, identity and the land, volume Proceedings of the Seventh FEL conference, Broome, Western Australia (pp. 36–40). Bath, UK: Foundation for Endangered Languages.

Nash, D. (2014a). Mandrulha. http:// dieriyawarra.wordpress.com/2014/06/ 30/mandrulha/, Posted on Ngayana Diyari Yawarra Yathayilha: Supporting the Dieri language blog on 30 June 2014 8:33am GMT.

Nash, D. (2014b). Reviving unique words. In J. Miller (Ed.), [Proceedings of 2013 Australex conference 'Endangered Words, and Signs of Revival', to appear] Adelaide: University of Adelaide.

Pusey, B. J. & Kennard, M. J. (2001). *Guyu wujalwujalensis,* a new genus and species (Pisces: Percichthyidae) from north-eastern Queensland, Australia.

Reed, A. W. (1965). *Aboriginal words of Australia.* Balgowlah: AH & AW Reed. http:

//babel.hathitrust.org/cgi/pt?id=
inu.39000005883553.

Roberts, A. & Mountford, C. P. (1969). *The dawn of time: Australian Aboriginal myths in paintings.* Adelaide: Rigby.

San Martín, G., Aguado, M. T., Murray, A., & Gardiner, S. L. (2007). A new genus and species of Syllidae (Annelida: Polychaeta) from Australia with unusual morphological characters and uncertain systematic position. *Proceedings of the Biological Society of Washington,* 120(1), 39–48. http://www.bioone.org/doi/abs/10.2988/0006-324X(2 007)120%5B39:ANGASO%5D2.0.CO%3B2.

SARDI South Australian Field Crop Evaluation Program (1999). Yitpi. a hard quality cereal eelworm-resistant wheat for South Australian growers. http://www.sardi.sa.gov.au/__data/ assets/pdf_file/0003/45993/yitpi.pdf.

Storey, R. & Weir, T. (1990). New species of *Onthophagus* Latreille (Coleoptera: Scarabaeidae) from Australia. *Invertebrate Systematics,* 3(6),783–815.http://www. publish.csiro.au/?paper=IT9890783.

Wilson, D. E. & Reeder, D. M., Eds. (2005). *Mammal species of the world, a taxonomic and geographic reference.* Johns Hopkins University Press, 3rd edition. http://www.departments.bucknell. edu/biology/resources/msw3/.

It's Harder in My Language but I Still Choose it

Te Taka Keegan
Department of Computer Science
University of Waikato
Hamilton. New Zealand
[tetaka@waikato.ac.nz]

Paora Mato
Department of Computer Science
University of Waikato
Hamilton. New Zealand
[pjm20@students.waikato.ac.nz]

Abstract

In New Zealand, the language that dominates most technologies is English. For a variety of reasons, interfaces have been made available in the Māori language for a range of modern technological tools. We have conducted usability studies on many of these products and fluent Māori users have almost unanimously stated that the products are more difficult and time consuming to use in the indigenous (Māori) language. They allude to unfamiliar instances and uses of Māori words, and to an ingrained familiarity with the English-language versions of these technologies, saying they would revert to the English-language interfaces if time is a factor. However, they also express a sense of pride at being able to see and use the Māori language in these various forms of media and state that although they experience some difficulty, the Māori-language versions would still be their first preference.

Introduction

Te reo Māori (the Māori language), is the native language of Aotearoa (New Zealand). In 2013, 21.3% of Māori (125,352) stated they could converse about everyday things using te reo Māori (Statistics NZ 2013). This level of fluency has decreased from 25.2% (2001) and 23.7% (2006) (Waitangi Tribunal, 2010: 103). According to *The Ethnologue* slightly over 70% of fluent Māori-language speakers are over the age of 45 (Gordon, 2005: 386). Given the assertions made by Fishman (1991; 2000) regarding the importance of intergenerational transmission to the health of a language, measures contained in *The Atlas for Endangered Languages* based on intergenerational transmission, and the observations of *Te Paepae Motuhake* (a team of Māori-language experts reviewing New Zealand's Māori Language Strategy 2003), te reo Māori can be classified as being somewhere between **definitely endangered** (children no longer learn the language as a mother tongue in the home) to **severely endangered** (the language is spoken by grand-parents and older generations; while the parent generation understand it, they do not speak it amongst themselves or to their children) (Moseley, 2010; Te Paepae Motuhake 2011: 17).

The use of translated modern technology as an avenue to promote the use of te reo would seem to cover off some fundamental areas in terms of increasing the use of the language. The technology can be continuously available, continuously shared, continuously updated, provided in a variety of settings and set in an environment that is most often used by younger generations. The use of translated technology would be somewhat ironic given that the use of modern technology has had the effect of promoting at least one of the major languages, English for example, at the expense of "local" Indigenous minority languages and "is often blamed for homogenising our ever-shrinking world, particularly when it comes to cultures and customs (Lee, 2011: 1)."

This paper shares feedback from speakers of te reo Māori who have participated in usability studies focussed on technological interfaces that have been translated into te reo Māori. Although the comments and discussion have been taken from a number of studies (five) across some very different technologies, common difficulties and common dispositions are apparent.

Usability Studies Feedback

The usability studies highlight some common themes regarding the use of te reo Māori interfaces. While each of the studies were performed on distinctly different technologies, with separate user groups, and using varying methodologies, similarities were evident in two particular aspects of the responses. Firstly, it is more difficult to use new technologies when it has been translated into te reo Māori, and secondly, the participants generally agreed that they would still prefer to use the technology, in the first instance, in their own language.

Given that the studies are separate pieces of research, the quantitative data generated from each could only be compared as trends, and the responses, while qualitative in appearance, should be regarded as anecdotal. The comments presented in this paper are representative of the general responses received from the participants in each of the particular usability studies. Paper length constraints have limited the number of comments that could be included here.

The five usability studies are presented in the following five subsections. A brief introduction of the technology and the usability study is followed by quotes from the participants regarding the difficulties they encountered and their disposition to the technology. Each section is concluded with commentary that discusses how likely the participants were to use the device in te reo Māori in the future. Where the quotes are in te reo Māori, English translations, shown in italics within square brackets, have been provided by the authors.

Study #1: Microsoft Windows & Office

Microsoft Windows XP and Microsoft Office 2003 were translated into te reo Māori in 2005. This required the translation of over 900,000 words in over 180,000 separate strings (character sequences). Subsequent versions of Windows (Vista 7 & 8) and Office (2008, 2010 & 2013) are also available in Māori.

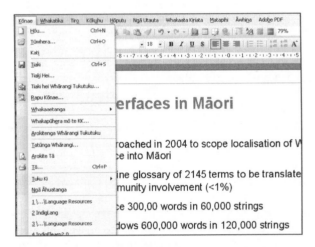

Figure 1: Microsoft Office in te reo Māori

Principals of Māori-medium schools in New Zealand were surveyed (by phone and email) to determine their use of te reo Māori on their computers and, in particular, their awareness and use of the reo Māori version of the Microsoft products (Mato *et al*, 2012). Responses were received from 47 (17%) of schools.

Difficulties Comments regarding the difficulties of using te reo Māori software in schools included:

> "Some staff struggle with the vocab and aren't confident users of IT or the Māori vocab. The kids have less problems; they are better able to adapt."

> "The new Māori words."

> "Knowledge about these resources; payment for them."

> "They [*teachers*] are used to the software already available on the computers."

> "Lack of understanding of the language that's used."

Disposition participants were asked if Māori-medium schools should use Māori-medium software:

> "Yes. Nothing is taught in English until high school years; as students are writing on computers all the time, these resources would make it easier for them."

> "Yes. In the initial and early stages, want to teach the reo in many mediums including computers; English is foreign to the younger children so it's good to have programs in Māori so they can read it; can then integrate them into English later."

> "Yes. It's our language of learning here and it would be an advantage to be able use computers in Māori."

> "Yes. It would be much easier to allow students to use the computer; they would have the words there and could go straight into their work. They don't want to break into English – important for maintaining the language; currently they say it and then point to the English word on the computer."

> "Yes. The current software is difficult for the children to navigate around as they are more familiar with te reo Māori as opposed to English."

Likely Use. The responses indicated that there was a general lack of awareness in Māori-medium schools that Microsoft software was available in te reo Māori. The anxieties faced by those schools that were aware of this interface were due primarily to the new vocabulary with some suggestion that teachers could be resistant as they had become proficient at using their computers in English and did not have the resources (time and finance) to upskill to using their computers in te reo Māori. However respondents unanimously agreed that te reo Māori software should be made available to Māori-medium schools to benefit the children.

Study #2: Two Degrees smart phone

In November 2011 a New Zealand mobile operator, Two Degrees Mobile Ltd, launched a smart phone with a te reo Māori/English interface. The device, a Huawei IDEOS X3 touch screen, provides an option that enables switching the interface language between English and te reo Māori.

Figure 2: Smart phone in te reo Māori

Usability studies were performed upon the phone between November 2013 and February 2014 (Naera, 2014). Of the twelve participants, nine were fluent/first language speakers of te reo Māori and three were classified as intermediate speakers of the language. The participants were asked to use the phone for a short period of time (2 hours – 2 days), complete some set tasks, then answer 10 questions regarding the phone's usability in te reo Māori.

Difficulties Comments from the participants regarding difficulties encountered included:

"If there were no pictures it would be hard to understand."

"There were some Māori words in there that I had not seen before…"

"Some words were too long therefore some of the words were not visible."

"Many words were new. Therefore it was difficult to use the interface because it took too much effort…"

Disposition Comments regarding participants' feelings towards using the smart phone in te reo Māori included:

"Tino harikoa te ngākau ki te kite i toku reo i runga i te waea pūkoro [*My hearts warms with joy at seeing my language on the mobile phone*]."

"Proud to be Māori. We need more of our reo out there."

"I think it's a good step for our Māori language being integrated with the technology world."

"Absolutely loved it. It's a positive avenue to the contribution of keeping te reo Māori alive."

Likely Use Although 12 out of 12 participants stated they found the English-language interface quicker and easier to use, 9 of them stated that if they had a bilingual smart phone they would select to use it in te reo Māori.

Study #3: 3M Library Kiosks

3M New Zealand have installed kiosks that enable library users to self-issue books and journals. The self-check kiosks are located throughout New Zealand in approximately 70 locations that include public libraries and educational institutes. The interfaces for these machines were updated in 2003 to include a te reo Māori option.

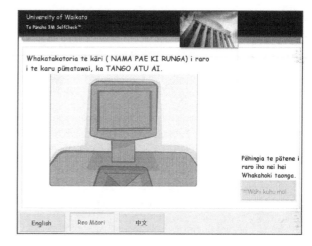

Figure 3: Library Kiosk in te reo Māori

A preliminary study on the usability of the Māori language interface of the kiosks was undertaken in 2013 (Mato, 2013). Six university students, fluent in te reo Māori, were asked to use these kiosks to self-issue some books using both the English and te reo Māori interfaces. The students then completed a short questionnaire regarding their experience and participated in an informal group discussion over a shared meal.

Difficulties Comments regarding the difficulties of using the kiosks in Māori included:

"A fluent speaker of te reo would understand the interfaces but it would be very likely that learners or those less fluent would struggle."

"Kupu hou [*new words*] made the instruction screens more difficult to follow."

"I wanted to use the Māori but I didn't understand what the machine was asking me to do."

45

"If you are going to translate it make it understandable."

Disposition The students were asked how it made them feel to see te reo Māori being used in these library kiosks:

"It was awesome to see my language used in this manner."

"This was cool! I didn't even know that there was an option to use te reo Māori."

"I'm going to use the Māori option from now on, and recommend it to other people, Māori and non-Māori."

"It made me feel proud."

Likely Use. Although 2 of 6 students were more comfortable using English, and 3 of 6 students said the English language was quicker and easier to use, all 6 students said they would prefer to use the interface in Māori. They recognised that this interface may have been slower for them and if they were in a hurry they may switch to English. However because they were Māori, studying the Māori language and quite proud to see their language in this environment, they would choose to use the te reo Māori interface first.

Study #4: Far Cry 3

Far Cry 3 is a first-person shooter game developed by Ubisoft for Microsoft Windows, Xbox 360 and Playstation 3. It was released 2012, is set in a tropical island, and features scenes where some of the local inhabitants speak in te reo Māori.

The testing group consisted of 8 secondary school Māori students, 6 male and 2 female, between the ages of 14 and 18 and fluent in te reo Māori. The game was set up in two separate rooms and played by the students with a particular focus on the scenes where te reo Māori was being spoken (Keegan & Mato, 2013). Five of the students had played the game before and 6 of the group classified themselves as 'gamers'. After almost 2 hours of group play we asked the students six questions in a discussion group environment, again, over a shared meal.

Figure 4: Māori avatar in Far Cry 3

Issues Negative comments from the participants regarding the encountering of te reo Māori in this environment included:

"The accents heard in the game were inconsistent and sometimes sounded random."

"There was a scene where they were doing a haka [*Māori war dance*] but they were using weird actions and unusual words…which is not right."

"They were just stereotyping our culture…"

Disposition Further comments regarding participants' feelings towards te reo Māori in the gaming environment:

"It was surprising to hear our language in a world-wide game."

"The chances of coming across a game that uses our language… is so slim."

"It would be better to have a game that was created by someone that had a knowledge of Māori language and an understanding of tikanga [*culture*]."

"If the game was from a Māori perspective, it would look quite different… there would not be the same [*gratuitous*] violence."

"The game has an emotional impact because it is our language."

Likely Use The students stated they would prefer to see (and play) games such as this in te reo Māori if it was spoken correctly and truly represented Māori culture. In this case they would be excited to play these games. However the students commented that because the gaming market is an international market it is unlikely this would happen.

Study #5 Google Translate

Google Translate is an on-line translation facility made available by Google. It uses statistical machine translation techniques to automatically translate between approximately 80 of the world's most spoken languages. In 2013 the facility was made available for te reo Māori translations with a te reo Māori interface.

Figure 5: Google Translate in te reo Māori

In February 2014, as part of a usability study, six Māori language experts agreed to undertake some preliminary testing of the te reo Māori translate facility (Ropitini, 2013). Four participants responded through email and two participants were interviewed in person. All questions, responses and interviews were conducted in te reo Māori.

Difficulties Comments regarding the issues of having te reo Māori on Google Translate include:

> "Āe e taea ana ngā kōrero te whakamāori, erangi te nuinga o ngā kōrero ka puta hapa mai. Kāore i te pai ki a au… [*yes, some text can be translated, however most of the text is appearing with errors. I am uncomfortable about that*]."

> "E nui ana ngā hapa kei te puta [*lots of errors are appearing*]."

> "Ko tētahi raru nui o tēnei mea kei te hapa ngā whakaputanga māori o tātau reo.[*the largest problem with this is the mistakes that are appearing in the translations of our language*]."

> "Ko te hē o te whakamāori te tino koretake o tēnei hangarau [*the mistakes in the translations is the most useless aspect of this technology*]."

Disposition The participants were asked how it made them feel to see te reo Māori being used in Google Translate:

> "Rawa atu he mīharo ki te kite atu i te reo e piki ake nei ki roto me waenganui o ngā hangarau nui a Pakeha [*very amazing to see the language ascend to be used in one of the most important technologies*]."

> "Ko te pai kei te rangonatia te rangatiratanga o to tātau reo ki tēnei taumata hangarau [*the benefit is that the status of our language is seen at this level of technology*]."

> "Kāore i kō atu i te mihi ki te au kaha mai o to tātau Reo i tōnā ekenga atu ki runga i te Kūkara nei kia tirohia mai e te ao kei te ora tō tātau reo. Ki au nei ka pai tōna ekenga ki reira, ērangi kei te āwangawanga ki te āhua o te tika o ngā whakaputanga whakamāori. [*Huge gratitude that our language is on Google because it shows to the world that our language is still alive. I think it is good that our language is there but I have concerns about the correctness of the translations*]."

> "Ko te ao e noho atu nei koe, e noho atu nei tāua he ao e kī ana i ngā momo hangarau katoa, kia kaua tātau te māori e whāiti, kia whānui te titiro me te haere. Ko te ao o aku mokopuna kei ngā hangarau katoa nei, nō reira me kimi huarahi e rata mai ngā mokopuna ki tō tāua reo maori i roto i te hanga o ngā hangarau nei. [*The world that we reside in is a world filled with lots of different technologies, our perspective and our approaches should not be narrow minded. The world of my grandchildren is a world filled with technology therefore we must find avenues that entices our grandchild to the Māori language from within technology*]."

Likely Use. While few of the participants specifically commented on whether they would use the resource in the future, there was a consensus that technology was rapidly changing and it was important that te reo Māori sought avenues to be part of those changes.

Conclusion

Two themes have clearly emerged from the participant feedback despite the comments being recorded from a diverse range of participants and the discussions covering a wide range of technologies. Firstly, it is more difficult to use modern technology in te reo Māori. Secondly, despite this difficulty, Māori still want to use modern technology, at least initially, in their own language.

The primary difficulties arose from words in the interface that were unfamiliar, often new and recently coined, and words that were used in an unfamiliar fashion. The resulting interface display and instruction was difficult to understand fully and, subsequently, more time-consuming to use. Feedback also mentioned a lack of awareness that the interfaces existed. Users of Far Cry 3 were disappointed with the inappropriateness of the language used, while users of Google Translate were concerned about the correctness of the translations that were being produced.

In spite of the difficulties, the over-arching sentiment of each group was pride. The participants were proud to see te reo Māori used in these types of environments and to know that te reo Māori was now available within these resources; it demonstrated that the language was alive and relevant in this modern world. As Māori, it was uplifting for them to see and use these new technologies in their own language1.

Despite the challenges and extra effort the translate interfaces presented, almost of all the participants stated they would prefer to use these interfaces in te reo Māori.

The feedback in these studies portrays a very real regard that Māori have in terms of their own language. The intent to persist in te reo Māori, despite the difficulties encountered, emphasises the importance of the language to Māori and perhaps reflects the value, importance and esteem that indigenous peoples in general place on their own languages. The feedback also highlights the realisation that for indigenous languages to survive in a modern technological world, they will need to embrace an active role within modern technologies.

Acknowledgements

We are grateful to Ngā Pae o te Māramatanga who have funded many of these usability studies and much of this research with grants, scholarships and internships. Also we continue to be indebted to the Computer Science Department at the University of Waikato for its ongoing support of Māori language HCI research.

References

Fishman, J.A. (1991). *Reversing Language Shift: Theoretical and Empirical Foundations of Assistance to Threatened Languages*. Clevedon, Multilingual Matters.

Fishman, J.A. (2001). *Can Threatened Languages Be Saved? Reversing Language Shift, Revisited: A 21st Century Perspective*. Multilingual Matters.

Gordon, R. (Ed.) (2005). *Ethnologue: Languages of the World* (15th ed.). Dallas, Texas, USA: SIL International.

Keegan T.T. & Mato, P., (2013). *Māori Perspectives on Using Te Reo Māori In Far Cry 3*. Unpublished report.

Lee, D. (2011). Micro-blogging in a mother tongue on Twitter. Retrieved from http://news.bbc.co.uk/2/hi/programmes/click_online/9450488.stm

Mato, P. (2013). *Library Kiosks in Te Reo Māori*. Unpublished report.

Mato, P., Keegan, TT., Cunliffe, D. & Dalley, T. (2012). Perception and use of software with a Maori-language interface in Maori-medium schools of New Zealand. In: *Language Endangerment in the 21st Century: Globalisation, Technology and New Media, proceedings of the Foundation for Endangered Languages* XVI Conference, Auckland, New Zealand, 2012: 87-92

Moseley, Christopher (2012). *The UNESCO atlas of the world's languages in danger: context and process*. World Oral Literature Project Occasional paper 5, University of Cambridge. Retrieved from www.dspace.cam.ac.uk/handle/1810/243434

Naera, L. (2014). *The Usability of a Māori Language Smart Phone*. Unpublished report.

Ropitini, W. (2014). *Ētahi Whakaaro Mō Te Google Whakamāori*. Unpublished report.

Te Paepae Motuhake. (2011). *Te Reo Mauriora: Te Arotakenga o te Rāngai Reo Māori me te Rautaki Reo Māori (Review of the Māori Language Sector and the Māori Language Strategy)*. Wellington: Te Puni Kōkiri

Statistics New Zealand (2013). *2013 Census QuickStats about Māori*. Retrieved from www.stats.govt.nz/Census/2013-census/profile-and-summary-reports/quickstats-about-maori-english/maori-language.aspx 2014/07/23

Waitangi Tribunal. (2010). *Pre-publication, WAI 262 Te Reo Māori*. Wellington: Waitangi Tribunal.

Tokunoshima Shima-guchi and Being

Satoru Nakagawa

University of Manitoba, Asian Studies & Kinesiology,
University of Winnipeg, Anthropology & Education
[Satoru.Nakagawa@umanitoba.ca]

Abstract

Undertaken on Tokunoshima, a Ryukyuan island colonized by Japan in the 17th century, my research speaks to the critical issue of Indigenous language loss. In general, people on Tokunoshima claim that the island is experiencing language and identity shift. In order to gauge the accuracy of these claims and the implications for the future of Tokunoshima islanders as a people, the research reported here used surveys (N=3509) and interviews (N=40) to assess and evaluate them. It was determined that while the language is being lost, Shiman-chu identity is not. The results are interpreted from within Western and Indigenous interpretive frames.

Introduction

The people of Tokunoshima in the south of Japan where I was born and grew up are losing their language. My generation of islanders was repeatedly told "Do not use Tokunoshima language (*Shima-guchi*) at school." We heard this so many times that we unconsciously internalized the message not to use *shima-guchi* outside school either. In many cases, including my own, this message traveled into our homes, with the result that favouring Japanese over *shima-guchi* became associated with success and cosmopolitanism. Like most of my peers, I learned not to respect my community language and scorned whatever opportunities I had to use it.

My generation seems to be the fulcrum for language shift on the island. As was the norm, I was 18 years old when I left Tokunoshima after graduation from high school. Identifying with the contempt for the island of our colonizers, I could not wait to leave. I was happy to go out to find success in the "real" world, which meant mainland Japan. My search led me to mainland Japan, Canada, and a Ph.D in language and Indigenous education. As an adult, I came to realize that we are a colonized and subjugated people.

I can say with pride that I speak *shima-guchi* when I compare myself to others in my own generation or in comparison with younger generations. However, when I compare myself to the older generations, then I am forced to realize that I speak very little. That is, my "gold standard" for judging my language knowledge shifts, depending on the comparison group I am using.

Background

In the summer of 2007 on Tokunoshima, I was conducting different research when the "gold standard" issue of language came up. Participants aged 60 and older noted that they did not consider themselves to be good *shima-guchi* speakers in comparison to their parents or grandparents. This was a revelation to me; I had considered my parent's generation, those aged 60 to 75, to be "gold standard" *shima-guchi* speakers.

Following this experience, I started to ask questions about who really speaks the gold standard of language. I kept returning to one answer; our parents, grandparents, and great grandparents all identify earlier generations as speaking the gold standard of language. Whatever generation, we made similar assumptions.

Method

Therefore, the purpose of my research became assessing the degree of language shift on Tokunoshima that is perceived to be experienced over approximately five generations, or within a given population's living memory. The guiding research question considered here is: "Is there a pattern of *shima-guchi* shift across generations, and if so, what appear to be significant factors?" I conducted surveys (N=3509), interviews (N=40), and multiple follow-ups with Tokunoshima islanders from 2008 until 2012.

I analyzed and interpreted the data from within both Western and Indigenous worldviews. Determining that multiple regression analysis would not permit islanders to engage with me in data analysis thus imposing a form of colonization on the results, I used a visual descriptive analysis using each of my variables as partitions, independently, to separate the responses. In that way, I was able to illustrate which demographic factors showed similar or different tendencies in relation to language shift.

After analyzing the survey data, I constructed interview questions designed to gain detail about the nature and extent of language loss/shift. I relied on my human network as well as contacting those who had indicated they would be willing to be interviewed on the survey. Over a four-year period, I researched, presented, consulted, and re-evaluated with islanders. Here, I am able to summarize only a small fraction of my findings.

Results

The overall survey results showed identifiable differences between several demographic partitions.

Findings

Age Regardless of their age, islanders have a strong tendency to see previous generations as having been "good" or "fluent" speakers of *shima-guchi*. They also have a tendency to see the next or later generations as not being "good" or "fluent" language speakers of either Tokunoshima language.

Sex There was almost no difference between women's and men's abilities to speak *shima-guchi* across the generations.

Generation Fluency in *shima-guchi* was related to the length of time that respondent's families had lived on the island.

Shima-guchi Self-assessment of *shima-guchi* fluency indicated that the older age groups are able to speak *shima-guchi* at the level of "fluent" or "quite well" compared to the reported abilities of the younger age groups. There were some clear defining age categorizations; 40-year-olds and older constitute a group that is "relatively fluent" to "fluent" in *shima-guchi*.

Japanese Most survey participants (over 80%) perceived themselves as fluent or good speakers of Japanese. Participants' self-assessment of their Japanese fluency was similar however there was a clear indication that advancing age (70s and older) was associated with progressively less comfort in Japanese.

Town There are three towns on Tokunoshima. Town of residence did not appear to be responsible for any differences in responses.

Occupation Public school teachers (normally from outside the island) expressed much less knowledge of *shima-guchi* than other occupations. Not surprisingly, farmers showed most *shima-guchi* fluency. Many occupations did not fit into the survey categories.

***Shiman-chu* identity** Overall, 67.8% of research participants agreed with the statement "I think I am a *shiman-chu*." Increased identification appeared strongly correlated with advanced age, length of residence, and fluency in *shima-guchi*, and, to a lesser degree, with occupation.

In both the survey and the interviews, residents of Tokunoshima reported a decline in their use of *shima-guchi* in accordance with a decline in age. However there were strong indications that *shiman-chu* identity exists independently from islanders' declared or assigned fluency in *shima-guchi*. Interview participants, many of them leaders, seniors, and experienced educators expressed the importance of passing down "*shima no kokoro*" to future generations. Translated as "heart of the community," this refers to island life as expressed in language and cultural forms, but appears not to depend on fluency in *shima-guchi*.

Discussion

Revitalization of language is the declared goal of many Indigenous peoples, including my islanders. While I was growing up on Tokunoshima people discussed how much the younger generations were losing *shima-guchi*, and how they could not speak or understand enough to

participate in the culture. For more than two decades after leaving Tokunoshima, I believed in the need for language revitalization, setting it as a personal goal in my doctoral studies. In keeping with Fishman (1991), I intended to master all variants of *shima-guchi* and then, with other speakers, teach the language.

Orthodox Approaches

Immediately apparent in my naïve vision is that there is a division between those who can and those who cannot speak or use *shima-guchi*, "authentic" and inauthentic speakers, with varying shades of gray in between (e.g., Wong, 1999). Having myself suffered from the invisible but clear distinction of "haves" versus "have nots," this division was not my intention. I realized that I had no wish to replicate the binary, and make some people feel like "lesser" islanders because they had not fluently learned to communicate in their grandparents' language. Communication itself was still taking place across generations, but people did not use *shima-guchi* for any official or community functions, so different generations developed different standards for judging fluency, referencing what they had known in their own lifetimes as the gold standard. Consequently, grandparents and great grandparents bemoaned the state of youth, but children still loved them and vice versa. It is clear that something was—and still is—shifting.

Time is an important thing to consider in arguments about the survival of languages. Often when people talk about the urgency of language revitalization, they cite the rapidly aging population of fluent language speakers in Indigenous communities. Yet, my earlier studies (Nakagawa, 2008) have strongly suggested that no gold standards of languages exist in either Indigenous or dominant languages. Even in what could be regarded as the most dominant language in the world, English, people do not fully understand written texts from only 500 years ago. For example, reading Shakespearian drama involves unfamiliar vocabulary and grammar, and questions about the meaning of his words and stories in light of the times he lived in. On the other hand, we think we can relate to some of the themes of European life that still exist today—love, loss, failure, triumph, deceit, honesty, loyalty, and courage. Looking at such texts, it seems safe to conclude that even a dominant language with a written form could not sustain itself in a standard form for only 500 years. That is, the particular forms of the language have been lost, but we retain the essential memory of the life, the identity.

Based on common practices in language revitalization and language pedagogy (e.g., Hinton, 1994), what is required to revitalize our language in the school system is easily imagined. The first step is to formalize the language in terms of grammar, pronunciation, vocabulary, and usage, meaning that islanders (or worse, outsiders will do it for us) have to choose the location on Tokunoshima that will provide the "standard" language, probably on the basis of numbers of speakers; all other variants would be deemed dialects. One difficulty with this is that it will pit islanders against islanders as each group (each individual *shima* or town) "...seeks to claim higher authority by promoting its version as superior to all competitors" (Wong, 1999, p. 96), meaning that a unique form of Indigenous hegemony could be established with standards of "right" and "wrong" ways to use *shima-guchi*.

Orthodox theories lead us to conclude that strong neighbors and groups with larger populations will have much stronger influence over subordinate societies', groups', and communities' language(s) and culture(s). Since Tokunoshima town has the strongest economic power and largest population when compared against Amagi and Isen towns, then, if these ideas are correct, residence in one town or the other provides their forms of *shima-guchi* with greater or lesser authority. Similarly, within each township, each *shima* would compete for authority and dynamics of struggle would emerge. My research so far strongly suggests that there is no rivalry or other conflict that has occurred between towns or between *shimas*, that people who are located in different towns showed consensus in their responses to the questions about being subordinated to mainland Japan.

This can be easily expanded to all of the Amami Islands. It is likely that, with a total population of only 27,000 people, Tokunoshima will need to look further afield for the dominant form of *shima-guchi*—to the island of Amami-Oshima with a population of 66,000 people, 47,000 of them concentrated in Amami City. At the present time, people in the Amami islands do not fight over language issues. Despite the economic equity issues created in the Amami Islands by the policies of mainland Japan (that is, most resources are consumed by the largest island of Amami-Oshima where the mainland government offices are located), there is little hostility. But standardizing the language form on the basis of power would ensure that the living standard of the language would be offshore and all languages on Tokunoshima considered dialects of it. This would then bring us to question why Tokunoshima islanders considered revitalization to be necessary in the first place.

The second step would be to make textbooks, train teachers, then provide students with various certificates as well as conduct a "modern" lifestyle in *shima-guchi*. The ultimate goal of such an education is to conduct every aspect of life in *shima-guchi* without losing any of the benefits of modernity. To make textbooks, it is important to write down the oral language meaning that, for our living language, time has to stop since written texts will likely capture one moment in time of our thoughts, the present. This will lead to questions such as whether it is possible to stabilize the oral language without changing the language we endeavour to save

and invalidating *shiman-chu* identity. By allowing the dominant ideology of the nation state into their communities, Indigenous peoples like my islanders will be unable to express their thoughts and ideas without the authority of written text demanded by their colonizer(s).

Once the language is written down, creating textbooks requires the mechanisms of mass production and decision about pedagogy and teaching materials. Who will take on the financial duty for the initial investment? The answer for Tokunoshima must be clear and simple. Textbook production relies on industries such as the printing and publishing industries, and standardized stocks of photos to provide visual support. Islanders will be forced to buy textbooks in order to learn their own languages, forcing us into the position of having to pay for what was stolen from us.

Adding complication to the production of textbooks is the issue of copyright of peoples' stories. Pedagogically, we know that methods stressing the teaching of language and culture together are the most effective (e.g., Emmett & Pollack, 1997). Clearly using the language of Tokunoshima to teach the (his)stories and content important to mainland Japan or any other dominator is an unworkable notion; therefore, the stories and songs of Tokunoshima need to be written down and formalized. Should story copyrights be ignored? If not, then should copyright be given to the storytellers who most often tell the stories within the community, or to some fictitious originator, or to the community itself? What about variations on the story? Is each variant recorded and copyrighted? And what of the stories that violate the norms of the dominant culture because they speak of taboo subjects such as perhaps cannibalism or a vibrant matriarchy? Are they censored or are they allowed to live?

Further to this question is who can be a teacher of Tokunoshima language? I might be a good example. In 2006, I obtained a certificate for Teaching English as second language, rendering me more qualified to teach English than are native speakers of English at large. I have spoken to many native English speakers who are not at all impressed with fact that I have more qualification to teach their language than they do. In comparison to many high school—or even university—graduates in Canada, I probably have more vocabulary, grammar, and academic language skills in English, but that does not mean I understand the ideology, worldview, or way of life in Canada more than they do.

Likewise, what is *shima-guchi* when a total outsider learns the grammar and lexicon of the language, and arrives on the island "armed" with a certificate to teach *shima-guchi* to new generations of Tokunoshima islanders? Does being *shiman-chu* then relate to language, or remain connected to genetic markers, geography, and worldview?

Non-orthodox Approaches

Engaging with the data with an Indigenous heart takes us to a different place altogether, much of which cannot be fully explained. It is undeniable that Tokunoshima islanders desire language revitalization for their endangered language—but they are also saying something more, that identity is not necessarily connected to language, and that revitalization requires energy and will, resources that are currently being poured into mere survival in the face of encroaching capitalism. As I have noted, treating revitalization as the mirror image of loss by teaching language in school and using it in the community while still remaining tied to the colonizer economically, politically, educationally, and emotionally requires our complete capitulation, colonization of our minds and spirits.

It is difficult to read outsider discourse about the ties that bind Indigenous language to Indigenous identity. Researchers who have no idea what it means to live and learn in a community make claims such as:

> … language is essential to identity, authenticity (including people's culturally grounded sense of authenticity), cultural survival, and people's learning and thinking processes because it encodes a cultural group's indigenous knowledge and, more important, its indigenous epistemology. (Gegeo & Watson-Gegeo, 1999: 26)

Such arguments serve the dominant cultures of the world, suggesting that without language, Indigenous people are without identity, inauthentic, on the brink of extinction, and without knowledge. Taking this argument to its logical conclusion, after learning our language, outsiders could claim identity and authenticity in our cultural groups. This will allow the dominant cultures to perform the final act in our colonization; they will take our identity, our Being.

Conclusion

I was taught while completing my science degrees that conclusions state only what can be proven without doubt. There is nothing in this study. However, after analyzing and discussing the data, it is possible to claim that no absolute gold standard of *shima-guchi* exists. In fact, it is reasonable to assume that there can be no gold standard in oral languages, since people use their own knowledge, information, and experiences to judge what they consider the standard to be. It appears that it is natural for people to use themselves as a reference point for judging others.

For revitalization to be successful, researchers argue, the earlier interventions are launched, the better, while the key language holders are alive. But, if we intervene with a standardized form of *shima-guchi* as early as possible in a child's life, then what is it that we're doing? Moreover, by doing so, we're asking the key language holders to speak a different dialect than the one they know, or we are privileging some language holders over other language holders. Once the language is standardized, it is no longer anyone's native language; it is everyone's foreign language.

When languages have a nation state then nation states can set their own standards through the use of policy. Unfortunately, given extant definitions and understandings of Indigenous-ness, this raises the question whether or not Indigenous people can remain Indigenous when they become the dominant culture in a modern nation state. Indigenous people have passed down their accumulated knowledge for millenia without relying on the nation state. Language learning took place within the family and community. Tease these things apart, invest certain islanders with titles and documents that declare them leaders or teachers, credential them with certificates of authenticity, and the whole reason to sustain language becomes moot.

I am not the only person who has come to this kind of realization. Littlebear (2007), in the preface to *Stabilizing Indigenous Languages*, wrote in poetry how all attempts to date have failed to slow the death of Indigenous languages (xi-xiii). It is important, therefore, to make decisions about what is really important—our Indigenous hearts and minds and souls—and how we can work toward sustaining those essentials into the future. If we do not, we will answer the question posed by Hinton and Ahlers (1999: 56) in the most negative way possible: "Can the use of the heritage language succeed in reflecting the traditional worldview in anyway, or does it become a hollow shell, inside of which nothing can be found but the dominant culture." That is, it is not the language that we need to revitalize, but the worldview, the ontology, and the ideology of island peoples. Nonetheless, it is clear that the majority of participants in the study want to retain *shima-guchi* for future generations, maintaining their ties to the past and their own unique relationship to the island land and ecology.

Acknowledgements

The author appreciates fellowship support from the Killam Foundation and the Social Sciences and Humanities Research Association of Canada.

References

Emmitt, M. & Pollock, J. (1997) *Language and learning: An introduction for teaching 2nd Ed.* Melbourne: Oxford University Press.

Fishman, J.A. (1991). *Reversing language shift.* Clevedon, U.K.: Multilingual Matters.

Gegeo, D.W., & Watson-Gegeo, K.A. (1999). Adult education, language change, and issues of identity and authenticity in Kwara'ae (Solomon Islands). *Anthropology and Education Quarterly, 30*, 22-36.

Hinton, L. (1994). *Flutes of fire: Essays on California Indian languages.* Berkeley, CA: Heyday Books.

Hinton, L. & Ahlers, J. (1999). The issue of "authenticity" in California language restoration. *Anthropology and Education Quarterly*, 30, 56-67.

Littlebear, R.E. (2007). Preface. In G. Cantoni (Ed.), *Stabilizing Indigenous languages* (rev. ed*)*. (pp. xi-xiii). Flagstaff, AZ: Northern Arizona University Press.

Nakagawa, S. (2008). *Social relationships are research ethics.* Paper presented at Canadian Society for the Study of Education, Vancouver, B.C.

Wong, L. (1999). Authenticity and the revitalization of Hawaiian. *Anthropology and Education Quarterly,* 30*,* 94-115.

Teaching Minority Indigenous Languages at Australian Universities

Jane Simpson

Linguistics, SLLL, and Centre of Excellence for the Dynamics of Language
Australian National University, ACT 0200
Australia
[jane.simpson@anu.edu.au]

Abstract

I describe the courses in Indigenous languages at university-level in Australia, dividing them into two principal types: "emblem language programs" focussing on learning a language which is being revived and re-created, and "communication language programs", directed to languages which are still spoken by children. Properties of the different types of program are outlined, considering the different audiences. While the audiences for the two program types have different needs, there is overlap, and they face similar challenges within universities. I outline some of the challenges, and describe an attempt to address them through the proposed University Languages Portal Australia (ULPA), to be run through the Languages and Cultures Network of Australian Universities (LCNAU). This aims to make courses in these languages more visible and thus more accessible to students across Australia.

Introduction

Languages are both emblems and means of communication. By "emblem" I mean that language can be a sign of belonging to a particular community. Linked to the uses of language as emblem is the view in many Australian Indigenous communities that a language is property inherited from parents and grandparents, and that languages are associated with land. Thus a language may be an emblem for a group because it is a shared means of communication, but it may also be an emblem because in the past it was a shared means of communication for the ancestors from whom the present-day group inherited their land.

As communities of speakers move from speaking Indigenous languages to speaking the language of government, Indigenous languages may lose their function as means of communication, but remain as emblems of identity. People stop using them for everyday conversation, but may retain emblematic uses such as singing songs in the Indigenous languages or using names from the Indigenous language for anything from people to places to institutions to wines to varieties of wheat.

Emblem languages and languages that are means of communication both deserve better representation at universities. In 1995 Bill Edwards, a long-term teacher of the Western Desert language Pitjantjatjara at university-level, wrote that Australian universities had "largely failed in their recognition and promotion of Aboriginal languages" (Edwards, 1995: 11). The situation has only minimally improved since then.

Representation of languages at universities includes not only teaching (to be discussed below) but also research. The teaching of languages at university-level is underpinned by research into the languages, and the history, society, and cultural and aesthetic traditions of the associated speech communities. This is the difference that university language teachers point to between themselves and their colleagues at intensive language schools. Research has a special place in teaching emblem languages, because, as Giacon observes, rebuilding a language requires considerable research into, and anlaysis of the sources (Giacon and Simpson, 2012). Practically, most speech communities are not in positions to undertake that research, and so often find it helpful to partner with researchers.

There are essential differences between teaching emblem languages at university and teaching communication languages, although there is some overlap between the ways of teaching them, the participants (teachers and learners), and the reasons for teaching them. Communication language courses include L1 courses aimed at first language speakers of an Indigenous language, and L2 courses aimed at Indigenous and non-Indigenous people wanting to learn an Indigenous language to communicate with speakers (Giacon and Simpson, 2012), as well as L2 courses for people, such as linguists, who want to learn about a language. Emblem language courses can be characterised as L2 revival courses aimed at Indigenous and non-Indigenous people wanting to learn an Indigenous language that is being revived or restored. I discuss each in turn.

Teaching languages for communication at universities

Indigenous languages as means of communication have several potential audiences at universities: non-speakers who want to learn to communicate with Indigenous people, Indigenous language speakers who would like to explore their own language more deeply (or learn a related language), non-speakers who are interested in Indigenous languages as objects of study, whether for better understanding of language, of Indigenous societies or Indigenous aesthetic practices.

Non-speakers who want to learn to communicate with Indigenous people

Awareness of the existence of Indigenous languages is essential for professionals such as teachers, legal and health professionals, and community workers working in communities where Indigenous languages are the everyday means of communication. Without an understanding of translateability and the complex linking of language, beliefs, knowledge and assumptions by speakers of other languages, these professionals cannot successfully help the Indigenous language speakers grapple with State education, health, legal and other institutional bodies. A simple example comes from Devitt and McMasters (1998) who describe the experience of Aboriginal renal dialysis patients in the Northern Territory.   Here is a story from the daughters of a dialysis patient.

> Cause sometimes if a doctor talks to her.. sometimes she doesn't understand a word what they are saying, and it is best for someone to stand beside her just to explain what it means. And you know it is hard for her.. Sometimes – you know what Europeans are like – they like to speak hard English.. [but] most of us now, we just know.. easy English – that [like] we speak now.. it's real hard sometimes for White people to understand [that]. (Devitt and McMasters, 1998: 148)

And here is a view from a renal specialist:

> Interviewer: Do [patients] routinely ask you questions?
>
> Specialist: Never. Never – very few. I mean a couple.. will probably ask a few questions, [generally] people who are a little more educated and urbanised. But the majority ..don't talk to me ... even sometimes when I want to make sure that the person understands, it is very difficult to get a positive feeling from my side, that this person does understand., and wants to do this, or doesn't want to. (Devitt and McMasters, 1998: 150)

Devitt and McMasters sum up the interactions as follows:

> It is true to say that in the examples given above both patients and carers understood "only half" of what was being communicated, rather than simply that patients were unable to understand carers' English. The carers' point of view and priorities in relation to health and well-being, among other things, were as opaque to the majority of the renal patients as the renal patients' perspectives were to their carers. (Devitt and McMasters, 1998: 151)

Similar gaps in understanding are found in interactions between Indigenous people and other professionals. Lawyers wrestle with explaining ideas such as "suspended sentence":

> Further, the concept of a "suspended" sentence remains a mystery to many. They serve a period in jail, are released and go home. Unfortunately, many are unaware that they are now subject to a Good Behaviour Bond. Even if they have this level of

understanding, they are often totally unaware it is requiring them to be of good behaviour for a particular period and, should this be breached, they must return to court and most likely serve the remainder of their suspended sentence in addition to receiving further punishment for the new offence. (Ford and McCormack, 2011 [2007]: x-xi)

Training in Indigenous languages, let alone tertiary-level training, is rarely available to professionals. As a result, they struggle with communicating vital information such as management of renal disease or bail conditions.   It also means that they may often have limited understanding of the people with whom they interact, e.g. speech pathologists who are not trained to detect the difference between children who happen not to speak English and children with a physiologically based language or cognitive delay. Devitt and McMasters suggest that this can result in Indigenous languages being seen negatively:

> Although we lack "hard evidence" on this point, there was also a recognisable attitude or ethos among service providers, albeit subtle and covert, that Aboriginal patients were somehow culpable in their linguistic difference; that Aboriginal language itself was perceived as yet another negative feature of that particular group of people. (Devitt and McMasters, 1998: 148)

The need for non-Aboriginal people to learn Australian Indigenous languages to communicate with their speakers was recognised in some missions in the 1930s, most notably by Presbyterian missions in the north of South Australia on the lands of people speaking the closely related Western Desert languages Pitjantjatjara and Yankunytjatjara. This led to the first tertiary-level course in an Australian Aboriginal language in 1966 when Pitjantjatjara began to be taught at the University of Adelaide (with materials prepared by a missionary linguist, Wilfred Douglas, and a pioneer of language laboratory teaching, Henk Siliakus) (Amery, 2007; Simpson *et al.*, 2008). The course has benefited from the availability of native speakers of Western Desert languages living in Adelaide, in particular Ngitji Ngitji Mona Tur, probably the first Indigenous tertiary-level language teacher in Australia.   At the height of interest, students could progress through up to six term-length courses, but in recent years this has been reduced to one level, taught as an intensive summer school run through the University of South Australia.

Perhaps the most successful L2 course has been the Yolŋu Studies program at the Charles Darwin University in Darwin.   Yolŋu Matha is the name for a group of related dialects and languages spoken to the east of Darwin in Arnhem Land. The program has done well, if success is measured through the number of student enrolments, the continued deep involvement of Yolŋu teachers, the possibility of taking up to six courses on Yolŋu language and culture, and continuation of this program over a number of years despite financial hard times in universities. Some factors in its success have been its innovativeness. Charles Darwin University is a relatively small university and so they arranged to offer the courses online, and to make it available through Open Universities Australia, thus increasing access to the course. An excellent publicly available webpage with links to resources has helped ensure knowledge of the course: http://learnline.cdu.edu.au/yolngustudies/

Another major innovation was "Teaching from country". This was an attempt to address two issues: the importance for Yolŋu of living in their country and teaching about that country as part of teaching the languages, and the need for access to natural interaction in the language as part of online learning of a language in order to communicate (Christie & Verran, 2010). Yolŋu teachers are able to address classes via Skype from their homelands as part of the course. Undoubtedly this has helped continue the deep interest of Yolŋu teachers in continuing in the program, although there are still logistic challenges.

Speakers who would like to explore their own language more deeply or learn a related language

Australian universities cater well for English speakers, who can explore aesthetic and cultural traditions using English language through courses on English literature, drama, film, and cultural studies. Their understanding of their own language, history and society is enhanced by studying them at university and sharing ideas with other colleagues.

Universities sometimes also cater for native speakers of immigrant languages through advanced courses in the language on history, music, art etc. (e.g. courses for background speakers of Korean, courses in Classical Chinese which native speakers may take, etc.). Whether they do this depends on factors such as the size of the immigrant community and the perceived prestige of the language (for example, despite the small size of the immigrant French community, French native speakers are well catered for at a number of universities).

However there is little provision for native speakers of Indigenous languages to explore their own language more deeply at university. Again, the Yolŋu Studies program at the Charles Darwin University in Darwin has provided this to some extent through guided research programs.

The general lack of such programs means that speech communities miss out on the enrichment that can be derived from systematic exploration of language and aesthetic traditions at university-level in collaboration with other scholars. While people can enrich their languages in their own communities, the lack of university-level recognition has long-term consequences for the languages both in terms of the perceived standing of the language, and in the available registers of the language.

Teaching Indigenous languages at university may also result in the longer term in developing a register of academic talk in those languages, which in turn increases the domains in which the languages can be comfortably used, and may also increase the prestige of the languages.

If Indigenous languages are taught at university, it can act as a sign that these languages are as rich and effective means of communication as any other language taught at university. This helps counter the misinformation and many negative stereotypes of Indigenous Australian languages that abound even in a well-off well-educated country such as Australia which has moved towards reconciliation with its Indigenous peoples.

Non-speakers who are interested in Indigenous languages as objects of study

Linguists, anthropologists, historians and so on may wish to study Indigenous languages, not for communication purposes, but rather for better understanding of language, of Indigenous societies or Indigenous aesthetic practices. These people are perhaps better catered for than the other two categories of student, first because there is an increasing body of material (learners' guides, dictionaries, reference grammars, YouTube videos) which allow people who are familiar with language learning to make considerable headway on their own, and second because many linguistics programs teach introductions to Indigenous languages generally.

Teaching emblem languages at universities

There has been increasing interest by Indigenous people in reviving heritage languages in Australia (Amery, 2000). Several revived Indigenous languages have been taught at university: Kaurna from 1997 (University of Adelaide), Gamilaraay (University of Sydney and Australian National University), Wiradjuri (Charles Sturt University). Amery and Buckskin (2013) give a vivid history of the elatons between a community wanting to revive a language and a university which eventually resulted in a memorandum of understanding between the two, a first for Australia.

An important audience for these courses are Indigenous people who want to teach their revived language to children at pre-schools and schools (Gale, 2011; Hobson, 2013; Poetsch, 2013), as well as non-Indigenous people wanting to learn more about Indigenous languages and societies. By taking part in the courses, people are creating the beginnings of communities reviving the languages, and their ideas, and materials they make in the courses, may well help shape the future of those languages. However, since in Australia there are many languages, it is hard to find enough students to make the courses viable at universities (Amery, 2007; Giacon and Simpson, 2012), even when they are offered online. Moreover, unless Indigenous students need to have certification that they have passed the course (say for teaching accreditation purposes), the cost of a university course may make private study groups a more useful and attractive option.

Visibility of Indigenous Australian languages at universities

It is a national embarrassment that it is so difficult for Australian students to study any Australian Indigenous language at tertiary level. As of 2014, only six Australian Indigenous languages are taught in any form at universities across Australia (three emblem languages, Kaurna, Gamilaraay and Wiradjuri, and three languages still spoken as a first language by children, Yolŋu Matha, Pitjantjatjara and Arrernte). Of these only Yolŋu Matha is taught as a major. While it is understandable that we do not yet have advanced courses in Indigenous languages comparable to the advanced university-level courses in French or Chinese that native speakers of French or Chinese can profit from, we should lay the groundwork for these to develop.

A first step is having courses available online which are as well organised and content-rich as online courses in other languages, and in which native speakers or language owners are heavily involved. The online Yolŋu Matha course at Charles Darwin University provides a model which may be attractive to other Indigenous communities - combining teaching using standard grammatical activities with interaction and teaching about Yolŋu society through on-country teaching.

The second step to getting this to work is for potential students to know that the courses exist and that they can be included in their degrees. A general problem with this has been the overall reduction in languages offerings at universities and the obstacles to collaboration across institutions (Dunne and Pavlyshyn, 2012; Hajek *et al.*, 2013; Lo Bianco and Gvozdenko, 2006).

In collaboration with the Languages and Cultures Network for Australian Universities (LCNAU http://www.lcnau.org/), our proposal (accepted by the Australian Office for Learning and Teaching) is to create "University Languages Portal Australia" (ULPA) to allow students and others to readily find information on:

1. which languages, including Indigenous Australian languages, are offered at which levels at which universities, and which are offered online

2. how to enrol cross-institutionally in these units of study from any university in Australia.

We want to make courses in Indigenous Australian languages a priority for sharing across universities, and so part of this work would be to help forge agreements across universities to simplify the process of cross-institutional enrolment in language units of study.

While there have been a number of attempts at sharing language units across institutions (Lo Bianco & Gvozdenko, 2006), including of Indigenous languages (Amery, 2007) several factors make it difficult (Hajek *et al.*, 2008; Winter, 2009), one of them being that competition by universities for students inhibits cross-institution sharing. Second, while online language learning is growing in popularity and attractiveness (e.g. Duolingo) there is little availability of attractive grammar testing and language strengthening activities in Indigenous languages. (However, a starting-place is the greater availability of texts through projects such as the Living Archive of Aboriginal Languages (http://laal.cdu.edu.au/)). To make the online courses attractive there needs to be more interaction (as in the Yolŋu Matha Skype sessions). Third, sharing Indigenous language units are subject to the constraints for collaboration on sharing units of study identified by Hajek et al (2008) and more globally in Winter (2009), namely (i) managing intellectual property rights on curriculum and teaching materials, (ii) the complexity of cross-institutional enrolment processes, which includes information on dates, enrolment processes, credit transfers, and fees.

These challenges will not go away, but a first step is the establishment of the University Languages Portal Australia, to allow people to find out information on what languages are taught where. Indigenous Australian languages will be taken as a test case for online delivery and cross-institutional enrolment.

Acknowledgements

I acknowledge the Office for Learning and Teaching grant "A national language studies portal for Australian universities", ID13-2845, and my collaborators on this grant, John Hajek, Anya Lloyd-Smith, Martina Möllering and Catherine Travis. I thank Rob Amery, Michael Christie, John Giacon, John Greatorex and David Nash for helpful discussion of these issues.

References

Amery, R. (2000). Warrabarna Kaurna!: Reclaiming an Australian language. *Multilingualism and Linguistic Diversity*. Lisse, The Netherlands: Swets & Zeitlinger.

Amery, R. (2007). Aboriginal language habitat in research and tertiary education. In G. Leitner & I.G. Malcolm (Eds.), *The Habitat of Australia's Aboriginal Languages: Past, Present and Future* (Pp. 327-53). Berlin: Mouton de Gruyter.

Amery, R. & Buckskin, V.K. (2013). Having it both ways: towards recognition of the Kaurna language movement within the community and within the university sector. In M.J. Norris *et al.* (Eds.), *Endangered Languages beyond Boundaries: Community Connections, Collaborative Approaches and Cross-disciplinary Research//Langues en péril au-delà des frontières:Connexions communautaires, approches collaboratives, et recherche interdisciplinaire. Proceedings of the 17th FEL Conference* (Ottawa: Foundation for Endangered Languages in association with Carleton University, Canada).

Christie, M. & Verran, H. (Eds.) (2010). Teaching from Country. *Learning Communities: International Journal of Learning in Social Contexts.* Darwin: Charles Darwin University.

Devitt, J. & McMasters, A. (1998). *Living on Medicine – A Cultural Study of End-stage Renal Disease among Aboriginal people.* Alice Springs: IAD Press.

Dunne, K. & Pavlyshyn, M. (2012). Swings and roundabouts: Changes in language offerings at Australian Universities 2005-2011. In J. Hajek, C. Nettelbeck & A. Woods (Eds.) *The Next Step: Introducing the Languages and Cultures Network for Australian Universities, Selected proceedings of the Inaugural LCNAU Colloquium, Melbourne, 26-28 September 2011* (Pp. 9-19). Melbourne: LCNAU.

Edwards, W.H. (1995). Teaching an Aboriginal language at university level. *Babel* 30(2), 4-11.

Ford, L. & McCormack, D. (2011[2007]). *Murrinh tetemanthay ngarra murrinh law kardu bamam thangunu: Difficult words that come from non-Aboriginal law Murrinhpatha — English Legal Glossary* [online text], Batchelor Press [Batchelor Institute of Indigenous Tertiary Education]. http://www.bowden-mccormack.com.au/WebsiteCont ent/articles-papers/murrinhpatha-legal-glossary.pdf (accessed 26 July 2014).

Gale, M.A. (2011). Rekindling warm embers: Teaching Aboriginal languages in the tertiary sector. *Australian Review of Applied Linguistics* 34. http://www.nla.gov.au/openpublish/index.php/aral/art icle/view/2278 (accessed 9 February 2012).

Giacon, J. & Simpson, J. (2012). Teaching Indigenous languages at universities. In J. Hajek, C. Nettelbeck & A. Woods (Eds.), *The Next Step: Introducing the Languages and Cultures Network for Australian Universities. Selected Proceedings of the Inaugural LCNAU Colloquium, Melburne 26-28 September 2011* (Pp. 61-73). Melbourne: LCNAU.

Hajek, J., Slaughter, Y. & Stevens, M. (2008). *Innovative approaches in the provision of languages other than English in Australian Higher Education. Evaluation of Model 2: Collaborative City-Based Model.* Melbourne: Deans of Arts, Social Sciences & Humanities.

Hajek, J., Nettelbeck, C. & Woods, A. (2013). *Leadership for Future Generations: A National Network for University Languages: Final Report.* Melbourne.

Hobson, J. (2013). Potholes in the road to an initial teacher training degree for Australian revival languages. Paper presented at the Languages and Cultures Network of Australian Universities (LCNAU) Biennial Conference 2013 (Canberra).

Lo Bianco, J. & Gvozdenko, I. (2006). *Collaboration and Innovation in the Provision of Languages Other Than English in Australian Universities.* Melbourne: Faculty of Education, University of Melbourne.

Poetsch, S. (2013). Why Aboriginal languages teaching sometimes works: a view from NSW. Paper presented at the Languages and Cultures Network of Australian Universities (LCNAU) Biennial Conference 2013 (Canberra).

Simpson, J., Amery, R. & Gale, M.A. (2008). I could have saved you linguists a lot of time and trouble: 178 years of research and documentation of South Australia's Indigenous Languages, 1826 – 2004. In W.B. McGregor (Ed.), *Encountering Aboriginal Languages: Studies in the History of Australian Linguistics* (Pp. 85-144). Canberra: Pacific Linguistics.

Winter, J. (2009). *Collaborative Models for the Provision of Languages in Australian Universities: Final report.* Perth: [Australian] Deans of Arts, Social Sciences and Humanities). http://dassh.edu.au/resources/uploads/publications/pr oject_reports/2009_CASR_Collaborative_Models.pdf (accessed 26 July 2014).

Language Revitalization across the South Pacific

Bruna Franchetto
PPGAS - UFRJ
Quinta da Boa Vista s/n - São Cristóvão
CEP 20940-040 - Rio de Janeiro/RJ Brazil
[bfranchetto@yahoo.com.br]

Rafael Nonato
PPGAS - UFRJ
Quinta da Boa Vista s/n - São Cristóvão
CEP 20940-040 - Rio de Janeiro/RJ Brazil
[rafaeln@gmail.com]

Livia Camargo Souza
Rutgers University
18 Seminary Place
New Brunswick, NJ
08901-1184 USA
[livia.camargo.rj@gmail.com]

Abstract

In this paper we present a project for fostering language maintenance and revitalization in Brazil. This project is inscribed in a collaboration recently started between Brazil and Australia in the area of language maintenance and revitalization. Similar histories of colonization in these two countries have led to comparable situations of language loss. Based on a three-month immersion experience in Australia, the authors of this paper argue that a Brazilian language maintenance and revitalization project should adopt a broad approach, in which linguists, traditional speakers of minority languages, federal government and civil society interact in order to propitiate an environment in which these languages can flourish back. In this paper we introduce the situation of two endangered and one extinct Brazilian languages and explain how we intend to deal with each of them in a pilot revitalization project. The languages are (i) Umutina, (ii) Yawanawa and (iii) Guató, and the techniques we intend to use in each case are, respectively, (i) language reconstruction based on historical registers and comparison with related languages, (ii) language nest and research of child-directed genres and (iii) emergency documentation.

Australia and Brazil have been shaped by similar colonial histories: by means of superior man-slaughtering technology and infectious diseases, European invaders exterminated most of the indigenous populations and, partially assimilating the survivors, created two of the largest "civilized nations" on the planet. In both countries, it happened as well that a fraction of the indigenous peoples managed to retain their identity up till current times, though suffering to varying degrees from cultural disruption and linguistic loss.

After a three-month field trip to Australia, which was the first phase of a program of cooperation in language maintenance and revitalization between Brazil and Australia, three Brazilian linguists specialized in Amerindian languages are reporting on a recently proposed project submitted to CNPq (*Conselho Nacional de Pesquisa*, the Brazilian National Research Council) for the revitalization of three Brazilian languages. The project aims at the integration of a number of spheres that are essential for the development of language programs and linguistic policies across the country. In this paper, we will make a qualitative comparison of language loss, language documentation, and language maintenance and revitalization efforts in Brazil and Australia, emphasizing how the Australian experience has helped elucidate not only methods and techniques in language revitalization, but also the essential and interdependet role of researchers, communities, government, and the general population for the fostering of language programs and linguistic policies.

By means of a cooperation effort between the Australian Institute of Aboriginal and Torres Strait Islanders Studies (AIATSIS) and the Brazilian National Indigenous Foundation (FUNAI), funded by the Australian Agency for International Development (AusAID), we were immersed in the Australian context of language programs and linguistic policies. For 3 months, we were hosted by AIATSIS and took fieldtrips across the country in which we became acquainted with different programs aimed at the maintenance and revitalization of native languages in varying degrees of vitality. The picture is vast: school-based programs interact with local communities to teach extinct – or "sleeping" – Wiradjuri and Woi Wurrung as second languages in New South Wales and Victoria; language centers in South and West Australia employ a number of techniques to work with communities and foster the use and revival of endangered Miriwoong, and Western Desert varieties, as well as resuscitating Kaurna and Barngarla; speakers and researchers of vital languages such as Warlpiri in the Northern territory and Kala Lagaw Ya in the Torres Strait Islands struggle against government impositions in order to strengthen their languages and ensure transmission. Not only did we become acquainted with the work that is being carried out in language centers, but also we interacted with academic researchers in the Australian Language Workshop and in seminars at The Australian National University, as well as with the government representatives responsible for the distribution of the national budget for language programs.

Thus, our experience in Australia has elucidated the fact that language maintenance and revitalization efforts necessarily involve and integrate several spheres of society. Linguists and other academic researchers are certainly a central piece in the puzzle. The involvement of researchers with local communities has been responsible, for instance, for the successful development of bilingual programs in schools across the Northern Territory and the publication of thousands of pedagogical books in Aboriginal languages, not to mention the reconstruction of extinct languages from archival sources and the ongoing work of language description and revitalization in language centers and universities across the country. Besides researchers, however, the effort of language communities is crucial for the maintenance of endangered languages. Speakers of Kala Lagaw Ya and Merriam Mer in the Torres Strait Islands, for instance, are currently struggling with limited government resources to develop two school-based bilingual programs and build a local language center. In addition, it is essential that these efforts of researchers and communities are also aimed at the general population. School-based programs have a crucial role in language maintenance and revitalization because of their capacity to reach beyond indigenous communities. Besides fostering tolerance and wellbeing in the school community, one of the main consequences of educating the general public on indigenous matters is influencing government policy. The government has a central role in language revitalization efforts for it is responsible for the development of national linguistic policies. For instance, in 2014 the Australian Ministry of the Arts allocated a budget of 10 million dollars for the development of language programs, but at the same time, a state law in the Northern Territory imposed that teaching must be solely in English in the first 4 hours of the school day, impairing the development of bilingual school programs.

While discussion and work on language maintenance and revitalization are quite advanced in Australia, with considerable governmental support and numerous language centers and school-based programs across the country, on the other side of the Southern Pacific, most of the efforts aimed at Brazilian indigenous languages have been limited to language documentation, with very little in the way of language maintenance and revitalization. There are at least two notable exceptions, both due exclusively to tribal efforts, without any support either from the government or from external organizations: (i) the Pataxó people of the Brazilian Northeast claim that they have reestablished their long lost language, which they now call Patxohã and (ii) in the Brazilian Amazon, the Yawanawa people have been living a linguistic renaissance triggered by the growth of shamanistic practices, cultural festivals, music and tourism, with the consequent rise of traditional linguistic genres.

The fact that language maintenance and revitalization programs are more advanced in Australia cannot be attributed only to their level of scientific development in this area (which is, nonetheless, notable, as can be deprehended from works such as Hobson *et al.* 2010). Indeed, the need for language revitalization in Australia is clearly urgent, due to the ever shrinking number of vital languages spoken in the country (see Marmion, Obata & Troy, 2014). In Brazil, on the other hand, there seems to be a notion that the large number of languages currently spoken (150, according to Moore, Galucio, and Gabas Jr. 2008) guarantees their vitality. Not much attention is drawn to the fact that 21% of these languages (also according to Moore, Galucio & Gabas Jr., 2008) are in risk of disappearing in the short term due to their reduced number of speakers and/or low rate of language transmission to the younger generations.

In spite of the endangered status of so many native languages, a major challenge we face as researchers in Brazil is the lack of government support for language maintenance and revitalization efforts. The absence of a comprehensive picture of the overall situation of languages across the country halts the development of linguistic policies. All that is known about language vitality comes either from academic research or from data collected in language documentation projects. Even though the Brazilian Constitution guarantees the right of indigenous peoples to speak their languages and have access to bilingual, differentiated education, very little practical efforts have been directed towards this goal by the government. Despite the emphasis attributed by FUNAI to land rights and indigenous cultures – especially concerning their ritualistic and material forms – indigenous languages are mostly invisible not only to the Brazilian government but also to the general population. As we discussed previously, these two spheres of society play essential roles in the fostering of language diversity and the development of national linguistic policies, thus our intention to contemplate them in the project in question.

As previously mentioned, most of the work directed at Indigenous languages in Brazil has concerned documentation. There are two main institutions in Brazil that have been supporting language documentation: Museu Paraense Emílio Goeldi (MPEG) and Museu do Índio, a branch of FUNAI in Rio de Janeiro. MPEG has teamed with Brazilian and international researchers in the description and documentation of circa 20 Brazilian languages, whereas Museu do Índio's Program for the Documentation of Indigenous Languages (ProDoclin) has been supporting collaborative documentation, the training of indigenous researchers, and the development of pedagogical material for 13 endangered Brazilian languages. Besides these two centers, much work has been conducted by scholars and funded by universities and international documentation programs such as ELDP at SOAS, University of London, and DoBeS, funded by the Volkswagen Foundation.

Apart from these projects aimed at documenting, archiving, and producing materials for a limited number of languages that are still spoken, no efforts have been made towards developing language maintenance and revitalization methodology, or language reconstruction from archival sources. Also, the discussion of national language policies is still at a very early stage in Brazil. The first major action taken towards this effort was the establishment of the National Inventory of Language Diversity (INDL) in 2010. By means of a major national census, the inventory intends to identify, document, and officially recognize the languages of the groups that compose the country's population, taking actions towards maintaining and valuing these languages. The first pilot projects are currently under development and our submitted project intends to collaborate directly with the inventory and the development of language policies.

Given the embryonic stage of development of government-supported programs, we have submitted a research project to CNPq (*Conselho Nacional de Pesquisa*), the Brazilian National Research Council. As mentioned previously, the project focuses on integrating the numerous spheres of society involved in the fostering of linguistic diversity: researchers, indigenous communities, the government, and the general population. Initially, the project will cooperate with the institutions involved in language documentation in Brazil, especially Museu do Índio, since its three proposers have been part of ProDocLin (Franchetto coordinates the program, Nonato and Souza are project leaders). We will be giving continuity to the model adopted by ProDocLin of developing collaborative research with community involvement and the training and active participation of indigenous researchers in the documentation of their language. In addition to integrating researchers and indigenous communities, our project involves the production of a book aimed at the general population about the indigenous languages of Brazil. Taking into consideration that a recent law makes mandatory the teaching of African and Indigenous cultures in Brazilian schools, this book may also be adopted as pedagogical material across the country. Thus, based on our experience in Australia, our proposal consists of a language revitalization project of three Brazilian languages that collaborates with the governmental sphere through the national inventory of linguistic diversity and attempts to involve scholars, indigenous communities, and the general population. Despite the broad spectrum of the project, our main focus in the following paragraphs will be to describe the situation of each of the languages chosen as objects of revitalization and the methodology to be studied and developed for each of them.

The first language to be contemplated in the revitalization project is Umutina, of the Bororo family, Macro-Jê stock, which has been extinct for decades. Resources on this language are scarce (ISA; Telles, 1995), but the community's desire to revive their language as well as the existence of closely related languages that are still spoken and are well documented make the reconstruction of Umutina a possible endeavor. The focus of the work with the Umutina community will be in recreating their language based on archival sources, following the format of numerous Australian language reconstruction efforts. The gaps in historical registers will be complemented by means of comparison with closely related languages such as Bororo (Nonato, 2007). This method contemplates mainly the reconstruction of the lexicon, but can also be applied for the reconstruction of the grammar, depending on the interests of the language's traditional owners. Grammatical grafts from Brazilian Portuguese are also a possibility, since this is the language spoken by the Umutina people today.

If compared to Umutina, Yawanawa (Panoan), the second language to be contemplated in the project, is in a very different situation, which reflects the reality of numerous Amazonian communities. The language is spoken by approximately 160 people out of a population of over 600, and transmission has suffered a generational rupture. Most fluent speakers are over 45 years old and with rare exceptions, children are no longer acquiring the language, making Yawanawa a highly endangered language (Souza, 2013). Souza has been working on the documentation of Yawanawa for the past 4 years and will give emphasis to language-nest methods in the revitalization of the language. Such methods have been employed, among others, in the revitalization of Austronesian languages Maori and Hawaiian (Hinton and Hale, 2001), as well as in the revitalization of Miriwoong, an Australian language from the Kimberly region. The work with Yawanawa will involve a documentary research of genres directed at children (songs, stories, games, lullabies, etc.) and the creation of a daycare in which women who are native speakers of Yawanawa work with young infants, thus restablishing language transmission and traditional story-telling customs.

Finally, the Guató language exemplifies yet another point on the scale of linguistic vitality. Nowadays it only counts with a handful of elderly speakers. Indeed, it is believed that only 5 people still speak the language, but data on the language and its last speakers are scarce and out of date (ISA). The Guató people were pushed out of their traditional territory in the 1940s and 1950s and afflicted by a series of epidemics, having been officially considered extinct until the 1970's. Today, there are three Guató nuclei in the states of Mato Grosso and Mato Grosso do Sul, as well as several individuals living in the outskirts of cities in the two states. It is estimated that the current Guató population sums circa 374 people (ISA). The focus of the work with Guató will be emergency documentation of the remaining speakers in order to complement the scarce description of the language available in the linguistic literature (Rodrigues, 1986; Palácio, 1984).

We returned to Brazil with the conviction that it would be an unfortunate strategy to wait until the situation of our languages is as fragile as that of Australia's before we start thinking about developing language maintenance and revitalization efforts. Programs aimed at the rescue of Brazilian languages are urgent and this is the gap that we intend to fill with the revitalization project and the continued cooperation with our Australian partners from AIATSIS.

References

Hinton, L. & Hale, K. (2001). *The Green Book of Language Revitalization in Practice*. Academic Press.

Hobson, J., Lowe, K., Poetsch, S. & Walsh, M. (Eds.) (2010). *Re-Awakening Languages: Theory and Practice in the Revitalisation of Australia's Indigenous Languages*. Sydney University Press.

ISA, Instituto Sócio-Ambiental. "Umutina [Homepage Na Internet]." *Brasil*. http://pib.socioambiental.org/pt/povo/umutina/2020.

————. "Guató [Homepage Na Internet]." *Brasil*. http://pib.socioambiental.org/pt/povo/guato/1972.

Marmion, D., Obata, K. & and Troy, J. (2014). *Community, Identity, Wellbeing: the Report of the Second National Indigenous Languages Survey*. Canberra: AIATSIS.

Moore, D., Galucio, A.V. & and Gabas Jr., N. (2008). "O Desafio de Documentar E Preservar as Línguas Amazônicas." *Scientific American (Brasil)* (3): 36–43.

Nonato, R. (2007). Ainore Boe Egore: Um Estudo Descritivo Da Língua Bororo E Conseqüências Para a Teoria de Caso E Concordância. Master's thesis, Unicamp, SP, Brazil. http://ling.auf.net/lingbuzz/001909.

Palácio, A.P. (1984). "Guató: a Língua Dos Índios Canoeiros Do Rio Paraguai." PhD thesis, Universidade Estadual de Campinas.

Rodrigues, A.D. (1986). *Línguas Brasileiras: Para O Conhecimento Das Línguas Indígenas*. São Paulo: Loyola.

Souza, L.C. (2013). Fonologia, Morfologia E Sintaxe Das Expressões Nominais Em Yawanawá (Pano). Master's thesis, UFRJ.

Telles, S. (1995). A Língua Umutina: Um Sopro de Vida. PhD thesis, UFPE.

Language Revitalization on Sakhalin and Hokkaido
as Seen by (Native) Speakers, Administrators and Researchers

Ekaterina Gruzdeva
University of Helsinki
[ekaterina.gruzdeva@helsinki.fi]

Riikka Länsisalmi
University of Helsinki
[riikka.lansisalmi@helsinki.fi]

Abstract

At present, the indigenous population of Sakhalin Island (Russia) is represented by the Nivkh, Uilta, Evenki and Nanai, whereas on neighboring Hokkaido Island (Japan) the Ainu are considered to be the only native people. Despite different historical contexts, the sociolinguistic situation on both islands nowadays is similar: all insular indigenous languages are either severely or critically endangered. We start with comparing the degrees of Nivkh and Ainu endangerment, making use of UNESCO's Major Evaluative Factors for Language Vitality. Next, we examine the (native) speakers' attitudes towards the maintenance/revitalization of autochthonous languages and consider the role of these languages in the preservation and reshaping of cultural knowledge and ethnic identities. Then we outline revitalization measures carried out by Russian and Japanese administrations and discuss their effect on the survival of Nivkh and Ainu. Finally, we consider the future of these languages from a viewpoint of researchers. Within a recently arisen theoretical framework of "superdiversity" we suggest addressing language revitalization as a continuum, ranging from small steps, aimed at maintenance of at least some functional links between languages and linguistic repertoires of choice and their respective environments, towards a complete preservation/restoration of language ecology in its full social, cultural and ecological context.

Sociolinguistic situation on Sakhalin and Hokkaido: Nivkh and Ainu

Nivkh (Giljak) and Ainu are both language-isolates that are generally classified as Paleosiberian. The UNESCO Atlas of World's Languages in Danger lists Sakhalin Nivkh as a severely endangered language, whereas Hokkaido Ainu is classified as critically endangered.[10] These results are based on assessment according to the six Major Evaluative Factors for Language Vitality.[11] For most of the factors the level of endangerment is evaluated on a scale of 0–5, ranging from *extinct* to *safe*.

With regards to Intergenerational Language Transmission (Factor 1), both languages are very vulnerable. Nivkh is still spoken (to a variable degree) by the older generation (grade 2), but has not been transmitted to the younger generation at least for the last fifty years. As for "living Ainu language", there is no language transmission either (grade 1) (Bunkachō, 2014: 2).

According to the last census of Russian population (2010)[12], there are 2,290 ethnic Nivkh on Sakhalin (of the total 4,652 in Russia[13]). The Absolute Number of Sakhalin Nivkh Speakers (Factor 2) is 118 (against 56 Amur speakers). The Proportion of Sakhalin Nivkh

Speakers within the Total Population (Factor 3) is very low, comprising only 5,2% (grade 2). It should be noted, however, that the evaluation of competence/incompetence in Nivkh recorded in the census is based on self-assessment of respondents. In reality, the language picture is much more complicated – Nivkh proficiency continuum ranges from (nearly) fully competent speakers from the oldest generation down to semi-speakers and rememberers from younger generations. Judging by a sociolinguistic survey (Gruzdeva & Leonova, 1990), the youngest fluent Nivkh speakers are nowadays about 65 years old. The number of L2/heritage language learners is limited to single persons (all of whom are ethnic Nivkh) irregularly attending language courses.

In Japan questions on ethnicity and language competence are excluded from censuses and corresponding statistical information is therefore absent. The actual number of people with Ainu heritage in Japan is hard to estimate, although Hokkaido government surveys on the living conditions of the Ainu listed 23,782 as "Ainu residing in Hokkaido" in 2006 and 16,786 people, "not representing the entire Hokkaido Ainu population", in 2013. Recent suggestions include 100,000 persons (Bugaeva, 2011: 74) and an "unknown" number (Satō, 2012: 29). The Absolute Number of Ainu Speakers (Factor 2) and correspondingly the Proportion of Ainu Speakers within the Total Population (Factor 3) are even more difficult to calculate (both grade 0–1). Tangiku (2012) suggests: "native speakers: none, passive knowledge: 10–100?, non-native speakers: 20–30?"; Shiraishi (2011)

---

[10] http://www.unesco.org/culture/languages-atlas/index.php

[11] http://www.unesco.org/culture/ich/doc/src/00120-EN.pdf

[12] http://www.gks.ru/free_doc/new_site/perepis2010/croc/Documents/Vol4/pub-04-21.pdf.

[13] The Nivkh also live in the Amur region of Russia.

estimates the number of speakers as "unknown (5?)" and Idutsu (2007) as "less than 5". Currently, speakers of Ainu should be conceived on an array displaying archival speakers, latent/old bilinguals, semi-speakers, token speakers and, perhaps most importantly, L2/heritage language learners with varying degrees of competence (Heinrich, 2012; Martin, 2011). Notably, nowadays many, if not most, learners of Ainu are ethnic Japanese (*wajin*) (Bunkachō, 2014: 3).

With respect to Trends in Existing Language Domains (Factor 4), both languages are used only in very restricted domains and for very limited functions (grade 1).

Presently, the Nivkh community has almost completely switched to Russian which totally dominates in all spheres of everyday life. Knowledge of Nivkh remains at best a passive reserve, whose use is restricted to rare occasions of communication among a few (fluent) speakers. The language is sometimes used during music performances and community festivals. A similar situation is typical of Ainu. As Bugaeva (2012: 462) notes, Ainu has not been spoken as a "community language" since the 1960s. Only a tiny fraction of Bunkachō's (2014: 71–73) survey respondents reported to be using Ainu at home or work. Its use pertains mostly to music, storytelling, prayer, ceremonies, festivals, speech contests and L2/heritage language learning (CAIS, 2010: 113).

Response to New Domains and Media (Factor 5), that includes among others educational activities, is from minimal to coping (grades 1–2), but varies essentially according to the language.

Nivkh is not used in broadcast media, as a result of which the language cannot be regularly heard by the community. It is nevertheless well presented in a long-term successful print media project, i.e. a monthly Nivkh-Russian newspaper *Nivkh Dif* ('Nivkh Word'). The newspaper has been published in the Sakhalin settlement of Nekrasovka since 1990, has a circulation of 250 copies and is highly valued by the community. Several issues are currently available online through a very informative and regularly updated website [14] created and supported by the Center for Preservation and Development of Traditional Culture of Indigenous Peoples of the North *Kykhkykh* ('Swan'). *Kykhkykh* also promotes Nivkh language and culture by making video-recordings of Nivkh speakers, by publishing booklets and teaching materials and by organizing language courses in Nivkh for the younger people (de Graaf & Shiraishi, 2013: 62).

Ainu is disseminated through weekly 15-minute beginner's level FRPAC/STV[15] radio courses, initiated in 1998 and targeting the general public. Podcasts of the programme and pdf format learning materials are available on the Internet. Among Ainu population, these courses are relatively well known, although many listeners land on them accidentally while looking for background listening. Though Satō (2012: 37) points out problems related to these courses (costs, non-existence of "standard Ainu", quality of research), they raise awareness of the language and its precarious state (Onai, 2014: 73). Other traditional media include bulletins published by various Ainu associations. Besides them, two important pioneers need to be mentioned: the Ainu language newspaper *Ainu taimuzu* and *FM Pipaushi* radio (Onai, 2014; Ueno, 2004). *Ainu taimuzu* 'Ainu Times' started off in Nibutani in 1997 and reached its 46th issue in 2013.[16] Texts are published both in Japanese *katakana* and Latin alphabet and letters from the readers are also accepted. The editors encourage readers with varying proficiencies to contribute irrespective of ethnicity. *FM Pipaushi* ('Place Rich in Shells') mini radio station broadcasts since 2001 from Nibutani in Ainu and Japanese once a month every 2nd Sunday for one hour.[17] Programmes include *yukar* sagas, music, "one point" conversation lessons, "seasonal topics", local news and interviews and are accessible online. Onai (2014: 77) concludes, though, that the media introduced here can hardly be considered as "ethnic media" advancing the cause of Ainu minority emancipation. When information on the Ainu is acquired, it is generally via mainstream television and newspaper reporting.

After a short period of teaching in the 1930s, Nivkh had no place within schooling until 1981 when it was reincorporated into the school curriculum as on obligatory subject, first, for primary, and later for secondary school. When, as a result of recent education reform, the schools got the right to assign more hours of the school syllabus to subjects that fall under the obligatory part of the Unified State Exam (Zamyatin, 2012: 37-38), it was done at the expense of 'a national language' (see section 3) that belongs to a variable part. Nivkh is now taught only as an elective subject one hour per week[18] in primary and secondary schools in Nekrasovka and Nogliki and in a primary school in Chir-Unvd. In 1984 Nivkh was introduced in several Sakhalin kindergartens, however, the issue of developing full-immersion programs and creating "language nests" for Nivkh community has never been

---

[14] http://kykhkykh.org/

[15] The Foundation for Research and Promotion of Ainu Culture (http://www.frpac.or.jp/english/) and Sapporo Television (http://www.stv.ne.jp/radio/ainugo/index.html).

[16] http://www.geocities.jp/otarunay/taimuzu.html

[17] http://fmyy.blogspot.fi/2006/04/fm_02.html

[18] Note that 'a native language' can potentially be taught for up to six hours per week (Zamyatin, 2012: 38).

raised. Unfortunately, the outcome of almost 35 years of systematic teaching of Nivkh is not very impressive – after the school course children are able at most to read the texts from the primers. Furthermore, school remains in fact the only place, where children have access to the language. Quite often the teachers themselves do not have full competence in Nivkh and like their own students use it only in the school context. One of a few community-based activities, i.e. summer camps, where Nivkh children had an opportunity to practice traditional way of life and to some extent language, ceased to exist in 2010 due to a new stringent legislation. After secondary school the study of Nivkh traditional culture and language may be continued in the Technological College of Handicrafts of the Peoples of the North in the Sakhalin town of Poronaisk. At the post-graduate level, the Institute of the Peoples of the North of State Russian Herzen Pedagogical University in St. Petersburg offers a program in Nivkh language, culture and pedagogy. It is worthy to note that after graduation potential schoolteachers often do not return to Sakhalin but stay in St. Petersburg. As Nivkh teacher Svetlana Poljetjeva pointed out, one of the urgent tasks is to create a special pedagogical department in Juzhno-Sakhalinsk (the administrative centre of Sakhalin region) and to organize on-site training of teachers in local pedagogical colleges.[19] This initiative, however, has not been followed by any development. Courses of Nivkh aimed at L2/heritage language learners of various generations have been organized on irregular basis in different Sakhalin settlements by local activists.

In Japan, Ainu is not a part of school education. Currently only some schools in Hokkaido incorporate learning about Ainu language and culture in their curricula. Promotion of the language lies mainly on the shoulders of the FRPAC and is divided into education and dissemination. Referring to the Ainu language as the "core" of Ainu ethnic identity, increasing the number of speakers and learners by training language instructors is mentioned as the main priority. Other objectives include language classes in community schools, Parent-Child Study (games, songs, etc.) and development of teaching materials. Dissemination refers to the above-mentioned STV radio course and the Ainu Oratorical Contest, which will be held in Sapporo in November 2014 for the 18th time.[20] Since 1998, the number of participants, including those under 30, has been increasing (Nakagawa, 2009: 2). In higher education, Ainu courses are offered at least in 7 Japanese universities and the number of Ainu language learners, including young people of Ainu heritage, is slowly increasing. Although some graduate testimonies illustrate positive and forward-looking objectives in

which the study of Ainu culture is connected to future professional aspirations,[21] attending Ainu courses is still rarely connected to direct financial, professional or social profit. Most Ainu instructors working in community schools have not studied the language in higher education (Bunkachō, 2014).

Materials for Language Education and Literacy (Factor 6) have been prepared for both languages, but accessibility to written materials is rather low: grade 3 for Nivkh and 2 for Ainu.

First Nivkh textbooks were written with Roman-based Nivkh alphabet and were used in schools in the 1930s. Current Cyrillic-based orthography was introduced in 1979 and starting from the 1980s several primers and textbooks have been published in the East-Sakhalin and Amur dialects. A series of new textbooks saw the light in 2008 after the adoption of a new school programme. In 2009–2013 the first multimedia textbooks and several school supplies for the Amur dialect were issued in Khabarovsk. Nivkh literature was developed mostly by Vladimir Sangi, whose last publication (2013) is the epic of the Sakhalin Nivkh.[22] Starting from 2006 Nogliki regional library has been publishing Nivkh tales and stories recorded from local speakers and illustrated by Nivkh children. Nivkh-Russian and Russian-Nivkh learner's dictionary prepared by Chuner Taksami was for the first time published in 1983 and passed through several editions. A serious obstacle for Nivkh revitalization is a lack of a learner's Nivkh grammar that could be used for training teachers and interested community members, as well as other up-to-date materials for adult L2/heritage language learners.

Following John Batchelor's (1887) and Chiri Mashio's (1956) introductions, modern Ainu language textbooks have been available since the 1970s, starting with Tamura Suzuko's *Ainugo nyūmon* (1979). Various means to transcribe Ainu, relying on the Latin and Cyrillic alphabet as well as Japanese *kana* syllabaries, have been employed (Tamura, 2000: 5). FRPAC primers now rely on *katakana* and Latin alphabet side by side, accompanied by translations into Japanese. These include textbooks for Chitose, Bihoro and Horobetsu dialects, all accessible on the Internet.[23] Learners appear to value 'locality' and variation, i.e. teaching of local dialects, and report the need to develop materials including everyday conversation (Bunkachō, 2014: 50). Other Ainu textbooks include primers by Chiri (1956), Nakagawa & Nakamoto (1997, 2007), Nakagawa (2013) and the Hokkaido Ainu Association (1994). Recent additions to the FRPAC website include

[19] http://www2.libsakh.ru/?div=indigen&subdiv=indigenteachinschool
[20] http://www.frpac.or.jp/about/details/post-169.html; http://www.frpac.or.jp/about/details/26.html

[21] Tomakomai Komazawa University: http://www.t-komazawa.ac.jp/org/apc/OBOG.html
[22] http://www.sakhalinenergy.ru/media/de82093d-9ee6-46c0-9ad4-46e389be0a8a.pdf
[23] http://www.frpac.or.jp/teach/index.html; Murasaki Kyoko's Sakhalin Ainu primer was published in 2009.

materials for children in the form of picture books with Ainu vocabulary, Ainu folktales in Japanese, games and quizzes, pictures for colouring as well as school materials introducing Ainu life and history.

Language revitalization as seen by (native) speakers

Current Nivkh and Ainu Community Members' Attitudes toward Their Own Language (Factor 8) and language revival are mainly positive, but somewhat ambiguous.

Assessing attitudes of (native) speakers, one should bear in mind that 'language' itself may be conceptualized in various ways. Both Nivkh and Ainu consider it as a valuable cultural attribute in par with music, dance and traditional clothing. The Nivkh, for instance, perceive language lessons as an addition to the lessons of history and culture, a kind of traditional life "wording". A similar view is manifested in Ainu living condition surveys in which respondents describe how they, indeed, learn *about* the Ainu language from elders or in courses, rather than conceptualize the language itself as the direct object of learning activity. Some elaborate their views even further, conceiving Ainu language as the "vessel" or medium without which understanding of Ainu culture and spirit (*puri*) would be impossible (Hokkaido Prefectural Government, 2013: 40; Idutsu, 2007: 64).

Nivkh and Ainu link the knowledge of the language with identity somewhat differently. The Nivkh are quite loyal towards a level of language competence but do not consider it as an indispensable attribute of ethnic identity. Moreover, most people do not claim the sole "possession" of Nivkh, leaving other peoples the right to speak it. Such tolerance may be explained by historical multilingualism on Sakhalin (Gruzdeva, 1996). The Ainu, by contrast, seem to be stricter in respect with language "ownership". In Bunkachō's (2014: 9) recent survey the Ainu language is conceptualized both as the most obvious medium to express one's true self and feelings (*honshin*) and a journey (*tabi*), a means to return to one's own roots – something which in this interpretation excludes *wajin* and other non-Ainu learners and scholars, who "cannot disclose and convey Ainu *kokoro*" ('heart, spirit, mind'). Yet another way of looking at the problem is expressed by those who do not essentialize the language but rather remark that "knowing about things like (…) the Ainu language does not make us Ainu" (CAIS, 2010: 111).

Many Nivkh community members support language maintenance (at least in words); others are indifferent and passive (grade 2–3).[24] There are community leaders

who have strong knowledge of Nivkh and support its preservation, but they are not able or do not know how to reverse a process that has gone too far. Difficult socioeconomic and ecological situation on Sakhalin turns the thoughts of indigenous population first of all on physical survival, not on language maintenance. Those who care about the fate of Nivkh rely almost exclusively on school teaching, though do not actually expect the children to learn the language at school. The teaching of Nivkh performs mostly a symbolic function, keeping up ethnic identities and proving that something is done for maintaining the language (Vakhtin, 2001: 313-314; Baranova & Maslinskii, 2008: 156-157). Informal community activities that would create a domain for language use are rare and irregular, though it seems that Nivkh language revival could be largely based exactly on a community-based approach involving those elders who are still fluent in the language.

Survey respondents of Ainu heritage seem to display enthusiasm with respect to language revitalization, maybe due to recent international and increasing national focus on their culture (see section 3). Attending language classes can also enhance regional group identification, feeling part of a community. It could be suggested that attitudes towards Ainu revitalization are likely to form a continuum, fluctuating on a scale of 1–3: some (activists/enthusiasts) are very positive, while others, the majority, are indifferent or prefer to conceal their Ainu heritage. Similar to Nivkh, for many Ainu battling with employment conditions, health risks and everyday livelihood is still a reality that overrides language revival activism (CAIS, 2010).

Language revitalization as seen by administrators

During the past decades both in Russia and Japan Governmental and Institutional Language Attitudes and Policies, Including Official Status and Use (Factor 7), have changed from active assimilation (grade 2) in Russia and forced assimilation (grade 0–1) in Japan to a form of differentiated support (grade 4), at least formally.

The status of one or another language is regulated in Russia by the Language Law[25] that was ratified in 1991 and re-ratified with minor changes in 1993. Russia's legislation does not use the term "minority language", but designates "a national language" that applies to the language one identifies with, that basically coincides with the language of one's ethnic group (Zamyatin, 2012: 22-24). By the Language Law, Nivkh does not

---

[24] Note that this information is based only on observations of a few researchers involved in Nivkh studies, since no in-depth investigation on the views of Nivkh community have ever

been performed. In Japan, by contrast, administrators such as the Council of Cultural Affairs and the Hokkaido Prefectural Government have attempted to ask or include questions on language attitudes in various surveys.

[25] http://constitution.garant.ru/act/right/10148970/

have any official status, but is "a national language" of the Nivkh community. In 2007, the Sakhalin Regional Duma adopted "A Law on the Languages of Indigenous Minorities Peoples of the North Living on the Territory of Sakhalin Area".[26] According to this law, Sakhalin state authorities are obliged to create conditions for the use of indigenous languages (henceforth IL) in different spheres of life, to promote scientific research aimed at their preservation, study and development, to publish textbooks, methodological and fiction literature in IL, to create media funds to distribute through mass media the materials on IL, to organize continuous training and education of the younger generation in IL and of national pedagogical personnel, to monitor the effectiveness of studying IL in school, to establish spelling and terminology commissions on IL, as well as the national editorial board for the publication of literature in IL, to open ethno-cultural centers for the preservation and development of IL. As can be seen, a legal framework for maintenance and revitalization of Sakhalin languages, including Nivkh, is most advanced and well developed. However, as rightly noted by Dmitrii Funk,[27] it does not correlate with a real life. Despite an existing open dialogue between the leaders of Nivkh community and authorities, most initiatives mentioned in the law have remained only on paper (see section 1). Furthermore, it seems that the government largely passed on care about Sakhalin indigenous population to the oil and gas companies that currently are the main sponsors of economic and cultural promotion (Gruzdeva, 2014).

Recent milestones in attempts to improve the situation of the Ainu include Shigeru Kayano's terms in the Japanese Diet in the 1990s, the "Ainu Cultural Promotion Act" in 1997, followed by the establishment of the FRPAC in the same year, and the "Resolution Calling for the Recognition of the Ainu People as an Indigenous People of Japan" in 2008 after the "UN Declaration on the Rights of Indigenous Peoples" in 2007. The 1997 Act focuses on the promotion of culture, which is defined as "*Ainu language,* music, dance, crafts, and other cultural artifacts inherited by the Ainu people, and cultural artifacts which developed from these", while the 2008 resolution "recognized that the Ainu people are an indigenous people who have lived around the northern part of the Japan, especially in Hokkaido, *with a unique language* as well as religious and cultural distinctiveness" (emphasis added). "Official Ainuness" is thus defined in terms of traditional culture, language being one *cultural* element. 2009 saw the establishment of the Council for Ainu Policy Promotion, "a high-level forum hosted by the Chief

Cabinet Secretary and composed of 14 members, including several Ainu representatives."[28]

FRPAC, which was established as a public service corporation and "the sole corporation in Japan with the authority to carry out the services provided in the law" (de Graaf & Shiraishi, 2013: 53), is currently the main government-funded agent in cultural promotion and has an office in Sapporo and the Ainu Cultural Exchange Centre in Tokyo. FRPAC activities were summarized in section 1. Although de Graaf & Shiraishi (2013: 1) suggest that "[t]he Ainu case can be compared and used as a model for possible (legal) measures to be taken regarding minority languages and cultures such as Nivkh with an outlook for future improvement", others are less positive. Satō (2012: 29) observes that the FRPAC avoids making reference to the legal situation of the Ainu and Morris-Suzuki (2014: 62-64) outlines problems related to the complicated application process for funding and practical concerns about the ways in which cultural projects are identified and approved. Establishment of "Ethnic Ainu schools", with systematic curricula for language and culture education, is suggested as a necessary future measure by some (Satō, 2012: 36), whereas others fear that such plans would only pave the way for continued discrimination and exclusion of the Ainu from "mainstream" society.

Another obvious problem is related to the current status of the language. At present Ainu legislation is not uniquely about language, and "rights" and "language" have not been combined into "language rights". The Japanese constitution does not mention language, which is "indicative of the stance in Japanese policy after 1945 to not take up language as an issue" (Kimura, 2011: 14, 18).

Language revitalization as seen by researchers

Over a century has passed since linguistic research of Nivkh and Ainu began, first in the form of glossaries, followed by compilation of oral texts and studies of toponymy, dialects, genetic relationship and language structure. The results are now available in the form of dictionaries, grammars, annotated translations, archival collections and linguistic publications, with respect to Ainu increasingly also in digital format. Amount and Quality of Documentation (Factor 9) for Nivkh may be assessed as fair (grade 3), whereas for Ainu it could even be evaluated on a continuum stretching beyond grade 3 (Bunkachō, 2014; Murasaki, 2012; Refsing, 2014).

Information and communications technology (ICT) is increasingly used in Ainu language documentation. In the Nivkh case it is still very moderate, the only web

---

[26] http://docs.cntd.ru/document/819021191
[27] http://yuzhno.sakh.ru/news/ys/89415/

[28] http://www.mlit.go.jp/hkb/ainu_e.html; http://www.un.emb-japan.go.jp/statements/hisajima052213.html

resource being the sound archive created by Hidetoshi Shiraishi [29]. Abundant materials of both languages (especially Ainu) still remain in closed archives or have not been processed. Systematical ICT-assisted Ainu language education is still in its infancy and is practically absent with regard to Nivkh. Idutsu (2007) offers as possible solutions "rural education" (as applied in American rural schools and communities) and "distance education" and calls for basic research for creating IT-assisted resources for Ainu teaching and learning – while admitting that copyright issues remain an obstacle. Another obstacle relates to manpower: finding and funding suitable candidates to carry out extensive time-consuming language data processing work is complicated.

The situation with Nivkh is aggravated by the fact that at the moment there are no academic researchers in Russia seriously involved in a systematic study of the language. The researchers working outside Russia deal mostly with language documentation and the study of language structure. Though the former plays an essential role in preserving language data, it must be acknowledged that the latter does not have any impact on language revival given that most scientific publications have exclusively research goals. One further problem is a general lack of vision, interest or regular support from Russian academic (non-pedagogical) fields that would be aimed at Nivkh revitalization.

In Japan Ainu revitalization rests on its own problems, since language revival measures suggested by various stakeholders do not necessarily coincide. Increasing support from (non-Ainu) scholars is geared towards a re-establishment of Ainu culture (inter-)nationally by allowing *everyone* to learn the language (Murasaki, 2012). Learning spaces, involving also non-Ainu, and opportunities for ethnic Ainu to learn and come together are equally highlighted (Bunkachō, 2014; CAIS, 2010; Nakagawa, 2009). As Satō (2012: 37-38) states, although some researchers refrain from participating in language education which has goals other than excellent proficiency, any command of Ainu should be valued. Similarly, Nakagawa (1995; 2007) relates the benefits of language learning to the understanding and mediation of Ainu world view and ways of thinking, irrespective of the background of the learner. Another, different objective of language learning then is that related to questions of identity. Many language learners with Ainu heritage wish to learn the language so as to be able to perform and recite traditional songs and legends, write song lyrics or carry out conversations. They thus have a commonly recognized L2 learning goal, namely, that of putting the language in actual use.

Scholars and administrators are in a key position to tackle the current weak and volatile status of Ainu studies in higher education. In academics the long history of discrimination and lacking research ethics translates into difficulty to carry out fieldwork, and study of the linguistic situation is further affected by the lack of reliable statistics. As balancing different views is not simple, linguists concentrate on researchable topics. However, calls for "forums for dialogue" between various stakeholders are also increasing. This is precisely what the interdisciplinary Center for Ainu and Indigenous Studies (CAIS), established in 2007, now attempts to provide via "national and international research and education programs featuring Ainu and other indigenous minorities while respecting their dignity".

Conclusion: 'Superdiversity' as a late modern sociolinguistic reality

In this short paper we briefly compared Nivkh and Ainu sociolinguistic situations at community, administrative and academic levels. We demonstrated that there are both obvious similarities and apparent differences in the state of these two insular languages. Besides purely practical questions connected with language revitalization, the analysis presented in this paper raises various theoretical issues pertaining to the notions of "speaker", "mother tongue", "language ownership" and perspectives of Nivkh and Ainu development.

While on Sakhalin it is still possible to speak about a distinctive Nivkh ethnic and even language community, in the current stage of the Ainu language, the usefulness of concepts such as "speaker", "speaking the language", and "group with which the speaker community identifies" must be readdressed. The concept of "community" is blurred by at least the following factors: most people of Ainu descent choose to conceal their roots; most of them are of mixed origin and have no knowledge of or even interest in the Ainu language (CAIS, 2010: 23-25); the umbrella term *Ainu* does not allow for internal diversity (cf. those in metropolitan areas outside Hokkaido or of Sakhalin descent).

At the moment, nobody learns either Nivkh or Ainu as a first language. Regarding Ainu, Nakagawa (2009: 4), from a scholarly perspective, suggests that the concept of *mother tongue* should be replaced by *"mother tongue"*, in quotation marks, a language which could *once* have been learned as a first language in different circumstances. This can be equally applied to Nivkh. These "mother tongues" could then become the ideal languages connected to Nivkh and Ainu identity and could be studied with the appropriate societal support by entire generations.

At this stage, the future of Nivkh and Ainu depends on the possibility of generating a critical mass of people who will take the responsibility for maintaining/learning and teaching the language, as well as for creating domains for language usage. This means that giving up the ideology of considering indigenous languages as

---

[29] http://ext-web.edu.sgu.ac.jp/hidetos/HTML/SMNStitle.html

"gifts", "possessions" or iconic representations of inherent human rights could increasingly be replaced by a new kind of acceptance such as tolerance of "superdiversity".

"Superdiversity" as a descriptor for new forms of socio-cultural and -linguistic diversity has recently been discussed in numerous pivotal studies focusing in particular on new types of speakers and learners, degrees of language ownership and "poly-languaging" (e.g. Blommaert & Backus, 2012; Blommaert & Rampton, 2011). Within this theoretical framework every speaker even with a rudimentary knowledge of language should be welcomed and supported. Language revitalization, then, can be seen as a continuum, ranging from small steps, aimed at maintenance of at least some functional links between languages and linguistic repertoires of choice and their respective environments, towards a complete preservation/restoration of language ecology in its full social, cultural and ecological context. For example, rather than labeling limited language use in restricted domains and functions such as music, storytelling, ceremonies and so forth as "folklorization", appreciation and reappropriation of the varying roles of such uses in individual language repertoires could be the path to follow. This, in its turn, could serve as a starting point of development into something *novel* by creating new societal cultures.

References

Baranova, V.V. & Maslinskii, K.A. (2008). Jazyk i sovremennaja jazykovaja situacija [The language and the current language situation]. In V.A. Turaev (Ed.) *Istorija i kul'tura nivkhov: istoriko-etnograficheskie ocherki* [The history and culture of the Nivkh: historical-ethnographic sketches] (pp. 148-158). Sankt-Peterburg: Nauka.

Blommaert, J. & Rampton, B. (2011). Language and Superdiversity. *Diversities,* 13(2), 1-21.

Blommaert, J. & Backus, A. (2012). Superdiverse repertoires and the individual. *Tilburg Papers in Culture Studies,* 24.

Bugaeva, A. (2011). Internet Applications for Endangered Languages: A Talking Dictionary of Ainu. *WIAS Research Bulletin,* 3, 73-81.

Bugaeva, A. (2012). Southern Hokkaido Ainu. In N. Tranter (Ed.), *The languages of Japan and Korea, Routledge Language Family Series* (pp. 461-509). London: Routledge.

Bunkachō (The Council of Cultural Affairs) / Hokkaido University. (2014). *Kikiteki na jōkyō ni aru gengo/hōgen no hozon/keishō ni kakaru torikumi nado no jittai ni kansuru chōsa kenkyū jigyō (Ainugo)* [Survey Project on the Preservation and Transmission of Endangered Languages/Dialects, Ainu Language]. (Report).

CAIS (Center for Ainu and Indigenous Studies/Hokkaido University). (2010). *Report on the 2008 Hokkaido Ainu Living Conditions Survey. Living Conditions and Consciousness of Present-day Ainu. Ainu Report,* 01. Hokkaido University.

de Graaf, T. & Shiraishi, H. (2013). Documentation and revitalization of two endangered languages in Eastern Asia: Nivkh and Ainu. In E. Kasten & T. de Graaf (Eds.), *Sustaining Indigenous Knowledge: Learning Tools and Community Initiatives for Preserving Endangered Languages and Local Cultural Heritage* (pp. 49-64). Fürstenberg/Havel: Kulturstiftung Sibirien.

Gruzdeva, E. (1996). The linguistic situation on Sakhalin Island. In S.A. Wurm, P. Mühlhäusler & D.T. Tryon (Eds.), *Atlas of Languages of Intercultural Communication in the Pacific, Asia, and the Americas II* (pp. 1007–1012). Berlin, New York: Mouton de Gruyter [Trends in Linguistics. Documentation: 13, 2].

Gruzdeva, E. (2014, in press). Explaining language loss. The Sakhalin Nivkh case. In H.F. Marten, M. Riessler, J. Saarikivi & R. Toivanen (Eds.), *Cultural and linguistic minorities in the Russian Federation and the European Union.* (pp. 265-287). Berlin: Springer.

Gruzdeva E. & Leonova Ju. (1990). K izucheniju nivkhsko-russkogo dvujazychija v sociolingvisticheskom aspekte [On the study of Nivkh-Russian bilingualism in sociolinguistic aspect]. In N. D. Andreev (Ed.), *Lingvisticheskie issledovanija 1990. Sistemnyje otnoshenija v sinchronii i diachronii* [Linguistic Studies 1900. Systemic relations in a synchrony and diachrony] (pp. 48-55). Moskva: Institut jazykoznanija AN SSSR.

Heinrich, P. (2012). *The Making of Monolingual Japan.* Bristol: Multilingual Matters.

Hokkaido Prefectural Government. (2006 & 2010). *Hokkaidō ainu seikatsu jittai chōsa* [Survey on Daily Life of the Hokkaido Ainu] (Report).

Idutsu, K. (2007). Ainu language education as a Rural Education: Basic research for creating IT-assisted resources for Ainu language learning and teaching. *Hekichi kyōiku kenkyū* [Research in Hinterland Education], 62: 61-17 (in Japanese).

Kimura, G. C. (2011). Language rights in Japan: what are they good for? In P. Heinrich & C. Galan (Eds.), *Language Life in Japan* (pp. 14-33). London & New York: Routledge.

Martin, K. (2011). Aynu itak: on the road to Ainu language revitalization. *Media and Communication Studies,* 60, 57-93.

Morris-Suzuki, T. (2014). Tourists, anthropologists, and visions of indigenous society in Japan. In M. Watson

(Ed.), *Beyond Ainu Studies* (pp. 45-66). University of Hawai'i Press.

Murasaki, K. (2012). The last stage of Sakhalin Ainu language and possibility of regeneration. *The Japanese Journal of Language in Society,* 14(2), 3-13 (in Japanese).

Nakagawa, H. (1995). *Ainugo o fīrudowāku suru* [Doing Ainu Language Fieldwork] Tokyo: Taishūkan.

Nakagawa, H. (2009). Ainugo gakushū no mirai ni mukete – kangaekata to annai [Towards learning Ainu Language: opinions and information]. *Ainu seisaku no arikata ni kansuru yūshokusha kondankai (Dai-5-kai), Shiryō* [Council for Ainu Policy Promotion, Materials] 2, 1-11.

Onai, J. (2014). Ainu to media kankyō [Ainu and media environment]. *Chōsa to shakai riron. Kenkyū hōkokusho* [Survey Research and Social Theory, Research Report] 31, 71-82.

Refsing, K. (2014). From collecting words to writing grammars. In M. Watson (Ed.), *Beyond Ainu Studies* (pp. 185-198). University of Hawai'i Press.

Satō, T. (2012). Ainugo no genjō to fukkō [Present state of Ainu language and language revitalization]. *Gengo kenkyū* [Journal of the Linguistic Society of Japan], 142: 29-44.

Shiraishi, T. (2011). The Northern Neighbors of Japan: Ainu, Nivkh and Uilta, presentation, Leiden University.

Tamura, S. (2000). *The Ainu Language.* Tokyo: Sanseidō.

Tangiku, I. (2012). Situation of Ainu Language, presentation, University of Helsinki.

Ueno, M. (2004). Ainugo no fukkō to fukyū ni okeru media riyō no torikumi ni tsuite [Utilization of media in Ainu language revitalization and spread]. *Waseda Daigaku daigakuin kyōikugaku kenkyūka kiyō* [Bulletin of Research Institute on Education of The Graduate School of Waseda University], 11(2), 23-34.

Vakhtin, N.B. (2001). *Jazyki narodov Severa v XX veke. Ocherki jazykovogo sdviga* [Languages of the North in the 20th century. Studies in language shift]. Sankt-Peterburg: Dmitrii Bulanin.

Zamyatin, K. (2012). The education reform in Russia and its impact on teaching of the minority languages: an effect of nation-building? *Journal on Ethnopolitics and Minority Issues in Europe*, 11 (1), 17-47.

The Shughnani Language: How it Survives and How it Affects the Cultural Life of the Inhabitants of the Pamirs

Parvonakhon Jamshedov
Dushanbe
Tursunzade Str. 52, Apt.16
Tajikistan/Tadjikistan
[pjam07@mail.ru]

Abstract

A group of Pamiri languages are spoken in Tajik and Afghan Badakhshan, and also in Pakistan and China. These languages belong to the East Iranian group, but became separated from the mass of Iranian languages long ago. The Pamiri languages comprise the Shughnani-Rushani sub-group, Yazghulami, Ishkashimi and Wakhi. The last two languages, Ishkashimi and Yazghulami, fall under the category of "seriously endangered". In 1989 the Language Law of the Republic of Tajikistan was issued. It allowed indigenous minorities to acquire education in their mother tongues. A newly adopted Language Law (2009) does not mention the local Pamiri languages at all. So, in fact only the Tajik language was, and still is, the language of school and mass media in the country. At the same time the Shughnani language, one of the largest languages of Badakhshan, serves as a language of communication and is used in cultural life of Badakhshan in both Tajikistan and Afghanistan. Today the main problem is to get Shughnani and other Pamiri languages employed in school education. This has not been solved by government structures, although several ABCs for mother-tongue speakers have been composed.

After the collapse of the USSR and the declaration of independence by the republics that had composed it, a substantially new geopolitical situation arose in Central Asia and Eurasia. In Europe two contradictory tendencies began to gain strength: toward integration, as endorsed by the majority of European countries; and toward disintegration, as characteristic of Eastern Europe. The creation of independent states from the republics of the former USSR did little to change the general political situation in the region that had been part of the former Soviet Union.

There are many narrow valleys along the valley of the upper Panj River – which separates Tajikistan from Afghanistan – where different Pamiri languages are spoken. These languages belong to East Iranian group, but separated from the mass of Iranian languages long ago. These indigenous languages are spread in Badakhshan (Tajikistan and Afghanistan), and also in Pakistan and China. They are: Shughnani-Rushani sub-group, Yazghulami, Ishkashimi and Wakhi. It should be noted that another two Pamiri s – Wanji and Darwazi were once spread in the area of the modern Wanj and Darwaz (close to modern Kalai Khumb). However, today they have been replaced by local dialects of Tajik language. The process of extinction of the Pamiri languages is continuing. The reasons of this process are:

1. All the inhabitants of Mountainous Badakhshan in Tajikistan are identified as "Tajiks": this is taken to imply that their mother tongue is Tajik language.

2. None of Pamiri languages are taught at school in Badakhshan (Contrast the situation in Pakistan and Afghanistan in Wakhi-speaking areas, according to B. Lashkarbekov).

3. Today in Tajikistan these languages have no officially adopted alphabet or script (in spite of the fact that in 1930, and again in 1995, there were attempts to establish alphabets and to introduce mother-tongue education at school).

4. Pamiri residents have emigrated worldwide.

In 1995 and later, Tajikistan declared the Tajik language as the official language of the Republic Tajikistan. After achieving independence, the official language of the country may have seen as a unifying symbol for the state. The Language Law of 1989 of the Republic of Tajikistan allowed indigenous minorities to receive education in their mother tongues. However, in fact Tajik language is the only language of school and mass media in the country. A newly-adopted Language Law (2009) does not mention the local Pamiri languages at all. It appears that nothing is going to be changed in the development and preservation of the above-mentioned indigenous languages and dialects.

The people of Badakhshan still use their mother tongues in everyday life and are trying to preserve them. But the influence of mass media and schools are affecting mother tongues. Ishkashimi and Yazghulami languages that have small number of speakers are loosing their position and now stand on the verge of extinction.

According to the widely employed GIDS (Graded Intergenerational Disruption Scale) classification, due to Joshua Fishman, the Pamiri languages, and in particular Ishkashimi and Yazghulami, fall under the category "seriously endangered". This means that the language is spoken only by grandparents and older generations. While the parent generation may still understand the language, they typically do not speak it to their children (e.g. Walsh, 2009, p. 136).

Shughnani is spoken along the bank of the Panj River from the village Dasht to Darmorakht and also in two big valleys Ghund and Shokhdara. On the Afghan side Shughnani is spoken along the right bank of the Panj River and a side valley in the area of the lake Shava (Shughnani Xeva). (The approximate number of Shughnanis is 100 000). Rushani is also spoken along the river Panj from the village Pastkhuf to Shipad (Rushani Xipuδ) on the border of Wanj region and in the Afghan side in the village Pajwar (up to 25 000 people are the speakers of Rushani). Both of these languages do not have written tradition with the exception of a period of eight years when in the 1930s was introduced a Latin-based alphabet for Shughnani. In these years ABC textbooks and other books were published in Tashkent and Stalinabad in Shughnani. In 1937 these scripts and books were banned by the Stalin regime.

The oral literature of the mentioned area was the subject of brief investigation from the end of the 19th to the 20th century. The first Shughnani tale was published by R.B. Show. In 1924, a Russian scholar I.I. Zarubin had collected 41 verses of Lalayik (Lullabay) and published them. He mentioned the specific character of the oral poems in Shughnani and Rushani languages. Dr Zarubin visited Shughnan and Rushan and collected interesting ethnographic materials (see, for instance, Zarubin 1960): (1) The tale "*Shahdukhtari moron*" ("The Snake's Princess"); (2) Six tales and a variant of the folk poem *Dargilmodic*.

Apart from Zarubin, the contribution of other scholars such as A. Semyonov, T. Pulody, J. Rupka, A. Habibov and others should be mentioned. Several monographic works have been published by Nisor Shakarmamadov (2005, 2007), a scholar from Academy of Sciences of Republic Tajikistan, who was a native speaker of Bartangi language. In 1960 the Academy of Sciences of Republic Tajikistan had organized the expedition to Shughnan and Rushan under supervision of Dr. Nurjanov. This expedition collected 40 folk poems (720 verses), 32 poems of local poets (470 verses), 194 rubai, 5 tales and 5 songs in Shughnani and Rushani.

The second expedition to Shughnan, Rushan and Ishkashim was organized by the Institute of Language and Literature of the Academy of Sciences. This expedition collected 171 songs (2046 verses), 161 poems (1332 verses) and 109 tales and stories which are available in the archive of the library of this Institute in Dushanbe.

As Shughnani language is oral and has no written tradition, the speakers keep their heritage (tales, songs, poems and rubai) in memory and spread them around by word of the mouth. That is one of the reasons why many songs, tales and rubais have variants and sometimes each valley or even village has a number of variants of the same songs or tale. The oral literature in Shughnani and Rushani languages can be divided into two groups:

1. Old traditional poems and tales inherited from ancestors and transmitted from generation to generation (Lalayik, Dargilmodik).

2. New poems, songs and stories created in the course of the last two centuries.

The first group includes the following topics: a) lyrics, and b) tragedy, associated with the longing for the beloved and complaining to the calamities of life.

Lalayik ('Lullaby') and *Dargilmodik* are the most popular songs in Shughnan. Everyone (except the youngsters) knows some verses and variants of these songs. The first is about a child and the wish for a happy future for him or her. *Dargilmodik* (*dargil* lit. 'longing', *modik* 'mammy') tells about the separation and longing of lovers and can also express different sides of life. The Wakhi version of *Dargilmodik* is called *Bulbulik* (lit. 'nightingale') it is very popular in Wakhan.

Shughnani language, one of the largest languages of Badakhshan, serves as a language of communication in the entire Badakhshan region and is actively used in cultural life of Badakhshan in both Tajikistan and Afghanistan. The local products have their local Shughnani names that are promoting the economy. The communication and menus in local restaurant and café are also in Shughnani.

Today the main problem is to employ Shughnani language in school education. This process still is not solved by the government, although a group of scientists composed an ABC for Shughnani speakers and offered it to the governmental structures.

References

Jamshedov, P. (2014). *Nomai Pazhuheshgah. Special Badakhshan issue*. Dushanbe.

Edelman, J.I. & Dodykhudoeva, L.R. (2009) Shughn(an)i. in G. Windfuhr (Ed.), *Iranian Languages*. London: Routledge.

Shughnan. (2014). M. Ilolov, P. Jamshedov (Eds.). Dushanbe.

Shakarmamadov, N., & Kurbanov, Kh. (1997). *Dargilik*. Dushanbe.

Shakarmamadov, N. (2005, 2007). *Folklori Pomer* I, II. Dushanbe.

Shambezoda, N. (1936). *Gulghuncha*. Tashkent.

Walsh, Michael, 2009, The Rise and Fall of GIDS in Accounts of Language Endangerment, In Ostler, N. & Elnazarov, H. (Eds.), *Endangered Languages and History, Proceedings of FEL XIII*, Bath, pp. 134-141.

Zarubin, I.I. (1960). *Shughnani texts and vocabulary*. Moscow.

Masaai Indigenous Knowledge Systems
Exploring the Value of Masaai Mara, Masaai Culture and Maa Language to the Masaai Speech Community of East Africa

Carolyne Adhiambo Ngara

University Of Nairobi – Kenya
C/o The Enduring Voices Foundation
P.O Box 38615 – 00100 Nairobi
Kenya
[carol.ngara@gmail.com]

Abstract

Chapter 2, Section 7(3), of the Kenyan constitution, of (The Republic of Kenya 2010) stipulates that the state shall develop, promote and protect the diversity of languages of the people of Kenya. Although this statement has no direct implication to the language of education policy in the Kenyan system of education, their implementation will largely affect the language policy in education. This paper explores ways in which the constitution can be used as a catalyst in the promotion; developments, protection of indigenous languages and at the same time use them as medium of instruction in schools in Kenya.

Introduction

The promotion of linguistic and cultural diversity of any people in the world constitutes the wealth of the entire mankind. The history of humanity in itself is not only a history of socio-economic activity but also a history of semiotic activity. As modernization bites its way into the heart of Africa, so does the western culture, globalization and industrial development continue to ravage indigenous peoples' cultures and languages in the continent. In Kenya, modernization has affected the social structure of the *Maasai* since independence.

In 2010, the government of Kenya (GoK) adopted a new constitution in which major changes were made in regard to the development, promotion and protection of indigenous languages in the country. This was done in tandem with the United Nation's affirmation of protection and promotion of cultural identity and linguistic diversity of Indigenous tribes as enshrined in the UN's Indigenous Peoples Rights Law.

This paper takes a six point approach in analyzing the effects of radical modernization on the Maasai Speech Community. First, it examines the role of the new Constitution and how instrumental it is in the development, promotion, protection, inclusion and teaching of indigenous languages like Maa in the first years of education system in the Republic of Kenya. Second, it explores the Maa Speech Community, analyzes specific affects on their decade-long-traditions, culture, environment, family and community structures. Third, the study discusses destruction of ancient Maasai Cultural heritage. Fourth, it elaborates the value of Maa as an indigenous language that orchestrated the Maasai Indigenous knowledge systems and developed solutions to daily challenges. The study gives an overview of the Maasai cultural identity, social customs and traditional structures as earlier related to an ideal traditional Maasai family. Finally, it examines the harmonious symbiosis between the Maasai (Indigenous folk), Maa (indigenous

Language), and the Maasai Mara (Indigenous Land) in an earlier period.

The Status of Indigenous languages in the Kenyan education system

The use of Indigenous languages in Kenya dates back to the colonial period. In 1935, the government of Kenya (GoK) issued a circular directing public schools in rural areas to use vernacular as a mode of instruction for the first four years of school life, (Mbaabu 1996: 81). However, the colonial policies at the time accorded supreme status to handful Indigenous languages only. In this regard, only four languages: Kiswahili, Kikuyu, Dholuo and Luluhya were given a priority. English was introduced as early as Standard 1 in some parts of the country.

Although done in total disregard of the Phelps-Stokes commission of 1924, which observed that all colonizing, nations in Africa had forced their languages upon the people of Africa and discouraged the use of Indigenous languages, (Adegbija 1994: 32). In 1953, UNICEF made a declaration supporting the use of indigenous languages in education as the best language of instruction for the learner. The declaration stated that:

> … it is important that every effort should be made to provide education in the mother tongue…On educational grounds we recommend that the use of the mother tongue be extended to as late a stage in education as possible. In particular, pupils should begin their schooling through the medium of the mother tongue, because they understand it best and because to begin their school life in the mother tongue will make the break between home and school as small as possible.

This was seconded in Article 6 (2) of the African Union Cultural Charter for Africa, which stated that member states should "promote teaching in national languages in order to accelerate their economic, political and cultural development" (quoted in Musau 1999: 118).

The language policy in the education system in Post-colonial Kenya pitted Kiswahili, Kikuyu, Dholuo, Luluhya, and English against each other. While Kiswahili still assumes official and national language status, Kikuyu, Dholuo and Luluhya play minimal role.

Currently, the policy for primary schools stipulates that the languages of instruction for the first three years of schooling shall be the language of the school's location while Kiswahili applies in urban areas. Thereafter, English shall take over (Mbaabu, 1996 quoted in Ngugi, 2009: 8). Since the colonial days, English language assumes a very supreme position in the Kenyan schooling system.

Indigenous language resistance in the Kenyan education system

The use of vernacular languages for instruction in most African countries has always been met with strong resistance from most sectors in the respective countries (Marivate, 1993). This is attributed to enormous factors discussed in the chapters below.

The elementary education policy in Kenya stipulates the usage of indigenous languages as medium of instruction in the foundation level of education-class one to three. Nonetheless, this policy bares some shortcomings that make the implementation of the policy overtly impossible. Many parents, teachers and policy makers themselves believe that indigenous languages stagnates the performance of pupils in their examination and their success in education (Luoch & Ogutu, 2002:89).

Since indigenous languages are excluded from important formal domains where focus is on the official language, these languages are not offered at the institute of higher learning. As observed by Matsinhe (2004) the number of students enrolling for African language courses has dwindled in the recent years in many universities across Africa. Due to these factors teachers, parents and learners generally have a negative attitude towards their own vernacular as languages of instruction. Most parents see the usefulness of English language in terms of its future utility for their children. In addition publishers decry the lack of readership and poor sales of books written in indigenous languages and thus do not want to invest in mother tongue languages (Ngugi 2009: 49).

Additionally, parents are in a dilemma, whereby they have to promote the use of indigenous languages at home, and provide their children with the opportunity to learn a language that will secure them some social mobility.

Another reason as observed by Djite (1993 quoted in Matsinhe, 2004: 18) is that approaches to development are usually defined in terms of economic growth, and in most African countries, Indigenous languages are not part and parcel of the efforts to achieve sustainable development and consequently, they warrant neither attention nor funding.

Although experts maintain that pupils are better placed to become literate when they start learning in their first language and the gradually move to another (Brooke-Utne, 2004: 1-12), Kenya, like many countries across Africa has a majority of her children going through an education system that fails to provide instruction in the language they speak at home or one that they understand best.

The place of the new constitution in the protection and promotion of Indigenous languages in Kenya

The issue of developing indigenous languages for literacy and education remains thorny in post- colonial Africa. In the recent past, calls for indigenous-based education have been supported by several international rights groups, which advocates for education reflecting the rights of people to develop their own language and culture (Minority Rights Groups, 2009 quoted in Pinnock & Vijayakumar, 2009: 15). These rights may imply both right of language and language right, (Ogechi, 2003: 277).

A large number of Kenya's indigenous languages have not been documented; only 22 out of 40 languages have been since 1950's (Kingéi, 2001: 129). In recognizing the diminishing use and status of Indigenous languages of the people of Kenya, the Government decided to take a positive measure of protecting and promoting the indigenous languages, by enshrining them in the new constitution that was enacted in 2010. As stated in the abstract, the new Constitution provides for the promotion, protection and the use of these languages in Kenya.

For a language to be considered as developed, it must have viable orthography, substantial literature and to be used in the domains as education, broadcasting, print media, administration, law and vice versa (Wollf, 2002: 14). Although the constitution doesn't offer practical guidance towards promoting the status of the indigenous languages, there is need for more action to be taken in order to promote, protect and use these languages as stated. Wollf argues that language use for all topics and domains, by all and consistently is the only effective strategy for any language promotion and or protection. This therefore means that the pronouncements in the new constitution of the Republic of Kenya are not enough.

Mazrui & Mazrui (1998: 15), states that the right of language(s) refers to the right of each and every language in a multilingual society to exist and the equality of opportunity for it to "develop" legal and other technological limbs and to flourish.

The new constitution therefore, needs to allow for practical promotion and protection of all indigenous languages in Kenya. There is an urgent need to have the statements implemented. In order to develop indigenous languages, the Kenyan Government should accurately establish the exact number of indigenous languages in Kenya. Muthwii (2002: 86). Mbaabu (1996) indicates that Kenya has 42 languages, Heine & Möhlig (1980) and Whitely (1974) talk of 30 and 34 languages respectively, recently Gordon (2005: 1) talks of 61 languages. In addition, ILO (2009: 5) maintains that the postcolonial Kenyan State pursued a policy of assimilation and integration of numerically smaller tribes into some dominant ones. Indigenous people such as the Endorois and others like the Ogiek, El Molo, Watta, Munyaya, and Yakuu were not legally recognized as separate tribes with their own linguistic identity (Wambua, 2012).

In chapter four of the constitution under The Bill of Rights, (The Republic of Kenya 2010), the Kenyan Government has obliged itself to protecting the rights of the minority and in section 56 (d) the constitution says that it shall put in place affirmative action programs designed to ensure that minorities and marginalized groups "develop their cultural values, languages and practices." Having determined the status of the languages spoken in Kenya, a plan of action must be put in place and pursued to the later, in order to achieve what has been enshrined and resolved in the constitution.

The Maasai: Understanding their origin, traditions, religion, linguistic and cultural assimilation

The Maasai are a Nilotic group of people found in East Africa. They are believed to be the descendants of Maasainta-the founder of the Maasai race (Masahren, 2009). They inhabit the southern part of Kenya and the northern districts of Tanzania. In Kenya, they presently reside in Narok, Kajiado, and Samburu. Some small groups like the Ilchamus (Njemps) live around Lake Baringo and Lakipia District (MCSF, 2004). In Tanzania, they reside in Longido, Monduli, Ngorogoro, Simanjiro and Kiteto (MCSF, 2004).

According to their own oral history, the Maasai originated from the lower Nile valley north of Lake Turkana and migrated south around the 15th century, arriving in a long trunk of land stretching from what is now northern Kenya to what is now central Tanzania between the 17th and late 18th century. Many ethnic groups that had already formed settlements in the region were forcibly evicted by the incoming Maasai, while other mainly southern Cushitic groups were assimilated into Maasai society (Wambua, 2012). The resulting mixture of Nilotic and Cushitic populations also produced the Kalenjin and Samburu groups.

The Maasai speak Maa language (Mol, 1996). Maa has two internal subdivisions. North Maa includes the Ilsampur (Samburu), and Ilchamus (Njemps). The south

Maa includes the Ilarusa, Ilmoitanik, Isiria, Ilwuasinkishu, Iloodokilani, Ildalalekutuk, Ildamat, Ilkaputiei, Ilmatapato, Ilkisonko, Iloitai, Ilpurko and Ilkeekonyokie (Vossen, 1988). The Maasai folk are further divided into clans whose members stem from the patriarch Naiterukop, the founder of the world or Oledukuya, (the first one). Naiterukop was believed to be the founder of the Maasai community. He had two wives and, as is their custom, they occupied different parts of the homestead (*enkang*) opposite each other (Masheren, 2009). One of the wives placed her house on the right side of the homestead and the other on the left. The one on the right was called *Nadomongi* (of the red cow) and the one on the left was named *Narok Kiteng* (of the black cow) (Masheren, 2009). From these sides came the lineage of the Maasai clans. Nadomongi gave birth to Ilmolelian, Ilmakesen and Iltaarosero. Narok Kiteng on the other hand gave birth to Ilukumai, Ilaiser, and Ilaitayiok (Masheren, 2009).

They are pastoralists, known for their intricate traditional costumes and jewelry and are famous for their fearsome reputations as warriors and cattle-rustlers. Like the Bantu, the Maasai have adopted many customs and practices from the neighboring Cushitic groups, including the 'age set system' of social organization and circumcision. Maasai society is strongly patriarchal in nature, with elder men making major decisions for each Maasai group. A full body of oral law covers many aspects of behavior. Formal execution is unknown, and normally payment in cattle will settle matters. An out-of-court process called *amitu* ('to make peace'), or *arop*, which involves a substantial apology is also practiced. The Maasai are monotheistic worshipping a single deity called Enkai or Engai. Engai has a dual nature: *Engai Narok* ('Black God') is benevolent, and *Engai Nanyokie* ('Red God') is vengeful. (Hodgson, 2005). The Maasai believe that Enkai is the originator and creator of everything on earth. The Black God and the Red God represent different aspects of Enkai; but they are not two separate deities (Hodgson, 2005). In the past, whenever the Maasai community faced difficulties that required divine interventions and during prolonged drought, *Enkai* ('God') was offered sacrifices to appease him for rain.

The central human figure in the Maasai religious system is the *laibon* whose roles include shamanistic healing, divination, prophecy, ensuring success in war and or adequate rainfall. Whatever power an individual *laibon* had, was a function of personality rather than position. Many Maasai have since adopted the Christian religion.

For the Maasai, the end of life is virtually without ceremony, and the dead are left out for scavengers. A corpse rejected by scavengers (mainly spotted hyenas, known as *Ondilili* or *Oln'gojine*) is perceived with suspicion and is liable to cause social disgrace. It is not uncommon for bodies to be covered in fat and blood from a slaughtered ox. Burial was previously reserved for great chiefs, since it was believed to be harmful to the soil.

Traditional Maasai lifestyle is centered on their cattle which constitute their primary source of food. The measure of a man's wealth is in terms of cattle and children. A herd of 50 cattle is respectable, and the more children the Maasai have, the better. A man who has plenty of one but not the other is considered poor. The Maasai believe that God gave them all the cattle on earth, rendering cattle-rustling an acceptable practice meant for reclaiming back what is rightfully theirs. A diminishing practice today.

Traditionally, the Maasai had generations that formed the peer traditional 'age-set' or 'age-group' system. The age groups are constituted over time. A new 'age-division' (*Olporror*) is opened every seven years, however, a more successive pair of 'age-sets' (*Olaji*) is done on a 14 year cycle (Spear and Waller, 1993). This system was very important because it provided an opportunity for the young Maasai warriors to grow, to build a sense of brotherhood and gain some solidarity. If a member of the 'age-group' lost his livestock to theft or sickness; he would be given other animals to start over by his comrades (Masharen, 2009). This group support system lasted throughout one's life. It was during occasions like age group festivals, 'ceremonial groups' (*Olamal*), circumcision ceremonies, weddings, and passage of rite into junior elders that young men got to learn *Inkoon* ('past stories and culture') (Masharen, 2009). It was within such "age group" that young Maasai men trained to be responsible adults by learning the great deeds of their ancestors, the myths and the legends of past generations.

One of the major cultural values which anchors the life of a Maasai is respect for oneself, others and society (Tarayia, 2004). The 'age sets' instilled respect among their members. Disgraceful acts that could dent the image of the age-group were punishable within the age-set systems (Masharen, 2009). Although Maasai women got married young, the men were born and groomed to be warriors and that's why there is a great age difference between husbands and wives. Women identified and belong to the age group into which they married (Masheren, 2009). Marriage of children sired by men from the same age group as well as clan were prohibited and considered a taboo. Families and children from the same age group considered themselves related and girls from that age group would never be married by men from their father's age group as it was considered incest and punishable by the Maasai traditional law (Tarayia, 2004).

Each "age group" had its own group of leaders called *Inkasisin*, who facilitate "age group" ceremonies. The *Inkasisin* was divided into three posts: the *Olaiguenani*, *Olotuno*, and *Oloboru Enkeene* (Masheren, 2009). Each of these leaders had his own specific duties and responsibilities. The *Olaigueanani* ('chief') was the first position to be filled as a new age group developed (Masharen, 2009). He was chosen as a chief because of his skills and abilities to handle disputes in the "age group" and within the community. He was expected not to rule as a dictator, but as a mediator in conflict (Masharen, 2009).

The focal point of Maasai social institutions were based on clans and each member belonged to a clan (Masharen, 2009). People from the same clan addressed each other as brothers and had very strong bond and responsibility for each other. Every family was identified by its clan. Maasai clans were believed to have their origin in the ownership of cattle. This was derived from the two major pillars of their society; *Oodo Mongi* (the 'Red Cow'), and *Orok Kiteng* (the 'Black Cow') (Hodgson, 2005) The Maasai traditional clan systems played a significant role in leadership and sustainable relationships. The clan system specified how marriage and other intimate relationships were conducted within the Maasai society (Hodgson, 2005). Traditional Maasai society had no centralized political structures and governance relied heavily on the "age set" system. All "age-groups" across all sections shared a name and their leadership was known to each other. Decisions regarding naming of "age groups" were made by senior elders in consultations with the *Oloiboni* ('traditional seer') who performed rituals to bind the age groups together, by performing traditional rituals which were strictly observed by all who prescribed to the age group.

The Masaai family and community structure

Before the colonial period, a Maasai settlement made each family (see Figure 1 below), live within the same homestead for psychosocial, economic support and security (Tarayia, 2004). The man was the head of the family and had absolute authority to choose partners for his children (Tarayia, 2004). By any standard, an ideal Maasai family was a tightly knit domestic unit, in which all members had defined roles. Girls, boys, men and women not only constituted a social structure but were equally an important unit of the family (Tarayia, 2004). Most families were polygamous and the more wives and children a man had, the higher was his status in the community and ability to cope with labor demands (Tarayia, 2004). Families were comprised of blood relations who included husband and wives, their children, the in-laws and their children as well as respective clans of the husbands which comprised hundreds of other community members (Tarayia, 2004).

The girl-child had no say on her choice of husband (Masheren, 2009). However, she had access to use the family property, but not right to inherit property at her parents' home (Tarayia, 2004). This was precautionary since she would marry off as approved by the family and would move to the *Manyatta* (kraal) of her husband (Tarayia, 2004). The same was true with the livestock;

she had access to the stock at her parents' home to maintain her livelihood, but not to own them (Tarayia, 2004).

Strong bonds were made between various members of the family by exchange of livestock - each of which they named after the person who gave it as a show of respect and bond (Hodgson, 2004). Each member of the family was responsible for the welfare of each other and for those that lived within a close proximity shared responsibilities which include childcare. Maasai settlement was identified on family basis with each family responsible for taking care of all shared resources (Masharen, 2009)

As indicated on Figure 1, Maasai families were connected within the geographic space as well as by intertwined relationships that made every individual belong to a family which made up a community. The common bond between families and communities existed in order to share common resources, roles and responsibilities which were guarded by a code of ethics and beliefs entrenched in the Maasai tradition and culture.

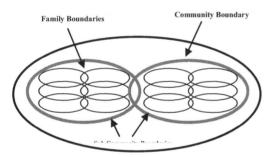

Figure 1. Source: Generated by the Author.
The structure of an ideal *Maasai* family and Community.

Maasai Traditional Education Systems

Peer-to-peer training has been an effective model for cultural education among the Maasai (Hudson, 1999). Among the Maasai, common methods of education were through observation, direct teaching, active participation, and cultural apprenticeship (Rogoff & Lave, 1999). Youngsters learnt through a rich oral tradition, which incorporated personal narratives, oral history, folktales, songs, parables, and cultural adages. Through these methods, adults transmitted cultural values and beliefs, and preserved stories about significant events and revered individuals from the past (Naimodu, 2012). These Maasai education traditions bore a great resemblance to many current best practices, such as oral communication, mentoring, problem-solving activities, active participation, personal examples, hands-on instruction, and experiential learning relevant to their daily lives (Bogonko, 1992; Kusuma-Powell, Powell & Phillips, 2000).

Rites of passage for both boys and girls played a key role in preparing children to become responsible adults and parents (Tarayia, 2004). Modern education systems

have since interfered with the traditional system of peer training as many Maasai now have access to modern education and are exposed to multi-cultural environment which do not reflect on Maasai cultural values (Hudgson, 1999). The interaction with other cultures has fostered multi-racial as well as multi-cultural marriages. Cross-ethnic families are common place now. This has greatly influenced the family structure and peer training (Sena, 1986), which is now done at schools and churches which delineates the children from their cultural orientation and creates a new culture and family set-up that is neither western nor Maasai. Cultural family values that were provided by traditional peer education are now being learned from diverse cultures and religions (Hudgson, 1999). These changes have created conflicts within families and between those adolescents who have had interaction outside the cultural setting and those who still get peer education from within Maasai cultural context (Hudgson, 1999).

The Cultural Value of Maa as an Indigenous Language

Maa played an important role in promoting the Maasai culture and giving Maasai children a sense of belonging and identity. The acquisition of Maa was part of the process by which a Maasai child absorbed his / her cultural environment. As observed by Letsie (2002: 198), any child will find it difficult to grasp any new concept that is alien to their cultural environment. Letsie goes on explaining explains that in learning any foreign language children may find it difficult to master the alien vocabulary and syntax sufficiently to express ideas in it. Swain (1982) as quoted in (Letsie, 2002: 198) observes that the mother tongue medium enhances the importance of local languages and identity.

The Maasai culture, ecological knowledge, customs and traditions found meaning in oral traditions and were mainly transmitted through Maa. In Kenya, the constitution recognizes culture as a foundation of the nation and as the cumulative civilization of the Kenyan people and nation. The Kenya Ministry of Gender, Sports, Culture and social Services is currently charged with the responsibility of promoting culture through various activities. However, the culture of the Maasai people has only been misused and exploited to earn the state some revenue in the lucrative tourism industry.

Globalization and its effects on the Maasai community

Globalization is a historical human process where competing ideologies which form the basis for global economic and political systems compete for dominance in resource ownership, access and control (Groody, 2007). It is a complex multidimensional process at many levels and involving multiple players, multiple cultures, diverse approaches and from different dimensions (Groody, 2007).

The end of the Second World War was followed by decolonization in Asia, Africa and the Middle East. The underdeveloped nations began to adopt the notion of development in order to be like the advanced nations of the West (Rozman, 2005). A process that was identified with economic growth. However, this process did not involve economic growth only, but it carried many other phenomena like social, cultural and political change (Gandolfo, 2009). It was a complex process of change that influenced a wide scope of life both of the individual and of society (Nyangira, 1975). This development led to the establishment of institutions in the underdeveloped countries that were meant to propel modernity (Nyangira, 1975). Modernization theories and Modernists regarded cultures of non-industrialized societies like that of the Maasai as obstacles to development. This was because of their kinship institutions that, according to the modernists, seemed to hinder individual enterprise and capitalism. They were perceived as traditional and barbaric to realize any development (Ntuli, 2002). According to Mittelmann (2000), globalization was characterized by economism, state-centricity and overemphasis within areas of interest. However, it is moral to note that globalization has not created a fair share of social ills. It has created inequalities (Groody, 2007), increased consumerism (Groody, 2007), ecological destruction (Groody, 2007), loss of cultural heritage (Jones, 2010) and pre-emptive wars to maintain economic, political and military dominance (Groody, 2007).

According to Bedelian (2012), Oxfam (2012), Thomson (2009), Galaty (1999) and Grandin (1986) the Maasai folk just like the rest of the communities in Africa, were introduced to modern conventions such as schools, large-scale agriculture, Western medicine, business, formal employment and a wage-based economy, and in the recent past, advanced telecommunication and cyber space. With such institutions, modernity has profoundly penetrated through the Maasai community and presented the modern values of life which have become the ultimate ideals of a "civilized" society. The colonial and post- independence governments have propagated these ideals and exerted pressure on the conservative communities like the Maasai to let go of their "primitive" ideals and traditions and instead embrace modernity (Naimodu, 2012).

Before modernization, a Maasai's personal identity revolved around the communal relationships he/she had with others. In pre-modern communities, a Maasai knew his/her position in the clan, family and community, but the modern age has since expanded the social roles (Hodgson, 2009). Linden (1991) also argues that when traditions are discontinued, cultural heritage and indigenous knowledge systems will be lost, unless the younger generations take interest in preserving their customs. He states that lack of interest in traditional knowledge, the "urbanization" and the "Westernization"

of the youth leads to a tribal culture without a soul (Linden, 1991).

Changing the Mara, Changing Maa, Changing the Maasai Cultural Structures

Before the formation of the colonial government, the life-style of most pastoral groups was spatially designed to provide a stable ecological foundation for their economy (Sindiga, 1984). The communal Maasai culture provided for an opportunity for socialization which was a process by which individuals become members of a particular culture and took on its values, beliefs, and other behaviors in order to function (Gardner & Kosmitzsky (2008: 54).

Traditionally, there was a high degree of interconnectedness between every member of the Maasai community either through birth, marriage, clan or age group; everyone belonged to a family, a clan, an age group, the community and tribe as a whole, the role of care giving was communal and the child's interaction was within family and other community members (Tarayia, 2004).

The Maasai tradition did not single out the responsibility of bringing up a child to the biological parents only. It was common to find an infant suckling several lactating mothers and as they grew up they slept together in groups, in houses belonging to elderly women in the homestead (Tarayia, 2004). While children were able to identify their biological parents, all women from the village were addressed as "mother" and all men as "father". Molding the children's character was a communal activity (Tarayia, 2004). Traditional practices meant to teach children cultural values, beliefs and social expectations were done communally through play and story- telling during specific moments by the elderly men and women (Sena, 1986).

In 1968, the Kenya Government came up with the (Group Representative) Act 1968 – which advocated for the formation of Group Ranches. Arising from the neoclassical economic theory and with the support of multi- lateral donors, a "group ranch" - was an organizational structure in which members held a collective title deed to an area of land while animals were owned and managed individually (Grandin, 1986). Day to day management of the ranch was the responsibility of a democratically elected committee with the right to incur debts and enforce its decisions on registered members (Grandin, 1986). This deviated from the traditional land management systems that was communal and disrupted the settlement patterns and family structure of the Maasai people (Galaty, 1999).

Saitoti (1981) states that though the Maasai have fought to maintain their traditional way of life for a long time, it is now evident that they can no longer resist the pressures of the modern world. The survival of Maasai culture has ceased to be a question (Saitoti, 1981). In truth, it is disappearing rapidly. According to Drinkwater (2010) the Maasai are currently struggling to maintain their traditions and are instead seeking alternatives means of survival by engaging in other forms of livelihood and practices that are unfamiliar to them. Mol (1996) argues that Maa language that once served as a powerful communication medium for the Maasai folk is gradually being corrupted by immigrant communities, placing it under stress.

Currently, research indicates that modernization has dispersed the traditional Maasai communities and converted Maasai settlements into individual family households - thus reducing the interaction between members of the larger Maasai community, and introduced new forms of socialization. The role of communal care giving in the Maasai community is gradually changing as many families begin to live in nuclear-family homesteads and child interaction is primary from the parents and siblings (Hodgson, 1999).

In the past, Maasai would help their clan members as well as age-mates or kin when times got tough by giving away their surplus, knowing that they would be helped in return (Masharen, 2009). However, these relationships are becoming stressed because many families are losing land and livestock at the same time and the Maasai folk have no place to turn to (Hogg, 1992; McCabe *et al.*, 1992). Cultural differences are emerging between the Maasai children who attend school and socialize in a multi-cultural environment and those who do not attend school or continue to be socialized within the traditional cultural context (Hogg, 1992).

Globalization has since brought in new dynamics. The characteristics of modern culture have brought new definitions for family. The gradual industrialization carried out by Local and Global Multi-national firms has pushed the Maasai out of Maasai Mara (ancestral land) and converted them into Nomads. The Valuable Maasai Indigenous knowledge systems acquired over generations is facing distinction. Radical modernization through schools and donor driven initiatives aimed at modernizing the Maasai community has brought in the emergence of new structures that are not in tandem with the Maasai settlement patterns (Nyangira, 1975). The presence of schools, religious institutions, business complexes and non-Maasai immigrant community cultures are now influencing most of the Maasai children, exposed to such environments. Change in livelihood patterns influenced by urbanization has forced many families to seek alternative employment other than relying on the traditional livestock-keeping for their livelihoods. Modern Maasai parents, with formal education, have lost their oral traditions and legendary story tellers are rapidly disappearing (Naimodu, 2012). Currently, Maasai men work away from their families, leaving women to for the needs of their children in the absence of their husbands (Tarayia,

2004). The modern Maasai families are becoming smaller as many men abandon polygamy and embrace Christianity and modernization (Naimodu, 2012). Communism has died and individualism has crept in gradually killing the ancient Maasai traditional knowledge systems, where everything was viewed from a communal perspective (Naimodu, 2012).

Summary and Conclusion

This paper sought to explore ways through which the new constitution of Kenya could be used as a catalyst in protecting and promoting the use of indigenous languages in Kenya. As elaborated, laws alone cannot develop and affect the use of these languages. More action needs to be taken in order to engagement all stakeholders. The Government of Kenya should come up with ways through which the article(s) on indigenous languages can be implemented.

To indigenous people like the Maasai, culture is a key ingredient not only in cognitive development but in the development of all aspects of their life. Culture gives them identity and a lasting connection between their cultural practices, patterns and traditional cognitive systems. Culture enables socialization which even though universal, is different from culture to culture (Bornstein & Lansford, 2010). This difference calls for an approach that is more inclusive of different cultures, and a need for appreciation of how different cultures conceptualize development and how cultural beliefs determine the holistic growth of a people.

Although Traditional institutions as well as indigenous issues are still critical to the Maasai people, globalization has contributed to the immense erosion of their culture, changed their community structures and negatively impacting family life. According to Robinson and Green (2011) globalization has restructured economic, political and social relationships at the indigenous level. Modernism, education and the movement of the indigenous people in search of better job opportunities have also undermined ancient indigenous communities. This modern social phenomenon has weakened the inter-connectedness and social bond of many communities around the world (Naimodu, 2012). Although the Maasai are arguably among the few ethnic groups in Kenya that bring the real picture and symbol of the "cultural" Kenya, their famous cultural identity is facing imminent challenges (Naimodu, 2012).

This paper reveals that the community is gradually abandoning their cultural values in favour of "progress". While there are positive aspects of modernization and development per se, the traditional Maasai family unit is facing greater challenges than ever before. Parenting which was once communal has become a sole responsibility of biological parents of the children; families are no longer large, peer training has been left to peers in schools and other non-traditional institutions

(Naimodu, 2012). While there exists no literature directly pointing out the impact of globalization on the Maasai child, Naimodu (2012) points out that Maasai children that have been exposed to other environments, have lost their culture, language, and respect for adults. Many of them are engaging in negative vices, once considered a taboo within the Maasai culture (i.e. Drugs abuse, early pregnancies, alcoholism, prostitution) etc.

References

Adegbija, E.E. (1994). *Language Attitudes in Sub-Saharan Africa: A Sociolinguistic Overview*. Cleveland: Multilingual Matters.

Asmara Declaration 2000 (2012). The Asmara Declaration on African languages and literature. In: C. Bedelian (Ed.), *Conservation and Ecotourism on Privatized Land in the Mara, Kenya. The Case of Conservancy Land Leases*. The Land Deal Politics Initiative.

Bogonko, S.N. (1992). *A History of Modern Education in Kenya (1895-1991)*. Nairobi: Evans Brothers.

Bornstein, M. & Lansford, J. E. (2010). Parenting. In L.S. Davids. L.S (200.), The Pedagogical Advantages of Mother Tongue Instruction in the Formative Years of Schooling: The Case of Khoekhoegowab. The University of Namibia.

Fafunwa, B.A. (1996). Using national languages in education: A challenge to African educators. In K. Legere (Ed.), *African Languages in Basic Education. Proceedings of the First Workshop onAfrican Languages in Basic Education. National Institute for Educational Development (NIED) Okahadja 18-23 September 1995* (pp. 151-164). Windhoek: Garmberg Macmillan Publishers.

Galaty, J.G. (1999). The rhetoric of rights: Construing Maasai land claims. *The Arid Lands and Resource Management Network in Eastern Africa*. 7: 1-13.

Gandolfo, A.J. (2009). Education-medium and African linguistic rights in the context of globalization. *Globalization, Societies and Education* 7(3), 321-336.

Grandin, B, de Leeuw, P, & Ole-Pasha, I. (1991). The Study Area: Socio-spatial organization and land use. In, Bekure, S., de Leeuw, P, Grandin, B. & Neate, P. (Eds.), *Maasai Herding: An Analysis of the Livestock Production System of Maasai Pastoralists in Eastern Kajiado District, Kenya* (pp. 57-70). Addis Ababa.

Heine, B. & Möhlig J.G. (1990). *Language and Dialect Atlas of Kenya* (Vol 1). Berlin: Dietrich Reimer Verlag.

Hodgson, D.L. (1999). *Once Intrepid Warriors: Modernity and the Production of Maasai Masculinities*. Pittsburgh: University of Pittsburgh.

Hodgson, D.L. (2004). Once Intrepid Warriors: Gender, and the Cultural Politics of Maasai Development. Bloomington: Indiana University Press.

International Labor Organization (2009). *The Rights of Indigenous Peoples: Kenya*. International Labor Organization and the African Commission on the Human and People's Right on the Constitutional and Legislative Protection.

King'ei, K. (2001). Challenges and opportunities in the development of African languages in Kenya: A contemporary perspective". In Mdee & Mwansoko (Eds.) *Makala ya Kongamano la Kimataifa la Kiswahili Proceedings*. Dar es Salaam: TUKI.

Koissaba B.R.O. (May 2013). Effects of Globalization in the Maasai Family. Clemson University.

Legere, K. (Ed.) *African Languages in Basic Education: Proceedings of the First Workshop on African languages in Basic Education. National Institute for Educational Development (NIED) Okahandja 18- 23, September 1995* (41-79) Windhoek: Gemberg Macmillan Publishers.

Letsie, M.M. (2002). African languages as media of instruction. In. F.R. Owino (Ed.) *Speaking African: African Languages for Education Development* (195-202). Cape Town: The Centre for Advanced Studies of African Society.

Luoch, T.O & Ogutu, E. (2002) The Use of Mother Tongue and Tribalism: A Misconceived Association. In F.R. Owino (Ed.) *Speaking African: African Languages for Education Development*. Cape Town: The Centre for Advanced Studies of African Society.

Matsinhe, S. (2004) Dwindling numbers of Students enrolling for African languages Courses: Problems and Possibilities. In B. Brock-Une *et al.* (Eds). *Researching the Language of Instruction in Tanzania and South Africa* (pp. 13-24). Cape Town: African Minds.

Masheren, S.O. (2009). *The Maasai Pioneers. The First Modern Cream*. Nairobi: Resil Print.

Mazrui, A.A. & Mazrui, A.M. (1995). *Swahili State and Society: The Political Economy of an African Language*. Nairobi: East African Educational Publishers.

Musau, P. (1999). Constraints on the Acquisition Planning of Indigenous African Languages: The Case of Kiswahili in Kenya." In: Eoghan Mac Aogain et al (eds.). *Language, Culture and Curriculum*. Linguistic Institute of Ireland. Vol. 12. No. 2. 117-127.

Muthwii, M. (2002). *Language Policy and Practices in Education in Kenya and Uganda: Perception of Parents, Pupils and Teachers on the Use of Mother Tongue, Kiswahili and English in Primary Schools*. Nairobi: Phoenix Publishers.

Mbaabu, I. (1996). *Language Policy in East Africa: A Dependency Theory Perspective.* Nairobi. Educational Research and Publication.

MCSF (2004). A memorandum on the Anglo-Masaai agreements: A case of historical and contemporary injustices on Maasai land. In F. Mol (Ed.) *Maasai Language and Culture.* Limuru (Kenya): Kolbes Press.

Mwangi, E. (2007). Subdividing the commons: Distributional conflict in the transition from collective to individual property rights in Kenya's Maasai land. *World Development* 35(5), 815-834.

Naimodu, J (2012). Unpublished Masters Dissertation.

Ngugi, P. (2009). Language and Literary Education: The State of Children's literature in Kenya.

Nyangira, N. (1975). Relative Modernization and Public resource allocation in Kenya.

Ogechi N. (2003). "On Language Rights in Kenya." In: *Nordic Journal of African Studies* 12(3): 277-295.

Republic of Kenya. (2010). *The New Constitution of Kenya.* Nairobi. Government Printers.

Saitoti T. (1981). *Maasai.* London: Elm Books.

Selepe, T. (2002). Constitutional provision versus practices: The South African experience with African languages. In Francis R. Owino (Ed.) *Speaking African: African Languages for Education Development* (pp. 203-212). Cape Town: The Centre for Advanced Studies of African society.

Sena, S. (1986). Pastoralists and education: School participation and social change among the Maasai. PhD. dissertation, McGill University.

Sindiga, I. (1984). Land and population problems in Kajiado and Narok Kenya. *Africa Studies Review* 27.

Tarayia, G.N. (2004). The legal perspectives of the Maasai culture, customs, and traditions. *Arizona Journal of International & Comparative Law* 21(1).

Thompson, M. Serneels, S., Kaelo, D. & Trench, P. (2009). Maasai Mara land privatization. T.P. Chevenix (Ed.), *Staying Maasai? Livelihoods, Conservation and Development in East African Rangelands.* New York: Springer.

UNESCO (1953). *The Use of Vernacular Language in Education.* Paris: UNESCO.

Vossen, R. (1988). *Maasai Language Dialects.* Hamburg: Buske.

Whiteley, W.H. (Ed). (1974). *Language in Kenya.* Nairobi: Oxford University Press.

Wolff, H.E. (2002). The heart of the "African language Question" in education. In F.R. Owino (Ed.) *Speaking African: African Languages for Education Development* (pp. 129-148.). Cape Town: The Centre for Advanced Studies of African society.

Zommers, A. (2010) Globalization and the foreignisation of space: Seven processes driving the current global land grab. *The Journal of Peasant Studies* 37(2): 429-447.

Indigenous Australian Stories and Sea-Level Change

Nicholas language

School of Behavioural, Cognitive and
Social Sciences
University of New England,
Armidale
NSW 2351, Australia
[nreid@une.edu.au]

Patrick D. Nunn

Sustainability Research Centre
University of the Sunshine Coast
Queensland 4556, Australia
[pnunn@usc.edu.au]

Margaret Sharpe

School of Behavioural, Cognitive and
Social Sciences
University of New England, Armidale
NSW 2351, Australia
[msharpe3@une.edu.au]

Abstract

Oral traditions, especially contrasted with written history, are typically portrayed as inaccurate. Commenting on native title claims in the US, Simic (2000) made the specific claim: "As a general rule, unwritten legends that refer to events more than 1,000 years in the past contain little, if any, historical truth". So can preliterate Indigenous languages tell us anything factual about the distant past, or does the transmission of historical facts become inevitably corrupted?

Changes in sea levels around the Australian coast are now well established. Marine geographers can now point to specific parts of the Australian coast and know with some confidence what the sea levels were at a particular time before the present. This paper reports on a substantial body of Australian Aboriginal stories that appear to represent genuine and unique observations of post-glacial increases in sea level, at time depths that range from about 13,400–7,500 years BP. This paper makes the case that endangered Indigenous languages can be repositories for factual knowledge across time depths far greater than previously imagined, forcing a rethink of the ways in which such traditions have been dismissed.

Oral Traditions and Sea-Level Change

Academically oriented history, as conceived of within literate cultures, once drew a clean line between "documented facts" and "oral traditions", and viewed the latter as having dubious worth over any significant time depth. In recent decades however, the idea that oral traditions might contribute to an understanding of natural phenomena has begun to gain increasing acceptance (Vitaliano, 1973; Piccardi & Masse, 2007). Perhaps the best examples involve cataclysmic events, such as the Klamath traditions about Mt Mazama in Oregon, USA, which appear to have endured in recognisable form for more than 7,000 years. Other traditions concerning now-extinct animals and extra-terrestrial objects are increasingly being considered as candidates for phenomena based on genuine observation.

Such stories, as well as those stories about flooding events described in many cultures, are good candidates to enter the oral tradition canon precisely because of their cataclysmic nature and great, and usually negative, impacts on the lives of people. By way of contrast, despite often being rapid in geological time, sea-level change may be barely detectable across a human lifespan, and therefore stories about it less likely to inform oral traditions.

There is now a wealth of scientific research focussed on coastal change in Australia, and changes in post-glacial sea levels around the Australian coast are now well established. The sensitivity of these changes to a range of glacio-/hydro-/isostatic processes, are also well mapped out, such that different parts of the Australian coast are understood to have undergone change at different times and rates (Lewis *et al.*, 2013). Marine geographers can now point to specific parts of the Australian coast and

say with considerable confidence that "Given known bathymetry, the sea here was X metres lower than present levels at Y time depth before the present day (BP)." However, there has been scant attention paid by the scientific community to how Indigenous oral traditions compare with these new scientifically informed sea-level change chronologies, despite the fact that Australia provides a surprisingly large number of relevant traditions.

This paper reports in brief on a wider research project interrogating Australian Aboriginal traditions of this kind, and comparing them explicitly with scientifically-derived chronologies in order to explore whether the ages for the initial observations underlying these traditions might be credibly determined.

Postglacial Australia: People and Sea Level

People arrived in Australia at least 50,000–40,000 years BP (O'Connell & Allen, 1998), perhaps earlier, but certainly before the Last Glacial Maximum (26,000 to 20,000 BP) when sea level reached its lowest point (120m below present). After the end of the Last Glacial Maximum, through the period 20,000–7,000 BP, the sea level rose (not always steadily) until about 7,000–6,000 years BP[30] when it reached a maximum around most parts of Australia. Over the last 6,000 years sea levels have been stable or trending downwards slightly. On a purely logical basis then, Australian coastal traditions about sea-level rise would reflect well what was actually happening during the period 18,000–6,000 years BP, but

---

[30] Years BP (Before Present) refers to calendar years before AD 1950.

would not be a good reflection of the actual stability of the last 6,000 years.

In the period prior to the sea-level high, say 18,000–7,000 BP, Aboriginal people have routinely occupied coastal environments which have since been covered by the sea, and in many cases buried by sediment. Such sites represent a part of the prehistoric record that is lost forever (Allen & Kershaw, 1996). The main sources from which we might learn about Aboriginal people's interactions with the coast during this period are oral traditions describing coastal change and the associated disruptions of coastal livelihoods. Such traditions tend to come in one of two forms: stories of narrated historical fact without obvious embellishment; or as myths in which observed changes are attributed to the acts of ancestral beings. As presented here, these traditions are from written records of orally-transmitted knowledge that date from early in the post-European contact history of Australia after 1788 when "curious, observant, and relatively unprejudiced individuals in all parts of Australia wrote down descriptions of Aboriginal ceremonies, recorded versions of Aboriginal myths and tales and sometimes gave the texts and even occasionally the musical scores of songs" (Clunies Ross, 1986: 233).

The 6 traditions

The Australian coastal traditions are generally of two thematic types:

1. stories about how a prior single landmass came to be two landmasses separated by a water gap. Here we discuss Fitzroy Island (Queensland) as such an example.

2. stories about how people could once cross a water gap by wading or swimming where such a feat would be impossible today. Here we discuss Rottnest Island (Western Australia) as such an example.

This larger project has unearthed a considerable number of such traditions. For this paper we'll discuss just the two listed above in some detail, and list in truncated form the assumed sea levels and dates for four others (Spencer Gulf, Bathurst and Melville Islands, Kangaroo Island, and Port Phillip Bay (see Figure 1).

Figure 1: Map of Australia showing the extent of the continental shelf exposed during the Last Glacial Maximum

We interpret these six Aboriginal traditions using local sea-floor bathymetry to estimate the minimum levels below present sea level at which these details would be true. By comparing these minimum levels to known post-glacial sea-level change, an age range for the most recent time at which the particular traditions could have originated is determined.

Tradition 1: Rottnest, Carnac and Garden Islands

There is an Aboriginal tradition that the Western Australian Rottnest, Carnac and Garden Islands, which were once settled by Aboriginal people then abandoned before European arrival, "once formed part of the mainland, and that the intervening ground was thickly covered with trees; which took fire in some unaccountable way, and burned with such intensity that the ground split asunder with a great noise, and the sea rushed in between, cutting off these islands from the mainland" (Moore, 1978[1884]: 8).

The detail that this dry-land connection was "covered with trees" does, if true, strengthen the interpretation of this tradition as dating from a time when sizeable areas of the present sea floor were beyond the reach of high tide and were able to support a lowland forest that could burn.

The bathymetry of the area is shown in Figure 2. For Rottnest island to have "formed part of the mainland", the sea level would have to have been 5–10m lower than present, most likely 7–8m lower than present if walkers kept to the (now-shallower) middle parts of the routes. Both Carnac and Garden Islands could have been reached when the sea level was 5m shallower than present.

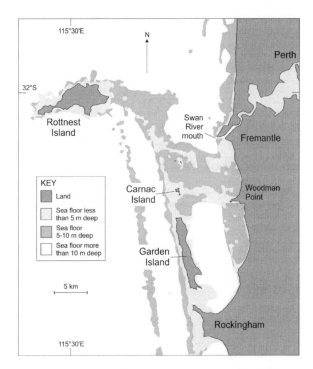

Figure 2: Part of Western Australia showing locations of Rottnest, Carnac and Garden Islands[31]

Assuming that the tradition described derives from an observation during a time when sea level was at least 7–8m below present, then this tradition must date from at least 7,500–8,900 years BP (see Figure 4), considerably older than an earlier published estimate for this tradition of 6,500 BP (Playford, 1983).

Tradition 2: Fitzroy Island

Off the coast of northern Queensland lies the Great Barrier Reef. In the Cairns region, where the edge of the Great Barrier Reef is 50km from shore, an early report states that "the Googanji natives … say that before the flood the Barrier Reef was the original coastline, and that a river entered the sea near what is known as Fitzroy Island" (Gribble, 1933: 7). More details come from a later story collected from the Yidindji people –

> a theme running through all the coastal Yidinj myths is that the coastline was once where the barrier reef now stands … but the sea then rose and the shore retreated to its present position. The only common noun denoting 'island' is *djaruway*, which also means 'small hill' – contrasting with *bunda* 'mountain, big hill'. The proper name of Fitzroy Island is *gabar* 'lower arm', so called because most of this geographical feature [a promontory of the mainland] was submerged and only one extension remains above water. Note also that there was a place half-way between Fitzroy Island and King Beach that was called *mudaga* ('pencil cedar') after the trees which grew there; it is now completely

submerged. Again Green Island is said to have been at one time four times as big as it is now – only the northwest portion remains above water. (Dixon, 1977: 14-15)

The present geography of the area is shown in Figure 3A. For Fitzroy Island to be connected to the mainland, as the latter tradition states, the sea level would need to be 23–25m lower than today. For the coast to be "where the barrier reef now stands", it is probably necessary for sea level to be at least 50m lower than today, depending on what people recognised as the "barrier reef".

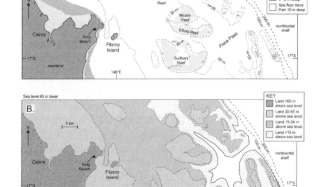

Figure 3: The area between Cairns and the nearby edge of the Great Barrier Reef, showing:
A. the present day geography of Fitzroy Island
B. the palaeogeography of the area when sea level was 65m lower than today approx. 13,355–12,560 years BP

It has been argued that during the Last Glacial Maximum, when what is now the Great Barrier Reef was emergent, the coast would have been bordered with cliff-line and unattractive to humans (Bowdler, 1995). Only later, as sea level rose over the edge of the continental shelf and a lowland terrestrial landscape developed that was both easy to access and contained diverse ecosystems, might people have been encouraged to occupy the area (Figure 3B).

If the stories quoted, and the others that Dixon (1977) alludes to, recall a time when the coastline was at the Great Barrier Reef, these would have to date from a time when sea level was perhaps somewhere in the range 30–65 m below present. As shown in Figure 3, most of the shelf/reef off Cairns would have been dry land when sea level was 65m lower, yet large parts of the area would still have been emergent when sea level was 30m lower. Much depends on how modern storytellers conceptualise what is and what was formerly meant by the (barrier) reef. The large range of former sea levels results in a large range of minimum ages for these particular traditions: 10,450–9,900 years BP if

---

[31] Here and in all figures Bathymetry is derived from Australian Hydrographic Service charts.

they refer to a time when sea level was 30m lower; 13,400–12,600 years BP if they refer to a time when sea level was 65m lower (see Figures 3B and 4).

Tradition 3: Spencer's Gulf

The Narrangga people tell a story that Spencer's Gulf was once a broad low-relief floodplain with a line of fresh-water lagoons, stretching northwards for a hundred miles or more, which was flooded by sea water.

If the tradition refers to the inundation of the mouth of Spencer Gulf, then the sea level would have been around 50m below that of today, requiring that the tradition date from as much as 12,450–11,150 years BP. Being more cautious, if the tradition referred to the inundation of just the northern part of Spencer Gulf, then its present maximum depth of 22m would suggest a time depth of 9,900–9,550 years BP.

Tradition 4: Bathurst and Melville Islands

The Tiwi story of the formation of Bathurst and Melville Islands involves an old blind woman, Mudangkala, *"who crawled between the islands as freshwater flowed in behind her, forming Clarence Strait. She continued to move over the land known as Bathurst Island till finally water flowed in to form what is now known as Apsley Strait"* (Sims, 1978: 165).

This story can be interpreted as recalling the discovery and occupation of these islands by Mudangkala and her family, by crossing Clarence Strait and later Apsley Strait without reference to watercraft, perhaps through a combination of walking, wading and swimming. For this to represent the activity of human ancestors, the sea level would need to be 12–15m lower in the Clarence and Apsley Straits than current levels, which was true between 9,650–8,200 years BP.

Tradition 5: Kangaroo Island

The Jaralde people have a story about how Kangaroo Island was once a dry crossing which became inundated and separated by the sea. The story concerns Ngurunderi pursuing his two wives westwards along the South Australian coast, when they sought refuge on Kangaroo Island which was then *"almost connected with the mainland, and it was possible for people to walk across"* (Berndt, 1940: 181). Ngurunderi caused the sea to rise and drown them, turning them into rocks in what is now the channel separating Kangaroo Island from the mainland.

If the Ngurunderi stories recall the submergence of the land connection between Kangaroo Island and the adjacent mainland, this would have occurred when the sea level was 28–32m below its present level, which it was been 10,650–9,800 years BP.

Tradition 6: Port Phillip Bay

There are numerous traditions about a time when Port Phillip Bay, at the head of which is the mouth of the Yarra River around which the city of Melbourne now lies, was dry land. The descendants of the Yarra and coast tribes *"recollected when Hobson's [Port Phillip] Bay was a kangaroo ground; they say 'Plenty catch kangaroo and plenty catch opossum there' ... the river [Yarra] once went out at the Heads, but that the sea broke in, and that Hobson's Bay, which was once a hunting ground, became what it is"* (Hull, 1859: 12).

An assumed sea level 8–12m lower than present for when postglacial sea level was just below the outer lip of the Bay at the western end of South Channel[32] places those traditions at 9,350–7,800 years BP. Dating of marine and freshwater palaeo-environmental indicators on either side of entrance to the Bay show that at the time when sea level reached the level of the entrance, this became blocked and inundation actually occurred at 7,217 years BP (Holdgate *et al.*, 2011).

The understood sea-level rise envelope within which the events described in these 6 stories might be plotted, is given in Figure 4.

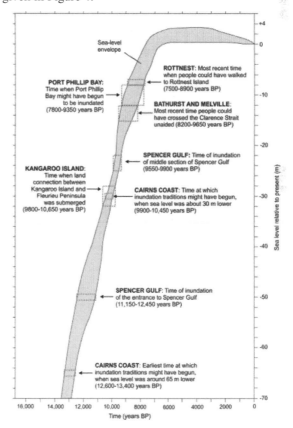

Figure 4: Post-glacial sea-level rise envelope, with datings of events that might be described in the 6 stories.

Discussion

Were there only a single isolated tradition known from Aboriginal traditions in Australia about coastal inundation

---

[32] Estimated from data in Holdgate *et al.* (2001).

that might be associated with postglacial sea-level rise, then in all likelihood it would be regarded as an anomaly, lacking credibility and probably invented significantly more recently. The 6 stories touched on here all point in a remarkably uniform way to sea-level changes that occurred in the few thousand years preceding the sea level high of 7,000 years BP. There are more Australian traditions reporting much the same thing, and a general lack of stories involving sea levels dropping and exposing land that was once under the sea. While there is understandably some uncertainty about the likely/possible ages of traditions from particular sites, there seems little doubt that they do actually recall the time when rising postglacial sea level attained the level of the continental shelf locally and rapidly inundated coastal lowlands.

The lack of any systematic analysis of these traditions, may be due to the scepticism with which most scientists might instinctively regard the attribution of scientific credibility to oral traditions that date back several thousand years. That scepticism still runs deep. For example, Andrei Simic, professor of Anthropology (USCLA, California), who specialises in the role played by folklore and oral tradition in the formation and development of the cultural identity of ethnic groups, commenting on native title claims in the north American context, in an affidavit on the Kennewick Man case writes:

> It is one thing to use folklore and oral tradition as a means of ascertaining or demonstrating what the members of an ethnic group believe (or once believed) about the world and their collective past. It is another thing entirely to use folklore and oral tradition as proof of the truth of what the group believes. As a general rule, folklore and oral tradition are not stable enough to be taken as inherently accurate witnesses of events from the remote past... As a general rule, unwritten legends that refer to events more than 1,000 years in the past contain little, if any, historical truth … (Simic, 2002)

The evidence provided in this paper of widespread, consistent, and datable stories describing events prior to 7,000 years BP, suggests that such a view is unnecessarily pessimistic. Rather, the extraordinary care with which Aboriginal people have passed down these stories over previously unimaginable time depths forces a rethink of the ways in which such oral traditions have previously been dismissed. While these examples should not be regarded as a licence for the incautious interpretation of the antiquity of oral traditions, or indeed for the belief all such stories have empirical foundations, it does allow for some traditions in some cultures to have survived far longer than it was once thought any such traditions could.

And the picture presented here is far richer than suggested, because to sea-level traditions we can add stories about other independently datable events: the eruption-linked formation of crater lakes on the Atherton Tableland (Queensland) which may date from 13,000 years BP (Dixon, 1991); the eruption of Mt Gambier (South Australia) 4,300–4,600 years BP (Smith, 1880; Sutherland, 1995); and Aboriginal traditions about encounters with extinct megafauna several thousand years ago (Flood, 1989; Vickers-Rich & Archbold, 1991; Sharpe & Tunbridge, 1997).

Australian Aboriginal people's wealth of such deep time-depth stories stands out as exceptional among the corpus of such traditions globally, inviting speculation about what kind of cultural attributes might have fostered the accurate carrying of information in this way. The practice and nature of Aboriginal storytelling is likely to be key, particularly the ways in which it was ritually embedded in cultural practice, both routine and occasional, and the explicit teaching of 'Law', the deliberate tracking of teaching responsibilities, coupled with high evaluation of unchangedness as a doctrinal principle, which encouraged the learning and onward transmission of particular traditions by successive generations (Berndt & Berndt, 1989).

The Australian case studies described in this paper all involve stories which were carefully nursed through millenia, and told in languages that currently are severely endangered or moribund. Having largely ignored these languages and their 'myths' for the last two hundred years, the scientific community has come late to the realisation that endangered Aboriginal languages might be storehouses of knowledge about current natural phenomena, with research institutions like the CSIRO showing keen interest in Indigenous fire management practices, and Indigenous perspectives on riverine ecologies, calendric cycles and animal behaviours, etc. The evidence presented in this paper further demonstrates that endangered Indigenous languages and their oral traditions can also be repositories for factual knowledge about natural phenomena across surprisingly deep time depths, with the potential in some cases to elevate the initiators of oral traditions from story tellers and myth makers to eyewitnesses to history.

References

Allen, J. & Kershaw, P. (1996). The Pleistocene-Holocene transition in Greater Australia. In L.G. Straus, B.V. Eriksen, J.M. Erlandson, & D.R. Yesner (Eds.), *Humans at the End of the Ice Age: The Archaeology of the Pleistocene-Holocene Transition* (pp. 175-199). New York: Plenum Press.

Berndt, R.M. (1940). Some aspects of Jaralde culture, South Australia. *Oceania*, 11(2), 164-185.

Berndt, R.M. & Berndt, C.H. (1989) *The Speaking Land: Myth and Story in Aboriginal Australia.* Ringwood, Vic: Penguin.

Berndt, R.M. & Berndt, C.H. (1996). *The World of the First Australians. Aboriginal Traditional Life: Past and Present*. Canberra: Aboriginal Studies Press.

Bowdler, S. (1995). Offshore islands and maritime explorations in Australian prehistory. *Antiquity*, 69(266), 945-958.

Clunies Ross, M. (1986). Australian Aboriginal oral traditions. *Oral Tradition*, 1(2), 231-271.

Dixon, R.M.W. (1977). *A Grammar of Yidiɲ*. Cambridge: Cambridge University Press.

Dixon, R.M.W. (1980) *The Languages of Australia*. Cambridge: Cambridge University Press.

Dixon, R.M.W. (Ed.) (1991). *Words of Our Country: Stories, Place Names and Vocabulary in Yidiny, the Aboriginal Language of the Cairns-Yarrabah Region* St Lucia, Qld: University of Queensland Press.

Flood, J. (1989). *Archaeology of the Dreamtime: The Story of Prehistoric Australia and Its People*. New Haven: Yale University Press.

Gribble, E.R. (1933). *The Vanishing Aboriginals of Australia*. Sydney: Australian Board of Missions.

Holdgate G.R., Geurin, B., Wallace, M.W., & Gallagher, S.J. (2001). Marine geology of Port Phillip, Victoria. *Australian Journal of Earth Sciences*, 48(3), 439-455.

Holdgate, G.R., Wagstaff, B. & Gallagher S.J. (2011). Did Port Phillip Bay nearly dry up between ~2800 and 1000 Cal. Yr BP? Bay floor channelling evidence, seismic and core dating. *Australian Journal of Earth Sciences*, 58(2), 157-175.

Hull, W. (1859). *Report of the Select Committee of the Legislative Council on the Aborigines*, (1858-9 Victoria). Melbourne: Government of Australia.

O'Connell, J. F. & Allen, J. (1998). When did humans first arrive in greater Australia and why is it important to know? *Evolutionary Anthropology*, 6(4), 132-146.

Lewis, S.E., Sloss, C.R., Murray-Wallace, C.V., Woodroffe, C.D., & Smithers, S.G. (2013). Post-glacial sealevel changes around the Australian margin: A review. *Quaternary Science Reviews*, 74, 115-138.

Moore, G.F. (1978[1884]). *Diary of Ten Years Eventful Life of an Early Settler in Western Australia; and Also a Descriptive Vocabulary of the Language of the Aborigines*. (facsimile edition). Nedlands, WA: University of Western Australia Press.

Piccardi, L. & Masse, W.B. (Eds.) (2007). *Myth and Geology*. London: Geological Society of London.

Playford, P.E. (1983). Geological research on Rottnest Island. *Journal of the Royal Society of Western Australia*, 66(1&2), 10-15.

Sharpe, M. & Tunbridge, D. (1997). Traditions of extinct animals, changing sea-levels and volcanoes among Australian Aboriginals: Evidence from linguistic and ethnographic research." In R. Blench & M. Spriggs (Eds.), *Archaeology and Language I: Theoretical and Methodological Orientations* (pp. 345-361). London: Routledge.

Simic, A. (2002). The Kennewick Man Case: Court Documents: Affidavits & Declarations. Affidavit addressing oral tradition and cultural affiliation. Affidavit of Andrei Simic. http://www.friendsofpast.org/kennewick-man/court/affidavits/oral-tradition-5.html

Sims, M. (1978). Tiwi Cosmology. In L.R. Hiatt (Ed.) *Australian Aboriginal Concepts* (pp. 164-167). Canberra: Australian Institute of Aboriginal Studies.

Smith, J. (1880). *Booandick Tribe of South Australian Aborigines: A Sketch of Their Habits, Customs, Legends and Language*. Adelaide: Government Printer.

Sutherland, L. (1995). *The Volcanic Earth*. Sydney: University of New South Wales Press.

Vickers-Rich, P. & Archbold, N.W. (1991). Squatters, priests and professors: A brief history of vertebrate palaeontology in *Terra Australis*. In P. Vickers-Rich, J.M. Monaghan, R.F. Baird, & T.H. Rich (Eds.), *Vertebrate Palaeontology of Australasia* (pp. 1-44). Melbourne, Vic: Pioneer Design Studios and Monash University Publications Committee.

Vitaliano, D. (1973). *Legends of the Earth: Their Geologic Origins*. Bloomington, IN: Indiana University Press.

The Encroachment of Personal Names and Naming System of the Hadzabe

Amani Lusekelo
Department of Languages and Literature
Dar es Salaam University College of Education,
P. O. Box 2329, Dar es Salaam, Tanzania
[alusekelo@duce.ac.tz]

Abstract

The culture of the Hadzabe people, the remaining hunter-gather "very minority" community of Tanzania, is highly endangered due to contacts with non-foragers. Endangerment appears in their onomastics as well. African communities cherish naming practices which are determined by, among others, circumstances-at-birth and kinship relationships. Findings reported herein indicate that foreign names and current naming systems amongst the Swahili speakers encroach the indigenous naming system of the Hadzabe. The Hadzabe of Yaeda Chini in northern Tanzania show three layers of personal names: (i) only a few Hadzabe people maintain their ancestral and traditional names, e.g. *Maroba, Zinzi, !ayaima and Tlaa*, a replica of the ancestral nomenclature in the community; (ii) many Hadzabe people use "joke names" as their formal names, e.g. *Shandalua* 'mosquito net', *Katambuga* 'shoes', *Mkuyu* 'baobab tree', *Tlutheya* 'man in the wilderness'; and (iii) to most Hadzabe, one of their formal personal name is either Christian, e.g. *Yohana, Joeli, Mathayo* or a borrowed name e.g. *Athumani, Isa, Akhwesu, Hamisi, Safari*. Changing of naming system is worse for names of school children because foreign names replace traditional Hadzabe names.

Introducing *Hadzabe* and their culture

Three factors, among other characteristics, distinguish the Hadzabe people. Firstly, the Hadzabe are the only remaining hunter-gather "very minority" community of Tanzania (Madsen, 2000; Marlowe, 2002; Petersen, 2012) who speak a *Khoisan* or *click* language (Brenzinger 2007b: 181). As for their livelihoods, anthropological findings point out that the Hadzabe maintain a system of livelihood similar to that of the first generation of the mankind because they "form a small nomadic people who live in camps" (Woodburn, 1970: 18). Additional information by Marlowe (2004: 366-367) indicates that the Hadzabe live in camps of about 25 people; with continuous changes of camp members and locations.

Another characteristic feature of the Hadzabe is that until today they have had contacts with non-foragers (the agro-pastoralists Afro-Asiatic Iraqw, pastoralist Nilotic Datooga and Maasai and agro-pastoral Nyiramba Bantu) at least for the past century and yet some 300-400 Hadzabe have persisted as full-time foragers (Marlowe, 2004: 366). It is argued that men and boys persistently hunt mammals and birds with bows and arrows and collect wild honey while women and girls steadily gather seeds, pick berries, dig edible roots and collect baobab fruits (Woodburn, 1970; Marlowe, 2004). In the camps, they share hunted and gathered food (Marlowe, 2004: 366).

The third distinguishing feature of the Hadzabe people is that they speak a fascinating language with "its rich consonant inventory, including clicks, ejective stops and affricates, and lateral fricatives and affricates" (Sands *et al.*, 1996: 171). Most of the languages with such properties are found in Southern Africa, mainly in Botswana, Namibia and South Africa (Sands *et al.*, 1996; Batibo, 2005; Brenzinger, 2007b).

In this article, I argue that continued and current contacts with a large number of pastoralists (Datooga and Maasai speakers), large populations of the Bantu speaking people (agro-pastoralists Nyiramba, Sukuma and Isanzu), the Cushitic speaking Iraqw, and many Swahili speaking non-foragers tend to influence Hadzabe culture. The influence is highly felt in areas connected to formal institutions such as schools and modernization processes such as trade. This article reports that change of the Hadzabe culture is also demonstrated in the way names and naming system of the Hadzabe change.

The customary *homeland* of the Hadzabe

Lake Eyasi area

The hunter-gatherer community of the nomadic Hadzabe customarily practise their livelihoods around Lake Eyasi in northern Tanzania. Since their population is very small, and non-foragers invaded the territory, it had been hard for the Hadzabe to establish and maintain their homeland.

Administratively, Lake Eyasi area is located in four regions in the country, which makes it hard to count them. Thus, their different population estimates is an indicator of endangerment. Most information in literature, both old and new, mention 1000 Hadzabe (Woodburn, 1970; Madsen, 2000; Marlowe, 2004; Peterson 2012). In my opinion, this estimate is too small. Muzale and Rugemalira (2008: 80) claim that the Hadzabe number 6289 persons. This is too large, in my opinion. My informants say Hadzabe speakers are estimated to be between 1500 and 3500. Given all these facts, I assume Hadzabe people are about 1800, scattered as follows:

Region	District	Ward	Population
Arusha	Karatu	Mang'ola	600
Manyara	Mbulu	Yaeda Chini	1,000
Shinyanga	Meatu	Pachi	100
Singida	Iramba	Mwonguli/ Mwengeza	100
Total			**1800**

The location and population of the Hadzabe

Earlier researchers such as Woodburn (1970), Madsen (2000) and Marlowe (2002) found that the Hadzabe occupy marginal-lands in dry-Savannah which is further degraded by human activities, mainly pastoralism practised by Datooga and Maasai and agriculture by Sukuma, Iraqw and Nyiramba.

The literature shows that one of the significant changes that occurred in Hadzabe homeland is an influx of pastoralists (Datooga) around 1950s (Young, 2008), agro-pastoral communities (Cushitic Iraqw) and agricultural communities (Isanzu Bantu) after villagization in the late 1960s and early 1970s (Ndagala, 1991; Madsen, 2000). This had had adverse impact on natural land in which Hadzabe gathered food staff and hunted wild game.

Yaeda Chini valley: The research areas

The encroachment of the Hadzabe is noticed even with my current findings from Yaeda Chini ward in Mbulu district. This area is located at the mid of Savannah dryland. It is bordered by a large dry-lake valley which is occupied mainly by Datooga people. The Hadzabe and other people call it *Mbugani*. There is a bush-land (savannah forest) which is mainly occupied mainly by Hadzabe, the hunter-gatherers. This part of the ward is traditionally referred to as *Mwituni*. Scattered homesteads are at the heart of the villages where I found mixed cultures, mostly Nyaisanzu and Nyiramba Bantu and Iraqw Cushites. The homesteads here are referred to as *Yaeda*.

The housing patterns, one of the cultures of African communities (Sisson, 1984), are different in the area. For instance, there are typical Hadzabe temporary homesteads (called *camps* in the literature (Madsen, 2000; Marlowe, 2002) which are made of grass and trees (bush). Such houses are different from Datooga homestead (called *gheda*) which "consists of a large, round, fenced-in compound containing houses for family members and enclosures for domestic animals" (Tomikawa, 1978: 5). Due to modernisation, *mixed cultures* houses are made of bricks, trees, grass, and corrugated iron sheets.

Administrative matters of this ward are situated at Yaeda. There are two government (public) schools at Yaeda, namely Yaeda Chini Primary School and Yaeda Chini Secondary School. A small dispensary and a veterinary centre are also situated at Yaeda Chini.

The situation at Yaeda Chini area permits language contacts between Hadzabe speakers and communities speaking Bantu, Cushitic and Nilotic languages. The establishment of the government institutions in the area (schools, veterinary centre and small dispensary) brings to the area Swahili culture. This contact situation has a lot to deal with in this paper because they cause encroachment to the Hadzabe culture.

Understanding *culture* via *onomastics*

The literature on African onomastics

The theory of anthroponomy in onomastics offers a good tool to analyse names and naming systems because it links language with cultural resources and community practises (Messing, 1974; Brenzinger, 1999; Agyekum, 2006). This is also tied to the fact that names and naming strategies is one of the cultural practises cherished in African communities (Swilla, 2000). This paper argues that since onomastics is tied to languages, the erosion of the traditional names and naming system is a sign of language endangerment.

Focusing on onomastics, the literature reveals that names and naming relate to culture. For example, based on findings from the Interlacustrine Bantu area, research by Muzale (1998: 28) shows that names have synchronic meanings and play a role in people's social life. This is indeed available in most of the literature on onomastics in African continent.

Thus, this research is informed by the naming system in various Africa communities, particularly on matters related to circumstances-at-birth and kinship names.

Circumstances-at-birth play a vital role in naming in African continent. For example, amongst Amhara of Ethiopia, Messing (1974: 79) says 20 percent of names are associated with circumstances-at-birth e.g. emotion of the mother. Amongst the Akan of Ghana, Agyekum (2006: 219) found that circumstantial names are attested; say for instance, location of the birth-place, e.g. *Agogo* 'district town name'. Amongst the Sukuma people of Tanzania, Manyasa (2008) found that circumstantial names express things such as death e.g. *Masalu* 'many deaths' and difficulties in life e.g. *Makoye* 'trouble'.

It is important to note that most African communities make use of circumstances-at-birth to assign names to children. Such names will always reflect the traditional lives practiced in these communities. Since naming make use of language, any change in the naming system will signal some kind of language endangerment. I argue that if such names come from foreign cultures, then encroachment of culture of the borrowing community will be noticed.

Another significant point surrounding language encroachment involves kinship names. In African communities, family names play a significant role in identifying the clan and the family from which one originates.

The literature shows that 50 percent of names amongst the Amhara are associated with relations for kinship members e.g. on defence (Messing, 1974: 80). In Sukuma community, Manyasa (2008: 53, 63) found that they identify a person by merely saying son or daughter of somebody, e.g. *ng'wana Mihayo* 'son of Mihayo'.

It is important to find out the way the Hadzabe names reflect kinship relationships. Also, this research investigated how family ties are reflected in names of the Hadzabe. I argue that the presence of a large amount of foreign names amongst school children is a sign of encroachment of the Hadzabe naming culture.

The contact situation at Yaeda Chini

Thomason (2001) succinctly shows that in contact situations languages tend to influence one another. The trend is that in most cases languages of wider communication tend to influence languages with minority speakers. Here the majority Swahili, Iraqw, Nyiramba and Datooga speakers are likely to influence the Hadzabe speakers who are a minority.

My findings demonstrate that all villages (Mongo wa Mono, Yaeda Chini and Domanga) of the Yaeda Chini Ward are no longer a typical Hadzabe homelands. This is because most of the inhabitants of the area are Datooga, Isanzu, Nyiramba and Swahili speakers who practise agriculture and pastoralism. This entails that the culture of the Hadzabe is highly encroached by these non-foraging communities. I managed to count only 6 families with 25 typical Hadzabe at Yaeda Chini village. Thus, contact (with Isanzu, Iraqw, Datooga) is obvious.

Findings point out that inhabitants of Domanga, Mongo wa Mono and Yaeda Chini villages keep animals, mainly cows, donkeys (careers and farm animals), goats, sheep and a number of fowls. Also, my findings show that the villagers own farms in which they grow soghum and maize. Nonetheless, it is obvious in my findings that some Hadzabe hunt wild animals and gather wild food.

I argue in this article that contra to Marlowe (2002), my research findings show that the Hadzabe at Yaeda Chini, Mongo wa Mono and Domanga villages have become partly sedentary farmers, growing *maize* and *sorghum*, and keep *cows, sheep, donkeys, goats,* and *fowls*. I will argue that this is a copying strategy due to human contact and societal changes. This copying strategy is consonant to Madsen (2000: 14) who writes that "in recent years Hadzabe diversify their income by limited gardening, small scale agriculture and trade with neighbours."

These observations from Yaeda Chini area seem to challenge Marlowe's (2004: 366-367) claim that the Hadzabe are nomadic living in camps. To date sedentary homesteads in Domanga, Mongo wa Mono and Yaeda Chini indicate that Hadzabe people cease, though in a slow pass, to be nomadic hunter-gatherers.

Personal names at Yaeda Chini

The data
The Hadzabe people of Mongo wa Mono, Domanga and Yaeda villages have such names as given below:

Name 1	Name 2	Name 3	Status
Salamii	Tlaa		*Hadzabe names*
Nakison	Kambala	Magadula	*Foreign name and Hadzabe names*
Katambuga	Ndulumo	Shandalua	*Joke (for foreigners) names*
Isa	Masaragi	Malapa	*Foreign name and Hadzabe names*
Paulo	Maliko	Musa	*Loan names (English, Swahili)*
Maliko	Musa	Zinzi	*Foreign names and Hadzabe name*
Nange	Shili	Jumapili	*Hadzabe names & Loan name (Swahili)*
Hamisi	Malala	Bagayu	*Loan name (Swahili)& Hadzabe names*
Eliza	Lameki	Musa	*Loan names (English and Swahili)*
Richard	Baalow	Mongulda	*English and Hadzabe names*
Yohana	Nange		*English and Hadzabe names*
Simon	C	Endeko	*English and Hadzabe names*
Athumani	Magandula		*Swahili and Hadzabe names*
Hashi	Mandago		*Hadzabe names*
!ayaima	Gipo		*Hadzabe names*

Personal names of villagers at Yaeda Chini

The contact situation in schools seems to impose more foreign names to Hadzabe children. Thus, Hadzabe school children have such names as these:

Name 1	Name 2	Name 3	Status
Regina	N	Safari	*English and Swahili names*
Yohana	M	Zinzi	*Swahili and Hadzabe names*
Mathayo	Ruben	Mahaza	*English and Hadzabe names*
Adam	M	Zengu	*Swahili and Hadzabe names*
Esther	M	Zinzi	*Swahili and Hadzabe names*
Godilizen	Melkizedek		*English names*
Paskali	Mathayo		*English names*
Sophia	Philimoni		*English names*
Joeli	Moses		*English names*

Personal names of school children at Yaeda Chini

Observations and comments on the data

It is obvious from findings given above that Hadzabe people maintain their ancestral and traditional names such as *Dundu, Maroba, Zinzi, !ayaima,Tlaa, Bagayu, Gipo,Magandula* etc. Also, it is obvious that some Hadzabe use "joke names" as their formal personal names as represented by *Shandalua* 'mosquito net', *Katambuga* 'shoes', *Mkuyu* 'baobab tree' etc. It is important to note that at least one of the formal name is either Christian e.g. *Yohana, Joeli, Mathayo* or borrowed one e.g. *Athumani, Lameki, Isa, Akhwesu, Hamisi, Safari*. This entails that a large number of personal names are foreign.

I think human contact, in line with Thomason (2001), affects the Hadzabe, similar to Khwe of Botswana and Namibia (Brenzinger, 2007a). This is because most school children have at least a foreign name, an English, Swahili or Datooga. This being the tendency (giving foreign names to school children), I wonder what will happen when all Hadzabe will have reached at least primary school!

On the naming system, it is fascinating to find that Hadzabe people maintain their traditional system. Thus, the traditional way of introduction is: *akhana be kwa*? [*akhana* 'to call', -*be* 'you' and *kwa* 'singular'] 'How are you called? OR 'What is your name'?

It is important to find that at least, some personal names in Hadzabe community are given to members of the family following the lineage (ancestry). Thus, the name of the first son is taken from the name of the grandfather, i.e. father's father. It is *akaye nepe akana* ('the name of the father's father'). The first daughter in the family takes the name of the mother's mother, i.e. *akana besa amamako* ('the name of the mother's mother'). The second born (son) is named after the name of the mother's father, i.e. *akana bema akaye* ('the name of the mother's father'). Likewise, the second born daughter takes the name of the grandmother ('the name of the mother's mothers').

I found this fascinating because the naming system in Hadzabe families tends to be ranked in a manner that respects both parties/parents, i.e. fathers-and-sons from both sides (this is a partial *patronomy* system) and mothers-and-daughters from both sides (this is a partial *matronomy* system). This is observed in the various families in both Mongo wa Mono, Yaeda Chini and Domanga villages.

Discussion

It is reported that the decline in number of wild game, the Hadzabe supplement meals with grains by barter trade with farmers (Isanzu, Iraqw) and fowl (meat) with pastoralists (Datooga) (Madsen 2000; Marlowe 2004). I argued that even contact with other communities (Datooga, Iraqw, Isanzu) have influenced both their naming system, the choice of names and their socio-economic materials.

I argued further that this is supported by my findings in that the number of families of Hadzabe which wish to settle has increased. Also, provision of cheap labour in towns (Arusha, Mbulu, Haydom) has become common. I argued that the consequence is that youngsters (who had been outside their homeland) despise their way of living hence the indigenous knowledge is no longer passed to new generations.

Lessons from Khoisan hunter-gatherers in Botswana are revealing. Chebanne (2002: 154) claims that Khoe people never perform well is schools and their culture is eroded by Setswana or Ikalanga cultures. Chebanne (2002: 151) claim that "for most of last century, the cattle-rich masters Setswana and Ikalanga speakers encroached into Khoe area and Khoe people are used as cattle herders."

Moreover, currently, traditional Batswana chiefs rule Basarwa and are responsible for the distribution of land and the administration of customary law, which created a situation of dependence of the weaker groups (Basarwa included) on Setswana culture (Batibo, 2005: 93). The consequence is that foraging techniques amongst the Khoisan of Botswana decline, together with the change in language because most youngsters and children no longer speak Khoisan languages (with its cultural richness) rather they use Setswana for communication in villages. This has implications on the loss of Basarwa culture, which, in a way would hinder our wish to amalgamate indigenous knowledge with modern knowledge for the betterment of Africans.

Conclusion

This article addressed the way foreign names and contemporary naming systems amongst the Swahili speakers encroach the indigenous naming system of the Hadzabe. I showed that the Hadzabe people at least maintain their ancestral and traditional names which is a replica of their ancestral nomenclature. I argued that some Hadzabe people use "joke names" as their formal names. I demonstrated that since at least one of the formal personal name is either Christian or borrowed one, a large number of personal names are foreign. I argue, in line of language contact that human contact affects the Hadzabe nomenclature because almost all school children at Yaeda Chini primary and secondary schools have at least one English or foreign name.

Results from Yaeda Chini Ward, are fascinating because the naming system in Hadzabe families tend to be ranked in the manner that respects both parties, hence they don't demonstrate patriarchy nor matriarchy system. The practise is that naming observes names of fathers-and-sons from both sides (this is a partial patronomy system) and mothers-and-daughters from both sides (this is a partial matronomy system).

Acknowledgements

Materials presented in this article were collected in the Mbulu District, northern Tanzania under the auspices of *Endangered Languages Fund* (ELF) whose financial assistance is highly acknowledged here. Research clearance was provided by the University of Dar es Salaam. I am grateful to Naftali Mandege for hosting me and Richard Baalow to act as an Assistant Researcher. This paper benefited from comments I received from participants of the Language of Tanzania Project, Workshop XIV, University of Dar es Salaam, 21st February 2014.

References

Agyekum, K. (2006). The sociolinguistic of Akan personal names. *Nordic Journal of African Studies,* 15(2), 206-235.

Batibo, H. (2005). *Language Decline and Death in Africa: Causes, Consequences and Challenges.* Clevedon: Multilingual Matters.

Brenzinger, M. (2007a). Vanishing conceptual diversity: The loss of hunter-gatherers' concepts. *Jornades 15 anys GELA (Grup d'Estudide Llengües Amenaçades)*, Recerca en llengües amenaçades.

Brenzinger, M. (2007b). Language endangerment in Southern and Eastern Africa. In M. Brenzinger (Ed.), *Language Diversity Endangered* (179-204). Berlin: Mouton de Gruyter.

Brenzinger, M. (1999). Personal names of the Kxoe: the Example of *tcóò*-names'. *Khoisan Forum,* 10, 5-18.

Chebanne, A.M. (2002). Shifting identities in Eastern Khoe: Ethnic and language endangerment. *Pula: Botswana Journal of African Studies*, 16(2), 147-157.

Madsen, A. (2000). *The Hadzabe of Tanzania: Land and Human Rights for a Hunter-gatherer Community.* Copenhagen: IWGIA.

Manyasa, J. (2008). Investigating the Basis of Naming People in Kisukuma. MA Dissertation, University of Dar es Salaam.

Marlowe, F. (2004). Mate preferences among Hadza hunter-gatherers. *Human nature,* 15(4), 365-376.

Marlowe, F. (2002). Why the Hadza are still hunter-gatherers. In S. Kent (Ed.), *Ethnicity, Hunter-gatherers and the "Other": Association or Assimilation in Africa* (pp. 247-275). Washington D.C.: Smithsonian Institution Press.

Messing, S.D. (1974). Individualistic patterns in Amhara onomastics: Significant expressions and their relationship to family and population problems. *Ethos,* 2, 77-94.

Muzale, H.R.T. (1998). Linguistic and socio-cultural aspects in interlacustrine Bantu names. *Kiswahili,* 61, 28-49.

Ndagala, D.K. (1991). The unmarking of the Datoga: Decreasing resources and increasing conflict in rural Tanzania. *Nomadic peoples,* 28, 71-82.

Peterson, D. (2012). *Hadzabe: In the Light of a Million Fires.* Dar es Salaam: Mkuki na Nyota Publishers.

Sands, B., I. Maddieson & P. Ladefoged. (1996). The phonetic structures of Hadza. *Studies in African Linguistics*, 25, 171-204.

Sisson, C.J. (1984). Economic Prosperity in Ugogo, East Africa 1860-1890. Doctoral Thesis, University of Toronto.

Swilla, I.N. (2000). Names in Chindali. *Afrikanistische Arbeitspapiere*, 63, 35-62.

Thomason, S.G. (2001). *Language Contact: An Introduction.* Edinburgh: Edinburgh University Press.

Tomikawa, M. (1978). Family and daily life: An ethnography of the Datoga pastoralists in Mangola. *Family Ethnological Studies*, 1.

Young, A.G. (2008). Young Child Health among Eyasi Datoga: Socio-economic Marginalization, Local Biology, And Infant Resilience within the Mother-Infant Dyad. Doctoral dissertation, University of Arizona.

Socio-Economic and Cultural Implications of Wolaita Proverbs
A Functional Analysis

Meshesha Make Jobo
College of Social Sciences and Humanities
Wolaita Sodo University
P.O. Box: 138
Wolaita Sodo, Ethiopia
[mesheshamake46@gmail.com]

Abstract

The purpose of this study was to collect and analyze some selected Wolaita proverbs for their socio-economic and cultural implications. The study analyzes the thematic implications of Wolaita proverbs for the three selected themes: social, economic and cultural realm of life in Wolaita. The subjects used for the current study were 222 theme-relevant proverbs collected by interviewing systematically selected 24 elders and through conducting participant-based observation being part of social interactions taking place in those villages. The descriptive research design was used to conduct this study using the qualitative method of data analysis. The result indicated that Wolaita proverbs embody different kinds of social, economic and cultural domains of life as a form of indigenous wisdom of Wolaita people. As social aspects of life, Wolaita proverbs imply faithfulness of people to each other, cooperation and relationship among people, principles of morality and respect to those who deserve it, promotion of good deeds, advice for the needy and non-conformity for the socially unaccepted values of the society. With regard to economic realm of life, Wolaita proverbs imply scarcity of resources and how Wolaitas manage it, unwise and wise use of resources, sources of wealth and economic inequality among people where as in the cultural facet of life, Wolaita proverbs embody the inheritance feature of Wolaita culture, the culture of Wolaita as the basic tool of identity for its members, the culture of marriage arrangement and its pattern and the effects of deviating aboriginal cultural practices on one's social life. Based on these findings, therefore, deep and series studies that promote the frequent use of Wolaita proverbs in all adequate contexts of interaction, awareness enhancement training for young generations of Wolaita for effective use of proverbs in the proper interactional situations, making proverbs as part of language curriculum in all levels of education and maintenance of Wolaita proverbs as vehicles of transferring indigenous wisdom to the next generation are recommended to be implemented by the all concerned bodies across the nation.

Introduction

Wolaita is one among Southern Nations and Nationalities of Ethiopia. The people of Wolaita lived independent being organized in socio-political and economic realm of life starting from the Stone Age (C.H. Stinger, 1910). Wolaita people have owned indigenous culture, beliefs, traditions, rituals, civilization and social identities that define them and make them distinct from other people in Ethiopia. These socio-political, economic and cultural realities of Wolaita have been transferred from generation to generation solely through oral tradition (Hailegabriel, 2007).

Wolaita people use oral tradition as a sole instrument to reflect their socio-economic and cultural realm of life. Among those oral traditions, proverbs remain a veritable tool in depicting the overall values of Wolaita people (Fikre, 2012). For instance, they use proverbs as a form of literary expressions to encourage, admonish, mock, advise, consol and generally to establish the verbal convention that is significant to their social order, historical circumstances and cultural values. However, the use of Wolaita proverbs in the aforementioned realm of life is in a continuous and alarming reduction that negatively contributes the transfer of indigenous wisdom, language, culture, heritage and other social realities to the next generation. That is why this study has been attempted to collect Wolaita proverbs, analyze them for their socio-economic and cultural implications and document them as vehicles for transferring indigenous wisdom, culture, heritage and other social realities of Wolaita to the next generation.

Methodology of the Study

The descriptive research design was used for this study. This is because it is suitable to describe the existing socio-economic and cultural realities embodied in Wolaita proverbs. For the analysis, 300 proverbs were selected using purposive sampling procedure based on their thematic relevance to the current study. Theses proverbs were collected using two tools of data collection: two-third (200 proverbs) were obtained through interviewing systematically selected 24 elders based on their deep knowledge of Wolaita socio-economic and cultural realities and for the remained one-third (100) of the entire sample, the researchers went to the remote villages of Wolaita and conducted participant-based observation being part of social occasions taking place in those villages. Then the proverbs collected were analyzed using qualitative method of data analysis.

Results and Discussions

Social Implications of Wolaita Proverbs

In this section, the researcher analyzed totally 138 theme relevant proverbs that imply some social values of Wolaita people. One of these social values implied by Wolaita proverbs is promotion of faithfulness. For instance, to avoid lack of trust and to develop a culture of trustworthiness among people, Wolaitas use the proverb **Ammanido mashshay tiriyaan Me'ees**, '*A knife highly trusted breaks on just cutting the liver (very soft part of animals' flesh)*'. This proverb entails to explain that Wolaita people pressingly use proverbs for social control and, as a hedge against failure of trust among the families, the relatives, friends and the society in general. It is also often used to let the members to keep the secrets of one another as legible social value. The core social implication of this proverb is to maintain one's commitment and trustworthiness as a good social value among the members.

The other social value that Wolaita proverbs imply is enhancing cooperation among people. By the fact that Wolaita people believe in social cooperative effort for the achievement of a set goal. Thus they say **Coray cuchich wonggiriyaa kunttees**, '*When all cooperates to add their saliva, they can fill a container*'. This proverb literally indicates that many is more important than some or one. The social context in which this proverb applied is to appreciate the activity carried out by cooperation with people. This is equivalent to the English proverb **Two heads are better than one** which has been used in another culture. The purpose of using this proverb in Wolaita culture is to encourage social cooperation to undertake certain activities.

As another theme of social value, Wolita proverbs imply long-stayed cultural traits of mutual respect within the society. For instance, Wolaitas say **Bonchchoynne borssay sooppe kiyees**, '*Respectfulness and disregard emanate from a family*'. This proverb implies that socializing children with the cultural traits of mutual respect is very important. In other words, it is also used to imply that the sense of mutual respect exist as far as two parties concerned have the same sense of regard to one another. Nevertheless, elders who are found to be disrespectful to even for youngsters are often warned by using proverbs in a certain social contexts of Wolaita. i.e., **Bonchchidi bonchchettettees**, '*One must suffer from or endure the results of his/her actions*'. The social function of this proverb is to regulate social values such as respecting elders, authority and family members.

Using theme-relevant proverbs, Wolaitas motivate good deeds and discourage bad behaviors. When such kind of situation occurs, Wolaitas proverbially say **Eeyyay balin eray zuuqqees**, '*Wise plants a seedling uprooted by a foolish*'. The special characteristics of human society are having the discourses of knowledge and wisdom. Similarly, people vary in scale of thought understanding and views to external social world. Apparently, people with good humor towards others often make things right when they find it is done wrongly by his/her fellow. The social implication of the aforementioned proverb is to socialize children to grow the behavior of acknowledging the views of others and when find them wrong, correct in the manner based on

the standard norm. Thus, the proverb provides an advisory function for the society in Wolaita.

Again as part of implying social values, some Wolaita proverbs view neighborhood relationships as more important than blood relationships and the others do the reverse. Both religious and cultural values encourage people to establish good relationships with neighbors and even to think about the type of neighbor before you build or buy a house. It is common in Wolaita that a neighbor might look after his neighbor's children and property when needed, shares pains and gains with neighbors, who borrow and lend from each other and exchange advice. In this regard, Wolaita people use their proverbial wisdom saying **Hahuwaanni de'iyaa dabbuwaappe matan de'iyaa allagay keha**, '*An enemy neighbor is worthier than a family far apart*'. This proverb reflects that Wolaita society has long adopted social value of cooperation and peaceful existence with the people living in the neighborhood, be it relative or with those who are from other groups, ethnically. This is attached to the social fact that the one at proximity is the first to help his/her neighbor at time of hardships and situations when immediate support is summoned.

As a general fact, in any social situations, truth and advice are considered difficult for adult people to accept. For this reason, parents in Wolaita consider educating and disciplining children with those social values at their early age is the most valuable thing for children's future life. Thus they proverbially express **Yellettdo gaallassa amaalee hayqqido gaalaassan attees**. '*He who grows with a bad manner, grows old with it*'. People use this proverb for commentary or social control, to encourage parents to teach their children good manners at the early age. They might also use it sarcastically to accuse a person that they grew up with bad habits. This proverb displays that what one learns when young will not be forgotten when becoming old. Another proverbial saying which deals with the same issue in child-care is **Maagee baagaa xonnees**, '*Feed your son properly and discipline him*'. This proverb advises that you have to look after your child by supporting him/her with good food and accommodation, but the most important thing is to teach him good morals and to discipline him. If a parent lets his child behave badly especially when some guests (visitors) are around, a relative may use this proverb to encourage the parents to discipline their children and to teach them good behavior at an early stage in their life.

Wolaitas deny to give confirmation to acts deviant to their accepted social values. Naturally when one lives in a given society having interaction with different individuals, there commonly exist some deviant acts which nullify standard social values of the people. When such kinds of situation happens, Wolaitas proverbially regret saying **Gaammuwaa qantan zeerusay yelettees**, '*There might occasionally be* *found unusual within usual'*. In social world what is accepted as a standard value is not perpetual as to the natural being does due to flux of changes resulting from the changing features of culture and other binding social forces. The underlying social implication of this proverb is to regret the unexpectedly happened occasion which is deviant to the usual social norm.

Economic Implications of Wolaita Proverbs

In this section, the researcher analyzed totally 100 theme relevant proverbs that imply certain economic realm of life of Wolaita. One among such economic issues that Wolaita proverbs imply is the scarcity of resources which is common fact to all other generations in the world. Whenever Wolaita people get demanding situation in their interaction, they frequently use proverbs that imply the scarcity of resources to strengthen their ideas and easily convince their interlocutors. For instance, they say *Abbaa pinttiya wozanay de'ishin abee son ashees*, *'How much wise a person is, he/she can't go further in any activity/business without his/her economic capacity'*. This proverb implies that resources, financial or material, play a key role for the accomplishment of any action in human life. On the other hand, this proverb also implies that the wisdom of an individual can't work if it is not accompanied by his/her economic capacity.

As a general fact it needs wise use of economic resources as resources are scarce by their nature across the nation (mentioned in the above paragraph). In the proverbial advice through endemic wisdom, Wolaitas discourage losing the chance of using resources at hand. They say, **Geleshshoppe aadhdhidi shaafaa qociyay baawa shin bari kushe meecetti erenna**, *'Even though monkeys are more exposed to rivers than anybody, they never wash their hands'*. Naturally monkeys live at the shores of rivers, but they do not wash their hands. The same is true for some people who do not exploit the resources that they are exposed to. Wolaitas count this kind of people as lazy proverbially saying, **Eeyyiya agido zaakkoy de'ishin haatta uyawusu**, *'A lazy woman drinks water having the drink she prepared at hand'*. The implication is lazy people are not conscious of resources in their hand and lose their chance of using it. Similarly, in Wolaita there has been said, **Bukkayda bullattay, agaydda sammettay**, *'Why make your skin tarnish and be thirsty having butter and water at your hand'*. The implication is that some people suffer from starvation not mainly due to shortage of resources rather than unconscious and unwise of using what they have at hand.

In their long-lived culture, Wolaitas believe that the reason why resources require wise use is due to high personal effort they need to be accumulated. Thus Wolaitas proverbially say **Aawu qaxxin baallee qaaxxees**, *'When one empowers him/herself to be strong, others become mobilized to support him/her'*.

This proverb depicts the value of self-empowerment for having one's intended prosperity in his/her economic life. Similarly it is said in Wolaita **Duunnee ottin mokkees, ogee hemettin aadhdhees**, *'A hard work makes a hill to produce, a quick walk makes a journey too short'*. This proverb has a similar meaning to **Daarinchchaa oottay dawullan makes**, *'One who exerts maximum effort by hard working, gets much production from a small plot of land';* hence it can be used alternatively in a demanding situation of interaction. With the same theme, to emphasis the importance of hard working for prosperity, Wolaitas say **Goyyiday tiyaa mees; shukkiday tiriya mees**, *'A hard working farmer eats unripe cereals, a butcher with similar quality eats liver'*.

On the other hand, as economic implication, it is obviously known that there exists economic inequality among people in the whole globe. The ground reality in Wolaita is not different. There exists a wide economic gap among people in Wolaita. Confirming this, Wolaitas proverbially say **Asi ubbi lagge shin dummaayiyay miishsha**, *'All human beings are equal, but what makes them different is their economic status'*. This difference makes people either suffer from shortage of their needs or overact due to excess of what they need. In this regard, Wolaitas say **Issuwa son shendderay porees; issuwa son shemppoy porees**, *'One suffers a lot from shortage of his/her basic necessities, another suffers a lot from the reverse'*. This proverb indicates that, in Wolaita, there exist the two extremely positioned people with regard to economic status, but that each has its own problems.

Cultural Implications of Wolaita Proverbs

As implication of certain Wolaita cultural facet of life, in this section, the researcher analyzed totally 62 theme relevant proverbs. One among such cultural issues that Wolaita proverbs embody is promotion of the inheritance of Wolaita culture. Wolaita people promote the inheritance of their aboriginal culture from generation to generation. Such an inheritance can be from parents to their children, from the given clan to next or even from the whole nation of Wolaita to its next generation. To such the trans-generational inheritance of their endemic culture, Wolaitas proverbially say, **Aawassi baynna togay na'aa aafuwan yeggees**, *'A practice of ridding not inherited from his father throws a son into cliff'*. This proverb has two implications: first, it promotes the maintenance of original culture by the coming generation and second, it reflects the importance of deriving experience from the previous generation to operate an activity that one has not yet exposed. With totally the same meaning, Wolaitas also say, **Aayeessi baynna sagaayoy na'eessi kushiya mentees**, *'A bracelet not familiar to a mother breaks an arm of a daughter'*, to indicate the importance of inheriting good experience of life from the previous generation.

As another element of cultural implication, there has been proverbial way of expressions in Wolaita for certain culturally adapted features/behaviors that define certain group of people in the society; either positively or negatively. They say, **Booddidi zin'iya deeshsha**, '*It is a goat that lies down after scratching*'. This proverb shows the identification of certain group of people based on the behavior that they display. Confirming the same argument, Wolaitas say, **Deshshay bari sheshshawu handdatees**, '*A goat swanks by its inherited behavior*'. Having similar implications, there are a lot of proverbs that have been frequently used in Wolaita to make a distinction of people in certain class of social categories: **Bone bukkenna, boori yelenna**, '*A winter can never rain, an ox can never give birth to a calf*', **Occoy ootteesppe attin zerenna**, '*A mole cultivates (digs) soil but never sow its grain*', **Yashshanchchay yedettennan woxxees**, '*A fearful runs without anyone chases him/her*'.

Again, as another cultural realm of life, in their long-lived traditional culture, Wolaitas promote the accurate match of the couple who marry each other as their marriage custom. They proverbially elucidate this saying **Dullee baynna kafoy xaphoy bayna mittan uttees**, '*A bird with ordinary background sits down on a tree without root*'. Even though it connotes negative meaning, this proverb implies the multidimensional socio-economic and cultural elements needed for matching of couples in marriage. First, it implies that the couples should have a compatible clan background that can make them to be matched with. I.e., both of them should be either from lower or from royal clan backgrounds for a peaceful and culturally relevant marriage to take place. Secondly, it also reflects the need to make a suitable match of the couple's parents economic backgrounds. Thirdly, it reveals the consideration of couple's social classes for their marriage to be acknowledged and approved by the society.

As the Wolaita people have great respect to its aboriginal culture, they strive to maintain it. Deviating culturally accepted pattern of life has many negative consequences which are proverbially elucidated. Wolaitas say **Haree kaciya kessanawu biidi hayttaa qanxxettees**, '*When a donkey makes a journey to add horn, it loses its existing ears in an occasion*'. Here the proverb implies that trying to deviate a long-lived cultural life pattern exposes one or a group to lose what they have already owned. There are other proverbs alternatively used in a similar context. For example, it has been said **Pilaataa darayiis giidi dadawu tooraa xonggeesa**, '*Acting overconfidently, one throws a spear to thunder*' which has a serious negative consequence in Wolaita culture. Again, we can use another proverb as an option, i.e., **Haree caanay dariis giidi waasuwawu biidi diddigaayiyaara tookkees**, '*When a donkey went for compliance thinking that its luggage is too heavy, the creator gave it additional luggage*'. In Wolaita traditional perception, this kinds of losses come from being unconsciousness. Thus, they proverbially reprimand **Hassayennan doommido gereessay zaarishin metees**, '*A chant started unconsciously, challenges one to complete it*'.

Conclusions and Recommendations

This chapter has two sections. The first section presents the conclusions as the key findings and the second section presents recommendations as possible solutions to the problems, based on the key findings of the study.

Conclusions

Based on the analysis and discussions of Wolaita proverbs, the following conclusions have been reached:

Wolaita proverbs embody different kinds of social, economic and cultural domains of life as a form of indigenous wisdom of Wolaita people.

As social aspects of life, Wolaita proverbs imply faithfulness of people to each other, cooperation and relationship among people, principles of morality and respect to those who deserve it, promotion of good deeds, advice for the needy and non-conformity for the socially unaccepted values of the society.

With regard to economic realm of life, Wolaita proverbs imply scarcity of resources and how Wolaitas manage it, unwise and wise use of resources, sources of wealth and economic inequality among people.

In the cultural facet of life, Wolaita proverbs embody the inheritance feature of Wolaita culture, the culture of Wolaita as the basic tool of identity for its members, the culture of marriage arrangement and its pattern and the effects of deviating aboriginal cultural practices on one's social life.

Recommendations

Based on the analysis and interpretation of Wolaita proverbs and conclusions made above, the following recommendations are forwarded:

There should be deep studies that promote the frequent use of Wolaita proverbs in all adequate contexts of interaction.

Awareness enhancement training should be given for the younger generations of Wolaita for effective use of proverbs in the proper interactional situations.

Proverbs should be made as part of language curriculum in all levels of education.

Wolaita proverbs should be maintained to serve the society as vehicles of transferring indigenous wisdom to the next generations.

Acknowledgements

Firstly, I would like to express my heart-felt thanks to overall management bodies of Wolaita Sodo University who established adequate research culture and sponsored this research. Secondly, my special thanks and appreciations go to Wolaita elders who provided me genuine and helpful information for this research. Last but not least, I thank all my family members, colleagues and friends for their moral and material support during my study.

References

Bezabi, M. (2011). *Wolayttatto Leemiso Haasaya*. Addis Ababa: HY Printing Enterprise.

Fikre, A. (2012). Analysis of Wolaita Proverbs: Function in Focus. Unpublished MA Thesis, Addis Ababa University.

Getachew, T. & Amenu, T. (1995). Wolaita Proverbs and their Amharic Translations: Addis Ababa: Artistic Printing Enterprise.

Haile, G.M. (2007). Monogamous Marriage among Wolaita Christians of Ethiopia (1894-2004); Doctoral Dissertation. Pontificia University Printing Press Rome.

Jeiylan, W. (2005). The Social and Ethno-cultural Construction of Masculinity and Femininity in African Proverbs. *African Study Monographs*, 26(2), 59-87.

Salzmann, Z. (1998). *Language, Culture and Society: An Introduction to Linguistic Anthropology*. Oxford, Westview Press.

Stinger, C.H. (1910). *The History of Wolayta People*. Köln: Rüdiger Köppe Verlag.

Chesaian, C. (1994.). *Oral Literature of Enabu and Mbeere*. Nairobi: East African Educational Publishers.

Dorson, R. (1972). *Folklore Life: An Introduction*. Chicago: The University of Chicago.

Fekade, A. (2001). The state of oral Literature Research in Ethiopia: Retrospect and prospect. *Journal of Ethiopian Studies*, 34(1).

Finnegan, R. (1970). *Oral Literature in Africa*. Oxford: Clarendon Press.

Lindfors, B. (1973a). *Yoruba Proverbs: Translation and Annotation*. Ohio: Ohio University Center for International Studies.

Melakneh, M. (2005). *Map of African Literature*. Addis Ababa, Addis Ababa University Press.

Mieder, W. (1999). *Proverbs are Never out of Season: Popular Wisdom in the Modern Age*. USA: Oxford University Press.

Miruka. O. (1994). *Encounter with Oral Literature*. Nairobi: East Africa Educational publisher.

Nandwa, J and Bo Kenya, A. (1983). *African Literature for Schools*. Nairobi: Longman.

Okpewho, I. (1992). *African Oral Literature. Bloomingto*: Indiana University Press.

Simyo.V. (1994). *Understanding Oral Literature*. Nairobi: Nairobi University Press.

"Why Can't I Read about Miyako History in our School Textbook?" Hisamatsu Community and Localizing Language Awareness

Sachiyo Fujita-Round

Rikkyo University, Graduate School of Intercultural Communication
3-34-1 Nishi-Ikebukuro, Toshima-ku,
Tokyo, Japan, 171-8501
[fujitar@rikkyo.ac.jp]

Abstract

This research in Hisamatsu community is an ongoing project and it aims to investigate to localize people's language awareness, as one goal, toward revitalization of the local dialect. It is an ongoing project and taking ethnographic approach to the "definitely endangered" dialects in Miyako Island. The purpose of the investigation was to ascertain awareness of their local area and language, and I set my study field at a school, the educational domain in the community. This linguistic ethnography of "local" community may give an implication toward multicultural awareness in this "globalized" age.

Introduction

This research in Hisamatsu community on Miyako Island, southern Okinawa, is a part of an ongoing project to investigate multicultural *"kyōsei"* ('co-existence, or living together') in 21st century Japan. I reconsider the meaning of how people in communities "live together" and go beyond the borders of plural cultures and languages in order to live and share multilingual identities in the same space called "Japan".

By the beginning of the 21st century, the diversity of language life in Japan and implications for education, have been successively described across a range of languages such as English, Korean, Chinese, Ainu, Ryukyuan (Okinawan), Japanese Sign Language, Portuguese, Spanish and Japanese as a Second Language (Fujita-Round & Maher, 2008). However, this diversity of languages is neither fully understood nor stable. Rapid societal change and the impact of decreasing populations have had a radical impact upon the local languages and cultures that are being handed on to future generations and communities. Some languages may vanish.

Miyako language and Hisamatsu variety

As in *The UNESCO Atlas of the World's Languages in Danger*[33], the Miyako language is one of 5 languages rated by "definitely endangered"[34]. Since this UNESCO's rating of the world endangered languages, the investigation on those nominated endangered languages in Japan was commissioned National Language Institute for Japanese Language and Linguistics (NINJAL), Hokkaido University and Ryukyu University by the Japanese Agency for Cultural

Affairs[35], and this urged to accumulate researches on those endangered languages since then. First, I will draw attention to the demography of the language speakers and geography of Miyakojima city to grasp the domain.

Demography of language speakers

Looking at the general demography of related region, Shimoji (2005) gives the general picture of total language speakers of languages of Ryukyus, in 2005 there are 1,452,288 (85,434 for Amami Region, 1,366,854 for Okinawa Prefecture including main island Okinawa and Miyako-Yaeyama). However, he noted that "as all the authors of this volume report, proficient speakers are limited to old generation, typically in their 50's and older, which means that the total number of speakers of Ryukyuan should much smaller that the figure of 1,452,288." (Shimoji, 2005: 2).

For Miyakojima city alone[36], the current population is 54,290, and for the community of Hisamatsu, 1,084 at the end of March, 2014[37]. The population of Hisamatsu community is, therefore, about 2% within Miyakojima City.

---

[33] For the detail is documented in the website, http://www.unesco.org/culture/languages-atlas/index.php (retrieved 2014/07/25)

[34] There are 8 languages in Japan recognized as endangered languages by UNESCO; apart from "definitely endangered" above, Yaeyama and Yonaguni under "severely endangered" and Ainu under "critically endangered" (UNESCO, 2010).

[35] The information of announcement of commission and final reports are provided on the website, http://www.bunka.go.jp/kokugo_nihongo/kokugo_sisaku/kikig engo/index.html (retrieved 2014/07/25)

[36] Officially, the city hall names their English name as "Miyakojima city", thus I will follow it in this paper. In 2005, 5 municipalities are consolidated to form a large Miyakojima city where includes 6 islands: Miyako (main) Island, Ikema Island, Ōgami Island, Kurima Island, Irabu Island, Shimoji Island. In addition, Tarama Island and Minna Island are independent as Tarama village, but these 6 islands of Miyakojima city and 2 islands of Tarama village, all together 8 islands as shown in the Figure 1, are categorized as 'Miyako Shoto (a group of Miyako islands)'.

[37] These figures are provided by Civic life division of Miyako Island city hall upon the author's inquiry.

Figure 1: Map of Eight Miyako Islands

Source: Creative Commons

Previous researches on Miyako language

Among those Miyako Islands, it is estimated that fluent active Miyako language speakers are above 60 years old, and under 60 years old they may be more passive, who understand but not speak fluently. Younger 20-30 years olds may not even be passive language speakers of Miyako language, but Japanese dominant (Aoi, 2013).

Aoi (2013) also introduces that Miyako language has 5 sub categories: Miyako, Oogami, Ikema, Irabu and Tarama, in addition to those varieties, he explains in each category there are varieties of communities. According to Pellard & Hayashi (2012: 13), "the dialects of Miyako is a part of South Ryukyu dialects and they are spoken within Miyakojima city together with Tarama village. Each community has different dialects and there are supposed to be between 30 and 40 dialects." Pellard & Hayashi (2012) reported about the extensive research on Miyako dialects mainly focused on the sites of 13 communities of Miyako city and collected rich data, by the research team of National Language Institute for Japanese Language and Linguistics (NINJAL). Hayashi (2013) particularly focused on Ikema dialect and she documented inclusive linguistic data from phonology, morphology, syntax, discourse examples and ethnographic data. These recent documentation on the Miyako language and dialects will help record the comprehensive present condition of Miyako language and its dialects of the early 21st century.

Hisamatsu community

Hisamatsu community is located on the west side of main Miyako Island. Hisamatsu's cultural heritage events are well recognized by Okinawa prefecture and Miyako city, however, uniquely Hisamatsu dialect itself is more associated with one popular singer who sings various genres of music with his Hisamatsu dialect, Miyako language and Japanese. Multilingual use of languages describes by Hisamatsu dialect with combination of Miyako language and Japanese language.

Matsubara (2001), who is ex-local politician and active bilingual of Hisamatsu variety and Japanese, wrote and compiled old folk tales into the book on the subject of history and life in Nozakimura, the old name of Hisamatsu community. Hisamatsu originally consisted of two villages, Kugai and Matsubara. Thus, the name of the community, Hisamatsu(久松), is a joint construct of each Kanji (Chinese characters) from, Kugai(久貝) ward and Matsubara (松原) ward. Earlier I mentioned the population of Hisamatsu in 2014 is 1,084, in which is the total number of Kugai, 484 and Matubara, 600. In his book Matsubara (2001) recollected that the peak of Hisamatsu population was the year of 1960, the total of 3,552, Kugai 1,442 and Matsubara 2,110. Over the 54 years, the population of the community decreased down to the one third of the peak.

This memoir of Matsubara coincided the number of Hisamatsu elementary school pupils' demography.

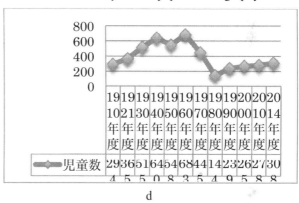

d

Table 1: Demography of Children in Hisamatsu Elementary School between 1910 and 2014[38]

The peak of the Hisamatsu elementary school children was 683 pupils in 1960, whereas 308 in 2014.

Ethnographic implication by the interviews at school

In this paper, I report on interview data collected, in 2014, from a group of 41 children, currently second grade pupils at Hisamatsu Junior High School. The purpose of the investigation was to ascertain awareness of their local area and language. Teacher interviews were also conducted. Prior to this study, my colleague provided classes, in school, once a year, for consecutive 5 years (2010-2014), for the same group of children from their grade 4, 5, 6 at the elementary school, then onto grade 1 and 2 at the Junior High School of Hisamatsu community. This special class conducted by the special guest is attempted for the purpose of

---

[38] The number is provided by the education authority of Miyakojima city hall upon author's request.

enhancing awareness of local identity.

As mentioned earlier, Hisamatsu village originally consisted of two villages, Kugai and Matsubara, and was a busy fishing community. The planting of sugarcane was also a local industry. In the interviews with School headteachers of Hisamatsu Elementary (6-12 years old) and Junior High School (12-15 years old) informed me that, currently, they recognized none of the parents of children are involved full-time in the "fishing" industry.

In this paper, I aim to discuss about localizing language awareness by my ethnographic data, in particular, how local language is tied to work practices in the community and how local language awareness is currently shaped. They are issues that a linguistic ethnography can reveal: as multilingual schools and communities in Japan seek new paths to multicultural awareness in this globalized age. Research and real-time implementation are necessary if Japan is to go beyond "the imagined community in which language policy emerges" (Fujita-Round & Maher, 2008).

Acknowledgements

This work is supported by JSPS Grants-in-Aid for Scientific Research between 2012 and 2014, Project Number 24520586, "Rethinking Multicultural 'Kyosei' in Japan: Towards a community which accommodates multilingual identities". Details on this project, see http://multilingually.jp

References

Aoi, H. (2013). 'Miyako-go' gaisetsu [Overview of Miyako language]. In Okinawa Daigaku Chi'iki Kenkyūjo (Ed.) *Ryūkyū shogo no fukkō* (pp. 87-98). Tōkyō: Fuyō Shobō.

Fujita-Round, S. & Maher, J. C. (2008). Language education policy in Japan. In S. May & N. Hornberger (Eds.), *Encyclopedia of Language and Education* (pp. 393-404). NY: Springer.

Garcia, O., Skutnab-Kangas, T. and Torres-Guzman, M. E. (Eds.). (2006). *Imagining Multilingual Schools*. Clevedon: Multilingual lMatters.

Hayashi, Y. (2013). Miyako Ikema hōgen no genzai [The present state of Miyako Ikema dialect]. In Y. Takubo (Ed.), Ryūkyū rettō no gengo to bunka [Language and Cultures of the Ryukyus] (pp. 157-176). Tōkyō: Kuroshio Publishing.

Heinrich, P. (2004). Language planning and language ideology in the Ryukyu Islands. In *Language Policy*, 3, 153-179.

Heinrich, P. (2012). *The Making of Monolingual Japan.* Bristol: Multilingual Matters.

Maher, J. C. (2005). Metroethnicity, language, and the principle of Cool. *International Journal of the Sociology of Language* 175/176, 83-102.

Maher, J. C. (2010). Metroethnicities and metrolanguages. In N. Coupland (Ed.), *The Handbook of Language and Globalization* (pp. 575-591). Chichester: Blackwell.

Matsubara, S. (2001) *Nozakimura Rekishi to Kurashi* [The History and Life in Nozaki Village]. Naha: Miebashi Publishing.

Pellard, T. & Hayashi, Y. (2012). Miyako shogengo no on'in. In N. Kibe (Ed.), *Shometsu kiki gengo no chōsa, hozon no tame no sōgō-teki kenkyū: Minami Ryūkyū Miyako hōgen chōsa hōkokusho* [Comprehensive Research for Investigating and Documenting Endangered Languages: Southern Ryukyu Miyako Language Research Reports]. Tōkyō: Kokuritsu Kokugo Kenkyujō.

Shimoji, M. (2010). Ryukyuan languages: An introduction. In Michinro Shimoji & Thomas Pellard (Eds.), *An Introduction to Ryukyuan languages* (pp.1-13). Tōkyō: Research Institute for Languages and Cultures of Asia and Africa (ILCAA), Tokyo University of Foreign Studies.

UNESCO (2010) *Atlas of the World's Languages in Danger* http://www.unesco.org/culture/languages-atlas/

Examining the Challenges of Language Learning, Retention and Revitalization Activities for Public Schools in Large Urban Centers

Peter Wilson

382 Second Avenue
Ottawa, Ontario, K1S2J4
Canada
[peterwilson@rogers.com]

Abstract

This paper seeks to redefine the concept of indigenous language study by encouraging urban Canadian high schools to engage indigenous students in language study within subject content courses. At present, indigenous language courses are only available in schools near indigenous homelands. The activities examined connect students with their homeland and contribute to maintenance of the language, the most unique aspect of each community in this age of assimilation. Inclusion of indigenous language activities into urban schools not only honors each student's ancestral identity, but also engages his or her family and provides a forum for sharing indigenous expertise and personal experience with non-indigenous classmates and the broader community. In addition, providing language opportunities in urban centers helps to fulfill the United Nations declaration supporting educational ancestral language opportunities for all indigenous peoples (United Nations, 2007).

Introduction

Canada contains approximately 80 indigenous languages that are spread throughout the country. *Ethnologue* reports that nearly 70 of these languages are in trouble or dying, and notes that intergenerational transmission is less and less common (Lewis, 2014). Language acquisition, thereby, is becoming, or needs to become, more commonplace in schools and adult education programs. This is increasingly important as schools target younger children (four and five year olds) and daycare centers are replacing traditional home-based early childhood rearing (OCDSB, 2013).

Although many indigenous peoples in Canada reside in their traditional homelands, known as "reserves," Statistics Canada (2014) reports that more indigenous peoples are currently living "off-reserve" than "on-reserve". The majority of these "off-reserve" families live in urban centers.

The migration of indigenous peoples to urban areas has affected traditional communities. When fluent speakers leave their home communities, they are less likely to use their language and are rarely able assist with language preservation (Sesín, 2014). In addition, when older fluent speakers relocate to urban centers they may lose touch with language activities This occurred with x̌aʔisla (spoken in Kitimat, B.C.) when two of the most competent speakers moved a great distance from their homeland, one to Vancouver and the other to Toronto (Robinson, 2014).

School Based Programming

School based indigenous language programming currently takes place in schools located in or adjacent to traditional communities. Indigenous students in urban schools are often geographically far from their traditional communities, and come from a variety of diverse nations and languages. Individuals living in urban communities, therefore, are rarely able to access programming in their ancestral language(s). In addition, indigenous students in urban schools usually lack age peers who share the same traditional community and language, and are often anxious about disclosing their indigenous heritage.

Although school-based indigenous language acquisition may be replacing role of the home in promoting heritage language learning, the efficacy of such programs remains in question and, as noted above, is non-existent for those living in urban centers. This lack of universal and effective indigenous language education among indigenous peoples throughout Canada has long been acknowledged both by linguists and educators. In 1979 Bob Levine, then Associate Curator of Linguistics at the British Columbia Provincial Museum, presented an address on the state of indigenous languages in British Columbia and the efforts to document and teach them (Levine, 2009). This report notes significant language loss and difficulties with language programming, especially in the context of British Columbia, which has nearly 30 distinct languages, the greatest linguistic variation of any province. This report was republished in 2009 along with comments from the editor noting the lack of effective language programming:

> In spite of much effort, the teaching of native languages is largely ineffective. With the exception of the very rare immersion primary schools and a few university-level courses, very few programs impart to their students a functional knowledge of the language (editorial comment, Levine, 2009).

In summary, indigenous language education is only available in traditional homeland areas and is not generally effective in developing functional competency. In addition, indigenous populations who reside in urban centers rather than traditional areas rarely receive any educational opportunities to develop even rudimentary knowledge of their traditional language. This fact is particularly disconcerting if school is the only place where young people have the opportunity to acquire the language.

2014

Indigenous education has become a significant national political issue in Canada in 2014, a year in which the general population of the country has become increasingly aware of the lack of services for indigenous populations, including education. Three stories in particular have caught the attention of the news media and the public. First, the proposed revision to the delivery of indigenous education on traditional homelands. Bill C-33, (Government of Canada, 2014) was rejected by many traditional communities and then withdrawn by the federal government in May, 2014. Second, a UN report on the welfare of indigenous people in Canada was released in April, (United Nations, 2014). This report was critical of numerous aspects of the treatment of indigenous people. And finally, the Truth and Reconciliation Commission concluded hearings into abuses which took place in residential schools, which provided education for indigenous students for nearly 100 years (April, 2014). The commission documented abuses that not only caused physical and emotional harm to the victims, but attempted to purge traditional language, religion, and culture from the indigenous populations.

Although these three stories received national attention through media outlets, a lesser-known story has begun to emerge, one in which the "off-reserve" peoples, the largest group of indigenous people, are given very few supports and virtually no opportunity to engage in activities that support their traditional language and culture. An examination in regards to services for indigenous peoples living "off-reserve" was conducted by the Senate of Canada Committee on Human Rights, which conducted hearings throughout the country in 2012 (Metro Newspaper On-line, 2012). Comments made during the hearings spoke of the lack of access to services including traditional language and culture, and drew attention to the lack of support structures, noting that off-reserve indigenous peoples do not fall under indigenous governance structures, including federal education programs, nor are they recognized as a distinct group within urban governance structures.[39] In addition, many individuals who identify as indigenous are without formal status, falling outside of the nationally imposed criteria of formal indigenous recognition. Although these individuals may be able to achieve such recognition through a recent change in legislation, they are nevertheless excluded from indigenous language education when they reside outside of formal traditional homelands. The negative impact of urban life away from traditional territories in regards to

indigenous languages is problematic throughout the Americas as well. A recent article in the *New York Times On-line* reported on indigenous language loss among adult speakers and the lack of indigenous language acquisition among children when resident in urban centers (Sesín, 2014).

Goals and Ideology

The goal to preserve and revitalize indigenous languages gained momentum as residential schools began to close in the 1960s and early 1970s and indigenous communities had greater input into education programs. This interest sparked the development of university-based language preservation activities and teacher training programs in the 1970's (Levine, 2009). Most recently, Maracle, proposed that language revitalization is the top priority for indigenous people (Maracle, 2014) and Hinton suggested that an important next step is to establish goals for the next generation of indigenous language learners (Hinton, 2014).

Currently, the goal to retain and revitalize the indigenous languages in Canada represents a generalized, long-term, national goal. The national and provincial governments view indigenous languages as heritage languages to be supported within the confines of a community, as do Australia and Colombia (see Liddicoat, 2014), except for Inuit in Nunavut Territory, where Inuit has the status of a language of governance. The other indigenous communities, through an education authority, develop language programming for their constituents. At present, there is a wide variety of programming, ranging from teaching basic vocabulary and phrases to immersion programs, among the over 600 reserves across the country. In all cases, programming in urban centers does not occur when those locations are distant from the traditional communities. The post-secondary academic community supports language documentation, teacher training and pedagogical materials with a goal to train indigenous peoples to implement a program that could lead to functional language capacity through such educational models as immersion, master-apprentice, and language crèche programs (Hinton, 2001). The K-12 educational community provides language programming in schools in traditional communities and cultural content in a variety of subject courses throughout the country (see, e.g. Ontario Curriculum Documents, 2014). Although these programs have received positive reports based on improved school retention and national language literacy, analysis in regards to indigenous language acquisition is not provided (see e.g. Bell, 2004).

Indigenous language education and revitalization activities in Canada reflect a process and ideology similar to those of other countries colonized by Western Europeans. Liddicoat (2014) describes programming in both Australia and Colombia, which reflects a similar context to Canada, in which indigenous languages are

---

[39] Although such structures may not be common, Ottawa includes an indigenous health centre (Wabano, 2014) and an Indigenous Education Advisory Committee (OCDSB, 2014).

taught in schools in traditional communities and not normally in urban multicultural areas. Liddicoat argues that this structure implies an ideology that indigenous languages are subservient to the national languages and are recognized only in the domain of their traditional territory. The discourse and structures in Canada, like those in Colombia and Australia, reflect an ideology that perceives the importance of indigenous heritage languages framed in terms of the traditional territory of each indigenous group. Indigenous languages are utilized and taught within the traditional nation while intercultural communication occurs in a national language and acquisition of indigenous languages is not pursued outside of the traditional community. As such, individuals who are not resident within the traditional territory are perceived within the domain of the national language and outside of the realm of an indigenous group. On-reserve, indigenous councils develop education authorities responsible for the development of language revitalization programs. Off-reserve, there are no structures to enable language maintenance or acquisition. This is particularly troubling as the majority of First Nations indigenous people reside off reserve and usually in urban centers.

The framing of indigenous language revitalization within traditional territories is consistent with the language programming provided by the academic community at universities as well as at provincial and federal schools. The academic community at universities targets language documentation and revitalization with fluency as its goal. Programs focus on traditional communities and, thereby, are consistent with the national ideology. Operationally, programs are based on the research on immersion-style programming, which suggests positive results in developing fluency in school-based settings in target European languages such as French, or in language crèches and master/apprentice relationships, which occur in more informal settings (see Hinton, 2001). Other than the master/apprentice methods, these procedures occur in situations where there is a significant population of potential students who share the same ancestral language, which only occurs in the traditional communities in Canada. In addition, the academic communities default to formal governance structures in indigenous communities, such as band councils and education authorities, as recommended by First Peoples Cultural Council (2013).

Provincial and federal schools focus on national language literacy in English or French. Indigenous language instruction only occurs in schools located near traditional communities and is only provided in the language of the local community. In urban centers, indigenous students are able to access indigenous topics in subject content courses including social studies and literature. These courses are taught in English or French with some guest supports from the indigenous community (OCDSB, 2014). Although there are curriculum guides for several indigenous languages (Ontario Curriculum Documents, 2014), urban schools do not provide language courses for the wide diversity of ancestral languages represented in their student body.

Language and Mindset

An alternative approach is needed in order to successfully provide indigenous language instruction in an urban setting. Changes could include:

- The recognition that every indigenous student has the right to ancestral language opportunities, regardless of residence, status, or family circumstances (i.e. with own family, in care, or adopted).

- The recognition in national and provincial policies of the right for indigenous language opportunities in one's ancestral language throughout the country, thereby raising the status of each language from the restrictive setting of a reserve to a national setting.

- The development of alternatives to immersion with a goal to expose students to their ancestral language and to enable them to engage in language documentation. Students would gain familiarity with some basic phrases and vocabulary as well as assist and encourage elders to share their expertise. These activities would need to account for the challenges that occur in urban settings, the most significant of which would be lack of fluent teachers and the possibility that numerous indigenous languages might be represented in any given urban school.

Language Goals and the Uniqueness of Urban Settings

Urban schools are unique from schools in indigenous communities and will require significantly different programs from the traditional "language class" or "immersion setting" [40] that are used in or near indigenous communities. Urban schools have a relatively small number of indigenous students who often come from very diverse nations and languages. Students may not be aware of their ancestry or come from a family that does not wish to identify. In addition, students may not be cognizant of the significant linguistic and cultural differences among the indigenous communities of Canada. Finally, it is necessary to develop curriculum to enable teachers to deliver such a program in the absence of fluent speakers.

Research Question and Methodology

In order to answer the question, "How can schools in urban centers incorporate effective language

---

[40] As exemplified in Hinton (2001).

preservation, revitalization, and retention activities into indigenous related programming?" this paper provides a case study of the indigenous programming at Nepean High School, one of the schools in the Ottawa Carleton District School Board, and proposes to supplement current courses that contain indigenous material with formal language activities that support language preservation, retention, and revitalization. Such supplements would be designed to readily adapt to the indigenous languages represented among the school's population.

Nepean High School is a comprehensive secondary school from grade 9 to 12 (ages 13 to 18) located in Ottawa, Ontario with nearly 1200 students. Second language classes include French immersion and Spanish language classes. Although this school usually has only 20 to 30 identified indigenous students, it is supportive of inclusion for indigenous programming.

This study focusses on an examination of two courses with significant indigenous programming, grade 9 enriched English and grade 10 native studies, both containing indigenous and non-indigenous students. The observations were undertaken in my role as Vice-Principal over the four year period ending in June, 2014. This examination is based on classroom observations as well as interactions with teachers, administrators, and students.

Case Study: Nepean High School

During grade 9 English classes, students in enriched classes study a unit on North American Indigenous literature. This unit includes contemporary authors such as Tomson Highway and Tom King, as well as traditional legends and mythology, and includes a focus on not only the literary aspects of these works but also provides students with the chance to examine traditional histories and ontologies, such as activities involving the sharing wheel, and opportunities to study and participate in present day concerns. This unit of study was developed by Connie Landry and Gwen Smidt, two English teachers at the school. The unit is designed to include a number of indigenous guest speakers, who engage the students with traditional legends and demonstrate cultural activities. In addition to guest speakers, students connect with indigenous communities by sharing their own stories with age peers and engaging with awareness campaigns relating to indigenous concerns. Two examples are "Books of Life" and "Shannen's Dream". "Books of Life" is a provincially sponsored program where urban students write their life stories and exchange these stories with life stories written by students on a reserve. (Ontario Teachers Federation, 2014). "Shannen's Dream" is a campaign advocating for improved educational opportunities for First Nations communities in support of Shannen Koostachin, an advocate for the Atiwapaskaat community in Northern Ontario who tragically died at 15 while travelling to a school outside

of her community (FNCFCS, 2014). The class brought this story throughout the school as well as to a nearby elementary school (Nepean High School, 2011)

In grade 10 students may choose the Native Studies Course (NAC2O) as their compulsory history course. This course is an approved course of the Ministry of Education for Ontario and has been taught by Connie Landry at Nepean High School. Units of study in this course include the history of colonization with topics on the residential school system and the negative impact that colonization has had on traditional North American languages, social structures, and culture. Students examine land claim issues, restrictive laws, and the work of the Truth and Reconciliation Committee. The course also continues the work of the grade 9 unit on North American Indigenous literature and delves further into the indigenous world view and ontology. Traditional foods, products, and home life are also studied.

For the past two years, the NAC2O course has developed connections with various traditional communities. In 2012-2013 students from Prince Rupert B.C. visited Nepean High School as guests of the NAC2O course. This year (2013-2014), NAC 2O students from Nepean High School visited a First Nations Cree community in northern Alberta and hosted students from that community in Ottawa in May. Among the preparations for the trip were guest speakers who introduced the students to the Cree language and traditional stories.

Although both the grade 9 and 10 classes noted above contain some informal exposure to indigenous languages (Algonquin, Cree, and Plains Cree), assessment and evaluation of the program is based on expectations and evidence from English. In addition, access to the languages is based on planned activities, and is not specifically adapted to the languages represented by the students in the class.

Formalizing Language Activities

In order to implement language-specific activities into the two courses above, discrete language goals are added into the current activities, and recommendations are made to identify the evidence that would be used to assess the students. Language activities are, therefore, integrated into content courses providing students with a functional setting for language development and supporting a variety of learning styles. In addition, this method utilizes technology as a supplement within the context of the functional, meaningful, and interactive "real-world" activities within a student's overall program of studies.[41]

---

[41] See Galla (2010) for analysis and recommendations regarding the efficacy of multimedia computer based technology in indigenous educational settings.

Grade 9: One possible starting point would be to begin with an introduction to Algonquin, the language from the area around Ottawa. Not only does this provide students with a connection to the local area, it affirms the importance of the traditional nation in which a school is located (Gardener, 2013). Cooperation with the Algonquin community has included guest speakers and field trips to indigenous events. This has enabled students to gain familiarity with legends, activities, and smudges. In order to introduce a language component, connections need to be extended to include language materials and activities from nearby programs from the Pikwàkanagàn First Nation and the Kitigan Zibi Anishinabeg First Nation.

At this introductory phase, students would be exposed to the sounds of the language and would gain familiarity with some short phrases. In order to accomplish this goal, an Algonquin language teacher could provide a short introductory lesson and phrases in Algonquin at the beginning of the unit on indigenous literature. The language goals could include phrases such as weather, and greetings, and, most importantly, phrases of thanks which could then be used when Algonquin speaking guests visit the class. During these visits, elders would then be encouraged to provide narratives or songs in Algonquin. Assessment of student language learning could be done collaboratively between the classroom teacher and the Algonquin language expert(s).

Grade 10: The curriculum of the grade 10 Native Studies Course includes an independent project. The project could be enhanced to include language content from a specific indigenous language chosen by the student. Teachers would ensure structure to the project and act as facilitators to enable students to acquire information on the languages. Projects could be varied based on the learning strengths of each student, including cultural as well language-based activities. Examples of projects could include making traditional items (cedar bark headbands, baskets, drums) and researching the correct language terms. Where possible, student family members could assist with projects and elders could demonstrate cultural, traditional or contemporary activities via the internet through on-line connections. When appropriate, students could record these experiences on video and share their discoveries on DVDs or on-line. Assessment of language and cultural criteria could be accomplished through collaboration with the student, the family, and community elders.

In addition, projects taking place in traditional communities could engage students in urban areas. For example, a recent video documentation project was completed at the ċ̓al̆ǧʷadi school in Port Hardy, B.C. High school students were trained to complete video projects engaging elders. Students developed several successful videos, which not only demonstrates the capacity of high school students to assist with language and culture documentation, a meaningful, functional and interactive "real-world" project, but one also possible in urban locations (Hemphill, 2014).

Summary

This paper has attempted to demonstrate that it is possible for schools in urban centers to provide activities supporting indigenous languages by integrating them into already existing programs and structures. Although the activities differ from traditional second language programming, bilingual / immersion programming, or master/apprentice relationships,[42] they do offer opportunities for students to acquire language skills which may lead to further languages studies in ancestral communities or post-secondary institutions, as well as to assist with language preservation through research and technology. Students engage in "real world" projects utilizing community supports and technology to develop a better understanding of indigenous communities, which may lead to an emotional connection for indigenous students to their ancestral communities. Such activities also engage members of the urban community as experts and collaborators in both classrooms and research settings. Incorporating language preservation, revitalization, and retention activities into urban schools, while perhaps not meeting the goal of developing fluency in indigenous languages, would provide positive activities for all students, connect urban students and their families with their ancestry and traditional communities, and provide opportunities for urban speakers of indigenous languages to contribute to both their traditional and urban communities.

References

Bell (2004). *Sharing Our Success*. Society for the Advancement of Excellence in Education: Kelowna, B.C. Retrieved from the Website: http://dspace.hil.unb.ca:8080/bitstream/handle/1882 / 8733/SOS2004.pdf?sequenc.

First Peoples Cultural Council (2010). *Report on the Status of B.C. Nations First Languages*. Retrieved from the First Peoples Cultural Council: Brentwood Bay, B.C. Retrieved from the Web site: http://www.fpcc.ca/files/PDF/2010-report-on-thehttp ://www.fpcc.ca/files/PDF/2010-report-on-the-status-of-bc-first-nations-languages.pdfstatus-of-bc-first-nations-languages.pdf

First Peoples Cultural Council (2013). *A Guide to Language Policy and Planning for B.C. First Nations Communities*. First Peoples Cultural Council. Brentwood Bay, B.C. Retrieved from the Website:

---

[42] For example, Hinton (2001) and Gardener (2013).

http://www.fpcc.ca/files/PDF/Language_Policy_Gui
de/FPCC_Policy_Guide_2013.pdf

FNCFCS (2014). "Shannen's Dream." The First Nations Child & Family Caring Society of Canada. Retrieved from the Website: http://www.fncaringsociety.ca.

Galla, Candace. (2010). *Multimedia and Indigenous Language Revitalization: Practical Education Tools and Applications Used Within Native Communities.* Doctoral Dissertation, University of Arizona.

Gardener, Blair, and LaFramboise-Helgson, (2013). *Being Cree in the 21st Century Through Language, Literacy, and Culture: Iyiniwoskinîkiskwewak (Young Women) Take on the Challenge.* Foundation for Endangered Languages, 2013.

Government of Canada (2014). *First Nations Control of First Nations Education Act.* Retrieved from the Website: http://www.parl.gc.ca/HousePublications/Publicatio n.aspx?DocId=6532106

Hemphill (2014). Personal communication.

Hinton, L and K. Hale (2001) *The Green Book of Language Revitalization in Practice.* Leiden: Brill.

Hinton, L. (2014). "Putting Languages to Use: Making sure the New Generation of Speakers is not the Last Generation." Keynote Address, Revitalizing Endangered Languages Conference, Northeastern State University: Oklahoma.

Levine, B. (2009). "Native Languages and Language Teaching in B.C." in *Northwest Journal of Linguistics.* 3(1), 1-7.

Lewis, M. Paul, Gary F. Simons, and Charles D. Fennig (eds.). (2014). *Ethnologue: Languages of the World, Seventeenth edition.* Dallas, Texas: SIL International. Online version: http://www.ethnologue.com. Ethnologue. (2014).

Liddicoat, A. (2014). *Language in Education Policies: The Discursive Construction of Intercultural Relations.* Bristol: Multilingual Matters.

Maracle, L. (2014). Interview on CBC National Radio re. Truth and Reconciliation Committee. May, 2014.

Metro (November 21, 2012) "Rights for off-reserve First Nations focus of Senate Committee meeting." *Metro Newpaper On-Line,* Vancouver, B.C. Retrieved from the Website: http://metronews.ca/

Nepean High School (2011). "Nepean Newsletter July 2011." Nepean High School, Ottawa, Ontario. Retrieved from the Website http://www.nepeanhighschool.com

Ontario Curriculum Documents (2014). *Native Languages.* Retrieved from the Website at http://www.edu.gov.on.ca/eng/curriculum/secondary/ nativelang.html.

Ontario Teachers Federation (2014). "Ontario Teachers' Federation Launches Books of Life." Retrieved from the Website: Retrieved from the Website: http://www.newswire.ca/en/story/1039367/ontariohtt p://www.newswire.ca/en/story/1039367/ontario-teac hers-federation-launches-books-of-lifeteachers-feder ation-launches-books-of-life .

Ottawa-Carleton District School Board (2013). *Strategic Plan 2013.* Ottawa-Carleton District School Board, Ottawa, ON. Retrieved from the Web site http://www.ocdsb.ca/abocdsb/annual_Reports/Pages/ default.aspx.

Robinson, Eden. (2014). "My White Accent: The Frontlines of Language Revitalization." Munro Beattie Lecture 2013-14 at Carleton University: March 3, 2014: Ottawa.

Sesín, Carmen. (2014). "With Migration, Indigenous Languages Going Extinct" *NBC News Online.* Retrieved from the Website at http://www.nbcnews.com/news/latino/migrationhttp: //www.nbcnews.com/news/latino/migration-indigeno us-languages-going-extinct-n52731indigenous-langu ages-going-extinct-n52731. NBCNEWS.

Statistics Canada. (2014). "2006 Census: Aboriginal Peoples in Canada in 2006." Retrieved from the Website at http://www12.statcan.ca/censusrecensement/2006/as -sa/97-558/p16-eng.cfm.

United Nations (2007). *Declaration of the Rights of Indigenous Peoples.* Retrieved from the Website: http://undesadspd.org/IndigenousPeoples/Declaration ontheRightsofIndigenousPeoples.aspx

United Nations (2014). *Report of the Special Rapporteur on the rights of indigenous peoples in Canada,* Retrieved from the Website at http://unsr.jamesanaya.org/country-reports/thehttp://u nsr.jamesanaya.org/country-reports/the-situation-of-i ndigenous-peoples-in-canadasituation-of-indigenous- peoples-in-canada

Wabano (2014). "Wabano Centre for Aboriginal Health." Retrieved from the Website: http://www.wabano.com/ (2014)

Re-awakening Australian Languages:
Economic, Educational, Health and Social Benefits to the Community

Michael Walsh
[michael.walsh@aiatsis.gov.au]

Doug Marmion
[Doug.Marmion@aiatsis.gov.au]

Jakelin Troy
[Jaky.Troy@aiatsis.gov.au]

AIATSIS Centre for Australian Languages
Australian Institute of Aboriginal and Torres Strait Islander Studies
Lawson Crescent, Acton Peninsula, Acton ACT 2601 Australia

Abstract

Indigenous Australia at one time was estimated to have had some 250 separate languages. A recent survey [http://www.aiatsis.gov.au/_files/site/nils2.pdf] indicates that only 13 of these are still strong in the sense that children are learning the language as a matter of course. The rest are in various states of vitality. Fortunately in recent decades there has been a considerable uplift in many languages so that these languages can be thought of as re-awakening. These re-awakenings have produced economic, educational, health and social benefits to the community.

At a general level economic benefits to the community have been assessed by Mühlhäusler and Damania (2004).[43] At the local level we have seen many instances of Indigenous people whose lives have been transformed through regaining their linguistic heritage. By their own reporting they have gone from being rather dysfunctional to becoming not only an economically viable unit but a person with renewed and enhanced identity. In these kinds of situation clearly there is also a social benefit because a dysfunctional individual will have disruptive effects on the community.

From an educational perspective there is increasing evidence that Indigenous students who have studies their heritage language show a marked improvement in their academic achievement across all learning areas. So Australian Languages have educational benefits in their own right but also benefit overall academic achievement.

There is an increasing awareness that the retention/revitalization of Australian Languages can yield substantial health benefits to Indigenous communities. For instance, the Social Justice Report 2009[44] indicates: "While Australia lacks research on culture and resilience, we do have longitudinal research data which demonstrates a correlation between strong language and culture in Indigenous homeland communities and positive health outcomes. A ten year study of Indigenous Australians in Central Australia found that 'connectedness to culture, family and land, and opportunities for self-determination' assist in significantly lower morbidity and mortality rates in Homeland residents." Work is in progress to further demonstrate how Australian Languages provide health benefits.

In the state of New South Wales a recent government report[45] indicates that Australian Languages are being taught to some 8,000 students. This is an extraordinary statistic in a country with an all too pervasive monolingual mindset! Interestingly 4 out of 5 of these students are non-Indigenous. Preliminary reports indicate that the corrosive effects of racism are giving way to increased social harmony so the learning of Australian Languages has considerable social value.

In this paper a range of examples will be presented of language re-awakenings that have produced economic, educational, health and social benefits to the community.

---

[43] [http://digital.library.adelaide.edu.au/dspace/handle/2440/40591].

[44] [http://www.humanrights.gov.au/publications/chapter-3-introduction-social-justice-report-2009]

[45] [www.aph.gov.au/Parliamentary_Business/Committees/House_of_Representatives_Committees?url=/atsia/languages2/report.htm]

Orientation

We would argue that the evolving situation for Australian Languages sits within what Truscott and Malcolm (2010) describe as "invisible language policy". Addressing the questions and issues that arise contributes to a more explicit language policy for Australian Languages and seeks to engage with "ethnographic monitoring" (McCarty, 2011). In addressing language re-awakenings that have produced economic, educational, health and social benefits to the community we favour the ethnographic monitoring approach:

> In McCarty's volume, ethnographic monitoring takes the shape of interventionist and advocacy ethnography. Ethnographers do not just observe what happens in education; they engage with the inequalities they observe and work collaboratively with the community in order to open new opportunities and horizons. In practice, this means that ethnographers challenge the dominant language ideologies they witness in educational practices, particularly in stratified multilingual environments where one language dominates the other (often indigenous minority) languages. (Blommaert 2013: 128)

Linguists as ethnographers can draw directly from their own observations but can also gain insight indirectly by drawing on Indigenous perspectives (see also Hermes, 2012). To that end we often present the words of Indigenous commentators directly. It is crucial to our enterprise that we demonstrate the economic, educational, health and social benefits to the community of language re-awakenings more fully so that these can be woven into a more explicit language policy. In this way we seek to become linguists as agents of social change (Charity, 2008).

Overview of the Australian Languages Situation

There have been many overviews and reports on the Australian Languages situation (e.g. Australia, 2012; Purdie *et al.*, 2009; Walsh, 2014) but space precludes rehearsing the situation in any detail. The main facts can be set out as:

- At first sustained contact, over 250 separate languages and many more dialects

- Now only around 120 still spoken

- Of these only 13 can be considered strong in the sense that they are learned by children as a matter of course (Marmion, Obata & Troy, 2014).

To demonstrate how language re-awakenings have produced economic, educational, health and social benefits to the community we present a number of case studies. We use the term, re-awakenings, because the majority of Australian Languages are said to be sleeping or in the process of revival.

Language in its place

Using an Australian Language on the territory of that language appears to be an important contributor to health and social benefits. Often observations along these lines fail to rise above the anecdotal. However research is beginning to appear that puts these observations on a much solid footing. One such study deserves quoting at some length:

> While Australia lacks research on culture and resilience, we do have longitudinal research data which demonstrates a correlation between strong language and culture in Indigenous homeland communities and positive health outcomes. A ten year study of Indigenous Australians in Central Australia found that "connectedness to culture, family and land, and opportunities for self-determination" assist in significantly lower morbidity and mortality rates in Homeland residents. The study compared the rates of cardiovascular disease in the Alyawarr and Anmatyerr people of the Utopia Homeland communities with the rates amongst the Indigenous population of Northern Territory. In the Utopia homelands, high value is placed on the maintenance of strong mother tongue languages and traditional cultural practices. The study found that residents of these communities were less likely to be obese, less likely to have diabetes and less prone to cardiovascular disease than Indigenous people across the rest of the Northern Territory. Interestingly, the study found that 'conventional measures of employment, income, housing and education did not account for this health differential. Strong connections to traditional ways of life were the predictors for the better health outcomes. (Social Justice Commissioner, 2009, see also Rowley *et al.* (2008))

This view is confirmed by a number of Indigenous commentators, for instance, Rosalie Kunoth-Monks, an Alyawarr/Anmatyerr elder:

> To the Alyawarr people, the land owning you means that through your song lines, you've got to know which part of the land owns you and where you are responsible for the wellbeing of that earth...Let me assure anybody who cares for the Aboriginal people of Australia that once we are moved from our place of origin, we will not only lose our identity, we will die a traumatised tragic end. (http://www.amnesty.org.au/indigenous-rights/comments/26142, accessed 17 July 2014)

Another perspective comes from a Waanyi man and medical anthropologist, Gregory Phillips:

> ... outstations are seen as an important intervention tool for grog, gunga and gambling. They are situated

out on the land, away from violence, noise pollution and the sedentism of the community. Culturally, it is perceived that being on the land provides physical, emotional, spiritual and mental sustenance: one young man told me about his grandfather: "... as soon as he goes bush, he talk/ language, chuck that walking stick away, can walk good again, he that happy for that land. When he come back here, leg swell up again, knee no good, he get low then". Thus connection to land is seen as a primary tool for intervention and wellbeing, and outstations are the natural expression of such a belief system. (Phillips, 2003: 102-103)

Yet another Indigenous observation is provided by a Gunai Elder, Dr. Doris Paton, Manager, Yirruk-Tinnor Gunai Community Language Program:

It's important that our people speak the language of the country. We could not go somewhere else and have the same relationship with another country because they speak another language. And in Victoria we have 38 different languages. Just think of the concept of a mini-Europe where there are many countries, many cultures, many languages and they are all unique and different. People will travel overseas, embrace the language. They embrace the words that go with the food; they embrace the celebration of the culture through language. I think people could think of Aboriginal languages in the same way. I think the value of reviving languages is not just for now – for the generations to come. (http://vimeo.com/45787761)

This view is echoed by one of us [Jaky Troy]:

On Friday 25 July 2014, Fraser Primary School in the Australian Capital Territory officially 'opened' the Ngunawal gardens at the school. For all in attendance it was an extraordinary event for the sense of overwhelming community wellbeing that it generated. As a Ngarigu person it was the first time I experienced the power of our shared cultural protocols as we were there participating as neighbours from the High Country bordering on what is now Canberra, welcomed in by our Ngunawal community in which we now live. The garden is part of a Ngunawal linguistic and cultural renaissance. I am part of that effort as a researcher in languages and linguistics. At AIATSIS we are helping the Ngunawal to reawaken their language using our technical expertise, collections of languages materials and the Ngunawal community's own retained knowledge and precious documents, including language recordings. Through language revival the community is regaining its health and strength as cultural leaders in Canberra. A much healthier, more culturally and linguistically robust future for all of us and particularly our children than any of us might have dreamed about even just a few years ago.

These examples present a range of possibilities for "language in its place". Many of the Alyawarr and Anmatyerr people of central Australia spend most of their lives on their own country and gain from the material and spiritual benefits of that land. Gregory Phillips' home country is in northern Queensland, the best part of 3,000 kilometres from his workplace in Melbourne. Nevertheless he is very much aware of the benefits of being on one's own country. Dr. Doris Paton and Dr. Jaky Troy live close by their traditional country and see it as a major touchstone in their lives.

"Cultural Wounds"

Australia's Indigenous peoples are certainly the most disadvantaged group within Australia and among the worst in the world. This is reflected across a whole range of indicators including lower household and individual income, lower rates of employment, residential overcrowding, disability and chronic disease, poorer educational attainment (e.g. SCRGSP, 2011). We adopt the term, cultural wounds, from a study conducted in Canada but readily applicable to Indigenous Australia:

… the sum total of malaise and ill-health suffered by Canada's (and the world's) Indigenous peoples is best understood, not as some simple aggregate or additive sum of the personal woes of separately damaged individuals, but as a culmination of "cultural wounds" inflicted upon whole communities and ways of life. (Chandler & Dunlop, to appear)

It is their belief that such cultural wounds need to be treated by 'cultural medicines'. For Chandler & Dunlop, these cultural medicines need to be administered by whole cultural communities. This appears to be the path followed by the Gumbaynggirr group of New South Wales (Walsh, 2001, see also Walsh (2003)) and also the Kaurna of South Australia (Amery, 1995, see also 2009). However it can happen that a language re-awakening starts at the level of a single family and then has the potential to spread out through the whole cultural community. A spectacular example is provided by the efforts of a Myaamia man, Daryl Baldwin, who resurrected his ancestral within his own family (e.g. Baldwin et al., 2013). Within Australia, a Kaurna man, Jack Buckskin, is currently teaching his young daughter her language from the earliest years so that she may become the first native speaker since the death of the Kaurna Elder, Ivaritji, in 1929 (http://www.abc.net.au/local/stories/2014/05/28/401410 0.htm). Such efforts indicate the need to engage with the emergent field of 'family language policy' (e.g. King, Fogle & Logan-Terry, 2008).

Healing cultural wounds is not restricted to communities in which the ancestral language is re-awakening. The Yolngu of northeast Arnhem Land in northern Australia have one of the strongest languages. It is one of the 13 which children are still learning as a matter of course. However a number of commentators have observed that Yolngu people suffer considerable difficulties and anxiety in attempting to interact with the wider Australian community:

> We believed then that if we just went to the Balanda [non-Indigenous people] schools and returned home at the end of high school with djorra' (paper/certificate) then that djorra' would bring this Balanda luck and power. We thought it was the certificate that would get you a vehicle, make you rich, and give you Balanda power and authority. This authority we thought would be like the power the superintendent had and the power that the Balanda used to push us off our lands. But when the young ones went through that education, it did not work. They got the certificate but they did not seem to work. No, on top of that they were more confused about the Balanda world than before. Many were so confused they started drinking or just dropped out. Others went mad trying to understand the strange mysteries of the Balanda world. (from the foreword by Rev. Dr. Djiniyini Gondarra, in Trudgen, 2000: 1)

The Yolngu community's response has been to develop resources which will help people understand areas of engagement with the Balanda world such as economics, governance, health and law.

Winning Hearts and Minds

One of the pleasing outcomes of non-Indigenous students learning an Australian language is the reduction in racism.

As Kerry Gilbert, Wiradjuri language teacher, Middleton Primary School, Parkes, observes:

> My brothers and I, we were treated badly some times by other children – racial taunts. I hardly see it now; it blows me away. I think it's to do with the Wiradjuri lessons; I think that can certainly change people's views on Aboriginal people. (https://open.abc.net.au/posts/our-mother-tongue-wiradjuri-02vw8hr).

A survey of Indigenous languages programs in Australian schools revealed:

> Over 16,000 Indigenous students and 13,000 non-Indigenous students located in 260 Australian schools are involved in an Indigenous language programme. Most of these students are located in government schools in the Northern Territory, Western Australia, New South Wales, and South Australia. … /More than 80 different languages are taught (Purdie et al., 2008: x-xi).

When this report came out we were heartened by what we saw as a relatively high take up of Indigenous languages in a country where the study of languages other than English at school is typically very low. We were also pleased to see the relatively high proportion of non-Indigenous students, roughly 45%, involved.

An even more recent report, *Our Land our Languages* (2012), presents even more encouraging figures and a wide ranging account of the issues arising in language learning. Surprisingly, some 8,000 students in New South Wales are learning an Australian Language of which four out of five are non-Indigenous students. This activity involves 13 Aboriginal Languages across 36 public schools (Australia. Parliament. House of Representatives. Standing Committee on Aboriginal and Torres Strait Islander Affairs, 2012: 88, see also Walsh, 2003).

The authors have been engaged with developing a Framework for Australian Languages which would potentially provide guidance for teachers across all the state and territory jurisdictions in Australia (Troy & Walsh, 2013). With the take up of the Framework we can anticipate many more students engaging with Australian Languages. In a country like Australia with its supposedly "monolingual mindset" (e.g. Clyne, 2008) this will be quite an achievement.

Limitations

While there are signs of wellbeing arising from the retention or revitalization of Australian Languages, solid proof of the connection remains elusive. This is partly through the difficulty of accurate measurement (e.g. Biddle, 2012, 2014; Biddle & Swee, 2012) but also through the lack of targeted research although Rowley et al. (2008) is a valuable exception. Nor are such problems confined to Australia (e.g. Ball & McIvor, 2013; McIvor, 2013). While there are beneficial effects from using language on its own territory, the overwhelming majority of Indigenous Australians do not live on their ancestral lands and often enough have not even visited them (Troy & Walsh, 2005). We have already mentioned that the take up of any languages other than English is quite low in Australian education. Regrettably this trend is likely to continue and poses a significant challenge for Indigenous languages (see also, McCarty, 2003). Another issue with regard to Indigenous language revitalization is its relative fragility, particularly on a longterm basis (Walsh, 2010).

Conclusion

We have attempted to present a range of case studies which demonstrate economic, educational, health and social benefits to the community. Improved wellbeing from retaining or revitalizing Indigenous languages is probably the greatest economic benefit to the community. The malaise experienced by so many Indigenous people in Australia has led to numerous impediments to economic independence. Among these are lower rates of employment, incarceration and substance abuse. When such impediments are removed economic benefits flow not just to Indigenous individuals and their dependants but also to the wider community in that there is reduced demand for a range of services provided by the state. Educational benefits can be seen in Indigenous students who have engaged with their ancestral language. Evidence is emerging that such students have improved attainment across the range of key learning areas, not just in languages but also in mathematics and science. The challenge now is to conduct rigorous evaluations of academic performance among Indigenous students. The same challenge applies to demonstrating the health benefits of retaining or revitalizing Indigenous languages.

References

Amery, R.M. (1995). It's ours to keep and call our own: Reclamation of the Nunga languages in the Adelaide region, South Australia. *International Journal of the Sociology of Language* 113, 63-82.

Amery, R. (2009). Phoenix or relic? Documentation of languages with revitalization in mind. *Language Documentation & Conservation* 3(2), 138-48.

Australia. Parliament. House of Representatives. Standing Committee on Aboriginal and Torres Strait Islander Affairs. (2012). *Our Land Our Languages: Language Learning in Indigenous Communities*. Canberra: Parliament of the Commonwealth of Australia. http://www.aph.gov.au/Parliamentary_Business/C ommittees/House_of_Representatives_Committees ?url=/atsia/languages2/report.htm.

Baldwin, D., Baldwin, K., Baldwin, J. & Baldwin, J. (2013). Myaamiaataweenki oowaaha: Miami spoken here. In L. Hinton (Ed.) *Bringing our Languages Home: Language Revitalization for Families* (pp. 3-18). Berkeley, California: Heyday Books.

Ball, J. & McIvor, O. (2013). Canada's big chill: Indigenous languages in education. In C. Benson & K. Kosonen (Eds.), *Language Issues in Comparative Education: Inclusive Teaching and Learning in Non-Dominant Languages and Cultures* (pp.19-38). Rotterdam: Sense Publishers.

Biddle, N. (2012). Measures of Indigenous social capital and their relationship with well-being. *Australian Journal of Rural Health*, 20(6), 298-304.

Biddle, N. (2014). Measuring and analysing the wellbeing of Australia's Indigenous population. *Social Indicators Research* 116(3), 713-729.

Biddle, N. & Swee, H. (2012). The relationship between wellbeing and Indigenous land, language and culture in Australia. *Australian Geographer* 43(3), 215-232.

Blommaert, J. (2013). Review article Policy, policing and the ecology of social norms: ethnographic monitoring revisited. *International Journal of the Sociology of Language* 219: 123-140.

Chandler, M. J. & Dunlop, W. L. (to appear). Cultural wounds require cultural medicines. In M. Greenwood, C. Redding & S. de Leeuw (Eds.) *Determinants of Indigenous Peoples' Health in Canada*. Toronto: Canada Scholars' Press.

Charity, A. H. (2008). Linguists as agents for social change. *Language and Linguistics Compass* 2, 923-939.

Clyne, M. (2008). The monolingual mindset as an impediment to the development of plurilingual potential in Australia. *Sociolinguistic Studies* 2(3), 347-366.

Hermes, M. (2012). Indigenous language revitalization and documentation in the United States: collaboration despite colonialism. *Language and Linguistics Compass* 6(3), 131-142.

King, K.A., Fogle, L. & Logan-Terry, A. (2008). Family language policy. *Language and Linguistics Compass* 2, 907-922.

McCarty, T.L. (2003). Revitalising Indigenous languages in homogenizing times. *Comparative Education* 39(2), 147-163.

McCarty, T. (Ed.) (2011). *Ethnography and Language Policy*. London and New York: Routledge.

McIvor, O. (2013). Protective effects of language learning, use and culture on the health and well-being of Indigenous people in Canada. In M.J. Norris, E. Anonby, M-O, Junker, N. Ostler & D. Patrick (Eds.), *Endangered Languages beyond Boundaries. Langues en Péril au-delà des Frontières. Proceedings of the 17th FEL Conference, Carleton University, Ottawa, Ontario, Canada, 1-4 October 2013* (pp. 123-131). Bath: Foundation for Endangered Languages.

Marmion, M., Obata, K. & Troy, J. (2014). *Community, Identity, Wellbeing: the Report of the Second National Indigenous Languages Survey*. Canberra: Australian Institute of Aboriginal and Torres Strait Islander Studies. http://aiatsis.gov.au/_files/research/report_of_the_ 2nd_national_indigenous_languages_survey.pdf

Mühlhäusler, P. & Damania, R. (2004). *Economic Costs and Benefits of Australian Indigenous languages*. Canberra: Australian Government Aboriginal and Torres Strait Islander Services. http://digital.library.adelaide.edu.au/dspace/handle/24 40/40591 (accessed 24 July 2014).

Phillips, G. (2003). *Addictions and Healing in Aboriginal Country*. Canberra: Aboriginal Studies Press.

Purdie, N., Frigo, T., Ozolins, C., Noblett, G., Thieberger, N. & Sharp, J. (2008) *Indigenous Languages Programs in Australia Schools: a Way Forward*. Canberra: Australian Council for Educational Research.

http://research.acer.edu.au/cgi/viewcontent.cgi?article=1017&context=indigenous_education

Rowley, K.G., O'Dea, K., Anderson, I., McDermott, R., Saraswati, K., Tilmouth, R., Roberts, I., Fitz, J., Wang, Z., Jenkins, A., Best, J.D., Wang, Z. & Brown, A. (2008). Lower than expected morbidity and mortality for an Australian Aboriginal population: 10-year follow-up in a decentralised community. *Medical Journal of Australia*, 188(5), 283-287.

Social Justice Commissioner (2009). The perilous state of Indigenous languages in Australia. https://www.humanrights.gov.au/publications/chapter-3-introduction-social-justice-report-2009 pdf (accessed 24 July 2014).

SCRGSP (Steering Committee for the Review of Government Service Provision) (2011). *Overcoming Indigenous Disadvantage: Key Indicators 2011*. Canberra: Productivity Commission. http://www.pc.gov.au/__data/assets/pdf_file/0018/111609/key-indicators-2011-report.pdf

Troy, J. & Walsh, M. (2005). Languages off country? Revitalizing the 'right' Indigenous languages in the south east of Australia. In N. Crawhall & N. Ostler (Eds.) *Creating Outsiders: Endangered Languages, Migration and Marginalization. (Proceedings of Ninth Conference of the Foundation for Endangered Languages, Stellenbosch, South Africa, 18-20 November 2005)*. Bath: Foundation for Endangered Languages, 71-81.

Troy, J. & Walsh, M. (2013). Embracing Babel: the Framework for Australian Languages. *Babel: Journal of the Australian Federation of Modern Language Teachers' Associations*. Australian Curriculum: Special Issue 48(2/3), 14-19.

Trudgen, R. (2000). *Why Warriors Lie Down and Die: Towards an Understanding of Why the Aboriginal People of Arnhem Land Face the Greatest Crisis in Health and Education since European Contact: Djambatj Mala*. Darwin: Aboriginal Resource & Development Services Inc.

Truscott, A. & Malcolm, I. (2010). Closing the policy–practice gap: making Indigenous language policy more, than empty rhetoric. In J. Hobson, K. Lowe, S. Poetsch & M. Walsh (Eds.) *Re-awakening Languages: Theory and Practice in the Revitalisation of Australia's Indigenous Languages* (pp. 6-21). Sydney: Sydney University Press. http://ses.library.usyd.edu.au//bitstream/2123/6949/1/RAL-chapter-1.pdf

Walsh, M. (2001). A case of language revitalisation in 'settled' Australia. *Current Issues in Language Planning* 2(2/3), 251-258. Also available at: http://www.multilingual-matters.net/cilp/002/0251/cilp0020251.pdf

Walsh, M. (2003). Raising Babel: language revitalization in NSW, Australia. In J. Blythe and R. M. Brown (Eds.), *Maintaining the Links. Language, Identity and the Land. Proceedings of the Seventh Conference Presented by the Foundation for Endangered Languages. Broome, Western Australia, 22-24 September 2003* (pp. 113-117). Bath: Foundation for Endangered Languages.

Walsh, M. (2010). Why language revitalization sometimes works. In J. Hobson, K. Lowe, S. Poetsch & M. Walsh (Eds.) *Re-awakening Languages: Theory and Practice in the Revitalisation of Australia's Indigenous Languages* (pp. 22-36). Sydney: Sydney University Press.

Walsh, M. (2014). Indigenous language maintenance and revitalisation. In H. Koch & R. Nordlinger (Ed.) *Languages and Linguistics of Australia: a Comprehensive Guide*. Berlin: Mouton de Gruyter.Chercheur, J.L. (1994). *Case-Based Reasoning*. San Mateo, CA: Morgan Kaufman Publishers.

"Our Ancestors Are Happy!"
Revivalistics in the Service of Indigenous Wellbeing

Ghil'ad Zuckermann
Chair of Linguistics and Endangered Languages
School of Humanities, University of Adelaide, SA Adelaide 5005, Australia
[ghilad.zuckermann@adelaide.edu.au]

Michael Walsh
Senior Research Fellow, AIATSIS Centre for Australian Languages,
Indigenous Social and Cultural Wellbeing (ISCW)
GPO Box 553, Canberra ACT 2601, Australia
[michael.walsh@aiatsis.gov.au]

Abstract

Hallett, Chandler and Lalonde (2007) report a clear correlation between lack of conversational knowledge in the native language and youth suicide in British Columbia, Canada. Whilst their research demonstrates a link between language *loss* and *reduced* mental health, there is an urgent need in the 21st century to examine whether there is a correlation also between language *gain* and *improved* mental health. To date, there has been no systematic study of the impact of language revival on mental health, partly because language reclamation is still rare, and Revivalistics is in its infancy. Revivalistics is a new trans-disciplinary field of enquiry, proposed by Zuckermann (see e.g. 2012). Revivalistics is far more than Revival Linguistics. It comparatively and systematically studies the universal constraints and global mechanisms on the one hand (Zuckermann, 2009) and culturally relative idiosyncrasies on the other hand (Zuckermann & Walsh, 2011) apparent in linguistic revitalisation attempts across various sociological backgrounds, all over the globe. This paper postulates language as core to a people's wellbeing and hypothesises that language reclamation often results in mental health empowerment, as evidenced in the case study of the current reclamation project with the Barngarla people of the Eyre Peninsula, South Australia (Zuckermann & Monaghan, 2012).

Introduction

Language is postulated as core to a people's wellbeing and mental health. The link between poor mental health and suicide has been clearly demonstrated. Furthermore, Hallett, Chandler and Lalonde (2007) report a clear correlation between youth suicide and lack of conversational knowledge in the native language in British Columbia, Canada. "The results reported … that youth suicide rates effectively dropped to zero in those few communities in which at least half the band members reported a conversational knowledge of their own "native" language." However, there has been no systematic study of the impact of language revival on mental health and suicide, partly because language reclamation is still rare.

Due to invasion, colonization, globalization and homogenization, there are more and more Indigenous groups losing their heritage. The Barngarla people of Eyre Peninsula are but one example of Aboriginal and Torres Strait Islander peoples suffering the effects of linguicide (language killing). Their language loss, consequent lack of cultural autonomy and intellectual sovereignty, as well as their dependence on the colonizer's tongue, increase the phenomenon of disempowerment, self-loathing and suicide.

From the last 200 years of systemic racism, abuse and cultural loss Australian Aboriginal and Torres Strait Islander peoples suffer greatly from many burdens, including poverty, discrimination, low life expectancy, poor health status and especially high levels of mental health issues (Australian Bureau of Statistics, 2010a; Purdie, Dudgeon & Walker, 2010). According to King, Smith & Gracey (2009), a strong sense of identity is a necessary condition for mental health however for the majority of Indigenous Australians this is not the case, especially when looking at the statistics of health and mental health.

Language has been identified as one of the key elements that make up ethnic identity (Phinney, 1990). Marginalisation of groups of people can easily be observed through the changes in the language system (Heinrich, 2004). Before the British settlement of Australia there were approximately 330 Australian Indigenous languages but post-colonization there are now only 13 language groups (4%) which are still going strong (Australian Institute of Aboriginal and Torres Strait Islander Studies & Federation of Aboriginal and Torres Straight Islander Languages, 2005; Indigenous Remote Communications Association, 2013). By and large, due to white colonization, the Aboriginal people living along the coasts, e.g. in the states of South Australia, Victoria and New South Wales, suffered linguicide more than those living in the Outback.

The Barngarla of the coastal area of the Eyre Peninsula (Port Lincoln, Whyalla and Port Augusta) decided to reclaim their "sleeping beauty" tongue and have worked in close collaboration with Professor Zuckermann since 2011. Studies on the effectiveness of Revivalistics in improving mental health for communities who urgently need to reinstate their own authority in the world, but who currently lack the language and linguistic knowledge with which to do so, have not yet been thoroughly conducted. While reclaiming the Barngarla tongue through Revivalistics, it is also possible to assess systematically whether language revival can reduce suicide by empowering people and communities and improve sense of identity and purpose.

Revivalistics (including Revival Linguistics and Revivalomics) is a new trans-disciplinary field of enquiry, proposed by Zuckermann (see Zuckermann & Walsh, 2011). It studies comparatively and systematically the universal constraints and global mechanisms on the one hand (Zuckermann, 2009) and culturally relative idiosyncrasies on the other hand (Zuckermann & Walsh, 2011), apparent in linguistic revitalization attempts across various sociological backgrounds, all over the globe. Revivalistics is far more than Revival Linguistics. It studies language revival from various angles such as law (see Zuckermann, Shakuto-Neoh & Quer, 2014), mental health, sociology, anthropology, politics, education, colonization, missionary studies, music and architecture.

Photo 1: Whyalla, South Australia, 2013. Barngarla participants in one of the Barngarla Aboriginal language reclamation workshops. (The Barngarla people have given their permission to use this photo.)

In 2014, the Second National Indigenous Languages Survey (NILS 2) Report showed the following as the goals of language activities, as viewed by Aboriginal people taking part in the Barngarla revival:

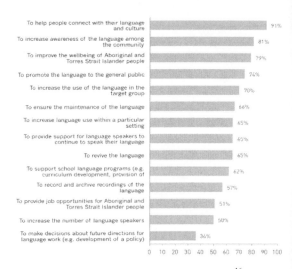

Figure 1:   Goals of Language Activities[46]

This paper suggests that there is an urgent need to systematically assess, both quantitatively and qualitatively, the mental health impact of language reclamation on Aboriginal people in Australia, e.g. the Barngarla people of Eyre Peninsula, South Australia. The primary hypothesis is that there will be significant improvements in mental health during the language revival process, reduced suicide ideation (i.e. people would be less likely to come up with the idea of suicide as a possibility), reduced self-harm and reduced instances of suicide. The demographic most at risk of suicidal behaviours are young people and should be a primary focus for studies in this area.

The Current State of Mental Health of Australia's Aboriginal and Torres Strait Islander People

Over three quarters of all Australians, who had been diagnosed with a mental illness during their lifetime, had symptoms and a diagnosis before the age of 24 years (Australian Bureau of Statistics, 2010b; headspace National Youth Mental Health Foundation, 2011). This fact has implications for the Indigenous community as the majority of the population (57%) are under the age of 25 years (Australian Institute of Health and Welfare, 2011). Due to the demographic distribution of the Indigenous population and overall disadvantage, Aboriginal and Torres Strait Islander adolescents are more likely to struggle with social and emotional issues than others. These issues influence the ability to maintain positive social and emotional wellbeing. These can include adverse life events such as the death of a loved one, forced removal of a loved one, discrimination, poverty, violence, abuse, gambling problems, incarceration, poverty, educational struggles and trauma (Purdie, Dudgeon & Walker, 2010). For

---

[46] Data drawn from the NILS 2 Report and analysed by Marmion, Kazuko, & Troy (2014).

example, one third of Indigenous youth have had a grandparent or carer who was forcibly taken away from their family as part of the Stolen Generations; the negative psychological impact is still evident in the higher levels of distress of both the grandparent and subsequent generations (Australian Health Ministers' Advisory Council, 2012; Australian Institute of Health and Welfare, 2011; Dodson *et al.*, 2010). Such cultural dislocation, trauma and loss can be passed down and accumulated in the next generation. The coping with cultural dislocation, trauma and loss are often displayed outwardly by behavioural aspects such as social withdrawal, anger, rage, violence, substance misuse due to high levels of hopelessness, depression, anxiety and complicated mental distress (Dodson *et al.*, 2010; Social Health Reference Group, 2004).

Collective crisis from a loss of identity, loss of purpose, loss of pride, and loss of self-esteem can lead to collective despair and collective suicide (Hunter & Harvey, 2002). In the Northern Territory between the years 2001 and 2011, 75% of all youth suicides aged 10-24 years were Indigenous persons (Hanssens, 2008; Hanssens, 2012). In some communities, such as the Kimberly region in north-west Australia, the rate was seven times higher than the average suicide rate (Australian Broadcasting Corporation, 2012; Tighe & McKay, 2012). One such community included Mowanjum, an area with a population of 300 people, which suffered five suicides within a few months (Australian Broadcasting Corporation, 2012). Indigenous communities can suffer from copycat suicides, or suicide clusters, at much higher rates than non-Indigenous communities and often do not have the resources to help people through grief (Hanssens, 2008; Hanssens, 2012).

The rate of suicide in the Indigenous population is almost three times greater than that of the non-Indigenous population. Rates are highest among young people (Australian Institute of Health and Welfare, 2011). In 2010, the ABS reported that Indigenous males aged 14-19 years were 4.4 times more likely to take their own lives, and 20-24 year old males were 3.9 times more likely, than the non-Indigenous population (Australian Bureau of Statistics, 2010c). For females it was even higher; Indigenous females aged 14-19 years were 5.9 times more likely, and, aged 20-24 years 5.4 times more likely, to take their own lives (Australian Bureau of Statistics, 2010c). For every five Indigenous youth, two of them have thought about killing themselves. This is a devastating statistic to comprehend. However, some research has identified key positive factors that can help to bring hope to this dire situation.

Cultural Identity, Language and "Cultural Continuality"

Positive factors which influence psychological wellbeing are few, but several comprehensive studies have helped to highlight key mental health elements that enable Indigenous individuals and communities to succeed in life (Human Rights and Equal Opportunities Commission, 1997; Purdie, Dudgeon & Walker, 2010; Trewin, 2006; Zubrick *et al.*, 2005). These factors include the knowledge and use of traditional language, connection to land, family connectedness, cultural strength and spirituality.

Hunter and Harvey (2002) explored Indigenous suicide in Aboriginal Australians and Canadians, as well as Inuit and Native American youth and found similar patterns regarding a lack of cultural involvement and suicide (Hunter & Harvey, 2002). Wexler, Difluvio & Burke (2009) explored reliance in marginalised youth and found that there was a connection between those who had better self-reported wellbeing and those who were actively engaged in their traditional culture. Two of the main issues of cultural transference in the modern era are increased globalization and remaining issues from colonization (de Souza & Rymarz, 2007). This transference of cultural knowledge is known as cultural continuality (de Souza & Rymarz, 2007). The lack of successful cultural continuality or transference can leave new generations feeling lost between cultures and creating an instable sense of identity (Wexler, 2006).

According to King, Smith & Gracey (2009) a strong sense of identity is a necessary condition for mental health. Language is reportedly the third highest contributing factor to ethnic identity for adolescents and young adults (after a sense of self, and family) (Kickett-Tucker, 2009) yet, in Australia, as a result of extreme linguicide, only 19% of all Indigenous Australians are able to fluently speak their language (Australian Bureau of Statistics, 2010a). Linguicide has resulted in many Aboriginal people not knowing their heritage, for example, 60% of Indigenous Australians identified with a language group but 35% did not know the specific Aboriginal tribe their ancestors belonged to. This is due to the unfortunate phenomenon of stolen generations and cultural dislocations (Australian Institute of Aboriginal and Torres Strait Islander Studies & Federation of Aboriginal and Torres Straight Islander Languages, 2005).

Revivalistics in the Service of Aboriginal Mental Health

The current situation reflects the pain and suffering endured by Aboriginal people since European colonization (cf. Sutton, 2009). One fundamental study conducted in 2007 in Canada helped to solidify any doubts about the connection between cultural continuity and mental wellbeing. Hallett, Chandler & Lalonde (2007) matched seven cultural continuality factors and measured them against reported suicide from 150 Indigenous Inuit communities and almost 14,000 individuals. These cultural continuality factors were self-governance, land claims, education, health care, cultural facilities, police/fire service and language. Of all the communities that this research sampled, the results indicated that those communities with higher levels of language knowledge (over 50% of the community) had lower suicide levels when compared to other communities with less knowledge. From the study, the 16 communities with high levels of native language skills had a suicide rate of 13 deaths per 100,000 people compared to low levels of language with 97 deaths per 100,000. When language skills were coupled with other cultural protective factors (mentioned above), there was an even higher protective effect against suicide.

These findings suggest that by facilitating the improvement of cultural identity through language, as one factor amongst other cultural protective factors, suicide rates in communities decrease. This could potentially be the case in Australia, as there has been some evidence for supporting this claim as well. In the 2005 study by Zubrick *et al.*, they found that those with higher levels of fluency in their language had decreased emotional and behavioural issues in childhood (Zubrick *et al.*, 2005). Decreased issues in childhood could mean early intervention to improve mental health into adolescence and adulthood. We can speculate therefore from this Australian study that those with fluency in their language, or those who knew at least sufficient knowledge of their native language, had a more stable sense of cultural identity.

The importance of language as a building block for community and individual identity relates directly to Australian Aboriginal people. Language reclamation of "sleeping" tongues is still rare and unique but it is becoming increasingly relevant as people seek to recover their cultural autonomy, empower their spiritual and intellectual sovereignty, and improve their wellbeing. Young Aboriginal and Torres Strait Islander language speakers report lower binge drinking, less use of illicit substances and are less likely to have been a victim of physical or threatened violence compared to those who do not speak their language (ABS, 2012).

Language revival is empowering for those involved, strengthening and validating their sense of cultural heritage; reclamation increases feelings of wellbeing and pride amongst disempowered people who fall between the cracks, feeling that they are neither *whitefellas* nor in command of their own Aboriginal heritage. As Fishman (1990) puts it:

> The real question of modern life and for RLS [reversing language shift] is … how one … can build a home that one can still call one's own and, by cultivating it, find community, comfort, companionship and meaning in a world whose mainstreams are increasingly unable to provide

these basic ingredients for their own members.

Zuckermann has noticed some people involved in Indigenous language reclamation, e.g. Kaurna and Barngarla, have improved self-confidence and are more likely to continue with other studies. Anecdotally, people have been spurred to begin language reclamation by a personal experience of suicide. Jack Buckskin experienced the suicide of his sister, which led him to begin work on the Kaurna language. Geoff Anderson had severe anxiety and depression before beginning classes to learn his Wiradjuri language; he says it saved his life. Both are now language teachers and have leading roles in language reclamation. Educational success directly translates to improved employability, "closing the gap" and decreased delinquency. These stabilizing factors give formal markers for personal success and enhance feelings of self-confidence and wellbeing.

Cultural Shift Through Revivalistics

Language reclaiming efforts to revive "sleeping" Aboriginal languages are often a result of people seeking to recover their cultural roots and to empower their identity by learning the language of their ancestors (Zuckermann & Monaghan, 2012).

To aid in the endeavor of language revival and reclamation of identity, there is an urgent need to develop linguistic tools and profound transdisciplinary (including evolutionary) understanding to support language reclamation. This paper contributes to the establishment of a new trans-disciplinary field of enquiry: Revivalistics. Revivalistics complements the established field of documentary linguistics, which records endangered languages before they fall asleep. This trailblazing field revises the fields of grammaticography (writing grammars) and lexicography (writing dictionaries) by placing the endangered-heritage people rather than the Western linguists at the centre. Grammars and dictionaries ought to be written for language reclamation, i.e. in a user-friendly way, for communities, not only for linguisticians. For example, we should avoid highfalutin, often Latin-based grammatical terminology. We should also offer communities a user-friendly spelling. Juxtapose Lutheran missionary Clamor Wilhelm Schürmann's 1844 user-unfriendly spelling *nunyara* for the South Australian Aboriginal Barngarla (Parnkalla) word for "recovery". This spelling resulted in the pronunciation *nanyara* (penultimately stressed and with the initial vowel as in *cup*) rather than *Noonyara*. While *nunyara* suits documentary linguists familiar with German and the International Phonetic Alphabet, *Noonyara* would be preferable from a revivalistic perspective, given that the current mother tongue of the Barngarla people is a form of English, the language of the invader and colonizer.

For linguists, the first stage of any language revival

must involve a long period of observation and careful listening while learning, mapping and characterizing the needs, desires and potentials of an indigenous or minority or culturally endangered community. Only then can one inspire and assist. That said, there are linguistic constraints applicable to all revival attempts, e.g. Hebrew, Barngarla, Kaurna, Ngarrindjeri, Māori, Hawai'i, Wampanoag, Manx and Cornish. Mastering them would help revivalists and First Nations leaders to work more efficiently; for example, to focus more on basic vocabulary (lexis) and verbal conjugations (morphology) than on sounds (phonetics) and word order (syntax).

The Barngarla revival activities so far constitute a strong pilot program, from the perspective of Revival Linguistics (see Zuckermann & Monaghan, 2012). The Barngarla case study demonstrates the potential for significant change within the field of historical linguistics, e.g. by weakening the Family Tree model, a biological metaphor (see Tree of Life) employed by linguists that may wrongly imply that a language ought to have only one parent. Any successful attempt to reclaim a hibernating language will result in a hybrid that combines components from the revivalists' and documenters' mother tongues and, of course, the target language.

Future Directions

There is a need for a longitudinal cohort study with ongoing language revival intervention. Mental health before, during and after language revival should be compared. Language reclamation should be assessed by measuring the success of the language reclamation according to linguistic criteria, e.g. fluency in Welcome to Country, rituals, spelling, translation, speech but also from the point of view of Indigenous empowerment and wellbeing. It is not the case that at the end, if any, of the revival process there is no all-encompassing native-speaking community that converses in the revived language in all semantic domains, will it automatically imply that the revival was a failure. The revival process is as important as the revival goals.

The hypothesis that there is interdependence between language revival and assessable benefits such as personal and community empowerment, improved sense of identity and purpose, and enhanced mental health, thus closing the health gap between Indigenous peoples and others cannot be proved without adequate, independent assessment. Unless we measure the impact of the language reclamation process on the mental health of the participants, as well as on their wider community, we cannot be sure about the extra-linguistic success of the language revival.

Acknowledgments

Caryn Rogers, Amy Finlay, Michael Wright, Leonie Segal and Gareth Furber.

References

Australian Broadcasting Corporation (2012). *7:30 Report: Spate of Suicides Grips Aboriginal Community* (http://www.abc.net.au/news/2012-09-06/spate-of-suicides-grips-aboriginal-community/4247358 06/09/2012). Perth, WA: ABC.

Australian Bureau of Statistics (2010a). *4704.0: The health and welfare of Australia's Aboriginal and Torres Strait Islander peoples, October 2010* (www.abs.gov.au/AUSSTATS/abs@.nsf/lookup/4704.0Chapter715Oct+2010, accessed 25 March 2014). Canberra, ACT: Australian Bureau of Statistics.

Australian Bureau of Statistics (2010b). *Measures of Australia's Progress 2010.* Canberra, ACT: ABS.

Australian Bureau of Statistics (2010c). *Suicides, Australia, 2010.* Canberra, ACT: Australian Bureau of Statistics.

Australian Bureau of Statistics (2012). *Publication 4725.0* (http://www.abs.gov.au/ausstats/abs@.nsf/Lookup/4725.0Chapter220Apr%202011, accessed 25 March 2014). Canberra, ACT: Australian Bureau of Statistics.

Australian Health Ministers' Advisory Council (2012). *Aboriginal and Torres Strait Islander health performance framework: 2012 report.* Canberra, ACT: Office for Aboriginal and Torres Strait Islander Health.

Australian Institute of Aboriginal and Torres Strait Islander Studies & Federation of Aboriginal and Torres Straight Islander Languages (2005). *National Indigenous Languages Survey Report 2005.* Canberra, ACT: Department of Communications, Information Technology and the Arts.

Australian Institute of Health and Welfare (2011). *The Health and Welfare of Australia's Aboriginal and Torres Stait Islander people: An overview.* Canberra, ACT: AIHW.

Commonwealth of Australia (2012). *Our Land, Our Language: Language Learning in Indigenous Communities.* Canberra, ACT: House of Representatives: Standing Committee on Aboriginal and Torres Strait Islander Affairs.

de Souza, M. & Rymarz, R. (2007). The role of cultural and spiritual expressions in affirming a sense of self, place, and purpose among young urban, Indigenous Australians. *International Journal of Children's Spirituality*, 12 (3), 277-288.

Dodson, M., Cox, A., Stewart, P., Walter, M. & Weir, M. (2010). *Trauma, loss and grief for Aboriginal children.* (http://www.earlytraumagrief.anu.edu.au/Indigenous

-children-and-families, viewed 30/04 2013). Canberra, ACT: Australian National University.

Fishman, Joshua A. (1990). 'What is Reversing Language Shift (RSL) and How Can It Succeed?', pp. 5-36 of Durk Gorter, Jarich F. Hoekstra, Lammert G. Jansma and Jehannes Ytsma (eds), *Fourth International Conference On Minority Languages*, vol. I. Clevedon (UK) and Bristol (Philadelphia, US): Multilingual Matters.

Fishman, Joshua (1991). *Reversing Language Shift. heory and Practice of Assistance to Threatened Languages*. Clevedon (UK): Multilingual Matters.

Hallett, D., Chandler, M. & Lalonde, C. (2007). Aboriginal language knowledge and youth suicide. *Cognitive Development*, 22(3), 392-399.

Hanssens, L. (2008). Clusters of Suicide. *Aboriginal & Islander Health Worker Journal*, 32(2), 25.

Hanssens, L. (2012). The impact of Suicide Contagion and Intergenerational Segregation on youth and young adults in remote Indigenous communities in Northern Territory, Australia. In paper presented at *3rd Australian Postvention Conference, Sydney*. Sydney, NSW.

headspace National Youth Mental Health Foundation (2011). Mental health and mental illness. In *headspace* (http://www.headspace.org.au/parents-and-carers/find-information/mental-health-and-illness, viewed 03-05 2013).

Heinrich, P. (2004). Language planning and language ideology in the Ryūkyū Islands. *Language policy*, 3(2), 153-179.

Human Rights and Equal Opportunities Commission (1997). Bringing Them Home Report: Report of the national inquiry into the separation of Aboriginal and Torres Strait Islander children from their families. Canberra, ACT: Commonwealth of Australia.

Hunter, E. & Harvey, D. (2002). Indigenous suicide in Australia, New Zealand, Canada and the United States'. *Emergency Medicine*, 14(1), 14-23.

from p. 1: ref for Indingenous Remote Communications Association, 2013

Kickett-Tucker, C. (2009). Moorn (Black)? Djardak (White)? How come I don't fit in Mum?: Exploring the racial identity of Australian Aboriginal children and youth. *Health Sociology Review*, 18(1), 119-136.

King, M., Smith, A. & Gracey, M. (2009). Indigenous health part 2: the underlying causes of the health gap. *The Lancet*, 374(9683), 76-85.

Marmion, D., Obata, K., & Troy, J. (2014). *Community, identity, wellbeing: the report of the Second National Indigenous Languages Survey*. Canberra, ACT: Australian Institute of Aboriginal and Torres Strait Islander Studies.

Phinney, J.S. (1990). Ethnic identity in adolescents and adults: Review of research. *Psychological Bulletin*, 108(3), 499-514.

Purdie, N., Dudgeon, P. & Walker, R.E. (2010). *Working Together: Aboriginal and Torres Strait Islander Mental Health and Wellbeing Principles and Practice*. Canberra, ACT: Department of Ageing, Office of Aboriginal and Torres Strait Islander Health.

Social Health Reference Group (2004). *National Strategic Framework for Aboriginal and Torres Strait Islander Peoples' Mental Health and Social and Emotional Well Being 2004-2009*. Canberra, ACT: Australian Department of Health and Ageing.

Sutton, P. (2009). *The Politics of Suffering: Indigenous Australia and the end of the liberal consensus*. Melbourne, VIC: Melbourne University Press.

Teichelmann C.G. and Schürmann, C.W. (1840). Outlines of a Grammar, Vocabulary, and Phraseology of the Aboriginal Language of South Australia, Spoken by the Natives in and for some Distance around Adelaide. Adelaide, SA: The Authors.

Tighe, J. & McKay, K. (2012). Alive and Kicking Goals!: Preliminary findings from a Kimberley suicide prevention program. *Advances in Mental Health*, 10(3), 240-245.

Trewin, D. (2006). *National Aboriginal and Torres Strait Islander Health Survey, Australia, 2004-05*. Canberra, ACT: Australian Bureau of Statistics.

Wexler, L.A., DiFulvio, G.T., Burke, T. (2009). Resilience and marginalized youth: Making a case for personal and collective meaning-making as parWexler, L. (2006). Inupiat youth suicide and culture loss: Changing community conversations for prevention. *Social Science & Medicine*, 63(11), 2938-2948.

Zubrick, S., Silburn, S., Lawrence, D., Mitrou, F.G., Dalby, R.B., Blair, E.M., Griffin, J., *et al.* (2005). *The Western Australian Aboriginal Child Health Survey:The social and emotional wellbeing of Aboriginal children and young people*. Perth, WA: Curtin University of Technology and Telethon Institute for Child Health Research.

Zuckermann, G. (2009) Hybridity versus revivability: multiple causation, forms and patterns. *Journal of Language Contact — Varia*, 2, 40–67 (www.zuckermann.org/pdf/Hybridity_versus_Revivability.pdf, accessed 14 March 2014).

Zuckermann, G. & Walsh, M. (2011). Stop, Revive, Survive!: Lessons from the Hebrew Revival Applicable to the Reclamation, Maintenance and Empowerment of Aboriginal Languages and Cultures. *Australian Journal of Linguistics*, 31, 111-127.

Zuckermann, G. & Monaghan, P. (2012). Revival linguistics and the new media: Talknology in the service of the Barngarla language reclamation. In *Foundation for Endangered Languages XVI Conference: Language Endangerment in the 21st Century: Globalisation, Technology & New Media* (pp. 119-126; http://adelaide.academia.edu/Zuckermann/Papers/1971557/Revival_Linguistics_and_the_New_Media_Talknology_in_the_service_of_the_Barngarla_Language_Reclamation). Auckland, New Zealand.

Zuckermann, G., Shakuto-Neoh, S. & Quer, G.M. (2014). 'Native Tongue Title: Compensation for the Loss of Aboriginal Languages', *Australian Aboriginal Studies* 2014/1: 55-71.

Kristang and Tourism – Mutual Roles and Effects

Mário Pinharanda Nunes
University of Macau, Macao S.A.R.
[Pinharanda.mario@gmail.com]

Eileen Lee
Sunway University, Malaysia
[eileenl@sunway.edu.my]

Abstract

Kristang, also referred to as Papiah Kristang, a Portuguese-based creole endogenous to Malacca is the heritage language of the Malayo-Portuguese community (MP). This community emerged as the specific socio-linguistic contact context that resulted from Portuguese rule over Malacca from 1511-1641. However, British rule and development of Malaya and successive policies since Malaysian Independence in 1957 brought modernization and economic prosperity which impacted on the maintenance of Kristang. Studies such as Nunes (1996), David & Noor (1999), Lee (2004), Baxter (2005), Pilai et. al. (2014) and Lee (2003, 2011) are unanimous as to the increasing disruption in the generational transmission of Kristang, entailing the inevitable reduction of active speakers and domains of use. In spite of the threat to the language element of the Kristang trinomial identity trait (language/religion/culture), the community has been in the limelight of the Malaysian tourism policies, promoted as one of the unique ethnic and cultural communities of this culturally diverse country. Such policies have contributed to the diffusion of Kristang folklore dance, cuisine and religious-related festivities. Our paper seeks to access the level of correlation between the cultural activities developed the Malacca Portuguese community and the promotion of Kristang within the community itself and among outsiders. The data was collected via semi-guided sociolinguistic interviews to the leaders of the two dance groups, owners of restaurants and food stalls in the Portuguese Settlement of Malacca, and members of the organizing committees of the community's traditional festivals.

Introduction

The Portuguese Maritime Expansion to the East (South Asia, Southeast Asia and East Asia) from the late 15th century to the mid 17th century gave rise to numerous miscegenated communities which generally fit into what has been termed creole peoples and creole languages. The heritage community of Kristang (MK), the Malacca Portuguese (MP), are one of such Luso-Asian communities. It came into existence during the 150 year rule of Malacca by the Portuguese, at during the peak of the spice trade between Europe and Asia. As in the case of the other Luso-Asian communities, the Kristangs were the result of ethnic and cultural miscegenation between European and Asian born Portuguese, local populations and also other migrant Asian peoples. In the case of this particular community in Malacca, Malay was the ethnic and linguistic substratum. Having been formed posteriorly to the South Asian Luso-Asian communities, from India and Sri Lanka (the first regions where the Portuguese established themselves in the Orient from the 1490s onwards), the MP community and K received much genetic, cultural and linguistic input from the latter Portuguese-based Asian creoles and their respective communities. MK also testifies the influence of the European colonisers who followed the Portuguese - the Dutch and the English. On par with the MP community's religion (i.e. Christianity, overwhelmingly Catholicism), cultural items, namely cuisine, music and dance, and the ethnic-cultural mix, MK has survived till the present as one of the community's identity markers.

Following the defeat of the Portuguese forces by the Dutch in 1641, Malacca ceased to be the stronghold of the Portuguese presence in Southeast Asia. The MP community of Malacca, by then spread out in other former Portuguese trading settlements throughout the Malay speaking world (Batavia, Tugu, Flores, Ternate, Timor) fled the new rulers; not least on account of their religion: Protestantism. Those who remained behind, maintained their cultural identity and heritage language alive throughout the Dutch as well the British rule, and in the post colonial era following Malaysia's independence in 1957. Having said that, in addition to modernization and economic prosperity, British rule provided the first and second generation of MP with an English-medium education up to Malayan Independence in 1957. Following that English continues to be a language of prestige despite the transition to a Malay-medium education. Even when English is taught as a second language in schools in present day Malaysia, English never lost its status with the community as a language of power and continues to be the dominant language for communication, especially for communication with the young (Lee, 2011). After Independence, as with most minority speech communities, maintaining the use of its ethnic/heritage language continues to be a challenge especially so in highly bilingual societies such as Malaysia where even the education system in some schools can consist of at least three medium of instructions: Bahasa Malaysia/Malay (the national language), English as a second language, and/or Mandarin or Tamil as the third language. On the other hand, the maintenance of MP culture, namely its cuisine, music, dance and (religious) festivities, is more feasible, taking into consideration the community's love for its cuisine and its belief in Catholicism and Malaysia's promotion of multiculturalism as a basis for national unity and "being truly Asia" as a niche for regional tourism.

In line with the discussions above, this study looks into the maintenance of MP culture ("Portuguese" dance, cuisine, festivals) at the Portuguese Settlement and how these activities perpetuate the maintenance of MP trinomial identity and heritage according to the their cultural agents.

The Portuguese Settlement of Malacca

Recent census data, places the number of MP living within the Portuguese Settlement of Malacca close to 1500. Obviously that many more live elsewhere throughout Malaysia, mainly in Kuala Lumpur and Penang. This diaspora within Malaysia commenced in the 1940s as other urban areas besides Malacca began to be further developed by the British, and was increased after Independence.

The Settlement was established in the 1933, when the Catholic Church, under the initiative of two priests serving the MP catholic community, bought 11 hectares of land at the seafront at Bandar Hilir area in Malacca to enable the residential concentration of the scattered community. The seafront location of the Settlement benefitted the community's primary occupation at that time – fishing; and helped preserve this trade within the community until now. Currently, however, the status of fishing as the primary occupation of the community has been dwindling. Based on opinions gathered through our interviews to community members, this has been a direct consequence of the land reclamation project for Malacca commenced in the 1990s which has cut the access of the community's fishing boats to the sea; forcing the MP fishermen to anchor them outside the Settlement's boundaries. Other reasons have been the increase of availability of jobs in the hotel and food and beverage industries which has boomed in the last 20 years. Malacca is fiercely promoted as a tourist destination by the State government of Malacca and by the central government of Malaysia. Following better education facilities for the youth, these have gained easier access to those careers, distancing them from the ancestral occupation of the MP.

The progressive higher level of education of the successive generations following Malaysian Independence, has increasingly lured them to enter all sorts of professional fields other than the ancestral fishing trade, as well as to migrate to other states within Malaysia, or even emigrate. This gradual physical distancing from the community's iconic territory and ancestral ecology has taken its toll on the maintenance of the generational transmission of KM within the MP families. An additional factor to the disruption of such transmission was the "prestige factor". The heritage creole of this community was deemed a lesser language by the generations of parents aspiring their children to obtain jobs within the British colonial civil service, from the early 20th century onwards. Thus, for many families, especially for those migrating out of Malacca to Kuala Lumpur and other Malaysian urban areas, the discourse

was one of devaluation of the heritage language to a point that it was highly discouraged by the parents to be used by their children: "Kristang was only allowed among the adults when we were growing up. They would switch to English when they realised we were listening", reported a MP interviewee, aged 83, who shifted to Kuala Lumpur at a tender age with the family. This report pretty much sums up the generational transmission disruption among the overwhelming majority of the MP living elsewhere in Malaysia, other than in Malacca.

Among the MP community in Malacca the spread of such disruption has been much slower. Specifically in the PS, the community concentration has fostered language maintenance considerably. However, the generation transmission disruption has visibly been in process for some time. Nunes (1996), David & Surdesh (1999), Lee (2004), Baxter (2005), Pilai et al. (2014) are unanimous in detecting an increasing disruption in the generational transmission of Kristang, entailing the inevitable reduction of active speakers and domains of use.

The following section gives a brief overview of how Malaysia has integrated Malacca and its heritage in the country's tourism promotion – a significant factor in the ongoing changes in the MP community.

Malacca, a UNESCO World Heritage site

Malacca is aptly named as the historical city of Malaysia due to its rich and colourful history – the 14th century Malacca Sultanate is the first sultanate in the Malay archipelago, following that Malacca is the only state in Malaysia which was colonized by three European powers – the Portuguese in 1511, the Dutch in 1645, the British in 1826. Further to this, as early as the 14th century there was much multiculturalism and bilingualism at the port of Malacca as it was actively engaged in the spice trade between the East and the West. Long before the Portuguese came to Malacca, there was already intense language contact among an international community of traders of Arab, Indian and Chinese origin trading at the port during the Malacca Sultanate. Coming from different parts of the world and having no common language, the traders communicated in Bazaar Malay, the lingua franca of the Malay Archipelago. Despite its non-standard status, Bazaar Malay continued to thrive over the centuries and up to this day it is the most common "language" of communication between the different races in Malacca. Another distinctive language that is the product of cultural assimilation is Baba Malay which is an interface of the Malay language and the Hokkien dialect a south China dialect) and closely resembles Bazaar Malay. Portuguese arrival in the 16th century and their policy of intermarriage with the local community expanded the people's linguistic repertoire. Today, the existence of three creole communities (the Kristangs/Malayo-Portuguese, the Peranakans/Baba Nyonya, the Chitty Melaka) in the second smallest state of the country clearly reflect the long term mingling of the different cultures and languages. Another tangible evidence of ethnic blending in Malacca is the delectable cuisine and the unique dressing of the creole communities. In recognition of their rich past, on 7 July 2008 Malacca and Georgetown (the capital of Penang) known as the historic cities of the Straits of Malacca, were listed as UNESCO World Heritage sites as

> "these two cities demonstrate a succession of historical and cultural influences arising from their former function as trading ports linking East and West. They reflect the coming together of cultural elements from the Malay Archipelago, India and China with those of Europe, to create a unique architecture, culture and townscape … With its government buildings, churches, squares and fortifications, Melaka (Malacca) demonstrates the early stages of this history originating in the 15th-century Malay sultanate and the Portuguese and Dutch periods beginning in the early 16th century" (wh.unesco.org/en/list/1223/).

All this resulted in a human and cultural tapestry that is expressed in a rich intangible heritage that includes languages, religious practices, gastronomy, ceremonies and festivals. In Melaka, a conservation area was first identified in 1979 and upgraded in 1985. In 1988 an international seminar was organized and the area of St Paul's Hill designated as a heritage zone and the State of Melaka established the Preservation and Conservation of Cultural Heritage Act. In 1993 this was placed under the newly established Melaka Museums Corporation. From this the Conservation Trust Fund was formed, and from 2001 this has been used to finance selected building conservation projects in Melaka. In 2013 Malacca recorded 13.7 million visitors thus, in the Visit Malaysia Year 2014 plans, the State government of Malacca is targeting 14 million (local and foreign) visitors. Naturally, the Portuguese Settlement, "Portuguese" cuisine and "Portuguese" music and dance are on the tourists' itinerary and menu.

As a further enhancement of the touristic promotion of the label "Portuguese" in Malacca, besides the recognition of the main Portuguese architectural relics – ruins of the Famosa Fortress Gate and the St. Paul's Cathedral, the Malaysian government also sought to showcase the PS as a remnant of the Portuguese presence in the State of Malacca. Such promotion was given a head start when former Malaysian Prime Minister Dr. Mahathir supported the building of what is now known as the Portuguese Square in the PS: a square on the then waterfront with facilities for restaurants and a centre stage for the dances. The emphasis on the Portuguese heritage link was so important to the government's tourism promotion intent, that a team of Malaysian architects was sent to Portugal to study the typical architecture of the old Portuguese squares.[47]

The promotion of "Portuguese" culture (at the Portuguese Settlement)

The most widespread promotion of "Portuguese" culture at the Portuguese Settlement is that of MP heritage cuisine. There are at least eight stalls/restaurants selling "Portuguese"[48] food and the stalls are highly popular with local tourists during weekdays, especially on weekends. In addition to the popularity of seafood, it is the delectable creole cuisine with influences from Malay, Chinese, and Indian cooking that is typical in multicultural Malaysian fusion menus. Another aspect of Portuguese culture that never fails to attract the tourists and the local media is the celebration of three religious festivities, namely San Pedro (St. Peter's Festival), San Juang (St. John's Festival), both held in June, and Intrudu (to mark the beginning of Lent and the time for fasting and penance).

Further to this, the most prominent part of "Portuguese" culture is the promotion of "Portuguese" music and dance. Here again we are confronted with the ambiguity of the term "Portuguese", for in the dance groups' repertoire these days, few are the dances and songs that genuinely can be traced to the MP ancestral heritage. The most well known today, probably because they are practically the only remaining ones are the Branyo and the Jingkli Nona. The former is traditionally danced at weddings or other special festive occasions and derives from a traditional folklore dance style from the Algarve region of Portugal. The latter is a song that carries the words and the tune common to other Luso-Asian creole communities in Southern India (Cochim) and Srilanka. The remaining so-called Portuguese dances and songs of the PS were in fact introduced to the community on the e early 1960s through the initiative of the last Portuguese Priest to have served in the PS, and supported by the then colonial Portuguese regime[49]. These dances and songs are, nowadays, the ones most associated with the dance and music component of MP culture, both within the community and by Malaysians in general and foreign tourists who attend the regular MP dance shows. These imported songs and dances have woven into and neatly blended with the popular image of the MP culture. The rhythms have been slightly slowed down and the words

---

http://www.expatgomalaysia.com/article/387/malaccas-portuguese-community-rocking-along-the-sands-edge

[48] It should be noted that "Portuguese" in reference to the cuisine of the MP, in no way indicates a clear link to Portuguese cuisine from Portugal. As with the denomination of the community and its language, "Portuguese" refers merely to their that portion of their their overall heritage that derived from the Portuguese. In fact, the MP cuisine is very much a fusion of the South Asian and Malay cuisines.

[49] Portugal held onto its five African colonies, and East Timor until democracy was finally installed after the fall of the Fascist regime in 1974. Until the end, this regime promoted the idea of a Portuguese Empire, supporting all types of initiatives that sort to promote traditional Portuguese culture, among which folklore.

---

[47]   referenced   in:

to the music are sung in varying approximations to their original standard Portuguese version, tainted by Kristang's creole elements.

Following our research object for the current paper, the entities involved in the promotion of MP culture who's activities benefit from tourism are two dance groups and the 10 restaurants / stalls within the PS. Currently there are two groups functioning from within the PS, entirely composed and managed by residents of the Settlement. The oldest of the two, was the very first MP dance group to be formed[50]. Its initial members, including the founder himself were youth who learnt the European Portuguese dances taught to the community in the 60s. It has been around for over 20 years. The other group is much more recent[51]. It was formed by former members of the first group and another now extinct group. In both cases the majority of the dancers are in their teens or young adults. As for the restaurants / food stalls, as mentioned above, the new area for such activity on the new waterfront of the PS (after the latest sea reclamation) houses 10 stalls. The Portuguese Square built in the 1980s also still houses another 3 restaurants.

In the analysis section that follows, we will discuss the significance, role and the extent to which these activities benefit MK.

Tourism and Malacca-Portuguese Culture

For the current study we considered the agents of MP culture to be a community run associations MPEA), MP dance groups (DGA & DGB) and food stall owners; all within the PS in Malacca. Our semi-guided interviews to theses agents aimed at answering the following research questions:

1. What type of exposure to Kristang do community members get from these various cultural activities?

2. How do the MP organizers and participants in these promotions view that exposure in terms of possible benefits for the maintenance of the language within the community and the promotion of its existence among other Malaysians and visitors ?

3. What is their level of awareness of their potential role as promoters of Kristang?

4. Are there different subgroups among the cultural agents? If yes, how do they differ and is there any common cultural project among them?

By applying these overall research question to the reported data collected, we aim to answer the specific question: Is tourism serving as a stepping-stone for language maintenance?

First and foremost it should be noted that the various MP cultural agents do not share a common promotion strategy, nor MP culture maintenance project. Each agent works on his or her own. This is visible from the Settlements' organising bodies down to the individuals who run their own cultural related business, as is the case of the dance groups and the food stall owners. There is no overall project. In the case of the latter, the marketing and profit realities speak higher than collaboration for the sake of a joint effort to preserve Kristang and the MP culture at large. Each group tries to sell their product - MP music and dance the best way possible, and gain performance contracts from local and international entities. The leader of the oldest group, DGA, takes pride that his dancers only showcase the 'true Portuguese' dances and songs from Portugal; and that some of the costumes are authentic folklore vestments donated to the group by Portuguese entities. The leader of the second group, DGB, on the other hand, claimed to dance and sing mainly traditional MP songs. Nevertheless, this group too has had to present the European Portuguese folklore introduced to the community in the 60s, for certain shows on request of the contracting organiser: 'When we dance for any function of the Chief Minister, we have to dance *Ti' Anica* and *Malhao-Malhao* and other Portuguese dances. For them these are the true Malacca Portuguese culture', says the leader of DGB. When questioned by us on the authenticity of these dances and songs as being truly MP culture, the group justifies such authenticity based on the fact that the 'dances have been adapted to local customs. They are slowed down, because the original rhythm in Portugal is too fast'. Even so, the dances retain some traits of the original rhythm and steps, making them stand out from other Malaysian folklore. 'Anyway, they wouldn't know', the DGB leader sums up, referring to the local audiences' ignorance on what is the exact original form in Portugal and regarding their relatively recent adoption by the MP community as part of their heritage folklore.

As for the dance and songs activity helping promote Kristang, both group leaders reveal that this is not at all a concern of the groups' activity. In-group promotion is not an issue, given that all members speak Kristang, albeit in varying degrees of proficiency, according to the leaders and group members interviewed. In DGB, however, according to its leader, the younger members are encouraged and reminded to speak Kristang when on tour to perform outside the PS: 'We must show we are Portuguese and have our own language'.

The 10 restaurants / food stalls, only two of which are not owned by MP, are the most visible element of MP culture to whoever visits the Settlement. They are, in fact the ultimate reason for tourists to go to that area of Malacca, offering an exotic cuisine on a seaside open air setting from sunset onwards. The only visual evidence of some Kristang in use in the restaurant business in the PS are the names of the food stalls, such as: *San Pedro, San Juang, Pescados* (Fishermen), *De Costa, El Chico*. The menus come almost exclusively in English. Dishes are referred to mostly based on their main ingredients, and

---

[50] We have labeled this group as Dance Group A (DGA)

[51] We have labeled this group as Dance Group B (DGB)

cooking style: Portuguese Baked Crab, Burnt Crab, Fried Fish, Portuguese Baked Fish; or the cooking style etc. When the dish is presented with a specific nomenclature it is given in Malay, like in: *Kangkong Belacan* or *Sambal Lala*. A mix of English and Malay is also visible for any one individual item on the lists, where in the main ingredient of the dish is given with the Malay word and English used to refer to the cooking style or seasoning: black sauce sotong, kangkong garlic, ginger lala. The only Kristang food name used in the menus of all the stalls is for the dish commonly known as curry *debil/debel*.

Questioned as to why they did not include more Kristang in their menus, the food stall owners were unanimous in considering there was not much use. According to them, given the big flux of customers at dinner time, it would not be practical to have foreign names for the customer to read and order from. These interviewees were also unanimous in considering that their business did not contribute considerably to the maintenance of Kristang within the families involved. 'Me and my sisters and husband we all speak Kristang to each other and to my children, too, even though fewer times. But here in the stalls, most children of the owners do not use Kristang at work, unless they need the customer not to understand', reported one of the interviewees. The general opinion that there is no need to consciously promote language maintenance of Kristang among the younger generations is based on the common opinion that their heritage language is picked up as long as they live in the PS, as the following quote from another food stall owner exemplifies: 'Once you live in the settlement. the language won't dye off. The environment is there. I speak Portuguese to my mother and husband, English to my Children, yet they do understand Kristang and can speak it a little, because it is all around here.'

Concluding Remarks

The oral reported data we collected for the current survey indicates that the promotion of Malacca, and specifically the MP community, as a relevant part of Malaysia's intangible heritage, has had significant effects on the MP community, most directly on the members living within the PS. The boom in tourism has directly caused the shift of the community from their ancestral trade, fishing, to other sectors. If this on the one hand is causing the disruption in the transmission of ancestral knowledge, culture and linguistic practices related to fishing, tourism has also brought new and more promising opportunities of better income to many of the families. Tourism related industries such as MP folk dance and songs and their ethnic cuisine has flourished easily under the umbrella of national and state promotion of Malacca, and consequently of the Portuguese Settlement. the emphasis on the uniqueness of this community is placed in the label 'Portuguese'. Although within the community 'Portuguese' as a denominator of the ethnic group and their culture is not consensual as some prefer to use Kristang equally for the language and for their ethnic identity, it is the former that prevails when promoting the community to outsiders. This conforms to the official denomination used by national tourism campaigns on Malacca and the MP. Such emphasis on the ancestral link with Portugal is welcomed by all the MP cultural agents alike. As we saw in the previous section, the cultural products sold to tourists are essentially dances, songs and cuisine; all material cultural objects. In none of them is there any particular concern regarding the use and promotion of the heritage language Kristang. Neither in the songs, nor in the visual artefacts used in the restaurant business in the Settlement: menus, restaurant signboards. On the contrary, the emphasis is on the 'Portuguese' element: European Portuguese lyrics and dance steps and, in visual terms, the reference to 'Portuguese food' and the Portuguese family names of the owners on the restaurant sign boards, as well as European Portuguese dance costumes or local copied versions thereof. The ultimate cultural image the MP community sells of itself appears to be in conformity with national tourism campaigns and promotions of the community as well. In summary, Kristang is not generally yet seen as an element in need of promotion through tourism by the MP; nor as a cultural element that can further benefit the industry within the PS. All MP cultural promotion by the PS residents is centred on the material artefacts mentioned[52]. Thus, in answer to our main research question, it appears that tourism is not serving as a stepping-stone for language maintenance, in the case of Kristang.

References

Baxter, A.N. (2005). Kristang (Malacca Creole Portuguese) – a long-time survivor seriously endangered. *Estud. Socioling.* 6(1), 1-37.

David, M.K., Mohd Noor, F.N. (1999). Language maintenance or language shift in the Portuguese Settlement of Malacca in Malaysia. *Migracijske teme* 15, 417-549.

Lee, E., (2003). Language Shift and Revitalization in the Kristang Community, Portuguese Settlement, Malacca. Unpublished PhD Dissertation, Department of English Language and Linguistics, University of Sheffield.

Lee, E., (2011). Language maintenance and competing priorities at the Portuguese Settlement, Malacca. Paper presented at the South Eastern Conference on Linguistics LXXV111 (SECOL 78), Department of Linguistics, University of Georgia, Georgia, USA.

Nunes, M.P. (1996). By how many speakers, by whom, with whom, and for what purposes, is Kristang still used in the Portuguese Settlement of Malacca? Paper presented at the CIEC Conference (Colloque

---

[52] An exception to this is the personal initiative taken on by Joan Marbeck, a MP not residing in the PS, who has on her own initiative sought fundings and support and publishes several books on teaching Kristang phrases and songs over the past two decades.

International d'Études Créoles), Guadaloupe, Carribean islands.

Pillai, S., Soh W.Y. & Katija, A. (2014). Family language policy and heritage language maintenance of Malacca Portuguese Creole. *Language & Communication* 37: 75-85

Language Loss and the Loss of Local Action Strategies in Amami and Okinawa

Yuko Sugita
Potsdam University
Germany
[sugita@uni-potsdam.de]

Abstract

This paper proposes a theoretical and analytical framework for exploring how "language loss" is linked to "knowledge loss" and, ultimately, to the reorganization of society. Hereby it is important to demonstrate what this process practically means for the people in the society of language shift. Knowledge is defined in terms of cognitive sociology here. It is a cognitive framework which one acquires through early and second socialization processes to organize lives. In this framework, language is fundamental for transmitting, organizing and sedimenting the knowledge in our mind. Language loss means that we inevitably organize our knowledge in somewhat another way or eliminate it as it can not function as references for lives any more. This ultimately leads to the change in strategies of action, and this change in action strategies can result in negative social changes.

Introduction

It cannot be emphasized often enough that the language loss is also the loss of knowledge and culture. Harrison (2007), Evans (2010) and many others sadly prove this with abundant examples from all around the world. Hence, linguists and researchers from other relevant fields are arguing for the maintenance of linguistic and cognitive diversity (e.g. Evans & Levinson, 2009). However, to what extent does language loss and knowledge loss actually matter for the people in the marginalized society to live their everyday lives? Language loss or knowledge loss is often not perceived as a problem in their everyday life as long as they are able to live and communicate in one way or another (e.g. by using the majority language). For many (younger generations), managing the life in the unstable social and living conditions is more impotrtant than "vague issues" such as language, identity, cultural knowledge, etc. that they have already lost. When the lamenting how much one has already lost starts, it is often too late to gain the language back to the society.

Therefore, it is important to point out from the very start of language endagerment that language loss can induce undesirable social changes in the ongoing lives as well. In order to link the micro level of language practices to the macro level of social change, this paper proposes a theoretical and analytical framework based on cognitive sociology (Zerubavel, 1997; Eder, 2007; Strydom, 2007) and discourse analytical approach to knowledge structures (Ehlich & Rehbein, 1977; Hoffmann 2010). This framework shall help us understand how the language loss is linked to the loss of knowledge, action strategies, and to the social change.

Theoretical Framework

Cognitive sociology is a domain of sociology that links cognitive science to social theory in search of accounting for the process of *cognitive socialization* and its change (Zerubavel, 1997: 15). It has been developed on the basis of different approaches that resulted in the so-called "cognitive turn" in sociology represented best by approaches such as Goffman's Symbolic Interactionism, Garfinkel's Ethnomethodology, the Sociology of Knowledge of Berger & Luckmann (1967) (Strydom, 2007). The ultimate goal of such an approach is to develop an integrative, multilevel approach to cognition that views people both as individuals, as human beings (i.e. practically seen as a biologically universal entity), and as social beings (members of "thought community") (Zerubavel, 1997: 113).

In cognitive sociology, knowledge and cognitive skills are something one acquires through early and second socialization processes as well as through diverse individual or societal experiences to organize lives (Zerubavel, 1997: 19). In this framework, language is essential for transmitting, organizing and sedimenting the knowledge in our mind that functions as references for choosing actions in everyday life (strategies of action)[53]. Through learning a language our cognition is tacitly socialized in a way which allows ud to become a member of the society as well (Zerubavel, 1997: 16). Language loss means, then, that we inevitably organize our knowledge in a somewhat different way, or eliminate this nowledge altogether, as it can not function as a reference for action any more. This ultimately leads to the change in action strategies what result in social changes.

Zerubavel (1997) introduces six possible domains of study of cognitive sociology: Perceiving, Attending, Classifying, Assigning meaning, Remembering, Reckoning the time. These domains are very similar to those that are often treated in researches of language loss and cognition (e.g. Harrison 2007). This similarity suggests that the framework is particularly compatible with the study field of endangered languages. Nevertheless, the sociological theory is lacking in methods for analyzing concrete knowledge in social practices in detail (cf. "situated knowledge" in Raffles, 2002: 332).

---

[53] Swidler (1986) defines the provider of such references (e.g. symbols, stories, rituals, world-views) for strategies of action as "culture."

Analytical framework

To meet this need, the types of knowledge in discourse analytical study will be employed complementarily as an analytical framework. Discourse analytical study also positions languages as an organizer and transmitter of knowledge, just as cognitive sociology does. Hoffman (2010) distinguishes types of knowledge for analyzing knowledge situated in concrete communication as follows (not exhaustive): 1. Knowledge from Observation (knowledge by obtained by seeing or hearing others), 2. Agent's Knowledge (knowledge from one's experiences), 3. Knowledge of Transfer (knowledge for reproducing other's utterances), 4. Knowledge of Processing (mentally transformed knowledge according to several different levels of sedimentation in mind and diffusion in the society), 5. Institutional Knowledge, 6. Knowledge of Action, 7. Linguistic Knowledge, 8. Discourse Knowledge. In this paper, I will focus on the type 4 Knowledge of Processing. To this knowledge type, Hoffmann (2010) deploys the study of Ehlich & Rehbein (1977) who propose the structures of agent's knowledge for analyzing originally institutional discourses. Only some those types that are relevant to the case study below will be introduced here.

Assessment (*Einschätzung*) is knowledge characterized as individual interpretation of certain parts of one's "reality": A knows B as C (or A knows that B is/has/does C) on the basis of Knowledge from Observation or Agent's Knowledge of the relation between B and C for A. Observing or experiencing a certain event repeatedly and having the mental résumé of this relation (assessing), one is able to predict such a relation in the future. They are expressions which give local, temporal, occasional frequency or are personal quantifiers (e.g. "here and there", "often", "sometimes"). Utterances with such expressions imply predictability for other cases (Ehlich & Rehbein, 1977; Hoffmann 2010).

A certain accumulation of assessments builds up a **Picture** (*Bild*) in the mind of agents. Picture is meant to be the firm state of "B as C" that exists in the mind of agents. Picture can be shared with others, becoming, then, socially generalized, an **Image** (Ehlich & Rehbein, 1977).

Sentential knowledge (*Sentenz*) is a Picture of "B as C" which "all" of the members of the group share as knowledge. Like proverbs, Sentential Knowledge works with the quantifier "all" as if the known relation were valid for all cases. Because of its characteristic of "consensus", Sentential Knowledge can function as a prerequisite for the members to cooperate in a society (Ehlich & Rehbein, 1977).

The type **Maxim** (*Maxime*) is developed from experiences of agents in the past as a lesson for future action. It is a type of knowledge which one can get by reflecting on some experience in the past. When an agent has to decide how to act, he makes use of maxim by recalling his choice in the past. In this sense, maxim plays an important role in our process of deciding how to act (Ehlich & Rehbein, 1977).

A (religious or spiritual) belief includes Sentential Knowledge and Maxim, but it is qualitatively very different from them as it can form and constrain one's way of living guiding directly his/her action, emotion, reasoning etc.

Applying the theoretical and analytical framework introduced above, the following case study shall illustrate that language loss can induce the reorganization of cognitive socialization and strategies of action especially regarding to Image, Sentential Knowledge, and Maxim that are socially shared.

Case Study

In what follows, two examples from the Ryukyu Islands are examined in detail, focusing on the causal linkage between language, knowledge, and negative social outcomes relevant to the current society of Okinawa and Amami[54].

(1) From interactional resources for Okinawans to the wrong sentential knowledge about Okinawans through the mistaken analogy

One example from Okinawa language shows how an idiomatic expression (Sentential Knowledge of Okinawans) has lost its original meaning in the process of language shift, how it was reinterpreted by the analogy of Mainland Japanese and has been connected to "Okinawaness", how this forms the (stereotype kind of) Image on Okinawan as "easy-going" (shared knowledge of the Mainland Japanese), and why it matters in the Okinawan society.

The expression in question is *nankuru naisa* in Okinawan. It is now known all over Japan after a famous Japanese writer, Yoshimoto Banana from Tokyo, had published a novel called *nankuru nai* in 2004. In this novel, Okinawa is presented as a "healing land" with the shining sun and the blue sea and sky where people are not so much concerned about the busy social life that is known to be "typical for Japanese". This turned out to be problematic for Okinawans.

First, despite still remained people's knowledge about the local language, most of the local people's loss of grammatical and lexical knowledge enabled the (more powerful) Mainlander(s) to reinterpret and distribute the expression to which a different meaning has been assigned. The reinterpretation is linguistically based on the analogy from Japanese language. Originally, *nankuru naisa* can be transliterated as follows:

---

[54] For detail study of the process of language shift on the Ryukyu Islands, see Heinrich (2014).

(1) original morphological transliteration

```
Nankuru              nai-sa
naturally,           become.APOC-FP
on its own
```

(Literally: It surely becomes naturally.)
It will be surely all right.

Nai is a so-called apocopate form (APOC) of the verb *najun* "become," a special grammatical form in Okinawan that is used when followed by particular particles such as *-sa* (utterance-final particle for discursive attitude; FP), *-si* (nominalizer) or *-ga* (question marker). In this case, *nai* is a non-finite form which projects the adding of further element mentioned above. That is to mean the next element (in this case *sa*) is syntactically obligatory. *Sa* is an utterance-final particle for expressing speaker's emphasis to what is said (similar to *yo* in Standard Japanese).

However, the analogy was caused by the fact that there are two similar forms in Standard Japanese, *nai* and *sa*, even if they are grammatically as well as semanto-pragmatically very different from Okinawa language; *na-i* is the finite form of the adjective expressing "non-existent" and *sa* is a utterance-final particle expressing "bystander's light-heartedness" which is added to a finite form of verb or adjective. In Standard Japanese, the final particle *sa* is, syntactically seen, facultative[55]. Therefore, the novel title *nankuru nai* written by the Tokyo-born author is perceived to be possible by people who do not have grammatical knowledge of Okinawan language, while the meaning of *nankuru* remains somewhat vague as this word does not exist in Japanese. Yet, due to the phonological similarity, *nankuru* is often interpreted as *nan to ka* "somehow" in Japanese.

(2) analogical misinterpretation

```
nankuru          na-i              sa
"somehow" (?)    not.exist-NPST    FP
```

No problem, you know.

The second problem is the semantic and pragmatic one. In Okinawa, many of older generation who actively use this idiomatic expression *nankuru naisa* understand it as to be used in the situation where one wants to comfort and pep up someone who has been distressed. To contrast, younger generation in Okinawa and also the Japanese from other prefectures understand *nankuru nai sa* as to mean "no problem" that can also be used in the situation that the speaker him-/herself who made a mistake becalms the other.

The third problem is a social one concerning the distribution and the subsequent forming of Image as shared knowledge. The "no problem"-type of understanding induced by the analogy of the famous writer had an impact on the distribution and the subsequent use of the expression in Okinawa and the Image of Okinawans. In January 2007, one popular local radio programme where listeners participate in the form of e-mail or fax messages answering and commenting on the topic of the day once asked the audience whether they use *nankuru naisa*[56]. The result was 30% answering yes and 70% answering no (to this programme, more than 500 persons regularly send messages. On this day, there were more reactions than usual also from the older generation phoning the broadcaster) (Sugita, 2011: 155).

The reason why many of the audience didn't want to use the expression was the Image that the (misinterpreted) expression transmits: "Okinawans living in the tropical island as happy-go-lucky and not hard-working." Such an Image has an impact in contact situations between Okinawans and people from other prefectures. Negative experiences with Okinawans are stereotypically verbalized by the people from other prefectures that Okinawans have mentality of *nankuru nai sa* (see Sugita 2011: 155-156 for details). The mistakenly analyzed and interpreted expression now has become a Sentential Knowledge of Mainlanders.

The above example shows that the language loss of local people can easily invite the misinterpretation of "exotic" expressions to local people's cost. It is not only the problem that the expression that has been very important for social interaction of comforting distressed friends, relatives or other is disappearing. It also matters because the Sentential Knowledge ("(All) Okinawans are not so much concerned.") easily obscures Okinawans' hardship that they have been bearing until now. The expression was completetly detached from its social, especially sociopolitical and historical context.

(2) From the spiritual belief to the commodification of spirits through the detachment of oral traditions

The next example demonstrates that, in the process of language shift, how the spiritual belief of the Ryukyuan people was detached from its oral tradition and its social context and why it matters for the local people.

On the Ryukyu Islands, folk tales about and the belief in tree spirits (a kind of supernatural monsters or magical creatures) are widespread, from Amami (*kënmun*), through Okinawa (*kizimun* or *kizimunaa*) to Yonaguni (*kidimunu*). Ethnographers have found out that there are various stories about the spirits (e.g. Akamine 1994). Many stories tell us that the spirits who live in trees avenge the human-beings when they burn down or cut

---

[55] As often pointed out (e.g. Miyara, 2011), it is evident that, in Okinawan, modality or speaker's discursive attitude is more incorporated into syntactical structure what is not the case in Standard Japanese.

[56] Podcast: Radio Okinawa (ROK) "Tiisaaji paradaisu" on 26/01/ 2007:
http://uruma.ap.teacup.com/applet/rokinawa/200701/archive?b=10

down the (banyan) trees where the spirits live. The awesome and respectful attitude towards trees or the nature to be learnt from the tales was evident in the varieties of stories.

As is often the case in the societies experiencing language shift, spiritual belief and oral traditions is linked to the knowledge that is important for living with the environment (e.g. Hirsh, 2013). According to Akamine (1994), there are also ritual ceremonies remained in Yaeyama and Yonaguni in which, when a new house is built, the tree spirits should be released from the wood used for the house (to ban the misfortune eventually caused by the tree spirits).

The necessity of such knowledge for the life in Amami can be seen in an example from an Amami's local FM radio, Amami FM D-Wave [57]. There is a few-minutes-feature on every weekday broadcasting conversation between a woman in her 90s and a moderator of younger generation born around 1975. In some of the broadcasted conversation, when it comes to the story about *kënmun* in Amami, the woman born in 1923 shows her unwillingness to speak of *kënmun*. When she has to mention it, she lowers the voice to whisper. This fact is to be conceived as that verbalizing the spirits is taboo. The same woman, in another broadcast, says how she generally rejects to cut down trees, especially banyan and pandanus, that are resistant to the salty wind from the sea.

The moderator of the radio reports afterwards how this woman once entreated some men not to cut down the banyan tree in front of her house. The men had to do it to come through a path with a crane in order to fix the house which was damaged by the torrential rain disaster in Amami in 2010. "Pandanus and banyan are treasure. Don't cut them down!" is a Maxim for the woman, and this Maxim is an important resource for the action strategy in her living environment at the seashore in Amami where typhoons often cause serious damage. Here we can recall what Maffi (2002: 388) makes the point: "[L]inguistic ecologies and biological ecologies are mutually related through human knowledge, use, and management of the environment and through the languages uses to convey this knowledge and practices."

Today traditional stories about *kizimunaa* or *kënmun* are rarely heard. Akamine (1994: 31) points out that the relationship between human-beings and trees/woods has become so loose in our modern society in Japan that it isn't regarded as relevant in the daily life. This is evident in the process how the spirits have been detached from the social context in which the trees and the human-beings were perceived to be more relational. Surely, it is a general tendency that people's interpretation of folk tales changes with time and the attached meaning changes as well according to the social context (as we can see, for example, in the case of Grimms' Fairy Tales). Yet, what we witness especially in Okinawa is somewhat tragic precisely because of the loss of linguistic knowledge and the unease transmission of oral traditions. *Kizimunaa*, who can be very cruel to human beings in the many versions of folk tales, has been "re-invented" as *kawaii* "lovely" mascots for commodity. The illustrations of innocently presented *kizimunaa* are found everywhere in Okinawa today, such as on a traffic sign board (Fig 1).

Figure 1: Sign board appealing to safe driving[58]

A pair of *kizimunaa* is complaining in the typical Okinawa-substrate Japanese (cf. Anderson, 2014) about the human beings driving too fast (Fig 1). Bright red hairs are said to be one of the characteristics of *kizimunaa* also found in many folk tales. However, only the wooden car they are driving somehow suggests us the connection to the sprits of trees, but not the name *kizimunaa*.

The contextual detachment became possible due to the lack of language proficiency. *Kizimunaa* comes from *kizimun* (< *kii mazimun* "magical, evil creature of tree", *munaa* < *mun or munu* with a final vowel lengthening – *aa* as suffix impying derogatory connotation "evil creature"). Due to the lack of semantic knowledge of Okinawan language, a random segmentation *kizimu* and *munaa* for naming the souvenirs is another consequence. It does not seem to be a problem for the company in Naha which produces the mascots of the following key chains in Figure 2.

Figure 2: Random segmentation *kizimu* & *munaa* and the commodification of the tree spirits in Okinawa[59]

The mascot pair is presented as a brother and a sister that are not found in the folk tales as such. Only their red hairs and the clothing made of "tree leaves" seem to have something to do with *kizimunaa*. However, the contextual detachment is so drastic that the belief in awesome and respectful tree spirits has no trace at all

[57] The simulcast per internet is available under: http://www.npo-d.org/index.html

[58] Source: http://en.wikipedia.org/wiki/Kijimuna
[59] Source: http://item.rakuten.co.jp/ryukyu-okinawa/1446319/

here. Examples like Figure 1 and 2 are yet abundant in Okinawa and in Amami[60].

The problematic situation I want to point out here is that the Sentential Knowledge (shared) or Maxim (individual or shared) that was learnt from the oral tradition and connected to the belief as well as the action strategies organized/constrained by the knowledge is disappearing even if the word *kizimunaa* or *kenmun*[61] remain. That is to say that it is not the loss of a word or an (idiomatic) expression itself that matters, but what is done with this word or expression matters. In the same vein, the loss of knowledge matters precisely because the action strategies which have been developed to live in the particular natural environment disappear.

This is not to mean that alternative ways to preserve the nature cannot be found. Nevertheless, it requires, then, as Mühlhäusler (1996: 206) points out, much more energy and endeavour for maganing the preservation. For example, in Amami, where *kenmun* has been partly commodified like in Okinawa as well, protecting the woods from big economic projects such as building wood chip factories for the pulp industry requires the people to mobilize effective protest actions constantly (e.g. Ishida *et al.*, 1998; Nankai Nichinichi Newspaper on May 3rd 2008) that also divides the local people's opinion. In such a situation, the lovely *kenmun* cannot help as it does not represent people's belief and knowledge any more.

Conclusion

In this paper, a theoretical and analytical framework for exploring the loss of knowledge caused by language loss was proposed. The advantage of this framework is first it can link the micro language use through socially shared knowledge (socialized cognition) and strategies of action to social change, and second it enables us to analyze language and knowledge loss in a more systematic, but also in a situated way. This is important for investigating the knowledge which appears always context-sensitive.

As cognitive sociologist Eder (2007: 403) metaphorically puts it, "language provides (…) the grammar of social life." Losing the language means, then, that the social life, relationship to people and to the environment, must be reorganized. This might lead to negative consequences for the people in the society of language shift as shown in the case study.

Acknowledgements

I would like to express my gratitude to the *Deutscher Akademischer Austausch Dienst/German Academic Exchange Service* (DAAD) for supporting my participation in the FEL VXIII symposium in Okinawa. Okinawan language instructor and language activist Fija Byron helped me with valuable information on the use of Okinawan.

References

Akamine, Masanobu (1994). Kijimunaa o meguru jakkan no mondai [Some problems on Kijimunaa]. *Shiryō kenkyūshitsu kiyō*, 19, 1-35. http://okinawa-repo.lib.u-ryukyu.ac.jp/handle/okinawa/7561

Anderson, M.R. (2014). Substrate-influenced Japanese and code-switching. In P. Heinrich, S. Miyara, & M. (Eds.), *Handbook of the Ryukyuan Languages*. Berlin/Boston: de Gruyter.

Berger, P. & Luckmann, T. (1967 [1966]). *Social Construction of Reality: A Treatise in the Sociology of Knowledge*. New York: Anchor Books.

Eder, Klaus (2007). Cognitive sociology and the theory of communicative action: The role of communication and language in the making of the social bond. *European Journal of Social Theory*, 10 (3), 389–408.

Ehlich, K. & Rehbein, J. (1977). Wissen, kommunikatives Handeln und die Schule. In Goeppert, H.C. (Ed.), *Sprachverhalten im Unterricht*. (pp. 36–113). München: Wilhelm Fink.

Evans, N. (2010). *Dying Words: Endangered Languages and What They Have to Tell Us*. Chichester: Wiley Blackwell.

Evans, N. & Levinson, S. C. (2009). The myth of language universals: Language diversity and its importance for cognitive science. *Behavioral and Brain Sciences*, 32, 429–492.

Harrison, D. (2008). *When Languages Die: The Extinction of the World's Languages and the Erosion of Human Knowledge*. Oxford: Oxford University Press.

Heinrich, P. (2014). Language shift. In P. Heinrich, S. Miyara, & M. (Eds.), *Handbook of the Ryukyuan Languages*. Berlin/Boston: de Gruyter.

Hirsh, D. (2013). *Endangered Languages, Knowledge Systems and Belief Systems*. Bern: Peter Lang.

---

[60] The commodification of *kizimunaa* detached from the cultural and social context of Okinawa resembles the situation in Hawai'i that Trask (1999: 136-147) provocatively but felicitously puts it as a "cultural prostitution. Recall also the expression *aloha* in Hawaiian. Trask (2009: 144) says that the expression has become meaningless as it has been removed from any Hawaiian cultural context. This "Erroneous Okinawan (Uchinaaguchi)" (Anderson, 2014) *mensoore* may have been invented for the Marine Expo 1975 and the subsequent development of tourism in Okinawa. Expo's official catchphrase was *mensoore* Okinawa meaning "Welcome to Okinawa." The phrase was chosen with the intention of creating a friendly, exotic image, ironically, equivalent to Hawaiian *aloha* (Tada 2003: 173).

[61] Nowadays most Amamian cannot pronounce the vowel /ĕ/, but pronounce /e/ as Japanese language.

Hoffmann, L. (2010). Wissensgenerierung: der Fall der Strafverhandlung. In U. Dausendschön-Gay, C. Domke & S. Ohlhus (Eds.), *Wissen in Inter-Aktion*. (pp. 249–280). Berlin/New York: de Gruyter.

Ishida, K., Sugimura, K., & Yamada, F. (1998). Amami Ōshima no shizen to sono hozen [Nature and Its Conservation of Amami Island]. *Seibutsu Kagaku* [Biological Sciences], 50(1), 55-64.

Maffi, L. (2002). Endangered languages, endangered knowledge. *International Social Science Journal*, 173(3), 385-393.

Miyara, S. (2011). Japonikku gozoku no naka no ryūkyū goha – keitō, taikei, oyobi genjō [Ryukyu language branch in the Japonic language family: Genealogy, structure, and the current situation]. In P. Heinrich & M. Shimoji (Eds.), *Ryūkyū Shogo Kiroku Hozon no Kiso* [Essentials in Ryukyuan Language Documentation]. (pp. 12-41). Tokyo: LingDy, The Research Institute for Languages and Cultures of Asia and Africa, Tokyo University of Foreign Studies. http://repository.tufs.ac.jp/handle/10108/69946

Mühlhäusler, P. (1996). Ecological and non-ecological approaches to language planning. In M. Hellinger & U. Ammon (Eds.), *Constrative Sociolinguistics*. (pp. 205-212). Berlin: de Gruyter.

Raffles, H. (2002). Intimate knowledge. International Social Science Journal, 173(3), 325-335.

Strydom, P. (2007). Introduction: A cartography of contemporary cognitive social theory. *European Journal of Social Theory*, 10(3), 339-356.

Sugita, Y. (2011). Shakai, bunkateki chishiki o gengo chūshaku ni toriireru [Annotation of socio-culturak knowledge]. In: P. Heinrich & M. Shimoji (Eds.), *Ryūkyū Shogo Kirokuhozon no Kiso* [Essentials in Ryukyuan Language Documentation] (pp. 147-165). Tokyo: LingDy, The Research Institute for Languages and Cultures of Asia and Africa, Tokyo University of Foreign Studies. http://repository.tufs.ac.jp/handle/10108/69959

Swidler, A. (1986). Culture in Action. Symbols and Strategies. *American Sociological Review* 51, 273–286.

Tada, O. (2003). Okinawa Imēji no Tanjō: Okinawa Kaiyōhaku to Kankō Rizōtoka no Purosesu [Emergence of the Image of Okinawa: Marine Expo and the Process of Making Okinawa as Tourist Resort]. Ph.D. Dissertation, University of Waseda. http://jairo.nii.ac.jp/0069/00006170

Trask, H-K. (1999 [1993]). *From a Native Daughter: Colonialism and Sovereignty in Hawaiʻi*. Honolulu: University of Hawaiʻi

Zerubavel, E. (1997). *Social Mindscapes: An Invitation to Cognitive Sociology*. Cambridge: Harvard University Press.

Minority Languages in Networks
of Overlapping, Hierarchical Communities in Colombia

Carl Edlund Anderson
Department of Foreign Languages & Cultures
[carl.anderson@unisabana.edu.co]

Enrique Uribe-Jongbloed
Faculty of Communication
[enrique.uribe@unisabana.edu.co]

Universidad de La Sabana
Campus del Puente del Común, Km. 7, Autopista Norte de Bogotá,
Chía, Cundinamarca, Colombia

Abstract

The fates of endangered languages are closely linked to conceptions of what value they provide to their communities. We examine how minority (particularly indigenous) communities in Colombia have understood themselves over time, as well as how the state as viewed them, and how definitions of communities and their relationships have historically been framed within hierarchical networks framed in terms of power and hegemony. More recently, national legislation has made considerable strides in recognizing and supporting Colombia's fundamentally multicultural character, opening the way to increased recognition and autonomy for minority language communtiies, especially in the areas of education. However, there has been a disappointing lack of accompanying action or real change; the attitudes on all sides that inform actions often remain mired in the past. In a rapidly globalizing world, greater communication and collaboration between all actors are necessary if endangered languages are to be strengthened. We make particular recommendations aimed to generate a more colaborative relationship between minority and mainstream communities, in the understanding that the whole of humanity is enriched (or impoverished) by the survival (or loss) of its languages and cultures.

Introduction

In Colombia, as elsewhere, the fates of endangered languages are closely linked to conceptions of what value they provide to their communities. How the various actors involved understand these concepts has a strong influence on outcomes for those languages. Any given individual can be understood as participating within multiple interacting communities where different values come into play. In Colombia, these overlapping communities have historically been framed within hierarchical networks framed in terms of power and hegemony. More recently, national legislation has made considerable strides in recognizing and supporting Colombia's fundamentally multicultural character, yet the attitudes that inform actions often remain mired in the past. In a rapidly globalizing world, greater cooperation and collaboration between all actors are necessary if endangered languages are to be strengthened.

That being able to use, retain, and indeed strengthen a language offers various benefits to its users is well documented. For example, it has been shown that minority languages maintenance provides speakers with physical and mental health benefits (Hallett, Chandler, & Lalonde, 2007; McIvor, Napoleon, & Dickie, 2009; Sánchez, 2014). Moreover, many members minority communities multilingual; in Colombia, the additional language is most commonly Spanish, but in many cases other minority languages are also known (de Mejía, 2006; Trillos Amaya, 1997), and recent research has revealed multilingual person exhibit certain cognitive advantages (Bialystok & Craik, 2010; Luk, Green, Abutalebi, & Grady, 2012). Nevertheless, the mere existence of such benefits does not imply they are *valued* (or even recognized). There has been an increasing amount of work on how economic value can be derived from minority languages and cultures, with a particular focus on tourism and environmental knowledge (Butler & Hinch, 2007; Coria & Calfucura, 2012; Mauro & Hardison, 2000; Ryan & Aiken, 2010). In Colombia, these have not (yet) become major issues, though existing experiences have not been wholly positive (Verner, 2009). Ostensibly, such endeavors should benefit the minority communities themselves, but there many complications and risks mediated through on the very different value systems that can be held by different communities involved. Indeed, the very terms *value* and *community* are often used as if they are well understood and agreed upon, though this is often far from the case.

Value

The concept of *value* has been variously addressed by among philosophers, anthropologists, psychologists, sociologists, and economists (of course), and even linguists, yet no real consensus on an underlying "theory of value" has been achieved (Graeber, 2001, 2005). For the purposes of this paper, it is understood that people assign *value* through the operation of a "symbolic system that defines the world in terms of what is important, meaningful, desirable or worthwhile in it … containing conceptions of what the cosmos is ultimately about and what is worth pursuing in it" (Graeber, 2005: 439, 444). For many who work with language, language itself holds an unassailable place amongst what is worth pursuing in the cosmos. "It is … an enormous human impoverishment when a language, with all its collective wisdom, beauty, and richness, falls silent" (McCarty, Skutnabb-Kangas, & Magga, 2010: 298). Yet not everyone shares such values—otherwise no individual would ever give up one or more of their languages, and no language would ever die.

Community

Community, too, is not a readily defined concept. Hillery (1955) identified 94 definitions of *community* whose sole unifying factor was that they "deal with people" (p. 117). *Community* has often been defined in contrast with (modern) *society* (Barrett, 2010; Stråth, 2001), and for much of the twentieth century, *community* was often equated with "village", while at the other end of the size scale, Anderson (2006) discussed the nation-state as a *community*. Communities can also be comprehended dialogically (Pallí, 2003; Sampson, 1993), in terms of how both insiders and outsiders perceive who is (or is not) a community member and how communities view and relate to each other.

Language researchers may most naturally think about *community* in terms of the *speech community*, although even this is a more challenging concept than is often appreciated (Eckert, 2008; Gumperz, 2009; Hanks, 1996). Nevertheless, if the "essential criterion for 'community' is that some significant dimension of experience be shared", then it might be agreed that "for 'speech community' that … shared dimension [should] be related to ways in which members of the group use, value, or interpret language" (Saville-Troike, 2003: 15). Admitting language as a factor in determining community membership further complicates questions of who is a member of a community, and the complications become even greater when additional communities are involved—as in the case of minority communities' relationships with the larger nation-states that encompass them.

Ethnic and supra-ethnic communities

The Spanish conquest of what is now Colombia in the sixteenth century effectively created the concept of an *indigenous* identity that implicitly united quite diverse native ethnic groups simply by defining them in opposition to people with a European-derived identity. During the colonial period, this new supra-ethnic identity in fact offered certain advantages, in that "Indianness was … a juridical and political position within the Spanish monarchy which opened avenues of collective political and judicial activity" (Saether, 2005: 58).

However, in the wake of independence, Colombia's post-colonial government promoted the consolidation of a culturally homogenous nation-state (and so, in a sense, itself a supra-ethnic imagined community), including an aggressive de-indigenization policy (de Mejía, 2004; Ortíz Ricaurte, 2004; Trillos Amaya, 1996; Zuluaga, 1996). Accordingly, "Indianness became a less potent instrument and was abandoned by many communities" (Saether, 2005: 58). Through the mid-twentieth century, persons pertaining to Colombian indigenous groups tended to claim membership in their specific ethnic group but resisted generalization as *indios* ("Indians") (Jackson, 2011).

The state was content to leave the mission of "civilizing" indigenous peoples largely in the hands of the Catholic Church until the 1960s, when the first governmental agency concerned with indigenous affairs, the *División de Asuntos Indígenas* (DAI), was established. Though the DAI performed poorly in its mission to promote indigenous interests (Triana Antorvez, 1978), it nevertheless marked the start of an increasingly progressive governmental attitude towards ethnic minorities in which academic criticism of existing government indigenous policies played a significant role (Correa, 2006). The process was not without conflict and setbacks (Jackson, 2011), but it culminated in the new Constitution of 1991 that effectively reversed previous homogenist policies by recognizing both the nation's inherent multiculturality and the state's responsibility to protect this (Asamblea Nacional Constituyente, 1991; Rodriguez & El Gazi, 2007).

Between the establishment of the DAI and the Constitution of 1991, a number of new supra-ethnic indigenous movements emerged out of earlier rural movements focused on issues of land rights and reform (Jackson, 2011). This was accompanied by a process re-indigenization (Chaves & Zambrano, 2006) in which an increasing number of people, some of whom might even have previously disassociated themselves from an indigenous heritage, began to claim supra-ethnic membership in an imagined community consisting of all Colombian indigenous peoples alongside membership in a specific ethnic group. This reassertion of a common indigenous identity was fuelled partially by awareness of other indigenous movements worldwide but also by the state's increasingly progressive policies on indigenous land rights—taking advantage of which required individuals or groups to present an indigenous identity that could be recognized by the national authorities (Jackson, 2011), much as had been the case in the pre-colonial period.

What are the communities, and who is in them?

In practice, just what is required for formal recognition of an indigenous group is not easily pinned down, though it generally requires demonstrating possession of "culturally distinct customary practices and traditions" (Jackson, 2011: 104). This is not always easy after centuries of acculturation, though use of a living language serves as something of a trump card. This motivates groups who have lost their language to seek some means of recuperating it, though it also leads to wrangling over who is, or is not, "indigenous".

Many Colombians have been affected by internal migration and displacement, not least the nation's ethnic minorities, for whom language loss and community fragmentation are amongst the many negative effects. For example, there are descendants of migrants from the Sierra Nevada de Santa Marta to the La Guajira peninsula who consider themselves ethnically Wiwa but whose communities have lost the Damana language still spoken by their relatives in the Sierra Nevada. There is tension not only within "Guajiro Wiwa" communities about whether re-indigenization might be desireable, but also tension with Wiwa communities in the Sierra Nevada, amongst whom there is likewise debate about whether it is possible to be genuinely Wiwa without speaking Damana to begin with (Pérez Tejedor, 2010). In another example, an Embera family that moved from their ancestral territory in Chocó to Caquetá subsequently split into urban and rural communities, though the rural group no longer considers their urban relatives to be "indigenous" (Piñeros, Rosselli, & Calderon, 1998). Such situations create added problems for well-intentioned linguists and government officials, who can hardly do anything without violating *someone's* beliefs about "the community".

Possession of a distinct language likewise plays a critical role in state recognition for Colombia's non-indigenous minority groups. Here, academic linguists have played critical roles in the formal recognition of the Afro-Iberian Palenquero creole and the Afro-English San Andres-Providence Creole as languages, rather than just "bad Spanish/English" (Bartens, 2013; Lipski, 2012).

Ethno-education

Another significant state concession to recognized minority groups in the wake of the Constitution of 1991 is a degree of autonomy in educational policy and practice, identified as *ethno-education* (Aguirre Licht, 2004; de Mejía, 2006; Liddicoat & Curnow, 2007; see also individual papers in Trillos Amaya, 1998). A number of Colombian universities now offer programs both on and through ethno-educational practices, and some universities (for example, the Universidad Indígena Intercultural de Colombia Jacinto Ortiz, and the Universidad Autónoma Indígena e Intercultural) have been established with specifically indigenous orientations (Moreno Rodríguez, 2011).

Some notable successes in ethno-education have been achieved. For example, between 1995 and 2009, the Cofán people (or A'i) of south-western Colombia, moved from the first linguistic description of their language (in a Master's thesis developed by a member of their community in a Colombian university) in 1995 to the development of a complete primary and secondary school curriculum that teaches Cofán language (A'inge) and culture alongside Spanish and the Colombian national curriculum, with teachers trained and qualified in both tracks and an considerable selection of specialized printed and digital materials (Ministerio de Educación Nacional de Colombia, 2009; Quenamá Queta, Queta Quintero, & Lucitante, 2011; Quenamá Queta, 2007, 2011).

However, the Cofán experience is something of an exception to the rule. Implementation of ethno-education policies has more generally been plagued with troubles, not least a shortage of appropriately trained teachers. The situation is exacerbated by segregation of ethno-education from mainstream education, with responsibility shared between the Ministry of Education and the Ministry of Culture. Moreover, the historical use of education as a tool for acculturation has hardly been forgotten. These factors likely contribute to the suspicion with which any kind of state-mediated education, including ethno-education, is viewed by many ethnic minorities (Kværndal, 2013; Ortíz Ricaurte, 2004; Trillos Amaya, 1996).

Recommendations

Historically, it is precisely the isolation and separation of minority communities that has most favored the preservation of their languages. Yet the evolution of transportation and communication technologies and infrastructures continue to bring more people into increased contact. It is questionable how much longer relative isolation will be able to provide much safety. This demands a hard look from all sides at how the various Colombian communities involved with minority languages—which, we would argue, is *all of them*—define and relate to themselves, each other, and indeed the wider international world. Accelerating processes of globalization demand new attitudes founded on historically unprecedented levels of cooperation—and thus trust—between all the actors involved.

Although Colombia has seen great advances in legislation and policy that support minority languages, there has been a disappointing lack of accompanying action or real change. To an extent, this is no surprise: the strength of governments is often more in the creation of policy than its implementation. Moreover, it is a truism that real success in language revitalization is achievable only when the communities themselves own the process. Yet Colombia's minority language communities often remain too isolated, fragmented, and poorly equipped with the knowledge needed to navigate the increasingly complex realities they face.

Ethno-education policies represent positive steps, but Colombian academia must do more to more close the gap between the state and minority language communities by offering knowledge, services, and training that can assist communities with their implementations of legislative policies. Tuhiwai Smith (1999) has famously questioned the participation of non-indigenous researchers within indigenous contexts, emphasizing the need for indigenous researchers working within their own knowledge traditions as agents for social justice. These are important points that deserve greater attention and appreciation, though in cooperation between indigenous and Western researchers, Western knowledge traditions can serve as a bridge between those of the particular indigenous community and the many varying traditions and experiences of other minority communities worldwide. This must not be a process of "academic imperialism"; the various knowledge traditions of minority communities should be in dialogue with and indeed inform those of the Western academic community. There is a very great need—in Colombia, and elsewhere—for improved understandings of how to manage this relationship. Nevertheless, partnerships between minority language communities and academia elsewhere have proven fruitful (Hinton, 2011; McAlpin, 2008; McCarty, 2008, 2013; Weinberg, De Korne, & Depaul, 2013), and the experience of the Cofán has shown that they can be effective in Colombia as well.

We would also argue that it is desireable to encourage mainstream (Spanish monolingual) Colombians to develop their own senses of collaborative responsibility for minority languages. This may be viewed as an inherently provocative suggestion, as there are many minority language groups who would resist (for various reasons) the notion that "outsiders" should have any relationship with their language. But we contend that endangered languages need friends—particularly amongst the communities that neighbor them and in which many of their own members share membership. Accordingly, we would recommend that policies and materials appropriate to improving awareness about minority languages and cultures be developed for use in mainstream schools. Similarly, policies and tools should be developed to help non-minority Colombians working in minority language contexts (such as doctors, social workers, law enforcement officials) use those languages appropriately and effectively where possible.

Moreover, though mass media can help bring endangered languages into new domains where intercultural and multilingual negotiations take place, catering to both existing minority language users and minority community members who have shifted to the majority language. There are also as yet unrealized opportunities for using ICTs to connect members of (often dispersed) communities with each other (via language-using platforms) to share experiences and knowledge and with potentially useful external actors (the state, and perhaps particularly academia).

Conclusions

Of course, the beliefs and preferences of any minority language community—and the right to self-determination—must be respected. Yet it can hardly be denied that majority language speakers already play an indisputable role in the fate of minority languages—and likewise stand to gain or lose (if less obviously so) from their eventual fate. Indeed, the whole of humanity is enriched (or impoverished) by the survival (or loss) of its languages and cultures. The integrated, overlapping nature of these various communities has often been obscured by their historical hierarchically mediated relationships. This is a difficult legacy to overcome. Though the way is no doubt fraught with challenges, we argue that approaches based on communication, cooperation, and collaboration—with accommodation, but not acculturation—amongst minority and majority communities represent the best chances for greater valuation of and chances of strengthening endangered languages.

References

Aguirre Licht, D. (2004). Estudios en lenguas aborígenes y etnoeducación en Colombia. *Revista Educación Y Pedagogía*, 39, 27-40.

Anderson, B. (2006). *Imagined Communities: Reflections of the Origin and Spread of Nationalism* (2nd ed.). London: Verso.

Asamblea Nacional Constituyente. Constitución política de Colombia, Pub. L. No. Gaceta Constitucional 116 de 20 de julio de 1991 (1991). Colombia: Gaceta Constitucional.

Barrett, S. R. (2010). Community: The Career of a Concept. *Anthropologica*, 52(1), 113-125.

Bartens, A. (2013). San Andres Creole English. In S.M. Michaelis, P. Maurer, M. Haspelmath, & M. Huber (Eds.), *The Survey of Pidgin and Creole Languages* (Vol. 1, pp. 101–114). Oxford: Oxford University Press.

Bialystok, E., & Craik, F. I. M. (2010). Cognitive and linguistic processing in the bilingual mind. *Current Directions in Psychological Science*, 19(1), 19–23. doi:10.1177/0963721409358571

Butler, R., & Hinch, T. (Eds.). (2007). *Tourism and Indigenous Peoples: Issues and Implications*. Oxford: Butterworth-Heinemann.

Chaves, M., & Zambrano, M. (2006). From blanqueamiento to reindigenización: Paradoxes of mestizaje and multiculturalism in contemporary Colombia. *Revista Europea de Estudios Latinoamericanos Y Del Caribe*, 80, 5-23.

Coria, J., & Calfucura, E. (2012). Ecotourism and the development of indigenous communities: The good, the bad, and the ugly. *Ecological Economics*, 73, 47-55. doi:10.1016/j.ecolecon.2011.10.024

Correa, F. (2006). Interpretaciones Antropológicas sobre lo «Indígena» en Colombia. *Universitas Humanística*, 62(1), 15-41.

De Mejía, A.-M. (2004). Bilingual education in Colombia: Towards an integrated perspective. *International Journal of Bilingual Education and Bilingualism*, 7(5), 381-397. doi:10.1080/13670050408667821

De Mejía, A.-M. (2006). Bilingual education in Colombia: Towards a recognition of languages, cultures and identities. *Colombian Applied Linguistics Journal*, 8, 152-168.

Eckert, P. (2008). Communities of practice. In K. Brown (Ed.), *Encyclopedia of language and linguistics* (pp. 683-685). Oxford: Elsevier. doi:10.1016/B0-08-044854-2/01276-1

Graeber, D. (2001). *Toward an Anthropological Theory of Value: The False Coin of Our Own Dreams*. New York: Palgrave.

Graeber, D. (2005). Value: Anthropological theories of value. In J.G. Carrier (Ed.), *A Handbook of Economic Anthropology* (pp. 439-454). Cheltenham: Edward Elgar.

Gumperz, J. J. (2009). The Speech Community. In A. Duranti (Ed.), *Linguistic Anthropology: A Reader* (pp. 66-73). Chichester: John Wiley & Sons.

Hallett, D., Chandler, M. J., & Lalonde, C. E. (2007). Aboriginal language knowledge and youth suicide. *Cognitive Development*, 22(3), 392-399. doi:10.1016/j.cogdev.2007.02.001

Hanks, W. F. (1996). *Language and Communicative Practices*. Boulder: Westview Press.

Hillery Jr., G. A. (1955). Definitions of Community: Areas of Agreement. *Rural Sociology*, 20(2), 111-123.

Hinton, L. (2011). Language revitalization and language pedagogy: new teaching and learning strategies. *Language and Education*, 25(4), 307-318. doi:10.1080/09500782.2011.577220

Jackson, J. E. (2011). Overview of the Colombian indigenous movement. *UniverSOS: Revista de Lenguas Indígenas Y Universos Culturales*, 8, 99-114.

Kværndal, S. M. (2013). *U'waenes syn på utdanning og deres utdanningssituasjon i Colombia: Parallellsystemer i praksis*. Universitetet i Oslo, Oslo, Norway.

Liddicoat, A. J., & Curnow, T. J. (2007). Language-in-education policy in the context of language death: Conflicts in policy and practice in Colombia. In J. Siegel, J. Lynch, & D. Eades (Eds.), *Language Description, History and Development: Linguistic indulgence in memory of Terry Crowley* (pp. 419-430). Amsterdam: John Benjamins Publishing.

Lipski, J. M. (2012). The "New" Palenquero: Revitalization and Re-creolization. In R.J. File-Muriel & R. Orozco (Eds.), *Colombian Varieties of Spanish* (pp. 21-41). Frankfurt am Main: Vervuert.

Luk, G., Green, D. W., Abutalebi, J., & Grady, C. (2012). Cognitive control for language switching in bilinguals: A quantitative meta-analysis of functional neuroimaging studies. *Language and Cognitive Processes*, 27(10), 1479-1488. doi:10.1080/01690965.2011.613209

Mauro, F., & Hardison, P. D. (2000). Traditional Knowledge of Indigenous and Local Communities: International Debate and Policy Initiatives. *Ecological Applications*, 10(5), 1263-1269. doi:10.2307/2641281

McAlpin, J. D. (2008). *Place and Being: Higher Education as a Site for Creating Biskabii---Geographies of Indigenous Academic Identity*. University of Illinois at Urbana-Champagne, Champaign, IL.

McCarty, T. L. (2008). Language Education Planning and Policies by and for Indigenous Peoples. In N.H. Hornberger (Ed.), *Encyclopedia of Language and Education* (Vol. 1, pp. 137-150). Philadelphia: Springer Science+BusinessMedia.

McCarty, T. L. (2013). Language Planning and Cultural Continuance in Native America. In J.W. Tollefson (Ed.), *Language Policies in Education: Critical Issues* (2nd ed., pp. 255-277). New York: Routledge.

McCarty, T. L., Skutnabb-Kangas, T., & Magga, O. H. (2010). Education for speakers of endangered languages. In B. Spolsky & F.M. Hult (Eds.), *The Handbook of Educational Linguistics* (pp. 297-312). Oxford: Wiley-Blackwell.

McIvor, O., Napoleon, A., & Dickie, K. M. (2009). Language and Culture as Protective Factors for At-Risk Communities. *Journal of Aboriginal Health*, 5(1), 6-25.

Ministerio de Educación Nacional de Colombia. (2009). Cofan: cultura, identidad, lengua. *Altablero*, 51.

Moreno Rodríguez, C. (2011). *Estudios sobre la Educación Superior Indígena en Colombia*. Brussels, Belgium: Centre d'Etudes Sociales sur Amérique Latine (CESAL).

Ortíz Ricaurte, C. (2004). Resistencia y procesos de integración indígenas: El caso de los kogui de la Sierra Nevada. *Boletín Antropológico*, 22(60), 72-88.

Pallí, C. (2003). Communities in Context: Undefinitions, Multiplicity and Cultural Difference. *Interamerican Journal of Psychology*, 37(2), 309-326.

Pérez Tejedor, J. P. (2010, April 29). Personal interview. Bogotá, Colombia: Ministerio de Cultura de Colombia.

Piñeros, M., Rosselli, D., & Calderon, C. (1998). An epidemic of collective conversion and dissociation disorder in an indigenous group of Colombia: its relation to cultural change. *Social Science & Medicine*, 46(11), 1425-1428. doi:10.1016/S0277-9536(97)10094-6

Quenamá Queta, V. (2007). *Enseñanza del cofán como segunda lengua (L2) en educación propia, escuela de Santa Rosa del Guamuéz - Departamento del Putumayo - Colombia*. Universidad Mayor de San Simón, Cochabamba, Bolivia.

Quenamá Queta, V. (2011). Propuesta de enseñanza de la lengua cofán y construcción de la gramática pedagógica. In *Ciclo de mesas redondas preparatorias del segundo seminario nacional de enseñanza y evaluación de lenguas nativas, Univerisdad Central, Bogotá, Colombia, 10-14 octubre 2011*. Bogotá, Colombia.

Quenamá Queta, V., Queta Quintero, I., & Lucitante, J. (2011). Proceso de revitalización de la lengua nativa y producción de material didáctico. In *Segundo seminario nacional de enseñanza y evaluación de lenguas nativas, Univerisdad Central, Bogotá, Colombia, 10-14 octubre 2011*. Bogotá, Colombia.

Rodriguez, C., & El Gazi, J. (2007). The Poetics of Indigenous Radio in Colombia. *Media, Culture and Society*, 29(3), 449-468.

Ryan, C., & Aiken, M. (Eds.). (2010). *Indigenous Tourism: The Commodification and Management of Culture*. London: Routledge.

Saether, S. A. (2005). Independence and the Redefinition of Indianness around Santa Marta, Colombia, 1750-1850. *Journal of Latin American Studies*, 37(1), 55-80. doi:10.1017/S0022216X04008600

Sampson, E. E. (1993). *Celebrating the other: A dialogic account of human nature*. London: Harvester Wheatsheaf.

Sánchez, M. A. M. (2014). Education and Health: A Case of Indigenous Cultural Identity in Colombia. *Procedia - Social and Behavioral Sciences*, 132, 166-170. doi:10.1016/j.sbspro.2014.04.294

Saville-Troike, M. (2003). *The Ethnography of Communication: A introduction* (3rd ed.). Oxford: Blackwell.

Stråth, B. (2001). Community/society: History of the concept. In N.J. Smelser & P.B. Baltes (Eds.), *International Encyclopedia of the Social & Behavioral Sciences* (pp. 2378-2383). Oxford: Elsevier.

Triana Antorvez, A. (1978). El Estatuto indígena; o La nueva encomienda bonapartista. *Controversia*, 79, 29-41.

Trillos Amaya, M. (1996). Bilingüismo desigual en las escuelas de la Sierra Nevada de Santa Marta: Problemas etnoeducativos. *Thesaurus: Boletín Del Instituto Caro Y Cuervo*, 51(3), 401-486.

Trillos Amaya, M. (1997). La Sierra: Un Mundo Plurilingue. In X. Pachon, F. Correa, & E. Benavides Gomez (Eds.), *Lenguas Amerindias: Condiciones Socio-Linguisticas en Colombia* (pp. 219-268). Bogota: Instituto Colombiano de Antropologia.

Trillos Amaya, M. (Ed.). (1998). *Educación endógena frente a educación formal: Mesas redondas sobre etnoeducación organizadas por el Centro Colombiano de Estudios de Lenguas Aborígenes (CCELA), Universidad de Los Andes, enero-mayo, 1996, Santafé de Bogotá*. Bogotá, Colombia: Universidad de Los Andes, Centro de Estudios Socioculturales e Internacionales, Centro Colombiano de Estudios de Lenguas Aborígenes.

Tuhiwai Smith, L. (1999). *Decolonizing methodologies: Research and indigenous peoples* (pp. 1-5). London/Dunedin: Zed Books/University of Otago Press.

Verner, D. (2009). *Tourism and indigenous peoples - lessons from recent experiences in eco and ethno tourism in Latin America and the Caribbean*. Washington, DC: The World Bank.

Weinberg, M., De Korne, H., & Depaul, S. (2013). "It's so alive right now": Community-university collaboration for Lenape language education in Pennsylvania . In *Third International Conference on Language Documentation and Conservation (ICLDC)*. Manoa: University of Hawai'i.

Zuluaga, O. (1996). *La enseñanza de lenguas extranjeras en Colombia en 500 años*. Popayán, Colombia: Taller Editorial, Unicauca.

The Yui Language, a Vehicle to Societal Cohesiveness and Survival Competence within the Yui Speaking Community

Ruth Kamasungua
Senior Tutor
Department of Language & Literature
P O Box 1078
Papua New Guinea
[kamasunguaruth@yahoo.com]

Abstract

The Yui language of the Salt Nomane District in the Simbu Province of Papua New Guinea is an endangered language. It has around 6500 speakers. It is employed for cultural effects in the domains of marriage feast songs; "Ama ha" (Girl-talk) Courting songs, "Hamil ha" or Traditional Speech oratory, "Kun-O" (Pig-killing) feast dance songs and others. This promotes societal cohesiveness through building up of self-esteem, identity, confidence, pride, self-worth, survival competence, strengthening of ties and relationships as well as other benefits within the Community. There are specific words and phrases that are attached to the ecology and geographical surroundings (landscape) – these are vitally attached to speakers of the Yui language. The extinction of these words or phrases means the severing of the umbilical cord. Only the Yui language (words and phrases) carry the link/meaning. This is a great cause for aiding Yui language revitalization. The Yui language ecology and language revitalization is invaluable to Yui speakers and their culture's preservation. It is the foundation of their identity. It reaffirms their sense of belonging and this gives them a sense of placement instead of feelings of displacement and loss of identity which are by-products of language loss. In this paper I aim to discuss on how Yui language is employed for cultural effects in the domains mentioned above and how this enhances the Yui society to be cohesive and to interrelate well and to survive competently within the community.

Introduction
Yui, an endangered language

The Yui language has around 6500 speakers. Yui speaking people are located in the south-eastern part of the Simbu Province in the central highlands of Papua New Guinea. Yui is an endangered language and unless it is documented it is surely dissipating. According to a research done in 2013 for a conference in Manokwari, Indonesia it was found that approximately 70-80% of all Yui speakers between the ages of 15-55 left their villages and migrated into towns and cities of PNG. The result of the research also showed that 60% of Yui adults and 100% of Yui school children and youths speak Tok-Pisin most of the time in the settlements. 70% of their parents admitted that their children do not speak Yui but Tok Pisin most of the time within the settlements (Kamasungua, 2013) The children of these migrants grow up in total ignorance of Yui since Tok Pisin is taking over in the settlements and English the language of instruction for the migrants' children at school. Also, the people still living in the rural areas within their villages are affected by the dominance of Tok Pisin and English. As a result, only the adults and the old people speak Yui but the majority of the children are turning to Tok Pisin and are speaking it in schools amongst their peers as well as speaking at home in their villages. The children grow up in total ignorance of the Yui language because Tok Pisin is the main creole language spoken in the urban areas of PNG. Simon Ager (1993-2013) stated that:

Tok-pisin is an English based creole spoken in PNG... The word tok means "word" or "speech" as in "talk", and pisin means "pidgin". ...Tok Pisin started out as a Pidgin – a simple contact language used by people who didn't share a common language. Over time it has evolved and become a creole acquiring more complex grammar in the process. The majority of Tok Pisin vocabulary comes from English, though it also includes words from German, Portuguese and a number of Austronesian languages such as Tolai and Malay. Tok-Pisin is used to some extent in the media and government. It is also the language of instruction for the first three years of primary education in some schools. (Simon Ager 1998-2013)

In this current trend, Yui is a dying language and will soon cease to exist. Therefore language revitalization as well as documentation are crucial. The prospects of Yui language revitalization are very minimal and therefore grim. However, the area of traditional courting songs, marriage feast songs, pig-killing dance and feast songs and speech oratories would be seen as one avenue of Yui language revitalization. In Yui society, due to the influence of western culture and mass migration, many things have changed. However, the types of songs mentioned as well as speech oratories are still functioning due to the fact that the Yui people in the rural areas are still practising the traditional courting system, traditional marriage ceremonies, pig-killing dance and feast songs and the speech oratory which is used for important ceremonies and meetings. These customary practices give hope for language revitalization. In the urban settlements where Yui migrants live, Yui speakers also have kept alive the practice of marriage feast songs, and traditional courting songs. For the pig-killing feast song and dance, the migrants have to go back to the rural areas to sing and perform as it is a very important occasion to the culture of the Yui speakers. Traditional speech oratory belongs strictly in the traditional society and therefore is not practiced by Yui speakers in urban settlements.

Courting songs, pig-killing feast songs, speech oratory – hope for Yui language revitalization and solution to social disharmony

I am from the Yui speaking society. Unfortunately I speak Yui as my second language since the national creole Tok Pisin took over being a national informal language. Tok Pisin is a language of convenience that gives the people of PNG a sense of unity since we have more than 800 different languages that come with their own distinct cultures segmenting us into hundreds of "micro nations" all huddled together in one country. Tok-Pisin threatens to eradicate our diverse languages altogether. And a more dominant and powerful English is intimidating Yui even more as people succumb to the lure of English as a prominent, privileged and official language. Tok Pisin and English are posing threats to Yui and its relation to the ecology and geographical surroundings (Landscape). As Yui words and phrases that are attached to the ecology are threatened to extinction by the influence of the powerful and dominating English and Tok Pisin, then this severs the umbilical cord of the Yui speakers, cutting them off from their identity, self-worth, self-esteem, pride, a sense of belonging, roots, and etc. This eradicates a sense of belonging which leads to cultural loss, and out of it emanates social implications such as crime, theft, prostitution, gambling, alcohol problems, mass migrations into towns and cities etc. Inspite of language dissipation, due to the above mentioned causes, there is still a fragment of hope in Yui revitalization as well as strengthening societal cohesiveness and survival competence, especially in the area of courting songs, pig-killing feast songs and speech oratory where the Yui language is employed for cultural effects. In this paper I will discuss on these three areas and talk about how the different types of songs and speech oratory hold together the invaluable link to societal cohesiveness, culture and the wellbeing of the Yui speakers.

Research Methods

I have done my research in terms of collecting songs from Pis wara settlement in Goroka town where Yui settlers dwell. Seven Yui people sang two (2) marriage feast songs and two (2) courting songs and one (1) pig-killing song. (These people explained the songs they sang and gave other valuable information. I recorded these songs and transcribed them. One Yui woman sang on the phone from Port Moresby, the capital of Papua New Guinea and I transcribed the song as she sang. For the speech oratory examples, I recalled the speech oratories given while I was growing up in the Yui society. Most of the information collected is from my own experience as a native Yui woman who grew up and experienced both the Yui and the western culture.

"Ama ha" (Girl-talk) Courting songs, Marriage feast songs and "Kun-O" (Pig-killing) feast dance songs

The Yui culture allows the Yui language to create a strong link between the Yui speaker and the surrounding environment and geography (landscape). The environment and landscape is integrated into the culture of the Yui speakers and is expressed through language (words / phrases) in the form of songs, proverbs and speeches. This is enhanced by the value attributed to "place" as opposed to dislocation. For the Yui, "place" is permanent and cannot be shifted. "Place" gives value to the wellbeing of its speakers in terms of stability, identity, self-worth / esteem, pride and survival competence amongst its neighbors and allies. This endows importance on certain geographical and environmental features such as rivers, mountains, animals, soil, food crops, trees, and etc within the boundaries of the Yui speaking society/tribe. The naming of these features creates an "umbilical cord" linking Yui speakers to their environment. These features are mentioned in songs, proverbs and speeches which express a strong link between place and culture. In this way it establishes and re-affirms tribal pride, competence, values, self-worth and the general well-being of the Yui speakers. For example, in the courting song, a group of young men from a neighboring tribe may sing a song calling the name of a river from their area, or a type of special food crop in that area – the mention of that environmental feature reflects tribal pride and enhances identity, as well as trying to woo over possible brides from a different tribe since Yui is a patrilineal society where the bride goes to live in the groom's village. Below is an example, of a

Ama ha ("Girl-talk") courting song sung by a group of Yui people in Piswara settlement, Goroka, PNG:

Yui Version	English Translation
Wai Yanda wai ya we we we (9 x)	Wai Yanda wai ya we we we
Dirma Barma mongo main yara we we we	Dirma-Barma hill
Arigigi mongo main yara we we we	Arigigi hill
Yobai Kul mongo main yara we we we (Stanza repeated)	Yobai mountain
Maina Kumo Ambu di yeiya we we we	Maina-Kumo Lady I dated
Bro Yori Ambu di yeiya we we we	Bro-Yori Lady I dated
Gil Begil Ambu di yeiya we we we (2 x)	Gil-Begil Lady I dated
Bro Yori Amubu di yeiya we we we	Bro-Yori Lady I dated
Maina Kumo Ambu di yeiya we we we	Maina-Kumo Lady I dated
Ole Umba Aurun baraula we we we	Ole Umba leaves I cut
Dui Simai Aurun baraula we we we	Dui Simai leaves I cut
Sil Sabia Aurun baraula we we we (2 x)	Sil Sabia leaves I cut
Dui Simai Aurun baraula we we we	Dui Simai leaves I cut
Ole Umba Aurun baraula we we we	Ole Umba leaves I cut
Wai yanda wai ya we we we (6 x)	Wai yanda wai ya we we we

In this courting song, names of hills and mountains, names of special trees, leaves and plants that are of significance to the Yui speakers of my tribe are mentioned. Yui speakers of my tribe live on high mountains, and *Dirma-Barma*, *Arigigi* and *Yobai* are mountains where my people's villages are situated on. *Ole Umba* is a special tree and people use its stem to make bows. *Dui Simai* is a type of flower that is common in my area. *Sil Sabia* is a common yellow *(tanget)* plant that is only grown in my village. It is highly favoured and used for decoration during singing and dancing in pig-killing ceremonies etc. All these environmental and geographical features have a significance in the cultural lives of the Yui speakers and so they have a significant link to the culture of the Yui speakers and especially their tribes. For example, when the above song is sung and the features of the environment and landscape are mentioned, it builds pride, self-esteem in the the singers and the tribe as a whole. This boosts the well being of the speakers, thus instilling in them a sense of survival competence amongst their neighbors and allies.

Another example would be in a marriage feast song where the bride's clan would sing a song that mentions the name of an environmental feature in their area.   Below, here is a song sung by a bride's clan (my clan, *Kebri Yori Girin*) during a marriage ceremony in 1980:

Yui Version	English Translation
Kamna Dirma mongo kulare	Dirima hill
Kamna Barma mongo kulare	Barma hill
Abe Dewa	Father Dewa
Abe Bare	Father Bare
Na igna bolgu	My home dismantled
Na igna sawai	My home dismantled
Na meule kama inata	Give me my black-bird of paradise
Na sinkral kama inata	Give me my belt of possum hair
Wi igne warinalaria	I have no relatives
Na Yol igne nalaria	I have no acquaintance
Na erinta pangwa alo	I have no roots
Na kuba pangwa alo	I have no roots
Na kia sre warinalaria	I have been displaced
Na waia sre warinalaria	I have been displaced
Daira sua	Struggle in pain

Dirima koibe daira sua	Struggle in pain in Dirima
Barma koibe daira sua	Struggle in pain in Barma
Mama Kina yo daira sua	Mother Kina, struggle
Mama Siria ya daira sua	Mother Siria, struggle

(Song by Bro-Yori women, quoted as sung by Erikina Kamasungua)

This song talks about the departing of the bride from her home to a new environment. *Dirima hill* is the name of the 'place' of the bride. The mention of the name of the place in the song by the bride's clan connotes the sadness felt by the bride's clan when she leaves her home for the groom's home as a vital part of the Yui marriage convention. This reaffirms the link this tribe has with their environment (*Dirima hill*) but the bride's departure from her home environment is a loss. On the contrary, the departure of the bride from her home is a gain for the groom's clan. Lines 5 and 6 talk about the bride's home where she was brought up in as being dismantled which means she is about to be dislocated. This line shows the value of "place" in the Yui society. In lines 9 and 10 talk about her departure to another area which would leave her all alone with no relatives / acquaintances. In line 11 and 12 talk about her as being displaced as a result of moving away from her home (*Dirima*) to the groom's place. Lines 13 and 14, talk about the struggle of pain the bride and her mothers' experience when she departs from her home. We clearly see the significance of place which is strongly linked to the Yui society. And in songs, names of places are mentioned to reaffirm their value to the Yui speakers and their culture. Also in line seven, the black bird of paradise (*Meule Kama*) is mentioned and in line eight the belt of possum hair (*sinkralkama*) is mentioned to show the worth of the bride. The black bird of Paradise is featured by its long black tail. For the Yui, the black bird of Paradise' tail and the possum hair with a plant used for decoration called *Sinkral* speaks of a young woman's beauty and worth.

(Black bird of Paradise and the possum hair and *sinkral* are of high value in the Yui Society.) These are displayed as part of the decorations on a young woman during dance such as the pig-killing feast dance. Therefore, the mention of the bird of paradise (*Meule Kama*), and possum (*haunugu*) and the plant (*sinkral*) which are features of the environment link the surrounding environment (plants, geographical features such as mountains/ hills and animals) to the Yui Speaker and enhance his culture. It thus creates the umbilical cord linking the Yui speaker to his culture. This thus gives him a sense of pride and self worth in the society. A third example would be the "Kun-O" (Pig-Killing) feast dance songs – this event happens every 5 – 7 years and is intended for the displaying of wealth, tribal strength, manpower and cultural pride. Since a pig's value is equivalent to monetary value according to the Yui culture and society, hundreds of pigs are slaughtered during this festival and every tribe comes out in their best traditional regalia to perform cultural dances to show their manpower, pride and wealth. Manpower and wealth are also valued in terms of strong young men and beautiful young women who are highly decorated to perform these dances which would take place not only in their own area, but they have the freedom to move around to neighboring villages. During this dance, songs are sung and certain features of the environment to which the dancing group belongs to are mentioned to enhance identity, wealth, pride, and competitiveness. Below, is a Pig-killing song from the Yui speakers living in Piswara Settlement of Goroka town:

Yui Version

Ere bonikulsunga ire, Ware sunga ire
Wari Kale yadraledungo O, Yaumauwe   (3 x)
Pu Aah

Ere bonikulsunga ire, Ware Sunga ire
Sirua Kabuyadrale dung O, Yaumauwe   (3 x)
Su Ah

Yobaikulberandi, DirimakulberandiAiya

English Translation

Ere Boni flower grows
Red Parrot sings, showing off
Pu Aah

Ere Boni flower grows
Bird of Paradise sings, showing off
Su Ah

Going around Yobai hill, Going around
Dirima hill Aiya

The above pig-killing song is one stanza of the many stanzas sung by Yui speakers during pig-killing ceremonies. Here a special flower plant *Eriboni* is mentioned. This flower is

141

common in our area. The red parrot "Kale" is mentioned. This bird's feathers are removed and carefully woven into a piece of cloth and worn around the head as part of the famous head dress in the Yui Society. The Saxony bird of Paradise is also mentioned in the above song. This bird's tail is unique because of its scale like tail which is worn into the pierced nose that gives the dancers a featured decorative look during pig killing dance. Also, the singers mention two mountains, *Yobai* and *Dirima*. These two mountains are significant because *Yobai* is a refuge place during tribal fights and *Dirima* is where my ancestors decided to build their homes. The names of plants, birds and mountains give the singers and their clan a sense of pride and self-worth in society. During pig-killing ceremonies representatives from all tribes within the Yui society form their own dancing groups and dance in an appointed area. The public is free to go to each of the villages to watch the dances. There is a sense of competition as every dance group represents its own tribe and has to perform to the best. It is the only time they show off their wealth, beauty in terms of young woman, strength and military power in terms of strong young man and they mentioned plants, animals, rivers and hills that are sacred to them and where they belong. It is showing off who they are and this gives them a sense of survival competence.

"Hamil ha" or
Traditional Speech oratory

Another venue where the Yui language brings/enhances societal cohesiveness and survival competence is the "Hamil ha" or the traditional speech oratory. This happens during important meetings such as bride price ceremonies, "peace ceremonies", compensation payment ceremonies and general village gatherings for other special events. The orators are a selected few and are comprised of village chiefs or elders who are given the role of tribal orators to speak at important occasions. These orators are known for their wisdom and eloquency of speech including the skilled use of proverbs. During speeches the orator would walk back and forth in front or in the middle of a crowd with the famous orator's sceptre and talk in a sing song voice. He uses proverbs and also mentions environmental features in his area such as, names of animals, food crops, trees, mountains and others. For the proverbs, especially people of another visiting tribe would ask around to find out what the speaker meant, for example, if it is a peace-making ceremony and two tribal enemies come together to make peace. The orator who represents the one tribe may explain why their tribe

decided to declare war on their neighbor. He would say something like:

Yui Version: *Meune nir ime habi kul holemda, ni kul si pre kuni gri iu nenda bani ni simnyo.*
Eng. Translation: 'We fought against you because you stole our ripe banana which grew near the river Meune.'

This would indicate that the other tribe was at fault by killing some one who went to the opponents' area for a friendly purpose, thus triggered the fight. The mention of the river's name and the type of banana would indicate to the accused tribe of their wrong doing. And it is through this proverb that they will eventually find out that they were at fault and this causes them to feel responsible to pay compensation to the victim's tribe. Furthermore, the mention of the particular river's name and the type of banana that gives the accused tribe a sense of burden that tells them that it is someone or a group of people from their tribe who committed murder and not someone from another tribe. Thus the name of the river and banana bears a strong link to the accused tribe causing them to act in order to clear their tribal name and it is also a provocation to them challenging them whether they are capable of paying compensation or not. It causes the accused to pay compensation to show neighboring tribes their competency and survival fitness. This enhances their pride, self-worth and creates peace. It also helps them to survive competitively within their society. Another example would be a bride-price ceremony where an orator from the grooms clan might give a speech which is made up alot of proverbs with metaphors. He might use "stone" to refer to "money", chicken to refer to "pig", "dog" to refer to "cow". He might say we offered two extra "chicken" to the girl's mother for raising her up. Or we killed "two dogs" for the bride's "feet". "Feet" refers to the value of the bride. For example:

Yui Version: *Awi ta ama dibin ban sikena tendi, wai pin tominyo.* English Version: 'For killing a "dog" for the girl's feet, we are grateful.'

It is showing appreciation of the fact that the bride is coming to the grooms clan to be part of it and is a gain to the groom's clan. In these proverbs, metaphors are used to sound graceful without stepping on the other clans' toes. The use of denotations may seem impolite and would sever good tribal relationships. Relationships between tribes are very important for the purposes of trade, exchange of brides, refuge stronghold during tribal wars, access to gardening land, tribal peace and harmony.

Conclusion / Recommendation

In conclusion, the use of metaphors in proverbs are a necessary incentive used to build good relationships among friends and allies within the Yui speaking society – this also enhances societal cohesiveness and survival competence within the Yui society. Within the domains of "Ama ha" (Girl-talk) courting songs, marriage feast songs, "Kun-O" or pig killing dance and feast songs, names of places, mountains, rivers, plants and animals are mentioned. This creates a link between the Yui speakers and their environment. The mentioning of the names of the geographical and environmental features in traditional songs and speeches plays an important role in bringing stability, peace and harmony into the Yui society. It also enhances relationships and ties between tribes and families and gives the Yui speakers a sense of self-worth in the society. For the Yui, place is stable and static, which has a strong link to the Yui speakers thus the mention of certain words such as these names intimately enhances the speakers sense of well being and survival competence. This is an invalueable asset to Yui revitalization. Since the Yui language is dying out, first of all awareness has to be made to the Yui people both in the villages of our society and in urban settlements throughout the towns and cities that the traditional custom of courtship, marital feasts, pig-killing festivals and different traditional speech oratories must be kept alive in order to maintain identity, self-esteem and pride which will consequently also keep the Yui society intact and make its speakers proud to be who they are. Secondly, as part of the revitalization process, the government should provide incentives such as funding cultural shows, building cultural centres and theatres where people can find avenues to take pride in their traditonal dances and songs. Thirdly, apart from Yui revitalization, the songs and oratory speeches should be recorded and kept for the future generation of Yui's who might never know the Yui language.

References

Ager S. (1989-2014)
http://www.omniglot.com/writing/tok pisin.htm
Date accessed: 21/11/13

Kamasungua, R., (2013) The Endangerment of the Yui Language – cited on 25/07/14 from wwwstaff.eva.mpg.de/-gil/wipl3/abstract/kamas ungua.pdf

Kamasungua R. (filed notes) Song by Bro-Yori women, quoted as sung by Erikina Kamasungua

Yui people in Piswara settlement, Goroka – 12/06/14

Noqanchis Magazine:
Using Print Media to Promote Cool and Quechua in Cuzco

Gabina Funegra
School of Humanities and Languages
Faculty of Arts and Social Sciences
University of New South Wales
[g.funegra@unsw.edu.au]

Abstract

This paper provides an overview of *Noqanchis* magazine. *Noqanchis* is written in Quechua and has been part of a funded project of the *Centro Huamán Poma de Ayala*, Cuzco, Peru, to promote Quechua in the city. In the magazine, all of the text is in Quechua and the images are all of indigenous people. The cultural studies concept of the principle of Cool is discussed in relation to the Quechua culture and *Noqanchis*. The preliminary results of interviews conducted with four members of the project team are presented. Initial analysis shows that the magazine has garnered considerable interest from the younger generations as well as the Quechua-speaking community in Cuzco. Moreover, the magazine has generated discussions on the language outside of Cuzco. Perhaps the most important finding is that the magazine has been a catalyst for resurgence of written Quechua in the city.

Introduction

This paper provides an overview of a print media strategy to revitalise Quechua in the city of Cuzco, Peru. *Noqanchis* Magazine was an initiative of the *Centro Huamán Poma de Ayala*, a Non-Government Organization (NGO) which for the last thirty-two years has worked towards the building of a just society for all people, placing emphasis on the most vulnerable people in the city of Cuzco.

The aim of this research study is to investigate how magazines, such as Noqanchis, can be used as vehicles to engage younger speakers of languages like Quechua as part of global language revitalisation strategies. The paper raises the principle of "Cool" in relation to the growing appeal of Quechua with the younger generations. Semi-structured interviews were conducted with nine members of the *Noqanchis* publication team; the preliminary analysis of four interviews is presented.

This paper builds on research that was conducted in Huallanca, Peru. Here, I extend my earlier research wherein I found that teenagers were the most difficult group to engage in language revitalisation strategies due to the pressure of globalisation and conformity (Funegra, 2011). What I wanted to investigate was why a magazine, such as *Noqanchis,* has worked as a strategy to engage younger generations in speaking, reading and being proud of their Quechua heritage.

Background

Efforts to revitalise indigenous languages is by no means a new or novel occurrence. In fact, there is a substantial amount of research that has been undertaken on efforts to promote languages. Studies, such as the seminal article by Krauss (1992), resulted in an increase in the focus of research in linguistics to raise awareness of the language revitalisation movement. There are numerous reasons why there is a global focus on language revitalisation efforts, such as initiatives like *Noqanchis*. This is perhaps best articulated by Dixon

(1997: 116), who stated that "language is the most precious human resource" and that each language is unique in that it has its own different phonological, morphological, syntactic and semantic organization. This value of language as a unique and priceless entity is further espoused by Crystal (2000: 34), who declared that "language is the most important part of human expression, rituals, music, painting, crafts and all other forms of behaviour all play their part, but language plays the largest part of all".

The relationship between language and culture is vital. It was argued by Miyaoka (2001: 9) that "The disappearance of any language represents a loss of intellectual heritage not only for the people but for humanity as a whole. It is evident that the vitality of the language as a form of cultural identity is extremely important". It is only by studying the various possibilities across all languages that we, as researchers, can gain a deeper understanding of the role that language has on culture and identity.

The Principle of Cool and cultural identity

"Ethnic absolutism is out. Cool is in" (Maher, 2005: 89). Maher (2005), in his study of metroethnicity in Japan, examined the role of "cool" in ethnic allegiance and how people use non ethnic criteria to feel affiliated to a language and cultural group. What he argues is that younger generations intentionally decide to align with a particular group on the basis of questions, such as: is it a cool thing to do? Or is it a cool thing to be? So identification with a group is more of an accessory that is subject to aesthetic demands, as opposed to a sense of ethnolinguistic duty. According to Maher (2005), being cool is to be quirky, innovative and tolerant. Cool is an attitude and it is also hope. So what is being put forth here in the principle of Cool is the idea that in ethnic minorities that are often viewed as being marginalised or disenfranchised there is a new cultural track emerging from younger generations that values the street credibility of the minorities (Maher, 2005).

Scholars of the theme of "cool" in general agree that the attitude cool came from Africa. According to McGuigan (2006), cool refers to composure in battle, heat, and life, and had particular relevance for young males. He explains that when Africans were forced into slavery in the Americas, the term "itutu" or cool became a way to maintain a sense of dignity in oppressive conditions. He further adds that there is an obvious connection between slavery, jazz culture and more modern forms of music, such as hip-hop and rap. The word "cool" has become an everyday form of approval, meaning "good" or "okay", so in this way the term which originally meant resistance to subjugation and humiliation is now a way into the hearts of young consumers (McGuigan, 2006). Younger generations easily adapt and construct identity through language choice (Hornberger & Coronel-Molina, 2004; Luykx, 2000). At one level, authority and social structures, including education and family, influence language use. Two ways that this manifests is through teenager peer pressure and the shift driven by the younger generation themselves through their increasing connections with the word beyond the community's boundaries (Luykx, 2000).

In my earlier research, for example, Funegra (2011), I found that teenagers were the most difficult people to engage with the Quechua language and culture as they wanted to belong to a cosmopolitan world, Consequently, they were the most challenging people to interview on this matter as they tended to deny or be embarrassed by their Quechua heritage. However, in this paper, I will discuss how a "cool" strategy of using print media has provided social currency for younger generations in affiliating with Quechua.

Print media as a language revitalisation strategy

The use of print media as a means of promoting a language may seem outdated with increasing access to the internet and the growth of social media, such as Twitter and Facebook. However, numerous studies have shown that there is still a significant divide between those that have access to such technologies and those that do not. For example, Selwyn (2009) in his argument against the myth of digital natives explains that females, those living in rural and remote areas and those that are from minority cultural and linguistic backgrounds have less access to technology. In this respect, the speakers of Quechua are most likely to fall into these minority groups that do not have access to technology. Hence, strategies to promote the value of the language need to be both visible and accessible to the target population.

Noqanchis Magazine

The title *Noqanchis* means *nosotros* in Spanish or *we* in English. The magazine was funded as part of an NGO project from 2011 to 2012. The project promoted social inclusion and equality of gender as well as cultural awareness. In a sense, the project can be aligned with Fishman's (1991, 2000) eight-stage model of language revitalisation. In stage six, Fishman (1991: 199) advocates focusing revitalisation efforts:

> Creating the intergenerationally continuous [Quechua] speaking community via providing and stressing the link to family life, residential concentration and neighbourhood institutions.

This project was supported by the Basque government in Spain through another NGO, *Solidaridad international del país vasco.*

Noqanchis started with the aim of breaking the popular stereotypes of Quechua speakers in mainstream society as being a parochial or backward language. The magazine was trying to compete with publications of the same kind that are directed to the middle class and the upper class of the Cuzco society and present a range of popular topics. The magazine had the same format of magazines, such as Vogue, and included fashion as well as editorials. Celebrities, such as actress/singer Magaly Solier, were interviewed for the magazine. The fashion spreads were modern and edgy, the models and backgrounds were intentionally appealing to younger generations in that they were aiming for cool rather than traditional. *Noqanchis* magazine was specifically directed to the sector of mainstream society that speaks Quechua in Cuzco. The images in the magazine depicted people of indigenous heritage and all text was in Quechua. In this sense, the magazine was unique in Peru in that all of the text was in Quechua and not Spanish. Moreover, the magazine had images of both males and females on the cover and in the photo shoots (see Figure 1) as a strategy to appeal to both a male and female audience.

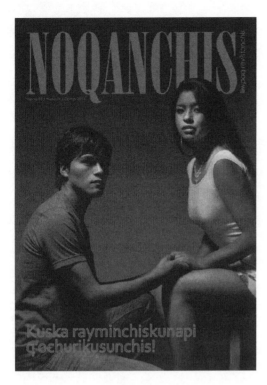

Figure 1: Cover image of
Noqanchis magazine

Noqanchis was a pictorial publication in that images of Cuzco residents featured throughout the editions. These included images of social events, traditional festivities in Cuzco, places of work, markets and sport events are all included in the magazine, along with the fashion shoots and short articles. The magazine featured children and adults in the social pages. All of the people who appeared in the magazine were Quechua speakers (Figure 2). The aim of the magazine was to both celebrate and normalise Quechua. So it combined high-end fashion with local events and people.

Figure 2: Social pages of
Noqanchis

The magazine was published quarterly and five editions in total were published in 2012. The project team had hoped for a few more editions. However, a lack of further funding from the European Union meant that the project did not continue. No further funding sources were found. *Noqanchis* was free. However, it had a publicity company who advertised on the radio and television. There was also an online version of the magazine. The magazine was distributed by hand to lower socio-economic areas where there was a high proportion of Quechua speakers. The magazine was also distributed to media outlets, juice stalls at the markets, coffee shops in the city, hairdressers and other places.The magazine was also distributed in Paris.

The long-term viability of Noqanchis

At the time of conducting my interviews with members of the magazine team, the future of the magazine was unknown. Financial problems within the European Union meant that there was doubt as to whether the project's funding was to be extended beyond one year. It was hoped a group of young people in Cuzco, who were interested in the magazine, would continue the project and publish the magazine. There was also interest from commercial areas to sponsor the magazine. The only condition of the project team was that the advertisements remain in Quechua.

Methodology

An interpretive ethnographical approach was used in this study. The core aim of this study was to capture the voices and stories of people, in a natural setting (Brewer, 2004). An interpretivist methodology was applied for this study. An interpretive approach was adopted as interpretive approaches rely heavily on naturalistic methods, such as interviewing and observation and analysis of existing texts. Semi-structured interviews were used in this study. The interviews were designed to elicit information on social life, the magazine, the participant's hopes for the magazine and their opinions about the value of print media to engage the younger generation of Quechua speakers. In the interviews discussed here, I used a set of questions that acted as a guide, but the interviews were more like a conversation that I changed to allow for deviations from the set questions as the interviews progressed (O'Reilly, 2005). This enabled the participants to provide a rich narrative of their experiences with Noqanchis.

The interpretivist method aims to ensure that there is an adequate dialogue between myself and the interviewees in order to collaboratively construct a meaningful reality. Angen (2000) put forward several criteria for evaluating research from an interpretivist perspective:

1. Careful consideration and articulation of the research question
2. Carrying out inquiry in a respectful manner
3. Awareness and articulation of the choices and interpretations the researcher makes during the inquiry process and evidence of taking responsibility for those choices
4. A written account that develops persuasive arguments
5. Evaluation of how widely results are disseminated Angen (2000) also proposed that to ensure moral validity that the inquiry should be undertaken in the discourse of the research community. These criteria were adopted for the study.

Participants

There were nine participants interviewed for the study. In this paper, I will provide an overview of the results of four of the interviews. All four participants participated directly in *Noqanchis*. One interview was conducted with Luis Nieto. Luis is the editor of several publications and periodicals in Cuzco. For example, he is the current editor of "Cronicas Urbanas", an annual publication on Quechua. He is involved in the promotion and distribution of *Noqanchis* and he is also on the editorial board. The interview was conducted in January 2013 in Cuzco. I conducted the second interview with Jorge Vargas, in Cuzco in January 2013. Jorge was in charge of the publication of the magazine.

The third interview was with Hilda Cañari. Hilda was the editor for the Quechua language in the magazine. She was a fluent Quechua speaker. Her interview was in Quechua, and Jorge Vargas acted as translator. Her interview was transcribed from Quechua to Spanish by a third party. The fourth interview was with Erica Valer Bárcena, who was a model in one of the *Noqanchis* issues. I transcribed all the interviews from Spanish into English.

Results

A preliminary analysis of the interviews is presented in the results. The main aim of the preliminary analysis is to identify how the initiative is being used to promote Quechua and how this form of print media may be used as an effective means of language revitalisation in a globalised world.

One of the main findings, at this stage, is that the magazine is gaining support from younger generations and is encouraging discourse in Quechua. Vargas stated that:

> *The models [with Quechua features] are young, beautiful, happy and rich. The Quechua culture is usually linked to poverty, old age and sorrow.*

This resonates with Maher's (2005) discussion of cool in that rather than being associated with the negative stereotype of poor, old and oppressed, Quechua is being presented as being attractive, wealthy and modern.

According to both Nieto and Vargas, there has been a strong interest in the magazine from the younger generations. Vargas and Nieto explained that all correspondence was conducted in Quechua and the people who write letters in Quechua to the magazine received responses in Quechua. They both feel that this was a rewarding exercise as younger generations were using Quechua and not Spanish to communicate. They explained that the younger generations not only wanted their photos included in the periodical, but they want to write articles as well. Vargas added that the magazine was supporting a new wave of Quechua learners, those who had missed the opportunity to learn from their parents. Now they have the opportunity to learn and embrace Quechua as it has a public voice.

These views on the role of the magazine on promoting Quechua as cool were echoed by Hilda who clarifies:

> *The reason we choose young people is because later on they will have kids, then if we reinforce*

the Quechua language, these young people will transmit it to their children, they will already have the idea. That's why we are focusing on young people.

Erica, who was pregnant at the time of the interview, perhaps provided the most personal reflection of the use of Quechua in stating that:

I would love that everyone was speaking Quechua in Cuzco. My children will be born in this city and they must also know Quechua. Friends, we must think and speak Quechua, everyone should know, we must teach our children. It is also what I want for my kids. They also will learn to speak Quechua, I will teach them, even their names will be in Quechua.

Nieto explained that the magazine was gaining attention from academics as well. He stated that academics have started researching the impact that the magazine has had not only in Cuzco, but in Lima and the United States, too. Interest is also coming from other forms of print media and television.

Figure 3: Models from an article in *Noqanchis* magazine

One of the more interesting findings arising from the interviews is that this magazine challenged the stereotypes presented in other magazines that Peruvians are of European heritage. According to Vargas, the advertising in Cuzco is targeted to the middle class, which is mainly at "white" people (10 per cent of the population), that is, people of European heritage. Normally, being white is associated with beauty, happiness and success. Vargas further explained that what this means is that even if you are beautiful, happy and successful there is a kind of rejection of "the colour of our skin, the colour of our eyes, of our height, the shape of our noses that prevents us from feeling completely fulfilled". We still lack that whiteness. *Noqanchis,* however, has shown that indigenous people are beautiful. The photos in the magazine show a range

of people from young to old in the social pages and the photo shoots show indigenous people modelling current fashions. Figure 3 shows an article from the magazine featuring both a male and female model.

What this means for the younger generation of Quechua speakers is that the beauty that they were once excluded from now includes them. As far as culture and identity are concerned, having beautiful people in magazines may seem like a shallow way to engage people in a language, but as younger generations are more greatly influenced by peer pressure and social influences, this may be one of the factors that has contributed to the success of the magazine.

There was some backlash against the magazine. Vargas said that some members of the public are citing "reverse racism", and that the magazine may be creating discrimination rather than preventing it. However, most of the support was overwhelmingly positive. Overall, according to Vargas, the magazine was a new avenue of empowering Quechua from speakers within the community. It also promotes the power of written Quechua within different strata of society.

Conclusions

What is presented in this paper is a very brief overview of the efforts of the *Noqanchis* project team to revitalise Quechua in Cuzco through the use of a magazine. The future of the magazine, at this stage, is unknown. The fact that it has garnered support from the Basque Government and external agencies means that there is recognition at an international level for the magazine as a revitalisation strategy. Both Vargas and Nieto explained that the magazine has also garnered interest from different strata of the Cuzco community.

Moreover, the magazine has been popular with younger generations, perhaps because Quechua has become cool. It has, in places, attained a status of being something to be associated with rather than being associated with the usual negative stereotypes. Younger generations have shown an interest in contributing to the magazine, and, as a consequence, revitalising written Quechua in Cuzco. This is perhaps one small step in the process; however, that small step means a lot to the indigenous people of Cuzco in finding a voice for their language, culture and identity. If cool works, then let Quechua be cool.

Acknowledgements

The author would like to thank César Itier, for his ongoing support in this research. The author would also like to thank Pablo Landeo, Jorge Vargas, Hilda Cañari, Erica Valer Bárcena and Luis Nieto for their generous sharing of their stories and their ongoing support.

References

Angen, M.J. (2000). Evaluating interpretive inquiry: Reviewing the validity debate and opening the dialogue. Qualitative Health Research. 10(3) pp. 378-395

Brewer, J. (2004). Ethnography. In C. Cassell & G. Symon (eds) Essential guide to qualitative methods in organizational research. London; Thousand Oaks: SAGE Publications. p. 312 – 322.

Crystal, D. (2000). Language Death. Cambrige: Cambrige University Press

Fishman, J.A. (1991). Reversing language Shift: Theory and Practice of Assistance to Threatened Languages. Clevedon: Multilingual Matters.

Fishman, J.A. (ed.) (2001). Can Threatened Languages Be Saved? Reversing Language Shift, Revisited: A 21st Century Perspective. Clevedon : Multilingual Matters.

Funegra, G. (2011). Language and Identity: The Shifting Face of Quechua in Peru. In Haboud, M. & Ostler, N. (Eds) Endangered Languages: Voices and Images. The 15th Annual Conference of the Foundation for Endangered Languages, Quito, Ecuador, pp. 25-32.

Hornberger N.H. & Coronel-Molina, S.M. (2004). Quechua language shift, maintenance and revitalization in the Andes; the case of language planning . International Journal of the Sociology of Languages, 167(1), pp.9-67.

Krauss, M (1992) The world's Languages in crisis. Language, 68(1), 4-10.

Luykx, A. (2000). Diversity in the New Word Order. State Language policies and the internationalization of Quechua. Paper presented at the 2nd Spencer Early Career Institute in Anthropology and Education: "Globalization and Education"

Maher, J. C. (2005). Metroethnicity, language and principle of cool. International Journal of Sociology of Language, 175/176. Pp. 83-102.

McGuigan, J. (2006). The politics of cultural studies and cool capitalism. Cultural Politics, 2(2), pp. 137 - 158

O' Reilly, K. (2005). Ethnography methods. New York: Routledge

Selwyn, N. (2009). The digital native: myth and reality. ASLIB Proceedings (2009). 61(4) pp. 364-379.

An Encounter with Extinction:
A case for the Preservation of the Diminishing Ngasa Language of Eastern Kilimanjaro in Tanzania

Carolyne Adhiambo Ngara
University Of Nairobi - Kenya
The Enduring Voices Foundation
P.O. Box 38615 – 00100
Nairobi, Kenya
[carol.ngara@gmail.com]

Gabriel Owiti Oguda
Enduring Voices Foundation
P.O. Box 45259 – 00100
Nairobi, Kenya
[gabriel.oguda@yahoo.com]

Abstract

The ability to communicate effectively in an individual's own language not only connects a person to his/her ethnic group but also helps in identity shaping and cultural preservation. The tribe, with which an individual identifies, in a great majority of cases, is always his/her tribal name. Before colonial rule spread across Africa, indigenous cultural heritage was passed down the generations by language; which was integral in affirming and maintaining well-being and a strong sense of generational identity. It bore complex understandings of indigenous cultures, environment, traditional and ecological knowledge. It connected an individual to his ancestral land. With the decline of their language and culture, the Ngasa – a nearly extinct indigenous folk found on the slopes of Eastern Kilimanjaro – has lacked the wealth of evidence that once supported their community. Since Tanzania is not a monolingual society, the Ngasa people have has gradually abandoned their diminishing language and adopted the language and cultural roots of the dominant Chagga, Pare and Swahili speech communities, thus losing their feelings of pride and self identity. While English and Swahili enjoy de facto official status, Tanzania's 1984 constitution neither establishes an official language nor protects indigenous languages in the country.

Introduction

The current linguistic "extinction crisis" is expected to decimate global cultural diversity. In a number of African countries, some dominant languages like *Setswana* in Botswana, Swahili in Kenya and Tanzania, Amharic in Ethiopia, Chichewa in Malawi and Somali in Somalia, have been promoted to the role of a national or official language. This promotion attributes to actual expansion and use of these languages in public functions, thus increasing their social status, prestige, utilization and value augmentation. This has given such languages more weight compared to the minority languages, making the latter more vulnerable and prone to extinction. In Tanzania, for example, the elevation of Swahili to national and official levels in the 1960s increased its predominance and influence over all other native languages, and as a result it expanded enormously throughout the country. Batibo (1992) and Mkude (2001) have described how the process of language shift due to *Swahili* domination has accelerated. As observed by Bernd Heine (pers. comm.), the main threat to indigenous languages in Africa today, is not the ex-colonial languages or the minor "areally" dominant languages, but rather the nationally and major areally dominant languages as these are often promoted and supported by the state. As illustrated by Mekacha (1993) for the case of *Swahili* (see Table 13), such languages are rapidly replacing both the ex-colonial and the minority languages.

The critical question addressed in this paper is whether Tanzania should disallow the loss of her linguistic diversity for the sake of Swahili as a single national language that is still equated with unity and identity of its citizens. In this paper, we elaborate the causes of gradual "language death" with reference to the Ngasa. We provide an overview on the current use of Ngasa language, its geographical and linguistic coverage in Tanzania, as well as shed light on the Ngasa people, their culture, traditions and particular motivations for their language shift to other more dominant neighboring native languages like Chagga, Pare and Swahili. We will explore the link between the Ngasa people, their language and culture; and discuss the value of the same and how it has shaped the cultural identity of the Ngasa speech community found on the Eastern Slopes of Mt. Kilimanjaro, Tanzania. We will also describe our current revitalization efforts on the Ngasa language and culture. Lastly, we will discuss the urgent need for the Republic of Tanzania, to recognize, promote and preserve her Indigenous languages that were spoken before the colonial era, as a valuable and historical part of Tanzania's cultural heritage.

The Situation of Indigenous Languages in Africa

Language, which is an important resource in human life, can be a source of great value for a nation as well as being part of national heritage. The Indigenous language situation in most African countries is characterized by three types of languages: an ex-colonial language; one or several dominant languages at national and areal local levels; and minority languages. African languages display extensive cultural wealth accumulated over centuries. They portray rare and unique linguistic features among the languages of the world. Each language reflects a unique world vision formed by its speakers through their long experience of their environment and at the same time manifests a rich range of artistic phenomena.

However, most African countries have paid minimal attention to their indigenous language and cultural issues. Although they are important linguistic, cultural, artistic resources and, potential vehicles for development, Indigenous languages in Africa have been grossly abused. The abuse includes their use for divisive politics between groups, to exclude others from participation in national affairs, to impede the social advancement of certain sectors of the population, to marginalize the speakers of other languages and to deliberately exclude others from participating in discussions with others. Usually, minority language speakers suffer the most. As a result, they tend to learn and use the dominant language as a second language or even shift to it at the expense of their "mother tongue". This is because they find the dominant language both socially and economically more attractive, rendering the fate of the minority languages to doom and extinction.

In this paper, Tanzania provides a great linguistic profile and example. Of the 128 languages spoken in the country, 80 are minority languages, while three are arealy dominant and one nationally dominant. The remaining languages are either severely endangered or extinct.

Language situation in the Republic of Tanzania

Tanzania is a medium sized country with a population of 35 million. It has 124 languages, with Swahili as the main official and national language and English as the second official language, mainly in higher education and international affairs. Swahili is also the nationally dominant language, spoken by over 90% of the population as first or second language. The only major arealy dominant language is Kisukuma, which is spoken in the northern part of the country by more than 12.5% of the population. The highly endangered languages include: Daiso (Dhaiso), Gweno (Kigweno), Hadza (Hadzapi, Kitindiga), Akie (Ndorobo, Kisankara), Kwavi (Parakuyo), Bondei, Doe, Burunge, Gorowa, Holoholo, Ikizu, Ikoma, Isanzu, Jiji, Kabwa, Kami, Kisi, Makwe, Manda, Mbungwe, Segeju (Sageju), Nghwele, Pimbwe, Rungwe, Suba, Alagwa (Wasi, Asi), Vidunda, Vinza, Zinza, Surwa, Sweta, Wanda and Zalamo (Zaramo). The extinct or nearly extinct languages are Aasax (Asax, Asak), Ongamo (Ngasa),

Kikae (Old Kimakunduchi), Kw'adza, Degere, Yeke, Hamba, Bahi and Ware.

Like many African countries, the tendency to neglect the minority languages in Tanzania, was driven by the desire to promote a strong national language. Swahili, which enjoyed the sole national language status, reached a point where there was no concern at a governmental level if the other languages disappeared in the process. President, Julius Nyerere, in his address to the Tanzania Swahili Writers Association in 1984, admitted that the empowerment of Swahili as the sole national language was likely to affect the other languages in the country. To him this was an inevitable development. The high rate of language endangerment and extinction in Tanzania is mainly a result of the dominance of Swahili as both official and national language (Batibo, 1992). The enormous prestige accorded to Swahili, exerted irresistible pressure on most of the minority languages in the country.

The status of native languages in the Constitution of the Republic of Tanzania

In Tanzania, minority languages are used primarily in the private family domains. The use of these languages is less prestigious. No explicit policy exists for minority languages like Ngasa; the dominant language Swahili prevails in the public domain. After gaining independence in 1961, Tanzanian Government encouraged assimilation to the dominant languages. The dominant language was and still is the sole official language, while non-dominant languages are neither recognized nor protected in the Constitution of the country.

As discussed on the Abstract, English and Swahili have de facto official status in the Republic of Tanzania. However, the 1984 Constitution does not reveal much on the protection, promotion and use of indigenous languages in the country. English and Swahili have remained the two major languages widely used by Tanzania's mainstream media, administrative, legal and education systems. Children are taught in Swahili at elementary school level and in English thereafter. The Constitution does not establish an official language and therefore, indigenous languages like Ngasa are not legally or constitutionally recognized in the Republic of Tanzania.

The Ngasa People: Their origin, traditions, religion, linguistic and cultural assimilation

The Ngasa folk, also known as the: Ongamo, Shaka, Ongg'amoni, Ongg'amo are a people resident on the Eastern Slopes of Mt. Kilimanjaro in Tanzania. They speak the Ngasa language. Their reported number varies from source to source. The Ngasa migrated from West Africa through Central Africa - from where they began expanding to other parts of sub-Saharan Africa around 2000 BC before settling in Tanzania. Their migration is believed to have been caused by the population bust in central Africa and influenced by personal quest for arable agricultural land. Although a cattle keeping people, their quest for fertile agricultural land was a viable alternative, prompting several successive waves of unplanned and instantaneous migrations over the following millennia, thus allowing plenty of time for the Ngasa people, their language, culture and traditions to spread across the region.

Geographically, the Ngasa language is spoken in three localities namely: - Ubetu, Reha and Kahe between the valleys Makuku and Machima near the border of Kenya and Tanzania border. UNESCO considers Ngasa language "moribund" - with only a few elderly speakers left. Its use and practical linguistic application began diminishing in the 1950s.

After many years of contact, the Ngasa people have been heavily assimilated by their more populous Chagga neighbours, to the point of a language shift having taken place among larger portions of Eastern Kilimanjaro. This has resulted to an extreme reliance on others for trade and survival.. The ethnic composition of the Ngasa is known as 'Ongamo' to the neighboring people. Nowadays the Ngasa language is no longer an intrinsic part of Ongamo ethnic identity. The only elderly speakers left are bilingual in Chagga, Pare and Swahili.

Although the Ngasa are "wildly" viewed as a sub-group of the 'Chagga' tribe, they are a people with a Language of their own. Their Ngasa language is genetically linked to the: Nilo-Saharan, Eastern Sudanic, Nilotic, Eastern, Lotuxo-Teso, Lotuxo-Maa, and Ongamo-Maa languages. Ngasa also has three varying dialects of its own - which are spoken at varying degrees and have lexical similarities with the Maasai, Samburu and the Chamus dialects of Kenya. Other languages used within the Ngasa speech community are: Chaga, Pare and Swahili.

European influence, which penetrated Africa, viewed the Ngasa as a sub-group of the Chagga. This further caused the Ngasa minority to lose recognition of their distinct culture. Since the Ngasa language was very different from other more dominant languages in the area, it came to be viewed as inferior. Education was always introduced in Swahili and later on in English, making many Ngasa people to lose the interest and the ability to speak their own language. Religions like Christianity too were brought to this area through the Chagga people – Thus sidelining the Ngasa folk. A lot has changed of the sociolinguistic state of the Ngasa language since the decline in usage began in the 1950s. Although older generation is struggling to keep a distinct ethnic and cultural identity, they lack all forms of infrastructure that could assist them in revitalizing and documenting their language.

Currently, it's viewed as a secret language of a few elderly people and is mainly spoken by older adults. While in most Tanzanian communities, the Ngasa language and culture is considered as endangered, in others it is more fitting to classify it as severely endangered or even extinct – this is due to the declining number of Ngasa folk willing to speak the language confidently in public. Ever since coming to this area, the Ngasa have been overshadowed by other dominant ethnic groups, particularly the Chagga, Pare and Swahili tribes.

The Ngasa adhere to their customs and traditions. For example in the past, Ngasa marriages were traditionally considered to be the most significant event in the lives of both men and women. It was thought inappropriate for any boy or girl within the Ngasa speech community to remain unmarried. Large families ensured adequate manpower and security for the Ngasa folk. Polygamy and large number of children guaranteed a spouse for every single person in Ngasa land. Arranged marriages for the Ngasa youth were common. The significance of 'dowry' (bride price) was paramount. Members of the Ngasa groom's family initiated a process of negotiation with the bride's family. This unfolded over many years. Negotiations were made intense, and for this reason, a 'go-between' or a 'middleman' considered to be neutral to the interests of each family, was contracted to carry out the task.

Cattle were primarily given as bride price. In determining the value of a prospective bride, several factors like health and beauty were taken into account. Failure of men to raise high bride prices prompted many of them to propose a "come-we-stay" (elopement). While many traditional African communities viewed divorce as a taboo – that could not be effected after the bride price had been exchanged among families and children born to the married couple, the Ngasa Speech Community viewed this differently. Even if separation took place, the Ngasa couple in question was still ideally considered married. Failure to have children, however, was thought to be the fault of the bride and for this reason she would be divorced after which the man marries another wife, mostly from the bride's family or clan.

Women played the primary role of child rearing and farming, girls were expected to help their mothers and their step mothers in farming land owned by their father, brothers, and paternal uncles. Men took total control over animals and were always occupied with rearing and grooming cattle for bride price, establishing trade partnerships with external communities; and handling commercial sales of the cash crops. Until male children turned five or so for boys and until adolescence for girls, Ngasa children had the most contact with their mothers, sisters, and other female relatives. Puberty ceremonies for boys and girls were practiced. Marking the transition to adulthood, such elaborate ceremonies involved circumcision of boys and several kinds of genital mutilations on girls.

Despite the severe decline of the Ngasa population, intermarriage with the Chagga and Pare people was common. When this happened, the Chagga-Pare customs were generally observed. However, the younger generation still wishes to marry within their Ngasa ethnic groups. In the past, Ngasa tribal elders caution against "intertribal marriages" - the more distant the ethnic group and customs of a bride was considered to be from that of the Ngasa speech community, the greater the cautionary warnings would be.

The Ngasa traditional way of life was considered as an important community cultural resource. Traditional songs were popular and music was the most widely practiced art in the Ngasa community. At any time of the day or night, music would be made and played. Music was functional and was mostly used for ceremonial, religious, political, or incidental purposes. Music was performed during funerals, to praise the departed, to console the bereaved, to keep people awake at night vigils, to express loss, pain and agony. Songs were sung during rituals like cleansing and chasing away evil spirits who visited the village at night, in rain making, and during divinations and healing.

The Ngasa played their traditional music during ceremonies like beer parties, welcoming back the warriors from the war, during wrestling matches and during courtship. Work songs performed during communal work like building, planting, weeding, harvesting and during individual work like pounding of cereals, or winnowing also existed.

In general, music was shaped by the total way of life, lifestyles, and life patterns of individuals within the Ngasa community. Because of that, the Ngasa music had characteristics which could be seen, heard, and felt in their melodies, rhythms, mode of presentation, dancing styles, movements and performances. This distinguished it from the music of other surrounding communities. The melodies in their music were lyrical, with a lot of vocal ornaments that was portrayed out clearly, especially if the music carried an important message for the people. Most of their songs were usually presented in solo performances and recitatives chants, with irregular rhythms and phrases, which carried serious messages. Another unique characteristic in their music was the introduction of yet another chant at the middle of a musical performance. As the singing stopped, the pitch of the musical instruments went down and the dance became less vigorous as an individual took over the stage in self praise.

Since there was no stigma associated with "nudity", the Ngasa wore animal hides that covered only their private parts. Walking barefoot was typical in the old days. Children were disciplined and brought up communally. The ability to control one's temper and emotions in public was highly valued. Elders were honored and respected by the rest of the community. Young men and women were not supposed to show mutual affection in public or in broad daylight. Women were not allowed to smoke tobacco, talk in raised voices or cross their legs while sitting or standing in front of/across the opposite sex.

Although the Ngasa community witnessed the increase of modern utensils and silverware, traditional customs prescribed eating all kinds of foods like rice, meat, soups and sauces using the right hand. Children who attempted to eat using their left hands were disciplined appropriately. This custom was related to their perceived symbolic purity of the right hand, compared to the left hand. The Ngasa practiced a custom known as the "tea time" – which they adopted from the British colonialists' in the 50's. They traded with the dominant neighboring communities like the Chagga, Pare; and the Swahili, exchanging their farm produce for animals, handicrafts, pots, and baskets. Their primary crops were maize (corn), millet, and sorghum. Coffee, tobacco, cotton, and sugarcane were important cash crops. Cattle were mainly used for bride price. Though periodic famine persisted yearly causing long, dry seasons prior to harvest, their staple food was *Ugali* - A meal made from corn meal, stirred in hot boiling water until it became thick and solid. *Ugali* was always served with meat, stew, fish or *sukumawiki* ('green vegetables').

Death was an inevitable loss for the Ngasa people. The "ancestors" assumed an extremely important role in relation to death. Ancestral spirits were believed to exert significant influence on daily lives of the Ngasa. They were remembered and called upon through various rituals. For example, before a beer drinking occasion, the Ngasa poured a small amount of beer on the ground, as a sign of respect for their ancestors. Otherwise, a small vessel of beer was left in a special location as an offering to the ancestors. In other cases, sacrifices of chicken or goat were regularly made to the ancestors in ceremonies that varied accordingly.

In the past the Ngasa men died in wars that were deemed necessary to protect the community from intruders. Today, the Ngasa folk like many African communities have been hit hard by the AIDS epidemic, causing frequent deaths. Often families are often lack the time and resources to follow traditional mourning and burial customs, which differ by religion and composition among many dominant ethnic neighboring groups that have since assimilated the Ngasa.

The Ngasa family and community structures have since been severely endangered too. Rules once set to guide the youth are often broken in urban centers. Boys and girls are commonly seen in public places holding hands as a sign of affection and friendship. The youth are increasingly challenging such customs as arranged marriages. Calls to stop traditional genital mutilation performed on girls have become louder and strongly discourage such practices due to unforeseen severe medical consequences. Cattle have a monetary value and are no longer primarily kept for bride price. Cash crops are sold to purchase items like: sugar, bread, and butter, which are then consumed with tea in tandem with the "tea time" tradition. Both boys and girls within the Ngasa community attend school if the parents can afford their school fees. If there is no sufficient funding for both to attend, the boy is given precedence, while the girl remains at home to help her mother until the time she can get married and move away.

Although, girls have access to formal education, they are still strongly associated with the land cultivation and are considered strong and experienced in farming as compared to their Chagga counterparts. The Ngasa clothing style and fashion is largely western in nature. Although people in rural areas dress according to their work routines, its common to spot people in remote areas of the slopes of Mt. Kilimanjaro fashionably dressed, in accordance to a person's social class, lifestyle and preferences.

The Ngasa enjoy dressing up for funerals and weddings and are considered to be the most fashionable across East Africa. In the modern contemporary set up, the Ngasa Artists compose and sing songs that praise and or lament over political, generational, economic, and cultural contradictions. Subsequently, there has been a great deal of disagreements over what culture, traditions and songs ought to be preserved and what ought to be changed. Customs centering on marriage and gender relations are strongly debated.

The Ngasa Language Shift

By the beginning of the colonial era, *Ngasa* was an active language spoken on the Eastern slopes of Mt. Kilimanjaro. *English* and *Swahili* prevailed in the urban areas. The division reinforced by the colonial administration, brought about distinguished linguistic and economic elitism and created a huge contrast between the rural and urban Kilimanjaro folk. It designed the social structure, marriage and migration patterns with the clan system predominating in the rural areas. Like many indigenous speech communities found in pre-colonial Africa, the "Ngasa speech form" was deeply in tandem with their traditional lifestyle. The richness of the Ngasa lexicon was chiefly connected with their own specialized way of life. There wasn't much connected with the cattle, the mountain, plants and food that they didn't have a word for, and they had a lot of weather terms that reflected the importance of decisions about whether to plant or harvest.

Unfortunately, by the end of the colonial era, the inevitable death of Ngasa language began when their niche was irrevocably altered by the political and economic dominance of actors and their interference with the traditional, political and economic systems in the Kilimanjaro region. Subsequent breakdown of the geographical "niche" for the Ngasa was closely linked to the drastic political and demographic changes with the creation of *Ujamaa*[1] (socialist state), eradication of *Ukabila* ('tribalism'), the associated establishment and promotion of Swahili to the role of a national or official language, access to education, industrial advancement, tourism and eventual calls for modernism across Tanzania were associated with increasing rates of Ngasa to "Chagga-Pare-Swahili" language shift.

The events leading to the Ngasa language extinction were caused by language shift rather than by the extinction of the population that spoke this language. What provoked the Ngasa shift was not cultural selection acting on grammatical or prosodic potential, but the Ngasa people shifting between three competing languages (Chagga, Pare and Swahili) because of their associated economic and social ecologies.

In current sociolinguistic studies, the terms "language shift" and "language death" are used as metaphors. Language shift is the process whereby members of a community in which more than one language is spoken, abandon their own original vernacular language in favour of another. It occurs when speakers abandon their language, willingly or under pressure, in favour of another language, which then takes over as their means of communication and socialization. Ujamaa[1] - This was the concept that formed the basis of Julius Nyerere's social and economic development policies in Tanzania after it gained independence from Britain in 1961. It means 'unity', 'oneness', 'uniting with your countrymen as one extended family'.

Language death refers to the state of extinction-where a language is no longer used as a means of communication or socialization. However, in historical linguistics, "Phylogenetic" (language death) explains that human populations have in the past undergone expansions, (with the mechanism of expansion being local population increase, "fissioning" and spatial relocation of some fraction of that population). Thomason (2001; cf. McMahon & McMahon. 2005: 78-79) has suggested that the effects of language contact can be arranged on a continuum from contact-induced language to language death, with people abandoning one language outright and shifting to adopt another, the non-use of the language in any domain and the disappearance of its speakers or the non-functioning of its structure.

The processes of language shift and language death are interrelated as usually a language becomes extinct when its speakers shift to another language. However, a language can also become extinct if all its speakers are eliminated like the case of genocide. The major driving factor of language shift is the decision to abandon a more local or less prestigious language, typically because the target of the shift is a language seen as more modern, useful or giving access to greater social mobility and economic opportunities (McMahon, 1994; Mufwene, 2001; Brenzinger, 2006). In the modern era, national states, globalization and selective migration (Boyd & Richerson, 2009), have been potent forces of language standardization and of minority language endangerment and extinction.

The historical reconstruction of *Ngasa*

In Tanzania and along the Kenyan-Tanzanian boarder, the original Ngasa-speaking populations were numerous. In the 1950s, the Ngasa people succumbed to external pressures which threatened their language, culture and identity. The elderly folk had fought assimilation pressure from the dominant languages and cultures in vain. As a result, monolingual Ngasa speakers began to decline towards extinction.

During the colonial era, Ngasa was widely spoken, and even in the 60's it was still possible to traverse the

Kilimanjaro and encounter parts of the region in which 50% of the residents spoke Ngasa. By mid 50's, economic adversity in the Kilimanjaro areas, the 'pull' factor of economic opportunities in the urban centers, the industrialization and Ngasa revivalism in the rural areas had produced a substantial Ngasa presence in the region, with only 30% of all Ngasa speakers resident in the eastern slopes of Mt. *Kilimanjaro* (where almost 60% of Tanzania's Chagga population now live), and 40% residing in the rest of Tanzania. The absolute numbers of Ngasa speakers in Tanzania have declined through this period, from about 1,000 (Tucker & Bryan, 1956:112) to about 300 speakers in the most recent (2009) census, making them one of Tanzania's smallest tribes.

Their pattern of decline was attributed to local geographical factors and the wider contrast in social and economic potential that participation in dominant Chagga-Pare-Swahili linguistic communities opened up, rather than to any specialized lexicon of these languages. The Ngasa speakers first adopted the Chagga-Pare-Swahili words as loanwords, and gradually disintegrated into assimilation.

Following the extinction of "informal within-household" transmission pathways, there is no known revitalization process that has ever taken place in the Ngasa speech community. Ngasa has become a subject of local revival efforts to try and bring the Ngasa indigenous language back into the community via exhibitions, arts and traditional community events. Although rough estimates put the current speakers at 300, the Ngasa people were never lexically impoverished. They had abundant terms for nature, the weather, the mountain and everything that associated with it. They knew their traditions and customs well and had words to describe the flora and fauna that surrounded their ecosystem.

Despite these facts, the historical shifts to Chagga, Pare and Swahili by Ngasa has never been studied nor documented. Virtually no major linguistic research has ever been conducted in Tanzania. As a result, almost no reliable linguistic data was available prior to the most recent survey done in cooperation with the University of Dar es Salaam's Department of Foreign Languages and Linguistics - (within the framework of the LoT² project) since 2003, dealing with names and uses of wild plants in Vidunda language - published in (Legère, S. Maganga & P. Mkwan'hembo, 2004; Legère, 2006a; Legère & Mkwan'hembo, 2006).

At the time when the sociologist H.A. Fosbrooke collected his first notes on the Ngasa in the early 1950s, Ngasa language started dying out, reducing its practical and linguistic application drastically. Tucker & Bryan (1956: 112) estimated their number (following Fosbrooke, 1954) to be about 1,000. A figure considered to have been far too high, owing to the fact that only elderly people were able to speak Ngasa at the time. The last monolingual speakers of Ngasa are believed to have died in the late 80's. A short word-list compiled by Fleming (1965), and single words scattered over a number of pages in Ehret (1971, 1974a) were incorporated into data presented by Heine & Voen (1975-76), who conducted field research during a short visit to Tanzania in February /March 1975. Occasional references were also made to an unpublished vocabulary by Ehret (1967).

LoT² stands for "Languages of Tanzania", which is a SIDA/SAREC (Swedish International Development Agency/Swedish African Research Cooperation) funded project that is jointly implemented by the University of Dar es Salaam and the University of Gothenburg. The current fieldwork and research on Ngasa language documentation and cultural revitalization carried out by Gabriel Owiti Oguda and the author (Funded by the Firebird Foundation For Anthropological Research), is being done in "post-Ngasa communities" - where Ngasa is severely endangered and dying out. Gabriel and the writer will spearhead the collection of Ngasa oral literature; document their traditional ecological knowledge in order to come up with a comprehensive Ngasa cultural dictionary on the *Roots of Ngasa Word's*.

Summary and Conclusions

While researchers are actively trying to reverse or modify language shift processes, academic linguists are increasing their efforts to record details and samples of endangered languages without written corpora before they disappear. Such languages are characterized by insufficient codification, limited domains of use, legacies of domination by other languages, low esteem, perception and negative attitudes towards them by their speakers and active bilingualism in the more publicly used languages.

Due to the lack of equity in the status and functions of indigenous languages of Africa, some find themselves in a disadvantaged position. Minority languages that are demographically inferior are often marginalized and considered unfit for public functions. As a result, speakers of minority languages tend to suffer several disadvantages, which include dilemma over self-identity through the use of their "mother tongue" or assimilation into the larger community by shifting to the dominant language.

Contradictory information on indigenous languages of Africa has made it impossible to be certain the stage at which languages get on the continuum. It is particularly difficult to decide or to ascertain whether the members of a given language group have disappeared altogether. Even if some are still alive, it is difficult to know to what extent a language is still being used. One good example is the case of Aasax in northern Tanzania, which was reported by Winter (1976) and Ehret (1980) to be extinct after the last speaker was presumed to have died of old age in 1976. However, Derek Nurse, as reported in Sommer (1992), found several Aasax speakers still alive in the 1980s.

Several misconceptions about minority languages in Africa have also ascertained reasons why minority languages are viewed as a liability rather than developmental assets; thus associating them with underdevelopment, tribalism and negative ethnicity. It is therefore not surprising that language policies of very few African countries make explicit reference to them in relation to national development. Most policies either ignore them completely, as in Botswana, and Tanzania. Some accord them mere symbolic status as national languages, as in Namibia, with no active role. As a result, most of these languages have become severely endangered as their speakers no longer see tangible value in them, hence abandoning them for other lucrative languages that offer greater socio-economic benefits.

In the case of the Ngasa, the language shift resulted when speakers of Ngasa abandoned their language, under pressure, in favour of Chagga, Pare and Swahili, which then took over as their means of communication and socialization, successively, attracting a gradual language death since1950. Besides demographic, socio-economic, political and cultural pressure exerted on any language, attitudes of the speakers play an important role - as a strong resistance to language shift is usually only possible if speakers have a positive attitude to their language and hold it in high regard.

Where a language is felt to have little socio-economic value or social prestige, speakers may put up little resistance and are often inclined to abandon it in favour of one with greater prestige. Thus, in Africa the most endangered languages are small, marginalized ones that lack demographic power, the economic attractions or the social status of dominant languages. The speakers easily cultivate negative attitudes towards them and encourage their children to learn the more prestigious languages instead.

With the Ngasa case studies, we analyzed two different scenarios. While the most recent (2009) census showed tremendous decline in numbers of surviving Ngasa speakers in Tanzania, our research data shows that Ngasa seemed to be maintained at minimalistic levels in a bilingual Chagga-Pare-Swahili sub-populations. Our final analysis on the *same* has shown that the key research issues for maintenance of Ngasa that ought to be emphasized are: i) to create or support social domains in which the Ngasa language will be the preferred medium of communication and ii) to increase the rate of inter-generational transmission of Ngasa language.

Of additional importance to language maintenance are the creation of economic incentives like creating jobs to implement language revitalization initiatives - which themselves require skills in the Ngasa language, and the establishment of corpora of written texts in the Ngasa language as a cultural archive and as a medium of continuing cultural self-expression. Without stabilizing a sustainable level of intergenerational transmission, future language researchers will have to rely on constant interventions in formal public domains to counter the continuing space flux from bilingualism by individual households. This is the current reality of intergenerational transmission in an environment where Ngasa language competes with very unequal external advantages. The success of our current research and interventions in reversing the continuous language shift and preserving Ngasa as a living language will be assessed when the Ngasa folk finally manage to spread the use of their "mother tongue" language into new domains. These can only be achieved through a positive change of attitude towards Ngasa language; strong sense of identity and increased participation of the current Ngasa folk in acquiring and reclaiming back their 'mother tongue'.

Acknowledgement

The Firebird Foundation for Anthropological Research's support for enabling the authors to embark on a field research on the *'Ngasa'* people and language in the Eastern Slopes of Mt. Kilimanjaro is gratefully acknowledged.

References

Abrams, D. M. & Strogatz, S. H. (2003). Modelling the dynamics of language death. *Nature* 424, 900.

Asher, R.E. und Moseley, C. (Eds.) (2007). *Atlas of the World's Languages*. London: Routledge.

Batibo, Herman. (2005). *Language Decline and Death in Africa*. Bristol: Multilingual Matters.

Brenzinger, M. (Eds.) (1992). *Language Death. Factual and Theorical Explorations with Special Reference to East Africa*. Berlin: Mouton de Gruyter.

Brenzinger, M. (2006). Language maintenance and shift. In K. Brown (Ed.), *The Encyclopedia of Language and Linguistics* (pp. 542-548). Oxford, UK: Elsevier.

Castello, X., Loureiro, L., Eguı´luz, V.M. & Miguel, M. (2007). The fate of bilingualism in a model of language competition. In S. Takahashi, D. Sallach & J. Rouchier (Eds.), *Advancing Social Simulation: The First World Congress* (pp. 83-94). New York: Springer.

Dimmendaal, G.J. (2007). *Eastern Sudanic and the Wadi Howar and Wadi el Milk Diaspora. Sprache und Geschichte in Afrika* 18, 37-67.

Dimmendaal, G.J. (2008). *Language Ecology and Linguistic Diversity on the African Continent. Language and Linguistics Compass* 2(5):842.

Dimmendaal, G.J. (to appear). *Nilo-Saharan and its limits*. In J.M. Hombert & G. Philippson (Eds.), *The Genetic Classification of African Languages Revisited*.

Fishman, J.A. (1991). *Reversing Language Shift: Theoretical and Empirical Foundations of Assistance to Threatened Languages*. Clevedon: Multilingual Matters.

Greenberg, J.H. (1966). Nilo-Saharan. In J.H. Greenberg (Ed.), *The Languages of Africa*, (Pp. 130-148). Bloomington: Indiana University.

Greenberg, J.H. (1963). *The Languages of Africa*, *International Journal of American Linguistics,*

Bender, L. (2000). *Nilo-Saharan*. In Bernd Heine and Derek Nurse (Eds.), *African Languages – An Introduction*. Cambridge: Cambridge University Press.

Kandler, A. & Steele, J. (2008). Ecological models of language competition. *Biological Theory* 3, 164-173.

Krauss, M. (1992). The world's languages in crisis. *Language* 68, 4-10.

Mira, J. & Paredes, A. (2005). Interlinguistic similarity and language death dynamics. *Europhysics Letters* 69, 1031-1034.

McMahon, A. (1994). *Understanding Language Change*. Cambridge: Cambridge University Press.

McMahon, A. & McMahon, R. (2005). *Language Classification by Numbers*. Oxford: Oxford University Press.

Minett, J.W. & Wang, W.S.Y. (2008). Modelling endangered languages: the effects of bilingualism and social structure. *Lingua* 118(1), 19-45.

Mufwene, S.S. (2001). *The Ecology of Language Evolution*. Cambridge: Cambridge University Press.

Mufwene, S.S. (2008). *Language Evolution*. London: Continuum.

Nettle, D. & Romaine, S. (1999). Vanishing Voices: The Extinction of the World's Languages. Oxford: Oxford University Press.

Haspelmath, M. (Eds.) (2013). Ngasa. *Glottolog 2.2*. Leipzig: Max Planck Institute for Evolutionary Anthropology.

Patriarca, M. & Heinsalu, E. (2009). Influence of geography on language competition. *Physica* A388, 174.

Patriarca, M. & Leppänen, T. (2004). Modeling language competition. *Physica* A338, 296-299.

Pinasco, J.P. & Romanelli, L. (2006). Coexistence of language possible. *Physica* A 361, 355–360.

Ruhlen, M. (1991). *A Guide to the World's Languages* (vol. 1). Stanford: Stanford University Press.

Schulze, C., Stauffer, D. & Wichmann, S. (2008). Birth, survival, and death of languages by Monte Carlo simulation. *Computer Physics Communication* 3, 271–294.

Sommer, G. (1992). A survey on language death in Africa. In M. Brenzinger (Ed.) *Language Death: Factual and Theoretical Explorations with Special Reference to East Africa* (pp. 301-417) Berlin: Mouton de Gruyter.

Thomason, S.G. (2001). *An Introduction to Language Contact*. Edinburgh: Edinburgh University Press.

Interactional Modality of "*shiyoo-ne*" in Okinawan Discourse

Katsuyuki Miyahira
University of the Ryukyus
1 Senbaru, Nishihara
Okinawa, Japan 903-0213
[miyahira@ll.u-ryukyu.ac.jp]

One of the peculiar features of present-day Okinawan discourse is the use of utterance-final form, *shiyoo-ne*. Although the same form may appear in Standard Japanese, it is used in a very distinctive way in Okinawan discourse. In Standard Japanese, this combination of utterance-final particles (*yoo + ne*) is used to mark speaker's intention to suggest to the hearer to do something together. Speakers of present-day Okinawan may use it in the same fashion. However, in addition, they can use it to indicate the speaker's intention to do something on behalf of the hearer or to do something on his/her own that merits the hearer. This article tries to unpack the subtle and contrastive modality functions of this utterance-final form along with some other similar forms like *shimashoo-ne* and *hazu-yo* by examining the effects of language contact and mixing between an indigenous Okinawan language and standard Japanese.

A collection of essays describing the unique style of speech that is commonly observed among Okinawan elderly served as a major source of data. It was supplemented by other essays, a radio drama, newspaper articles, and some samples of everyday conversation among university students that were collected by the researcher. Takaesu (2002) explains that an utterance ending with *shiyoo-ne* is formulated with the grammatical structure of substratum language (i.e., indigenous Okinawan) and with the lexicon supplied by standard Japanese. The result is the utterance-final form that is identical to Standard Japanese expression and yet idiosyncratic in its use of the grammatical properties of modality. The article first delineates the grammatical properties of the modality pertaining to these utterance-final forms along the following four salient dimensions as was discussed in Cornillie and Pietrandrea (2112) and Palmer (2001): (1) proposition vs. event modality, (2) epistemic vs. deontic modality, (3) realis vs. irrealis factuality, (4) interactional dimension of modality. It does so by comparing and contrasting Okinawan usages with and against those of standard Japanese. The analysis led to a finding that some trances of modality marking in vernacular Okinawan language can be observed in the present-day Okinawan use of the utterance-final forms, *shiyoo-ne* and *hazu-yo*. The substratum effects on modality marking help establish a unique status of an Okinawan variety.

Uchima (2001) argues that in such substratum effects remains a distinctively Okinawan, cultural code of speaking; in the case at hand, a preference for speaker-hearer identification. The article demonstrates how it plays out in everyday talk and it further argues that modality marking is a discourse strategy that sets Okinawan variety apart from other linguistic varieties in Japan.

References

Cornillie, B. & Pietrandrea, P. (2012). Modality at work: Cognitive, interactional and textual functions of modal markers. *Journal of Pragmatics*, 44, 2109-2115.

Palmer, F.R. (2001). *Mood and Modality* (2nd ed.). Cambridge: Cambridge University Press.

Takaesu, Y. (2004). *Uchinaa-Yamatuguchi* – dōshi no asupekuto tensu mūdo [Aspect, Tense, and Mood in Uchinaa-Yamatuguchi]. In Kudo, M. (Ed.), Nihongo no asupekuto tensu mūdo taikei: Hyōjungo kenkyuu o koete [The System of Aspect, Tense, and Mood in Japanese: Beyond the Study of Standard Language]. Pp. 302-329. Tokyo: Hitsuji Shobō.

Uchima, C. (2011). Ryūkyū hōgen to uchi/soto ishiki [Ryukyuan dialect and uchi/soto consciousness]. Tokyo: Kenkyūsha.

The Possibility of an "Orthography" for Ryukyuan Languages: Considering the Writing System from the Viewpoints of Tradition and Universality

Satoshi Nishioka

Okinawa International University
Ginowan 2-6-1, Ginowan City, Okinawa,
Japan
[nishioka@okiu.ac.jp]

Historical material of Ryukyuan languages

Historical material of Ryukyuan languages can be classified into five corpora on the criteria of the written letters or characters: 1. The joint use of *kanji* (Chinese characters) and *kana* (Japanese syllabic letters) used mainly by Ryukyuan people; 2. *kana* only; 3. Chinese characters only with Chinese pronunciation written mainly by Chinese or Ryukyuan people; 4. *hangeul* letters used mainly by Korean people; 5. Roman alphabet used mainly by Western people (missionaries in the early times).

The main written examples of pre-modern Ryukyuan (16-19th century), most of which are in the Okinawan language (the Okinawa Central and Southern dialects) except the "Collections of folksongs", are the following.

Script	Examples of Ryukyuan corpora
joint use of *kanji* and *kana*	ofstone monuments, *Omorosōshi*, *Yuraiki*, *Ryūka* collections, *Kumiudui* play books, collections of folksongs
kana only	lyrics in *kun-kun-shī* (Ryukyuan score) Bible translated by *B.J.Bettelheim*
kanji only	glossary by *sappūshi* (Chinese envoys)
hangeul	glossary of *go-on-hon-yaku*
Roman alphabet	Ryukyuan-French dictionary written by *T-A. Forcade*

Table 1: Scripts used in Ryukyuan texts

An appropriate writing system for the modern Ryukyuan languages

The possibilities of an "orthography" for modern Ryukyuan languages are the threefold: 1. Joint use of *kanji* and *kana*; 2. *kana* system; 3. Roman alphabet system. This is connected to the fact the Ryukyuan indigenous speakers already know the Japanese writing system (Ogawa 2011:103) and the fact that the younger generation is increasingly accustomed to the Roman alphabet (Ogawa 2011:104). This author believes that all three scripts should be accepted as orthographies for Ryukyuan languages. Teaching of Ryukyuan languages needs to make use of two or three writing systems: the combined *kanji-kana* system or a pure *kana* system which is easy to read for elderly people who are the best language teachers, and the Roman alphabet system which is accessible to young people who are the successors of the languages.

The history of the joint *kanji* and *kana* writing system of in the Ryukyus

Omorosōshi (compiles in the 16-17th centuries), a collection of sacred ceremonial songs in the Middle Okinawan language, had mostly *kana* letters and few Chinese characters in the writing system. The number of Chinese characters in the collections of *Ryūka* ('Ryukyuan lyric poetry') and the plays of *kumiudui* ('Ryukyuan musical drama') increased in the 18-19th centuries). The joint use of *kanji* and *kana* was established at this time. The movement to apply Chinese Characters to Ryukyuan words semi-frivolously made radical progress in the writing system of *Ryūka-Hyakkō* (1795), but this use of *kanji* was restrained in later collections of *Ryūka*. The difference of register between literary style and colloquial style of Ryukyuan languages should be recognized when considering this traditional Ryukyuan literature.

The history of the use of the *kana* script

Most letters in *Omorosōshi* are *kana* with so few *kanji* so that it can be said to be a *kana* writing system. Even after the age of the *Omorosōshi*, *Ryūka* poems written in *kun-kun-shī* ('Ryukyuan musical scores'), are written in the *kata-kana* script to indicate the pronunciation. Bettelheim (1811-1870), who visited and stayed in the Ryukyu Kingdom, mastered the Okinawan language and translated the Bible into Okinawan using the *kata-kana* script.

The history of the use of the Roman alphabet

In the age of Pre-modern Ryukyu, the Ryukyuan glossary with English translation embedded in *Account of a Voyage* by Basil Hall (1788-1844) and the unpublished Ryukyuan-French dictionary written by T-A. Forcade (1816-1885) are important Ryukyuan documents in the Roman alphabetic script.

Opinions on the writing system of Ryukyuan languages

I introduce proposals from three researchers on the writing system of Ryukyuan languages and give my opinion at the end.

Karimata writes the following:

> No matter how much one improvises with *kana* letters, a writing system using the Roman alphabet is the best way for the young who learn the Miyako dialect for the first time because the teacher who has phonetic knowledge must phonetically instruct the pronunciation of the Miyako dialect. As far as the Miyako dialect is concerned, everything can be written with 26 alphabetic letters. The elderly may be reluctant to use the Roman alphabet, but the negative feeling must be much less for the younger generation whose first language is not the Miyako dialect. (Karimata, 2011: 202)

Karimata's comments are limited to the Miyako language, but he shows an understanding of the elderly who are reluctant to use the Roman alphabet, but claims that the Roman alphabet should be used for the linguistic instruction of the younger generation.

Ogawa (2011:103) is not a promoter of the Roman alphabet to the extent that Karimata (2011) is. He thinks it is important to create a system based on *kana* letters and another based on the alphabet, with an accurate correspondence between the two, as soon as possible. Ogawa (2011: 104) postulates that in the Ryukyuan languages where written language was not developed, the method of associating *kun* (indigenous)-readings with Chinese characters was not invented, unlike in Japanese, but I am against his postulations because since *Omorosōshi* (16-17 centuries), even in the Ryukyus, the method of associating *kun* (indigenous)-readings with Chinese characters was developed. It is just that researchers have not yet managed to classify how Ryukyuan indigenous readings were associated with Chinese characters.

Nakahara writes the following on the issues of developing orthographies:

> what we should consider to be the most important thing when we write is not simply to 'record' but to think constantly "what should we do in order to convey our ideas to readers". Furthermore, it is not useful if readers find it difficult to read a script even if writers think the script is adequate. In the future, I want to devise a user-friendly *kana* writing system which is easy to understand for the young who learn the Ryukyuan dialects or the middle aged who want to teach children the traditional languages, and which will be familiar to the elderly who speak the Ryukyuan languages. (Nakahara, 2013: 31)

My opinions are the following four points. I think it desirable to retain Chinese characters in the Ryukyuan writing systems because it will enable the diverse Ryukyuan languages to be loosely connected with one another. For example, the character 肝, which means 'human mentality' in the Ryukyuan languages, can serve to connect the indigenous readings of each region.

I think it would be ideal to devise three writing systems: a joint *kanji* and *kana* system, *kana* letters alone, and Roman alphabet. By linking each writing system, corpora will be accessible to all age groups.

New and unique letters which are modifications of *kana* created in order to adapt to Ryukyuan syllables, such as the *Okinawa-moji* ('Okinawan written characters') created for the Okinawan languages, have been proposed. However, the problem of character manipulation in computers must be solved. The creation of complicated *kana* letters makes it unclear how to order words when compiling Ryukyuan dictionaries, for example.

Although Ryukyuan languages are claimed to be the basis of Ryukyuan culture, how to revitalize them is not as clear as with other aspects of traditional culture. It is necessary to establish target grades of *Shima-kutuba* literacy and have explicit standards to be met in learning Ryukyuan languages.

References

Karimata, S. (2011). On'in-kenkyū to hōgen-shidō kara Miyako-hōgen no hyōkihō o kangaeru [Thinking over a notation of Miyako dialects from the point of view of phonemic research and dialect teaching]. In P. Heinrich & M. Shimoji (Eds.), *Ryūkyūgo kiroku hozon no kiso* [Essentials in Ryukyuan Language Documentation] (pp.194-204). Tōkyō: Research Institute for Languages and Cultures of Asia and Africa, Tokyo University of Foreign Studies.

Nakahara, J. (2013). Okinawa chūnanbu-hōgen no kana-hyōki no mondaiten. "Okinawago kana-zukai ni mukete [Issues on kana orthography of central and southern dialects of the Okinawan language. Towards "The use of kana in the Okinawan language). *Nantō Bunka* [Bulletin of the Institute of Ryukyuan Culture], 35, 19-39.

Ogawa, S. (2011). Kore kara no ryūkyūgo ni hitsuyō na hyōkihō wa dono yō na mono ka [Developing a Writing System for Ryukyuan Languages]. *Nihongo no kenkyū* [Studies in the Japanese Language], 7(4), 99-111.

Tense, Aspect, and Evidentiality
in the Masana Dialect of Okinoerabu Ryukyuan

Gijs van der Lubbe

901-2424 Okinawa-ken, Nakagami-gun Nakagusuku-son
Minami-Uebaru 995-2, China Apaato 105
[gijs.van.der.lubbe@gmail.com]

UNESCO recognises 6 Ryukyuan languages: from north to south, Amami, Kunigami, Okinawan, Miyako, Yaeyama, and Yonaguni. The Okinoerabu language is subsumed under the Kunigami language, however the existence of Kunigami as a separate branch within the Ryukyuan languages is controversial. Pellard (2014) argues that the languages of Yoron Island and Okinoerabu Island are to be regarded as varieties of the Amami language, based on innovations in the lexicon that they have in common. The language spoken on Okinoerabu can be subdivided into individual village dialects. The village dialects display small differences in pronunciation, intonation, and vocabulary. These differences are no obstacle for mutual intelligibility, however they are a strong source of identity for the speakers. Masana dialect speakers are very much aware of the features that set their dialect apart from other Okinoerabu dialects. The youngest speakers of the Okinoerabu language in Masana are around 50 years of age; but the language they speak is often considered to be a form of "Okinoerabu koiné" rather than Masana dialect. Because only speakers over 70 years of age use features that define the Masana dialect, research on the Masana dialect must be conducted now.

This presentation is to outline the tense, aspect, and evidentiality system of the Masana dialect of the Okinoerabu language. These 3 categories are marked in the verb morphology of the language, and display marked differences with other Ryukyuan languages and with Japanese. The existential verbs *ʔaːmu*, for inanimate things, and *wuːmu*, for animate things are the subject of grammaticalisation in verb forms that indicate tense, and aspect, as is the case in most other Japanonic languages. *ʔaːmu* is also used in its grammaticalised form in verb forms that indicate indirect evidentiality, as is also the case in Shuri Okinawan (Kudō *et al.*, 2007). The verb *ʔakkimu* 'to walk' is also grammaticalised in some aspectual forms. This is also the case some other (N.) Ryukyuan languages. For instance, Shimabukuro (1997) mentions a grammaticalised form of 'to walk' in a frequentative meaning for Nakijin Ryukyuan, and Hashio mentions one in a progressive meaning for Iejima Ryukyuan (Hashio, 1992). The case of the Masana dialect differs from these two instances in the fact that there are restrictions on the grammaticalised use of 'to walk', amongst others in terms of animacy.

This kind of grammar research will allow for comparisons between Ryukyuan languages from a grammatical perspective as opposed to most previous comparative research, based on phonology and lexical innovations. A comparison of grammatical features among the languages that are classified as either Amami, Kunigami, or Okinawan will allow for a more thorough comparison and classification of the varieties that UNESCO considers to be part of Kunigami.

The outline of my system of non-spatial setting is based on my fieldwork, conducted during the past 2 years using elicitation and analysis of spontaneous discourse. This fieldwork is the first inventory of the system of tense, aspect, and evidentiality for Masana dialect and Okinoerabu language in general. It contributes to comparative research of the N. Ryukyuan languages based on grammatical features. The analysis is carried out according to Kudō's framework, as in Kudō (2014).

References

Hashio, N. (1993). Iejima Hōgen no tensu, asupekuto ni ikkōsatsu [A study of tense and aspect in Iejima dialect]. *The Journal of Social Sciences and Humanities* (243), p. 23-45.

Kudō, M. (2014). *Gendai nihongo mūdo, tensu, asupekuto ron* [Mood, Tense, and Aspect Systems in Japanese]. Tokyo: Hitsuji Shobo.

Kudō, M., Takaese, Y. & Yakame, H. (2007). Shuri hōgen no asupekuto, tensu, evidensharitii [Aspect, tense, and evidentiality in the Shuri dialect]. *Ōsaka Daigaku Daigakuin Bungaku Kenkyūka Kiyō*.

Pellard, T. (2014). The linguistic archaeology of the Ryukyu Islands. In Patrick Heinrich. Shinshō Miyara, and Michinori Shimoji (Eds.), *Handbook of the Ryukyuan Languages.* Mouton de Gruyter

Shimabukuro, Y. (1997). Okinawa Hokubu hōgen [N. Okinawan dialect]. In Kamei, T., Kōno, R., & Chino, E. (Eds.), *Gengogaku daijiten serekushon: nihon rettō no gengo* [Selection of Linguistic Encyclopaedia: the Languages of the Japanese Islands]. Tokyo: Sanseidō.

Miyakoan Legacy Cast in the Language: Proverbs and Metaphors

Aleksandra Jarosz
Adam Mickiewicz University Poznan
Komisji Edukacji Narodowej 35, 07-410 Ostroleka
Poland
[aljarosz@amu.edu.pl]

Source Material of the Study

Nikolay Nevskiy (1892-1937), a Russian ethnographer and linguist who became a pioneer in the linguistic study of the Ryukyus, apparently chose the Miyakos as his research subject because the local language seemed archaic and possibly held a key to the past of Japanese, as well as from the simple fact that this language had not been studied before (Baksheev, 2013: 225-226). He gathered huge amounts of Miyako language materials, many of which unfortunately still remain unedited and/or unpublished (and some possibly even have not yet been discovered). One of these are the handwritten and tentatively edited by the author himself *Materials for the study of the Miyako language* (Russian *Матерьялы для изучения говора островов Мияко*) from the 1920s. His comprehensive lexicographical records of Miyakoan, all the more valuable because of the period of their compilation, as Nevskiy conducted his fieldwork back in the day when the local varieties were still used as the L1 by all generations of the islands' population. The usage of many lexemes was illustrated by example sentences extracted from natural speech or from traditional songs, and some of the entries include Nevskiy's derivational analysis or commentary referring to their etymology.

The purpose of this paper is to present the lexical richness of traditional Miyakoan varieties by introducing figurative expressions from Nevskiy's *Materials* as retrieved, analyzed and translated into English by this author. This presentation will be limited to only two of a few conceivable categories of such expressions: proverbs and metaphors.

Proverbs

Proverbs are the fixed utterances (usually complete sentences) used to explain particular extra-linguistic circumstances in a way that classifies them as a representation of a general rule. They are often based on metaphors, but what makes them a distinct utterance category is the clear assessment and assertive commentary upon the situation which they contain, along with their perceived universality. Proverbs usually reflect common beliefs on popular matters held by the members of a given community. Miyakoan proverbs most often seem to relate to the nature or a man's ties with it, cp. *A:-kara muzza uin* 'No wheat will grow out of millet', *Takagi-n-du kaza: kakal* 'It is against the tall trees that the wind blows the fiercest', or *Izi-nu azsu-ga-du upuzz-u:ba tuz* 'Those who catch big fish are those who have the patience'.

Metaphors

Metaphors are the expressions used for comparisons; they expand the meaning of a concrete lexeme or phrase in order to clarify or enhance the description of the object or phenomenon they refer to. Miyakoan displays interesting astrological and meteorological metaphors, such as *tin-nu uputzu* 'the Milky Way' (lit. 'the heaven's great canal') or *timbav* 'a rainbow' (lit. 'a heavenly snake'), possibly expressing the community's beliefs about origins of these phenomena.

Figurative usages of a language encode a population's perceptivity and ingenuity passed on for generations. Further study of Miyakoan proverbs and metaphors, including an actual fieldwork conducted with contemporary informants, could thus explain a lot about the speakers' beliefs, worldviews and living conditions, and the results might be incorporated into language revitalization programs or school lessons on Miyakoan cultural heritage.

References

Baksheev, E. (2013). Н. А. Невский – рюкюанист и его *"Матерьялы для изучения говора островов Мияко"* [Nikolai Nevsky as a Ryūkyūanist and his materials for the study of the Miyako Islands dialect]. In E. C. Бакшеев, В. В. Щепкин (Eds.), *Николай Невский: жизнь и наследие. Сборник статей* [Nikolai Nevsky: His Life and Legacy. Proceedings] (pp. 225-244). St. Petersburg: St. Petersburg State University, Faculty of Filology.

Nevskiy, N. (2013). *Nikolay Nevskiy's Miyakoan Dictionary as Recovered from its Manuscript by Aleksandra Jarosz. Preprint.* Stęszew: IIEOS.

Language Revitalization in the Ryukyus through the Okinawan Diaspora in Hawai'i: "Imagining the Homeland", Remaking Identities, and Taking Cues from the Native Hawaiian Campaign

Howard K. Higa
Chubu Gakuin University
[howard_higa@yahoo.com]

This presentation will describe the movement within the Okinawan diaspora for supportive "return" in the homeland, especially toward language revitalization and cultural renewal. This influence from abroad through the diasporans is significant because diasporans often adhere to a nostalgic view of the homeland and are not hindered by assimilation with the Japanese national entity as in the homeland. As such diasporans more freely explore and uphold truisms attached to the homeland, e.g, language legitimacy. I will also argue that the nostalgic view through "homeland imagining" is justified for at least two reasons. One, certain aspects of traditional Okinawan culture have been preserved in the Hawaii setting. And two, the approach to cultural exploration by a burgeoning sector of the youth generations of the diaspora is bolstered by academic study and practice of the cultural arts. In addition, the Okinawan diasporans in Hawaii have had a first-hand view into the movement to save the Hawaiian language from extinction – as participants in the campaign and as observers in the community. This presentation will highlight the successes of the Native Hawaiian campaign and the intriguing similarities between the plights of the Native Hawaiians and the Okinawans in the homeland. These insights provide valuable directives for the Okinawan people, starting with language revitalization and cultural renewal but having far reaching ramifications.

I will argue that the role of language and culture in this pivotal position for social deliberation and movement is important because it introduces a different dynamic into movements in Okinawa on many fronts. To date, the major campaigns in Okinawa have rallied around acute tragedies, e.g., the crash of a US military helicopter into an Okinawan university in 2004. Focusing on language and culture maintains and carries the momentum through acts of celebration – the practice of cultural arts and the learning of indigenous languages – rather than the campaigns which rely on tragedies and may not have lasting power. This is one of the lessons that can be learned from the Native Hawaiian movement which Okinawan diasporans in Hawai'i have special insight into. Therefore, it is noteworthy that the University of Hawai'i offered the first academic courses in the world on an indigenous language of Okinawa through the inauguration of the Center for Okinawan Studies in 2008. Also, in 2013 the main daily in Hawai'i carried an article entitled "LANGUAGE REVIVAL" (with capital and bold letters). With the success of the Hawaiian language campaign, the newspaper title probably sought to attract readership through the sentiments attached to the theme in the Hawaiian community. In an opening paragraph, the article stated: "The class at Jikoen Hongwanji Mission (in Honolulu) might just be the beginning of a cultural revival thousands of miles east of the source." Okinawan diasporans in Hawaii recall that the revitalization of the Hawaiian language seemed impossible through the start of the campaigns in the 1980s. Today, that dream has been nurtured into reality and is now widely recognized as the status quo – with wide and developing aspects ongoing. This presentation will focus on this diasporan perspective for language revitalization and its potential for influencing social change in the homeland.

Okinawan (Uchinaaguchi) Particles from the Perspective of Cognitive Linguistics

Yuka Ando

Duisburg-Essen University
Institute of East Asian Studies
47048 Duisburg, Germany
[yuka.ando@uni-due.de]

This study examines Okinawan's particles, *nakai, kai, nkai* and *ni,* from the cognitive linguistic perspective by comparing them with the prototypes of the Japanese case particle *ni* obtained empirically based on the Prototype Theory.

The Prototype Theory is a theory describing the human beings' cognition of categories. According to this theory, there exist both typical and untypical members within the same category and the former is a prototype. A category has a radial structure with its center occupied by prototypical members and this is called prototype effect (Lakoff, 1987).

The current prototypes of the Japanese case particle *ni,* as claimed by research so far, are mostly theoretical in nature and based on the intuition of the researchers. Thus an online questionnaire survey was conducted in order to obtain empirical prototypes for *ni.* 182 Japanese native speakers sorted out 36 functions of *ni* on the basis of functional similarities. These 36 functions were defined based on the semantic syntax analyses (Muraki, 1991; Waki, 2000) and morphosyntax analysis (Rickmeyer, 1995). A multidimensional scaling analysis was conducted and four prototypical functions of *ni* were observed, namely, "locative", "goal", "partner" and "time". Each functional category has a radial structure with its center occupied by prototypical members.

This result is yet more crucial to our understanding of the Okinawan particles as each of four prototypes of *ni* has its matching particle in the Okinawan language, part of the Ryukyuan branch of the Japonic language family. A speaker of Okinawan provided the Okinawan translation for the sentences in the questionnaire used for finding out the empirical prototypes of the Japanese case particle *ni.* There were 38 Japanese sentences containing *ni* and they were all translated into Okinawan. Examining the Okinawan translation as well as four publications such as dictionaries (Handa, 2000; Kokuritsu Kokugo Kenkyūjo, 1983; Nishioka, 2004; Uchima, 2006) showed that different particles were used in Okinawan which were all expressed by *ni* in Japanese. In Okinawan "locative" was expressed by *nakai,* "goal" by *kai,* "partner" by *nkai* and "time" by *ni.* This means, Okinawan still holds the grammatical differentiations that reflect human cognition of the speakers of the Japonic languages. The fact that all four prototypical functions are expressed by *ni* in Japanese, therefore, should not automatically mean that there exists one superordinate prototype even though there is debate among the researchers to decide on the superordinate prototypical functional category of *ni.*

Furthermore, *nkai* whose core function is "partner" is observed to take over the functions of *nakai* for "locative" and *kai* for "goal". Not only that *nkai* offers a variety of functions like the Japanese particle *ni* as seen in the dictionaries used to cite the example sentences but also that 31 Japanese particle *ni* out of 38 in the questionnaire mentioned above were translated with *nkai* at first. Does this imply a cognitive extension of speakers from "partner" to "locative" and "goal", that is, an extension from "animate" to "inanimate" objects? This line of thought is interesting from the view of cognitive linguistics since the currently accepted view is that human cognition distinguishes stasis and kinesis in space (i.e. Levinson, 2006). The former leads to the concept of location of existence which is expressed by *nakai* in Okinawan and by "locative" *ni* in Japanese, and the latter leads to the concept of motion which is expressed by *kai* in Okinawan and by *ni* of "goal" in Japanese. Kabata and Rice (1997, 2007) also offer the same view, from the grammaticalization theory point of view, that "locative" and "goal" express the basic spatial relation and present a network model of *ni* in which two main functions "locative" and "goal" exist and the rest of the functions of *ni* are extended from either one of them. The analysis of this study shows, however, the distinctions between animate and inanimate of human cognitions might be as dominant as or even more dominant when choosing an appropriate particle than the distinctions of stasis and kinesis. If this were the case, how do these two contrasting human cognitions, "animate and inanimate" and "stasis and kinesis" intertwine? This is to be an interesting line to follow for the future research.

In this study, it is shown that not only cognitive linguistics help understanding Okinawan within the theoretical framework but also Okinawan contributes to cognitive linguistics from the perspective of typology. That is, it changes the current situation where only Japanese data is considered for considerations of Japonic languages. This research serves as an illustration that the loss of linguistic diversity undermines our understanding of language, cognition and how speakers place themselves in the world differently via the languages they speak. Clarifying this is yet another important factor why the Ryukyuan languages should be valued.

References

Handa, I. (2000). *A Luchuan Dictionary*. Tokyo: Daigaku Shorin.

Kabata, K. & Rice, S. (1997). Japanese *ni*: The particulars of a somewhat contradictory particle. In M. Verspoor, K. D. Lee and E. Sweetser (Eds.), *Lexical and Syntactical Constructions and the Construction of Meaning* (pp. 107-127). Amsterdam: John Benjamins.

Kokuritsu Kokugo Kenkyūjo (1983). *Okinawago jiten* [Okinawan Dictionary]. Tokyo: Printing Bureau of the Ministry of Finance.

Lakoff, G. (1987). *Women, Fire, and Dangerous Things*. Chicago: University of Chicago Press.

Levinson, S. & Wilkins, D. (2006). *Grammars of Space*. Cambridge: Cambridge University Press.

Muraki, S. (1991). *Nihongo dōshi no shosō* [Various Aspects of Japanese Verbs]. Saitama: Hitsuji Shobō.

Nishioka, S. (2004). Okinawago Shuri hōgen no joshi "nkai" "nakai" "ni" "ga" "kai" – kyōtsugo no joshi "ni" "e" to taishō sasetsutsu [Particles of Okinawan Shuri dialect "nkai" "nakai" "ni" "ga" and "kai" in comparison with Japanese particles "ni" and "e"]. In: *Okinawa kokusai daigaku nihongo nihon bungaku kenkyū* 9(1), 1-11.

Rice, S. and Kabata, K. (2007). Crosslinguistic grammaticalization patterns of the ALLATIVE. *Linguistic Typology* 11, 451-514.

Rickmeyer, J. (1995). *Japanische Morphosyntax*. Heidelberg: Julius Groos Verlag Heidelberg.

Uchima, C. (2006). *Okinawago jiten* [Okinawan Dictionary]. Tokyo: Kenkyūsha.

Waki, T. (2000). Ni-kaku meishiku no imi kaishaku o sasaeru kōzo-teki genri [The structural principle behind the interpretation of 'NP-*ni*' in Japanese]. *Nihongo kagaku* [The Science of Japanese] 7, 70-9

Do Surtitles of Traditional Okinawan Theatre Contribute to Language Revitalization in Okinawa in General?

Shoko Yonaha
University of the Ryukyus
Nishihara, Okinawa
[shinasaki@goo.jp]

(based Upon Traditional Okinawan Theatre Production in Hawai'i and the National Theatre Okinawa)

On 27 October 2013, the all female Okinawan theatre company "Unai" had a chance to perform at Hawai'i Okinawa Center. They performed the traditional Okinawan comedy *Teijo-gwa* and Ryukyuan 'Opera' (*kageki*) *Nachijin Nundunchi* along with three Ryukyu dances and Ryukyu folk music. For two plays' performances, English subtitles were prepared. Most of the audiences were Okinawan Americans from the first to the fifth generations. The production in Okinawan languages (mainly spoken in Shuri-Naha languages) was successful, and part of the reason was because Unai prepared surtitles for the shows.

This was clearly indicated in my survey. Among 171 polled in the audiences, many were found to appreciate the surtitles, and this experience made me focus on the issue of surtitles.

"Subtitles" or "captions" are familiar from screen broadcasts, but surtitles is the special term for the stage-subtitles. So I'll use surtitles in this paper.[62]

Need for surtitles: in productions overseas and in mainland Japan

The theatre troupe Unai which has been performing mainly *Okinawa shibai* ('play') and Ryukyu dances since 2004 was founded after the legendary all-female Okinawan theatre company *Otohime Gekidan* which lasted for 52 years from 1949 to 2001. In 2012, the troupe had performed in Taiwan and Osaka with surtitles in Chinese in Taiwan, and in Japanese in Osaka. Because of these experiences, the leader Ritsuko Nakasone decided to project the surtitles in Hawai'i in English, even if it was believed that many older Okinawan Hawaiians still understand Okinawan languages.

The results were the same: many audiences in those three different places appreciated the surtitles. It was simply, first, that Taiwanese could understand the meaning of the stage drama performed in Okinawan languages, and likewise, those in Osaka, mainly Okinawan Japanese who've lived there since the first generation to the present, understood through the surtitles. It was obvious for those Okinawan Japanese, Okinawan original languages were not easily understood since their mother tongue is Japanese, and the same things came out in the Hawai'i performance.

The audiences of Okinawan descendants have enjoyed the original songs and dialogues through the surtitles. Though my assumption was that they should have got used to listening to Ryukyu folk songs and seen Ryukyu dances, but still it was difficult for them to follow the sung dialogues and stories without surtitles. To sum up, audiences in Taiwan, Osaka, and Hawai'i enjoyed the comedy and Ryukyu opera with surtitles.

According to Gottlieb Henrik, subtitles are defined as "the rendering in a different language of verbal messages in filmic media, in the shape of one or more lines of written text presented on the screen in sync with the original written message" (quoted in Delia, 2009, 148), and it's commonly appreciated by Okinawans, too. For many filmgoers, rental DVD lovers, and Internet users, subtitles are very popular as well as dubbed versions. However most of them are Japanese subtitles and original English languages like TED, and it's rare to access Okinawan language subtitles on the screen. However, it was familiar with us to see Japanese subtitles on the *Okinawa shibai* production on the air by NHK "Okinawan songs and dances" programs. Occasionally NHK Okinawa has televised Okinawan traditional performing arts on TV, and Japanese subtitles are common for more than 40 years. To understand the real content of traditional Okinawan performing arts, NHK was the front runner to subtitle them not only to the majority of Japanese but to Okinawans whose comprehension of their own native languages is getting lower.

Because of that, when the National Theatre Okinawa which opened in 2004 made surtitles in Japanese for their production, it was welcomed by the theatre-going Okinawans who had less comprehension of the classic performances, and so were some guest Japanese.

Surtitles of *Kumi-wudui* and *Okinawa shibai* at the National Theatre Okinawa

According to Manabu Oshiro who was in charge of the research and project section at the National Theatre Okinawa at its opening, it was properly accepted to set

---

[62] Editor's note: *surtitles* (aka *supertitles*) is a term for textual glosses projected simultaneously with spoken or sung dialogue, as in traditional Chinese opera. Live opera productions using SURTITLES™, a system of the Canadian Opera Company, have been widely popular since the 1980s.

up the surtitles. "It is a sort of service for those who don't understand classic Okinawan languages used in *kumi-wudui* ['Okinawan opera']" he added. Of course, there were some who were against the surtitles, but Oshiro insisted that it is necessary for new audiences who visit Okinawa from various places to see *Kumi-wudui*. The majority of Japanese and young and middle generations in Okinawa are not used to seeing *Kumi-wudui* and *Okinawa shibai*. And the purpose of constructing the National Theatre was to increase the number of tourists, as well as the preservation, revitalization, and re-creation of traditional performing arts. The Asia-Pacific inter/cross cultural community interactions are also placed in the foundation of the National Theatre. For this purpose, all the more, multi-linguistic surtitles will be required.

Conclusion

The main issue is whether or not the procedure of surtitles is beneficial for the revitalization of Ryukyu/Okinawa languages. Certainly it's necessary not only for those whose native languages are not Okinawan but also for more than half of the Okinawan population who cannot understand and speak their native languages. The rate of Okinawan people who are alienated from their own ancestral languages is increasing, since assimilation to Japan has somehow been accomplished linguistically within 135 years. UNESCO's warning of the endangerment of Ryukyu languages in 2009 appears to have inspired Okinawans to revitalize their indigenous languages. But in a likely bilingual outcome, both Japanese and Shuri-Naha languages in Okinawan traditional performing arts, would coexist in Okinawa.

Shinsho Aniya, performer of the Ryukyu kingdom's *Omoro* (the oldest Ryukyu poems, which are chanted) claims that surtitles should be in the original Ryukyu/Okinawa languages: this could pose a different challenge for the National Theatre.

In sum: first of all, Japanese surtitles are necessary; but the next step should be a further commitment, to represent the original dialogue in *Kumi-wudui*; finally, a global audience might bring a requirement for surtitles in English.

References

Delia, C. (2009). Issues in audiovisual translation. In Jeremy Munday (Ed.), *The Routledge Companion to Translation Studies*. London: Routledge.

Translating *Uchinaaguchi/Shimakutuba* in Contemporary Okinawan Literature

Kyle Ikeda
University of Vermont
Department of Asian Languages & Literatures
479 Main Street
Burlington, VT 05405, USA
[kikeda@uvm.edu]

Translators of modern Okinawan literature into English often face the challenge of rendering in one language the polylinguality in another. In other words, the translator is faced with trying to reproduce in a single target language the appearance of Okinawan words and speech, or *Uchinaaguchi*, in a story primarily written in Japanese. To be sure, regional dialects appear in mainland Japanese literary works, but almost all translators of mainland Japanese literature into English render everything monolingually into "standard" English.

This presentation begins by reviewing how existing translations of Okinawan literature into English have dealt with Okinawan literature's polylinguality, analyzing the strengths and weaknesses of various approaches, and drawing from Lawrence Venuti's critique of the "invisibility" of the translator, I analyze the particular repercussions the dominant mode of translation has on Okinawan literary texts in translation. I contextualize the issue of Okinawan language/ *Uchinaaguchi* use within Okinawa's history of colonization by and assimilation into mainland Japan, particularly Japanese military massacres and executions of Okinawan civilians for speaking *Uchinaaguchi* during the Battle of Okinawa. I argue that the variety of attempts to reproduce the polylinguality of Okinawan literature in English translation can be read as a sign of the tension between the homogenizing monolingual expectations of literary translation and the politicized meanings and importance of *Uchinaaguchi*'s distinction from Japanese in relation to issues of identity and resistance in Okinawa.

Foundation for Endangered Languages

Manifesto

1. Preamble

1.1. The Present Situation

At this point in human history, most human languages are spoken by exceedingly few people. And that majority, the majority of languages, is about to vanish.

The most authoritative source on the languages of the world (Ethnologue, Gordon 2005) lists just over 6,900 living languages. Population figures are available for just over 6,600 of them (or 94.5%). Of these 6,600, it may be noted that:

- 56% are spoken by fewer than 10,000 people;
- 28% by fewer than 1,000; and
- 83% are restricted to single countries, and so are particularly exposed to the policies of a single government.

At the other end of the scale, 10 major languages, each spoken by over 100 million people, are the mother tongues of almost half (49%) of the world's population.

More important than this snapshot of proportions and populations is the outlook for survival of the languages we have. Hard comparable data here are scarce or absent, often because of the sheer variety of the human condition: a small community, isolated or bilingual, may continue for centuries to speak a unique language, while in another place a populous language may for social or political reasons die out in little more than a generation. Another reason is that the period in which records have been kept is too short to document a trend: e.g. the Ethnologue has been issued only since 1951. However, it is difficult to imagine many communities sustaining serious daily use of a language for even a generation with fewer than 100 speakers: yet at least 10% of the world's living languages are now in this position.

Some of the forces which make for language loss are clear: the impacts of urbanization, Westernization and global communications grow daily, all serving to diminish the self-sufficiency and self-confidence of small and traditional communities. Discriminatory policies, and population movments also take their toll of languages.

In our era, the preponderance of tiny language communities means that the majority of the world's languages are vulnerable not just to decline but to extinction.

1.2. The Likely Prospect

There is agreement among linguists who have considered the situation that over half of the world's languages are moribund, i.e. not effectively being passed on to the next generation. We and our children, then, are living at the point in human history where, within perhaps two generations, most languages in the world will die out.

This mass extinction of languages may not appear immediately life-threatening. Some will feel that a reduction in numbers of languages will ease communication, and perhaps help build nations, even global solidarity. But it has been well pointed out that the success of humanity in colonizing the planet has been due to our ability to develop cultures suited for survival in a variety of environments. These cultures have everywhere been transmitted by languages, in oral traditions and latterly in written literatures. So when language transmission itself breaks down, especially before the advent of literacy in a culture, there is always a large loss of inherited knowledge.

Valued or not, that knowledge is lost, and humanity is the poorer. Along with it may go a large part of the pride and self-identity of the community of former speakers.

And there is another kind of loss, of a different type of knowledge. As each language dies, science, in linguistics, anthropology, prehistory and psychology, loses one more precious source of data, one more of the diverse and unique ways that the human mind can express itself through a language's structure and vocabulary.

We cannot now assess the full effect of the massive simplification of the world's linguistic diversity now occurring. But language loss, when it occurs, is sheer loss, irreversible and not in itself creative. Speakers of an endangered language may well resist the extinction of their traditions, and of their linguistic identity. They have every right to do so. And we, as scientists, or concerned human beings, will applaud them in trying to preserve part of the diversity which is one of our greatest strengths and treasures.

1.3. The Need for an Organization

We cannot stem the global forces which are at the root of language decline and loss.

But we can work to lessen the ignorance which sees language loss as inevitable when it is not, and does not properly value all that will go when a language itself vanishes.

We can work to see technological developments, such as computing and telecommunications, used to support small communities and their traditions rather than to supplant them.

And we can work to lessen the damage:

- by recording as much as possible of the languages of communities which seem to be in terminal decline;
- by emphasizing particular benefits of the diversity still remaining; and
- by promoting literacy and language maintenance programmes, to increase the strength and morale of the users of languages in danger.

In order to further these aims, there is a need for an autonomous international organization which is not constrained or influenced by matters of race, politics, gender or religion. This organization will recognise in language issues the principles of self-determination, and group and individual rights. It will pay due regard to economic, social, cultural, community and humanitarian considerations. Although it may work with any international, regional or local Authority, it will retain its independence throughout. Membership will be open to those in all walks of life.

2. Aims and Objectives

The Foundation for Endangered Languages exists to support, enable and assist the documentation, protection and promotion of endangered languages. In order to do this, it aims:-

(i) To raise awareness of endangered languages, both inside and outside the communities where they are spoken, through all channels and media;

(ii) To support the use of endangered languages in all contexts: at home, in education, in the media, and in social, cultural and economic life;

(iii) To monitor linguistic policies and practices, and to seek to influence the appropriate authorities where necessary;

(iv) To support the documentation of endangered languages, by offering financial assistance, training, or facilities for the publication of results;

(v) To collect together and make available information of use in the preservation of endangered languages;

(vi) To disseminate information on all of the above activities as widely as possible..